NORTH AMERICAN F-86 SABRE

AVIATION SERIES

North American F-86 SABRE

Duncan Curtis

The Crowood Press

First published in 2000 by
The Crowood Press Ltd
Ramsbury, Marlborough
Wiltshire SN8 2HR

**British Library Cataloguing-in-Publication
Data**
A catalogue record for this book is available
from the British Library.

ISBN 1 86126 358 9

Frontispiece: **Dwarfed by a Convair B-36 bomber, this
aircraft is from 27th Fighter Squadron and sports a
yellow fuselage flash. Early tests with F-86As
intercepting B-36s showed that the Sabre had little
or no chance of catching the bomber and this
indirectly led to the installation of the Ground
Controlled Intercept system. Note that 48-131 still
features the intake-mounted pitot probe. During
October 1950 this aircraft was routed through NAA's
Long Beach plant, where a wing-mounted probe
was installed.** A.J. Jackson

Edited, designed and produced by Focus
Publishing

Printed and bound by Bookcraft,
Midsomer Norton

Dedication

To my great friend and mentor Pete
Hutting.

Acknowledgements

I thank Mike Fox for his continual
support, proof-reading and the loan of
material, and also John Henderson, NAA
tech rep, who generously provided a
considerable amount of material from his
personal archives. John also answered my
many queries in a supremely prompt and
professional manner. Finally, to my wife
Tanya a big thank you for proof-reading
and for putting up with me.

My sincere thanks also go to: Bill Allen,
Sr, Maj Gen Fred Ascani, USAF Retd,
Mike Bennett, Lawrence Biehunko,
Duane Biteman, Jack Brauckmann, Air
Cdr D.F.M. Browne, Wei-Bin Chang,
Bernard Chenel, Stephen Darke, Don
Exley, Eric Falk/GE Aircraft Engines,
Peter R. Foster, Clarence J.P. Fu, Craig
Fuller, Roque Garcia, Jr, George Getchell,
Lee Gollwitzer, Jennifer Gradidge, Col.
Laverne Griffin, Richard Gross, Wayne
Heise, Leif Hellstrom, A.J. Jackson, Mario
Canongia Lopes, Jim Low, Dave McLaren,
Frank McMeiken, Bill Madison, Andy
Marden, Barry Mayner, Dave Menard,
Ron Mock, the National Air & Space
Museum, Archie Nogle, 'Oakie' Oakford,
Jorge Felix Nunez Padin, Dave Roberson,
Harry Runge, Frosty Sheridan, Peter
Sickinger, José Carlos Carias Silva, Elliott
P. Smith, Roger W. Sudbury/MIT Lincoln
Laboratory, Zeev Tavor, Brian Austria-
Tomkins, Themis Vranas, W. Yip and
Benjamin Yu.

Contents

Seen at McChord AFB in 1970, this 104th TFS Maryland ANG F-86H was one of the last Sabres in US military service. The extra 'zero' in the serial number differentiates this 53-Fiscal Year machine from those procured in 1963. Ken Mock

Introduction: a Brief History of North American Aviation, Inc.

North American Aviation was incorporated in Delaware on 6 December 1928 by Clement Keys to become a holding company for a number of aviation-related interests. Keys was considered something of a financial guru, and investments of $4.5 million were represented in aircraft-related shares, including those of the Curtiss Aeroplane and Motor Company, Transcontinental Air Transport and the Douglas Aircraft Company. In March 1930 North American Aviation, Inc. (NAA) was listed on the New York Stock Exchange.

The company continued to expand in the post-depression period and in 1932 The General Motors Corporation bought a 29 per cent interest in NAA and pursued the manufacture of Fokker Trimotors at its Dundalk plant in Maryland. With airmail forming a large part of the business, the revisions in the whole postal system during 1934 led to major changes at NAA. In May of that year a new ruling prevented airlines affiliated with any part of the aircraft manufacturing industry from holding an airmail contract after the end of the year.

As a result, North American Aviation was set up with the sole purpose of aircraft building, and 39-years-old 'Dutch' Kindelberger became president, having previously served as vice-president of engineering at Douglas Aircraft. When Kindelberger moved to NAA, he took with him two key aircraft designers from Douglas, Lee Atwood and J.S. Smithson. The Dundalk plant was abandoned too, and Kindelburger moved eighty-five of the employees out to a 159,000-sq ft facility on 20 acres at Inglewood near the edge of the Los Angeles Municipal Airport.

The new NAA team had a daunting challenge ahead for, up to this point, North American had never sold a single aeroplane. For sure, it had done some modification work on obsolete Berliner-Joyce P-16 pursuit aircraft, but that was really all. Therefore the company's first government contract was not for a complete machine, but for 161 sets of floats for US Navy observation aircraft.

Work began in temporary manufacturing quarters while the original Inglewood factory was expanded and modernized. The new premises were occupied during January 1936, with 250 people on the payroll. Kindelberger felt that NAA would have the best chance of success if it concentrated on small, single-engined craft and his vision paid off; an Army Air Corps contract for forty-two basic trainers was awarded and this allowed the company to further modernize the plant at Inglewood.

Starting life as the company project NA-16, a fixed-gear, two-place, low-wing monoplane, which flew on 1 April 1935 (and, coincidentally, the first North American model-numbered to fly), the NA-16 evolved into the Army's BT-9 trainer; eventually more than 250 of the type were delivered, beginning in 1936. Further continued development of the BT-9 design led to the BC-1 combat trainer and eventually to the superlative AT-6 Harvard advanced training aircraft.

With a major war impending, North American forged ahead to new production records, but it was the British that really put the company on the map. Their request in April 1940 for a new fighter aircraft (the NA-73) eventually led to the P-51 Mustang, and the rest, as they say, is history. North American built some 41,000 aircraft during World War II and was ideally placed at its end to lead the way in advanced aircraft design and manufacture.

CHAPTER ONE

The XP-86 and the F-86A

XP-86 Prototype

Background to the Design

The F-86 Sabre design can be traced back to North American Aviation's (NAA) project NA-134, an aircraft originally drawn up for the US Navy. The NA-134 was planned to be a carrier-based jet capable of supporting the invasion of Japan planned for May 1946. More importantly, it needed to be superior in performance to existing shore-based interceptors. As jet-powered aircraft were still in their infancy, the Navy had earlier hedged its bets by pursuing different designs from several manufacturers. Thus the pure jet Chance Vought XF6U-1 Pirate and the McDonnell XFH-1 Phantom were born. In addition, compound fighters were also drawn up, which were to be equipped with a piston engine for quick carrier response and a jet for high altitude, high-speed operation. Ryan's Fireball met this latter requirement, although it should be said that none of these designs ever saw widespread service use, with only the FH-1 going on to better things in the shape of its F2H Banshee derivative.

Work on the NA-134 project began in late 1944, and the NAA designers came up with a fairly conventional design featuring a straight, thin-section wing set low on a rather stubby fuselage. A straight-flow pitot-type nose intake fed air to the jet engine, which then exhausted under the unswept tailplane. The US Navy ordered three NA-134 prototypes under the designation XFJ-1 on 1 January 1945, and on 28 May also approved a contract for a hundred production FJ-1s, known by NAA as the NA-141.

Meanwhile, the US Army Air Force (USAAF) issued a design request for a medium-range, day fighter that could also cope with the escort fighter and fighter bomber missions. A top speed of 600mph (965km/h) was stipulated, and on 22 November 1944 NAA put forward its RD-1265 design study for a version of the XFJ-1 to meet this requirement. Assigned the NAA number NA-140, the USAAF authorized Letter Contract AC-11114 on 18 May 1945 to cover three prototype aircraft. The USAAF designated these aircraft XP-86s.

Both North American fighters were designed around the General Electric J35 axial flow turbojet, but their jointly developed design soon led to compromises. The Naval version required considerable strengthening to cope with high sink-rate carrier landings, and the Air Force aircraft, being less constrained in this area, emerged with a thinner wing and slimmer fuselage, although it shared its tail surfaces with the XFJ-1. Armament for both aircraft would be six .50-calibre machine-guns mounted three on either side of the nose intake, although the XP-86's gun muzzles exited the fuselage further to the rear.

In the XP-86 a 10 per cent thickness to chord ratio wing was utilized to extend the critical Mach number to 0.9. The wingspan was 38ft 2½in (11.63m), the length 35ft 6in (10.8m) and the height to the tip of the vertical tail 13ft 2½in (4.01m). Four-speed brakes were to be installed, which would extend above and below the wings, in a similar fashion to those found on the A-36 dive-bomber. The initial climb rate was quoted as 5,850ft/min (1783m/minute) and the service ceiling was to be 46,000ft (14,020m). The combat radius was 297 miles (477km) with 410gall (1537l) of internal fuel, and this could be increased to 750 miles (1,206km) by adding a 170gall (637l) drop tank to each wingtip. Critically although, at a gross weight of 11,500lb (5,215kg), the XP-86 was estimated to be capable only of reaching 574mph (923km/h) at sea level and 582mph (936km/h) at 10,000ft (3,048m). Clearly, further design work was necessary if the XP-86 was to reach the Air Force's ambitious requirements. Despite this, a mock-up of the straight-wing XP-86 was built and approved by the USAAF on 20 June 1945. Mock-up Review Boards took place in a large work bay on the ground floor of NAA's Engineering Building, located at the south-east corner of Mines Field (nowadays Los Angeles International Airport).

At this point in the life of the XP-86 design a decision was made which would move the aircraft into a different league: that resulted in swept wing and tail surfaces being fitted to cope with the USAAF's higher speed requirement. The radical redesign evolved from one simple fact: even with a thinner aerofoil section the straight-winged aircraft would still not be able to reach the 600mph stipulated.

The idea of sweeping wing surfaces to reduce drag and compressibility effects was not new. However, although a swept wing did reduce the drag coefficient and increase the speed capability, it brought such problems as wing-tip stall and instability in low-speed and high yaw conditions. The understanding and solution of these problems had yet to be fully realized, and on 24 August 1944 the NAA chief aerodynamicist Ed Horkey had travelled to the National Advisory Committee for Aeronautics (NACA) research station at Langley Field, Virginia to study the effects of airflow over a very thin wing operating at high Mach numbers. In conversation with NACA's assistant chief of full-scale research Ira Abbott, Horkey soon discovered that little research had been done into such phenomena and thus little data existed. A tentative programme was set out for Horkey, to include the testing of NACA 1408, 1410 and 1412 aerofoils in the two-dimensional, low-speed wind tunnel. Abbott also suggested that tests should be carried out on NACA 64-section aerofoils and, in modified form, this section was incorporated in the XP-86.

It was at this point that considerable amounts of captured German research documentation began to fall into allied

Swept Wings: Theory into Practice

A conference had been held in Rome during September and October 1935 to discuss high-speed flight, and at this Volta Congress a talented young German engineer from Lubeck named Adolf Busemann had predicted that a swept 'arrow wing' would function effectively inside the shock waves stretching back from the nose of an aeroplane at supersonic speeds. The V-shaped bow waves of ships navigating Lubeck's harbour had initially inspired Busemann. Since there was no contemporary engine capable of propelling an aircraft fast enough to take advantage of this effect, Busemann's theories were not put into practice. But with the advent of the jet engine in the early 1940s his papers took on new meaning and the Germans were not slow in putting the wheels of science and industry into motion.

Concurrently in the United States, a Russian immigrant, Michael Gluhareff had been first to realize the promise of the swept wing while working for Igor Sikorsky. In a 1941 memorandum to his employer, Gluhareff described a possible pursuit-interceptor which would have a delta-shaped wing, swept back at an angle of 56 degrees. His reasoning was simple: to attain 'a considerable delay in the action of the compressibility effect'. A wind tunnel model was built, but the USAAF was too busy with a myriad of other designs and Gluhareff was forced to consolidate his theories instead into the 'Dart' design, the basis for an air-to-ground glide bomb in 1944. This time the Army showed considerable interest and, by a further twist of fate, Gluhareff's Dart was brought to the attention of the NACA aerodynamicist Robert T. Jones at Langley.

With more theoretical work, Jones validated Gluhareff's theories, showing that at supersonic speeds, the swept wing stayed clear of the shock wave and the air flow around the wings remained subsonic. The study of this concept was complete in January 1945, and on 5 March Jones wrote to the NACA's director of research George W. Lewis with the historic words, 'I have recently made a theoretical analysis which indicates that a V-shaped wing traveling point foremost would be less affected by compressibility than other planforms.' Using a modified P-51 Mustang, Langley scientists mounted small test aerofoil sections on the aircraft's wing which would experience accelerated flow close to the wing surface in a dive. Coupled with wind tunnel tests, the results conclusively proved the theories put forward ten years earlier by Busemann. The results of these tests were issued on 11 May 1945, just before the arrival of captured German data. However, the worth of the German data cannot be underestimated; that country had, after all, managed to produce and fly swept-wing aircraft during the war. More importantly, it had managed to solve many of the practical problems associated with wing sweep. Such proven knowledge proved invaluable for the XP-86 design team.

hands, and Air Materiel Command in the USA began to assimilate these data, passing them initially to Boeing. Ed Horkey learnt of the data through George Scharier at Boeing. In addition, as World War II ended, many German scientists started to work on American research and development (R&D) projects and their expertise in swept-wing design was put to good use. As an example of the Germans' progress into high-speed research, they had already put two swept-wing fighters – the Messerschmitt Me 163 and Me 262 – into operational service before the end of the war. In particular, the Me 262 was produced in large numbers and incorporated a 15-degree wing sweep in its design. More importantly, its designers had largely solved the low-speed stability problems of its swept wing by installing automatically operating, leading edge slats. These airfoil-shaped devices were held shut at high speed by aerodynamic forces, but extended at low speeds to increase the effective chord of the wing and thus increase lift. It is worth pointing out that the leading edge slat was a British invention, pioneered by Handley-Page from 1920. The adoption of a slatted wing for the XP-86 transformed it into a

practical fighter with a transonic capability; the information on slats was passed to NAA from the Air Force at Wright Field, Ohio. By June 1945 a swept-wing design was introduced for investigation in parallel and independently of the straight-wing design.

The North American design team was led by John 'Lee' Atwood, and comprised Horkey as chief aerodynamicist, Tony Weissenberger as project engineer with A.C. 'Art' Patch as his assistant. Harrison Storms, Walt Fellers, Larry P. Greene, Dale Meyers and Bill Wahl also gained credit for major inputs into the aircraft. In August 1945, the project aerodynamicist Larry Greene, encouraged by positive wind tunnel results, proposed that a swept-wing configuration for the P-86 should be adopted. Horkey and his group then managed to persuade the USAAF that sweeping the wings would put the XP-86 over the top speed they required, and on 18 August 1945 NAA received an R&D grant to develop the swept-wing XP-86 under design study RD 1369. The following month a wind tunnel model of the new design was tested, and the results were as expected: drag and compressibility effects had been

lowered enough to bring the XP-86 into the 600mph range.

North American's next step was to choose the aspect ratio (the ratio of wing span to chord) of the swept wing. A higher aspect ratio would give better range, a lower (broader) one better stability, and the correct choice would have to be a trade-off between the two. The initial wind tunnel tests had involved a 5.0 aspect ratio wing and, although an anticipated instability at high lift coefficients was present, the incorporation of leading edge slats achieved satisfactory stall characteristics. Further testing was then carried out from late October to mid-November using a 6.0 swept wing, incorporating the Mustang's NACA laminar-flow aerofoil and increased taper to reduce structural weight. A comparative evaluation between the 5.0 and the 6.0 ratio wing then clearly showed that the latter possessed a much higher and advantageous lift/drag ratio, but with violent pitch-up tendencies. The slat testing experience gained on the 5.0 ratio wing was then put to good use and incorporated into the 6.0 ratio configuration, which was adopted as the basic design during October and proposed to the USAAF.

Unfortunately, continued wind tunnel evaluation of the slatted, 6.0 ratio wing failed to overcome the pitch-up problem, despite the fact that 150 different slat designs had been tested. Reluctantly, in March 1946, the design reverted to a shorter 5.0 aspect ratio wing as the starting point. Further wind tunnel work and refinement brought the production wing's aspect ratio to 4.79:1, with a sweepback of 35 degrees and a thickness/chord ratio of 11 per cent at the root and 10 per cent at the tip. At this time high-speed model tests were being carried out in NACA's Ames wind tunnel and it became apparent that full span trailing-edge flow separation was occurring. The cause was quickly pinned down to the relatively high trailing edge angle of the chosen aerofoil section. The solution was simple: a constant 4in chord extension over the full span effectively reduced the angle and maintained flow adhesion. This aerofoil modification also changed the wing plan form and represented the final production configuration of the wing until the advent of the '6-3' wing some years later.

On 1 November 1945 NAA had received permission from Lt Gen Laurence C. Craigie, the head of Air Force R&D at Wright Field, to proceed with the swept-wing XP-86. Ray Rice, NAA's chief engineer, had advised Craigie that the swept-wing development would put the XP-86 programme back by six months compared with the Navy's XFJ-1; but the Air Force agreed that the massive performance gain justified the wait. In the event, the XFJ-1 took to the air for the first time on 27 November 1946 and the first XP-86 nearly a full year later. On 20 December 1946 Letter Contract AC-16013 was approved for thirty-three production P-86As, along with 190 P-86Bs; the latter would have a slightly wider fuselage to accommodate larger main undercarriage units. As it turned out, advances in wheel, tyre and brake technology negated the need for a new design and the order was changed for 188 further P-86As and two P-86C Penetration Fighter prototypes. All these aircraft were constructed at NAA's Inglewood, Los Angeles plant.

Construction

In order to cope with the stresses of high-speed flight, the XP-86 design team had to face new challenges. The thinness of the aircraft's wing effectively ruled out conventional rib and stringer design, and NAA's head of structures Dick Schleicker came up with a revolutionary idea. He created a machine-milled, homogeneous, double-skinned structure which featured integral top hat stiffeners from tip to tip through the centre section. The wing skin was machined to taper in thickness from ¼in (6.4mm) at the root to 0.032in (0.81mm) at the tip, and this form of construction enabled strength requirements to be closely tailored in each area of the wing. A side effect of this design was that it was easier to accommodate wing fuel tanks. The all-important wing-mounted leading edge slats were installed as four independently opening units on each mainplane. The wing-mounted speed brakes of the original XP-86 design were replaced on the actual prototype by hydraulically actuated airbrakes mounted on each side of the rear fuselage. In addition, a single brake panel was fitted in the ventral position, just rear of the wing trailing edge. The speed brakes opened concertina-like from the rear and it was

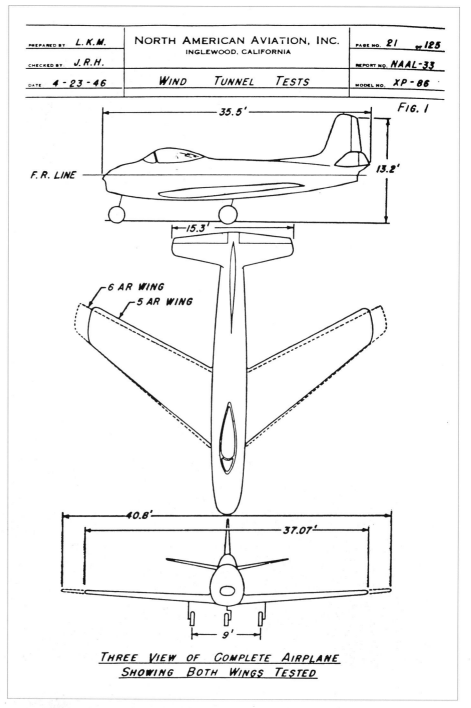

Interim XP-86 configuration from April 1946 showing 5 and 6:1 aspect ratio wings tested. The 5:1 ratio wing was eventually settled upon. NAA via John Henderson

planned that they could be actuated at any attitude and speed, including the supersonic range. However, after the assembly of the first prototype had begun, wind tunnel data showed that this design of airbrake was unsatisfactory. A more conventional, side-mounted, front-hinged airbrake was designed, but flight-testing schedules meant that the no.1

XP-86 would have to fly with the original design. For flight testing, the airbrakes were rendered inoperative and their joints taped over.

To assist in engine removal, the whole rear fuselage could be removed from a point just aft of the wing. The engine exhausted under the swept tail surfaces, just forward of the trailing edge, so that a

This is how the first XP-86 looked before its first flight, late September 1947. Note the original airspeed probe location on the vertical fin. NAA

Another preflight view showing the lack of a fuel dump pipe. The fuel dump was soon fitted just below the leading edge of the left-hand horizontal stabilizer, but moved slightly aft on production machines. Note also the fin-mounted navigation lights; these were relocated to the base of the fin on the P-86A. John Henderson

slight lip was present on the upper edge of the jet pipe. This aspect of the design was said to eliminate snaking at high speeds as well as improving the take-off thrust. The surface finish also received close attention and flush-fitting rivets were installed throughout the external surfaces of the XP-86. These rivets were then milled fully flush after assembly.

From the start of the XP-86 design external fuel tankage was a high priority. With the change from straight to swept wings, however, it became difficult to mount such tanks on the wing tips and maintain a satisfactory centre of gravity. Therefore external fuel-tank pylons were fitted as far inboard as was practicably possible, and this also led to the aircraft's relatively narrow undercarriage track.

The cockpit of the XP-86 was fully pressurized, utilizing air from the engine's eleventh compressor stage at a rate of 10lb/min (4.5kg/min) at 'full cool' or 14lb/min (6.3kg/min) in the 'full heat' setting. Air was routed either through a turbine refrigeration unit for cold settings or bypassed for hot. During the aircraft's test phase considerable problems were experienced in maintaining adequate canopy sealing and, for much of the time, the system was rendered inoperative.

First Flight

The XP-86 prototype 45-59597 was ready for its flight test on 8 August 1947 and would initially be powered by a Chevrolet-built J35C-3 with 4,000lb static thrust. Although the first taxi tests

A poor quality shot, but one that appears to depict the XP-86's first landing at Muroc on 1 October 1947. Note that the aircraft is not using the rear-opening speed brakes which were rendered inoperative for flight testing. Author

Touching down at around 117 knots (216km/h), ground observers were relieved then to see the nose gear slowly extend as the airspeed decreased. At 78 knots (144km/h) Welch reported that he had a 'down' indication in the cockpit, and the aircraft was settled into a normal attitude. '597 rolled to a stop, undamaged.

Subsequent investigation revealed that the nose gear 'down' supply restrictor piston had been badly damaged and the nose gear door sequence valve actuating rod was broken. This rod had caused further damage at bulkhead station 41.5. It soon became apparent that NAA engineers had fitted a retraction jack that was less powerful than that specified. The quick retraction of the nose undercarriage with insufficient hydraulic power to slow the leg against the airflow also damaged several frames on the bottom of the intake duct. Corrective action was taken before

were undertaken at Mines Field in Los Angeles, the prototype was transported by road to Muroc Army Air Field for its first flight at NAA's Flight Test Section. The company test pilot George Welch took the first XP-86 into the air for a ten-minute mission on 1 October, accompanied by a P-82 chase plane. However, soon after take-off undercarriage problems became apparent.

Welch had climbed to 10,000ft (3,048m) and, upon raising the gear at approximately 160 knots (296km/h), found that he did not obtain a cockpit indication of full retraction. This was verified by the chase plane, which also reported an unusually high retraction speed for the nose undercarriage leg. Several cycles of the undercarriage were then made in an attempt to raise the gear fully, but without success. It was then noted that the nose gear would not extend beyond 20 degrees for airspeeds above 130 knots (240km/h). Clearly, although the accumulator pressures were normal, there was simply not enough hydraulic power to extend the nose leg fully into the airstream at even these relatively low speeds. The undercarriage was finally made to raise when Welch cut power to 6,200rpm (note that engine speed was measured in rpm at this time rather than 'per cent', as would become customary for jet engines).

Welch's problems were not yet over though, for although the undercarriage had been retracted successfully, it was

For flight number 26 on 21 November 1947, a long boom was fitted to the tail-mounted pitot probe. Considerable effort was taken during the early days to ensure accurate airspeed readings. NACA ground-based theodolites were used late in 1947, and finally from flight number 78, a 10ft (3.04m) nose-mounted probe was fitted. NAA

then discovered that the nose gear would still not fully extend, even with the use of the emergency system. At this point it was decided to attempt a landing at Muroc with the main gear extended, while trying to hold the nose off the ground for as long as possible. Thus, following a flight that had lasted for forty minutes, Welch brought the stricken machine in to land.

the second flight and included the fitting of a 1gall flow restrictor in the undercarriage 'up' supply line (against the 3gall restrictor previously fitted). Further wind tunnel tests were undertaken to ascertain the air loads on the undercarriage at the maximum lowering speed. It is thought that this investigation led to a redesigned, two-piece, folding nose gear fairing door, introduced on the production P-86A.

At this point it is worth raising an interesting and controversial point. Although history records that Chuck Yeager was the first man through the sound barrier in the Bell XS-1 rocket plane on 14 October 1947, there is now evidence that George Welch beat him to it soon after the first flight of the XP-86. Officially, the XP-86 did not achieve the feat until 26 April 1948, even although NACA personnel at Muroc had tracked the aircraft at Mach 1.03 on 21 November 1947. More importantly, Welch had been flying these same flight patterns (un-monitored by NACA) in the days before 14 October. It is also worth dispelling a commonly held belief here: it is often stated that 'a visiting British pilot' carried out the flight on 26 April. However, the first British pilot to fly the XP-86 (45-59598) was Roland Beamont, and he did not take to the air – and even then for one flight only – until 21 May 1948.

The flying characteristics of the new machine were generally favourable, and soon after the XP-86's first flight, George Welch had this to say:

The plane's so clean you never have trouble. Reduce drag to a minimum and you don't have to worry about effects of compressibility shock waves. Spin recovery is easy when pressure on the elevators is released. [On take off] it seems at first as if the nose is pointed too high and you might stall. You soon get used to it though.

In general, Welch's only concern was that the prototype aircraft did not have enough power. Considering that the J35 engine fitted in '597 produced over 1,000lb (450kg) less thrust than the J47 proposed for production P-86s, this was not too much of a problem. Flight number two was not completed until 9 October and, even then, as a result of the undercarriage problems encountered on the maiden flight, the gear was locked down. Following completion of NAA Phase I testing, Phase II testing by USAF pilots commenced in early December 1947. Maj Ken Chilstrom flew the first and the second flight of Phase II on 2 December, after test flying had moved to Muroc's North Base due to flood conditions on the main site. Although the runway at the North site was much shorter, no problems were encountered. The USAF tests were completed in six

days, comprising eleven flights and ten hours and seventeen minutes of flying time. Chilstrom declared himself highly pleased with the results, although the cabin pressurization system was again inoperative and the aircraft's oxygen system had trouble coping with such a condition. In early 1948 the second and the third prototype – 45-59598 and -599 – were assigned to the test programme.

Following flight number 77 in January 1948, the first XP-86 was grounded for a 25-hour engine inspection. The opportunity was taken at this time to incorporate several modifications and among these was the fitting of a new rear fuselage with the standard airbrake. These side-mounted airbrakes (and the deletion of the ventral brake panel) would become standard fit on all subsequent P-86s plus

the two later XP-86s. Ken Chilstrom has confirmed that the original airbrake system was never used, the wide expanses of Muroc meant that they were not needed in any case.

First tests on the XP-86 showed that the new speed brakes could be safely extended at speeds ranging from 250 to 450mph (407 to 724km/h), although buffeting was reported to be excessive above 400mph (643km/h) with brakes fully extended; their operation was deemed satisfactory up to 450mph (724km/h) when extended 60 per cent. Other modifications carried out to the first XP-86 at this point included the fitting of a 10ft (3.04m) nose boom extension in order to ascertain the gauging of airspeed accuracy. The boom enabled airspeed readings to be taken safely out of any shock-wave effects at

---

George S. Welch (1918–54)

George Welch was born on 18 May 1918 in Wilmington, Delaware. He was the son of George Louis Schwartz and Julia Welch Schwartz. As a result of the ill feeling towards those of German ancestry during World War I, George Schwartz Sr had the last name of his children legally changed to their mother's maiden name Welch. Thus George Louis Schwartz Jr became George Schwartz Welch. George's father was a senior research chemist with Du Pont, indeed he and his family were close friends of the Du Ponts. George was educated in expensive prep schools and graduated from St. Andrews in June 1937. He entered Purdue University that September and proved to be an excellent student. Yet his heart was already lost to aviation and in May 1939 he signed up for the Army's aviation cadet programme. Due to the overwhelming number of volunteers, Welch knew that the wait would be a long one and returned to Purdue in the fall. Finally, at the end of the first semester he was called up.

After earning his wings, 2nd Lt Welch ('Wheaties' to his friends) reported to the 47th Pursuit Squadron at Wheeler Field on Oahu in January 1941. Under control of the 18th Fighter Group, the 47th Pursuit flew Curtiss P-40 Kittyhawks. Francis Gabreski, a fellow pilot said of Welch: 'He was a rich kid... and we couldn't figure out why he was there, since he probably could have avoided military service altogether if he wanted to. George was a real hell-raiser, but he was also an excellent fighter pilot.' In early December 1941 Welch and 2nd Lt Kenneth Taylor moved their P-40s away from the main airfield at Wheeler to a nearby auxiliary field at Haleiwa as part of a gunnery exercise.

On the morning of 7 December the Japanese launched their famous attack on Pearl Harbor, which included the airfields at Hickam and Wheeler Fields. The majority of the American fighters were destroyed on the ground, densely parked in neat rows to make their guarding easier. Hearing of the attack, Welch got into his car with Taylor and set off immediately to Haleiwa. Strapping into their P-40s, the pair managed to get airborne while the attack was still in progress. Welch and Taylor tore into the attacking Japanese formations, landed to rearm and refuel when the first wave of attackers left and were back in the air waiting when the second wave attacked. Only three other American fighter pilots managed to get airborne on that day; while each of these scored confirmed kills, Welch was the most successful with four (plus two probables), while Taylor scored three. Their actions were briefly depicted in the 1970 film *Tora! Tora! Tora!*

Welch was nominated for the Medal of Honor for his actions at Pearl Harbor and Air Force Chief Gen Henry H. Arnold supported the nomination. However, for reasons unknown, intermediate commanders declared that Welch had taken off without proper authorization and could therefore not be awarded the nation's highest military award; instead he received the Distinguished Service Cross.

Welch later shot down three more Japanese aircraft while flying P-39Ds with the 36th FS near Buna. Welch added nine more flying a P-38 with the 80th FS, which included another four-kill mission on 2 September 1943. These proved to be his last, and Welch was then sent home suffering from a severe and prolonged bout of malaria. In 1944, now discharged, he joined North American Aviation and became the chief test pilot at the Inglewood, Los Angeles plant. He then began testing the prototype XP-86 and was closely involved in Sabre test flying for the company until the arrival of the F-100 Super Sabre, which he took into the air for the first time on 25 May 1953. Sadly, the danger of test flying caught up with 'Wheaties' Welch. On 12 October 1954 he was carrying out a maximum performance test dive in an F-100A. A high-g pull-out followed the dive, and it was at this point that the aircraft disintegrated. Although he managed to eject, Welch was mortally wounded by flying debris. Thus ended the life of an extraordinary man and the one who may well have been first through the sound barrier.

This early shot of the no.1 XP-86 shows the taped-up rear-opening speed brakes originally planned for production. They were never used in flight, and in January 1948 a production-standard rear fuselage was fitted to '597. USAFM

high speeds. Returning to the test programme on 29 January, '597 completed flight number 78 on that day, when elevator instability was reported; a short-chord production elevator was fitted subsequently. This showed satisfactory performance. A further seven test flights were then flown until 13 February, when it was ascertained that accurate airspeed readings had indeed been obtained from the wing-mounted probes. It is interesting to note that an official report to the USAF XP-86 Project Officer Col George F. Smith, dated 17 February 1948, stated that the maximum speed thus far attained by the XP-86 was Mach 0.937.

Spinning trials were carried out by George Welch in late May, and comprised

five turns each way with the centre of gravity fully forward on 19 May, followed by the same number on the next day with the CG fully aft. Welch described the recovery characteristics as 'excellent', with only a small amount of elevator reduction being required to bring the aircraft out each time. Spin rate was approximately four seconds per turn. It is thought that '597 received the J47 at some time in its life, but not before October 1948, some time after the first flight of the first production P-86A with J47 power.

The number one XF-86 was delivered to the Air Force on 3 December 1948, having been redesignated from 'P for Pursuit' to 'F for Fighter' on 1 June.

Likewise, when the US Air Force (USAF) became an independent service on 18 September 1947, Army Air Fields were renamed Air Force Bases (AFB). '597 passed to the charge of Wright Patterson AFB on 12 December 1948 for test use, and then in April 1951 it returned to 2759th Air Base Wing at Edwards AFB as a test-support aircraft. Finally in May 1952 the first prototype was assigned to 4901st Support Wing at Kirtland AFB in New Mexico for static testing. It was tested to destruction there on 3 October 1952. The total flying time on the airframe was 241 hours. Note that this airframe was definitely not lost in a flying accident as is often stated.

Two further XF-86 prototypes joined the test programme, differing in some respects. The second and the third aircraft were equipped with AN/ARN-6 radio compass receivers in place of the BC-453B radio

Specifications: XP-86

POWERPLANT
J-35A-5 engine of 4,000lb (1,818kg) thrust

WEIGHTS

empty weight:	9,730lb (4407kg)
design gross weight:	13,395lb (6,074kg)
maximum take-off weight:	16,438lb (7,455kg)
internal fuel capacity:	435gall (1,631l)
external fuel capacity:	2 x 206.5gall (774l) drop tanks

DIMENSIONS

wingspan:	37ft 1in (11.3m)
length:	37ft 6in (11.43m)
height:	14ft 9in (4.49m)
wing area:	274sq ft (25.4sq m)
dihedral:	3 degrees
root chord:	9.9ft
tip chord:	63.47in
incidence:	+1 degree at root; -1 degree at tip
airfoil section:	NACA 0012.64 at root (modified) NACA 0011.64 at tip (modified)
aileron range:	25 degrees up and 18 degrees down
horizontal stabilizer range:	3 degrees up and 9 degrees down
wheelbase:	167.3in (4.24m)

PERFORMANCE

maximum speed:	
at sea level:	591mph (951km/h)
at 14,000ft:	618mph (994km/h)
at 35,000ft:	575mph (925km/h)
stalling speed (slats open, 40 degrees flap, undercarriage down):	107.8mph (173km/h)
service ceiling:	41,200ft (12,557m)
take-off run:	3,030ft (923m)
distance required to clear 50ft (15.2m); obstacle:	4,410ft (1,261m)
maximum rate of climb:	4,100ft/min (1,249m/min)
combat range (with drop tanks):	1,750miles (2,815km)
combat radius (with drop tanks):	575 miles (925km)
limiting flight loads:	+7.33g, -3.00g

ARMAMENT (THIRD PROTOTYPE)
6 x 0.50-calibre M-3 machine-guns capable of 1,200 rounds/min
2 x 1,000lb bombs
20 x 5in unguided rockets
Type A-1A gunsight; AN/APG-5C gunsight radar

Early P-86A production at Inglewood. At the front of this line is the fourth production aircraft, 47-608. Immediately behind is the unarmed 47-609, which later passed to NACA. NASM

range receiver installed on the first prototype. The number two machine, 45-59598, was retired to the 6570th Chemical & Ordnance Group (Air Record & Development Command) at Aberdeen Proving Ground in Maryland during March 1953 and the following month was transferred to the US Army. Total airframe hours were 202. Persistent reports indicate that this machine still exists in some form on the Aberdeen ranges.

The third XF-86 aircraft, 45-59599, flew during May 1948 and was accepted by the USAF on 17 December. It was immediately assigned to 2759th Air Base Group at Muroc (later to become Edwards AFB), where it remained in several test programmes, notably in armament testing, until August 1951. It subsequently underwent depot maintenance and modification at the San Bernardino Air Materiel Area, Norton AFB until April 1952. Like the first prototype, it too was transferred to 4901st Support Wing at Kirtland where it was tested to destruction on 31 August 1952. Total airframe time was just 75 flying hours.

Production and Service: the F-86A

The XP-86 design went into production as the P-86A, and one of the most important differences between these two models was the introduction of the General Electric J47 as the P-86's powerplant. In addition, the airspeed pitot probe was relocated on production P-86As – from the vertical fin to the inner surface of the engine intake. In addition, the one-piece nose-ear door of the XP-86 was redesigned as a folding, two-piece item. The P-86A was also equipped with the standard armament fit – six .50-calibre machine-guns with 300 rounds each. To preserve the streamlined form of the P-86, flush-fitting panels covered the gun muzzles. When the pilot fired the guns these panels were opened automatically and then closed after each burst. Although they often proved temperamental in use, they were installed on every production P-86A. Later, most

fin on the 'A' model. Finally, the four separate slat sections of the prototypes were joined on each wing to act as one item on the production models. Internally, many systems and cockpit changes were also made and the empty weight of the P-86A-1 increased to 10,077lb (4,569kg) although maximum take-off weight remained the same. However, with J47 power the first P-86As could climb nearly 5,000ft (1,524m) higher and the rate of climb was a much-improved 7,800ft/min (2,377m/min). NAA listed the P-86A-1's top speed at sea level as 585mph (941km/h) – over 70mph (112km/h) faster than the prototypes. The P-86A-1 was the first 'block' of aircraft delivered, the '-1' signifying this. Subsequent P-86As (and later models) were therefore further assigned 'block' numbers to signify when significant changes had been made to the basic design. Thus, in line with general USAF policy, the next variant of the P-86A would be the –5, and so on, raising in

as the NA-151, with serial numbers 47-605 to -637. The first aircraft from this batch took to the air from Inglewood on 20 May 1948 powered by a J47-GE-1 engine and, eight days later, this and the second production aircraft were delivered to the USAF. They were, however, immediately returned to North American for test work. Under the USAF aircraft designation changes of 1 June 1948, all P-86A 'pursuit' aircraft became F-86A 'fighters', although it was not until 16 July that the first F-86A was actually assigned to the Air Force. This machine, 47-608, went straight to the 3200th Proof Test Group at Eglin AFB in Florida. It then undertook most of the cold weather testing for the F-86A in Eglin's climatic test facility, being subjected to temperatures as low as -65°F. 47-617 also took part in cold weather tests, this time at Ladd AFB in Alaska during January 1949.

Although many F-86A-1s were later assigned to operational squadrons, they were primarily service test aircraft and most were assigned to research programmes. In particular, the third aircraft, 47-607, was retained at NAA for use as the static test airframe, later being transferred to Wright Patterson AFB in September 1948 for a similar purpose. Other testing duties were: performance and stability test (47-610 at Edwards AFB), armament test (47-611), maintenance evaluation (47-614 and 615 at Chanute AFB), structural test (47-619) and engine control (47-621 with NAA). In addition, two F-86A-1s were handed over to the National Advisory Committee for Aeronautics (NACA): 47-609 was assigned to the Ames Laboratory for variable stability testing and 47-620 to Langley, Virginia. The last Fiscal Year (FY) 47 F-86s delivered were 47-637 and 47-619, on 1 and 21 March, respectively.

47-608 was assigned straight to 3200th Proof Test Group at Eglin AFB on 20 July 1948 for cold weather testing. On 5 September Maj Richard Johnson attempted a new world speed record in this aircraft at Cleveland. Though he failed that time, just ten days later he was successful in another F-86A. Just visible in this shot is the pre-1 June 1948 'PU-' buzz number. W.T. Larkins via J.M.G. Gradidge

surviving aircraft were modified to accept a more conventional, open muzzle.

Other improvements on the production aircraft included the navigation lights, which had been fitted to the trailing edge of the fin tip cap on the XP-86. These were relocated to the engine exhaust's 'pen nib' fairing at the base of the vertical

increments of five with each production change. In addition, if a significant modification was carried out after production the number gaps between each block number could be used, so that a modified P-86A-5 would become a P-86A-6.

The initial production block of thirty-three P-86A-1-NAs were known by NAA

Speed Records

On 25 August 1947 a new world air speed record was set at 650.796mph (1047km/h) by US Marine Corps pilot Maj Marion Carl, flying the Navy's Douglas D-558-1 Skystreak research aircraft. By September 1948 that record still stood and in that month the Air Force decided to try to go one better, by breaking the record again, but this time with an operational aircraft – the F-86A Sabre.

Early F-86 Engine Development

From its inception, the XP-86 was designed around the TG-180 engine, which itself resulted from a US Army request in 1943 to produce a 4,000lb (1,814kg) thrust jet engine. The General Electric company took up the challenge, even though before this GE had produced only a small number of gas turbine engines, notably the I-16 engine which powered Bell's P-59A Airacomet. At this point the I-16 produced just 1,600lb (724kg) of thrust. GE tackled the 4,000lb thrust problem with two designs; one, with a centrifugal compressor, would be built at the Lynn, Massachusetts plant. The second, featuring an axial-flow compressor, was slated for production at the Schenectady, New York factory.

The centrifugal flow engine, by now designated I-40, was quickly produced, and started testing on 9 January 1944; reaching 4,200lb (1,904kg) thrust the following month. This design was immediately a success and flew in the XP-80A aircraft on 10 June 1944. Placed into production, the engine became the J33 and in September 1945 production was transferred to Allison.

Meanwhile, GE's axial-flow engine, although even more promising than the I-40/J33, was taking more time to develop. Designated TG-180, this unit comprised an eleven-stage compressor of constant tip diameter with aluminium alloy discs and steel blades. A magnesium alloy casing enveloped the compressor. Driving a single-stage turbine, the TG-180 featured eight separate combustion chambers of Nimonic alloy. The first TG-180 was run in April 1944 and weighed

2,300lb (1,043kg) for a thrust of 3,620lb (1,641kg). This power level was quickly improved upon, and the TG-180 flew for the first time at around 4,000lb (1,814kg) thrust in the Republic XP-84 prototype on 28 February 1946. Adopted for production, the engine was redesignated J35 and manufactured also by Chevrolet and Allison. Eventually production of this engine was fully transferred to Allison, but it was a Chevrolet-built J35 that powered the first XP-86.

This left GE in a somewhat unenviable position. Despite designing two excellent jet engines, both had been taken away for mass production in order to develop Allison as a viable competitor.

Undeterred, GE then set about building a new Aircraft Gas Turbine division at the Lynn plant under Harold D. Kelsey. It soon became apparent to Kelsey that a development of the J35 engine could swiftly and economically be designed to produce 5,000lb (2,267kg) thrust with better fuel economy.

Therefore the design of the new TG-190 engine went ahead on 19 March 1946, led by Neil Burgess. Using the same frame size as the J35, the TG-190 would be easy to fit in place of the earlier engine, although the compressor and turbine design would be entirely new.

The axial flow compressor of the TG-190 featured twelve stages and the lubrication system also came in for improvement. Although weight reduction was also high on the agenda, the first TG-190 was actually

heavier than the J35, but with a great deal more potential for development.

The USAAF quickly accepted GE's new engine proposal and funded it into production as the J47. The first engine started testing on 21 June 1947 and made its first flight in the first production F-86A on 20 May 1948. Although initial J47 production was carried out at Lynn, it soon became apparent that further production capacity was needed, as the engine had also been chosen to power the B-47 bomber in addition to the F-86. GE then came upon the old Wright engine plant at Lockland, near Cincinnati, Ohio. With fourteen engine-test cells, 150 GE engineering staff moved in and, on 28 February 1949, Lockland (later renamed Evandale) reopened as a General Electric facility. The first Lockland-produced J47 for the USAF was accepted in that same month. This plant quickly became the main General Electric aeroengine headquarters.

The J47 went on to be one of the most successful jet engines in history. Packard and Studebaker also manufactured it and, in total, 35,832 were produced of all marks. It was also the first US jet engine certified for civil use. J47 engines provided auxiliary power for a number of larger aircraft, including the B-36 and the B-50 bomber, as well as the KC-97 tanker. Indeed, the USAF J47 story ends with the KC-97. On 23 June 1978, with the retirement of the Air Force's last KC-97L to the Davis Monthan boneyard, the final USAF J47 engine was also retired.

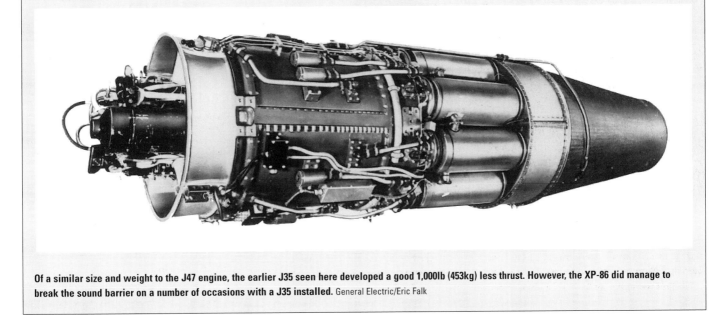

Of a similar size and weight to the J47 engine, the earlier J35 seen here developed a good 1,000lb (453kg) less thrust. However, the XP-86 did manage to break the sound barrier on a number of occasions with a J35 installed. General Electric/Eric Falk

The Air Force decided to make the attempt during the Cleveland National Air Races, held over the Labor Day weekend at Cleveland Airport, Ohio. The fourth production F-86A-1-NA (47-608), a 3200th Proof Test Group aircraft from Eglin AFB was selected to make the attempt, and Maj Robert L. Johnson was to be the pilot. To satisfy Federation Aeronautique Internationale (FAI) rules, a 3km course had to be covered twice in each direction in one continuous flight to compensate for wind. Such runs also had to be carried out below 165ft (50.3m) altitude to enable precise timing with cameras to be made. On 5 September 1948 Johnson took his F-86A out on six low-level passes over the course in front of a crowd of 80,000. Unfortunately, timing difficulties prevented three of these runs from being clocked accurately, even though Johnson had averaged 669.480mph (1077km/h); thus the record could not be certified by the FAI.

A further attempt to set an official record at Cleveland was frustrated by bad weather and by excessively turbulent air. A few days later the undeterred USAF team moved its speed record attempt out to Muroc Dry Lake, where weather conditions were far more predictable and the air was less turbulent. Richard Johnson was again selected for the attempt, although this time he would use F-86A serial 47-611, which had been assigned to Muroc's 2759th Air Base Group on 14 September. The following day he finally set the record at 670.981mph (1079km/h) by flying his aircraft the required six times over a 3km (1.86 miles) course at altitudes between 75 and 125ft (22.9 and 38.1m). This time the cameras worked without any problems and the FAI certified the record.

Record breaker. 47-611 was the aircraft in which Maj Richard Johnson set a new speed record of 670.981mph on 15 September 1948. After an eventful test career this historic aircraft ended its days as a ground instructional airframe with 195th FBS, California ANG at Van Nuys. Donald A.S. MacKay via J.M.G. Gradidge

This 71st FS aircraft, F-86A-5 s/n 48-184, is carrying the rarely-seen 206gal (772l) ferry tanks. Note how these lack the anhedral fins of later models. Dave Menard

Front Line Assignment

The first actual squadron deliveries began on 14 February 1949. At that time 47-627 and 47-628 were assigned to 1st Maintenance Support Group of the 1st Fighter Group at March AFB, California.

They were then transferred to the first squadron to receive the F-86 – the 94th 'Hat in Ring' Fighter Squadron, replacing F-80 Shooting Stars. Between 15 February and 3 March a further eight FY47 F-86s were assigned – they remained with the 1st FG until July 1950, when newer

F-86As arrived with the Group. All except for one aircraft were passed on, mainly to Air National Guard units for familiarization.

The remaining aircraft, 47-635, had been written off in a crash on 8 March 1950 while with the 94th FS, and thus continued an unenviable trend. Despite these problems, from the outset the F-86 proved to be a real pilot's plane.

Jack Owen flew F-86A Sabres with the 81st FIW in England:

I flew F-86As, which had been stationed at Bentwaters before being returned to the US, for over a year. It was a delightful aircraft, uncomplicated; reminded you of a powerful sports car. On my third flight in the F-86 I had a fire warning light and vibrations. So I shut it down and glided about 80 miles [129km] from 30,000ft [9,100m] and made a non-powered landing. It worked just as the book said it would. All the North American aircraft that I flew I thought outstanding: the AT-6 Harvard, B-25 Mitchell, P-51 Mustang and F-86 Sabre.

The first true production version of the F-86, the A-5, started to be delivered in March 1949, with completion of deliveries achieved in September. The 188 aircraft in this batch differed primarily in being fitted with the J47-GE-7 engine. In addition, the windshield glass, which had been rounded on the XP-86 and the F-86A-1, was changed to a vee-shaped item on the F-86A-5. A modified sliding canopy was also introduced which could be jettisoned in flight, and this also featured a shorter Perspex section and a correspondingly longer aluminium fairing at the rear so that an upper position light and the cabin pressure relief outlet could be mounted there. The A-5 also introduced underwing pylons capable of carrying up to 1,000lb bombs or underwing ferry fuel tanks of 206gall (772l) capacity. A heating system was provided for the gun compartments and stainless-steel, fire-resistant oil tanks and feed lines were introduced. Beginning with the hundredth F-86A, which was delivered in May 1949, an improved canopy defrosting system was installed and a special coating was applied to the engine intake ring to reduce the effects of rain erosion. This airframe also marked the introduction of an improved nose-wheel steering system. Earlier airframes were modified to incorporate many of these changes. All F-86A-5s had provision for mounting the AN/ARN-14 radio receiver and the AN/ARN-19 radio set.

Spin testing of F-86As had shown an unexpected problem with the slat system. When the leading-edge slats opened or closed, instead of this being a gentle operation, aerodynamic forces often 'slammed' them in or out. To remedy this, from the fourth F-86A-5 onwards a rubber snubber was installed along with a revised slat track radius. The 116th F-86A, 48-211, was the first to feature a new wing slat mechanism that eliminated the slat lock and provided fully automatic operation.

Deliveries of FY48 F-86As to the squadrons began on 1 March 1949, and by early August seventy-two F-86A-5s had been assigned to the 1st Fighter Group. Starting in late March 1949, seventeen F-86A-5s were also assigned to the 31st Fighter Escort Wing at Turner AFB in Georgia. For a short period confusion reigned, as the 31st was due to receive F-86s from the 1st Fighter Group, which would then revert to F-80s. However, it appears that few of these machines ever reached the 31st and, in any case, the unit continued flying the straight-wing Thunderjet for a few more years and the 1st FG remained in the F-86 business. All the remaining 31st FEW F-86As were reassigned to the 1st Fighter Group on 21 April 1949.

The 1st FG was busy during 1949, not only in coming up to readiness on the F-86A but also in ferrying Sabres for other units, notably 4th FG at Langley. They also had to cope with the Sabre's teething problems, such as turbine wheel failures, drop-tank feed problems and hydraulic failures. Initially the aircraft were restricted to an altitude of 35,000ft (10,668m) while NAA installed new canopy seals at March AFB, and the aircraft were grounded twice in July 1949 while the drop-tank feed problems were sorted out. Many F-86As were to be lost in the early years of service, and even by the end of September 1949 the Group was down by five Sabres as a result of accidents. 2nd Lt Robert Farley of 71st FIS also gained a dubious honour – he became the first pilot to eject from a Sabre on 29 August 1949. 1950 proved no better for the 1st FG, with six F-86As lost in flying accidents and one on the ground.

The torrid time is best summed up by Robin Olds, famous as a P-51 ace in World War II and later to become a MiG-killer in Vietnam. He was operations officer with the 94th FS in the early days:

Looking back, I admit that our methods at that time were verging on the primitive, as compared to the computerized operations of today. Yet we managed to get the job done. We enjoyed a hiatus in those days, a gap between the wars of that era. Life was not without peril and sacrifice. The F-86 was new; its characteristics pushed the boundaries of operational knowledge and maintenance capabilities. We suffered too many losses for complacency. But we were a happy unit and faced each day with spirit and eagerness.
Then came Korea. Like a thunderbolt. We scarcely knew what that far-off place meant in the scheme of things and had little mental preparation for our coming involvement. By

1st Fighter Group F-86A Incidents:1949

Date	Aircraft s/n	Pilot	Circumstances
18 Apr	48-181	Robert DeLoach	hydraulic failure on take-off from Inglewood; pilot killed
10 June	48-135	Capt William Higgins	mid-air collision with 48-191 near Gorman, CA during B-50 intercept; pilot killed
10 June	48-191	Capt Richard Barr	mid-air collision with 48-135 near Gorman CA during B-50 intercept; pilot thrown clear and broke back
18 July	48-161	2nd Lt Richard O'Leary	elevators locked and pilot unable to eject or release canopy; crash landed near Beaumont, CA. Pilot OK.
29 Aug	48-173	2nd Lt Robert Farley	lost hydraulic boost, went into spin after one drop tank hung up, ejected near Indio, CA; pilot OK
? Aug	48-186?	n/k	landed short at night after windshield fogged up; hit runway marker and damaged wing
6 Sep	48-184	n/k	pilot overshot and landed in bean field aftergo-around, Chanute AFB
? Sep	n/k	n/k	drop tank fell off and damaged wing
12 Dec	48-153	n/k	nose-gear collapse
13 Dec	48-151	n/k	nose-gear collapse

then I had moved over to take command of the 71st Squadron. Our whole group moved up to the desert at George AFB, stayed a short while, moved to Griffiss AFB in upstate New York, leaving the 94th behind, and found ourselves assigned to the distasteful task of air defense. Ultimately, my unit was sent down to the armpit of America, Pittsburgh. The upshot was the total dissolution of the 1st Fighter Group. We became separate units, operating in isolation from one another, and serving mostly as replacement training units for the F-86 squadrons in Korea.

Up to this point, the F-86 had been unofficially known as the 'Silver Charger' by NAA personnel, continuing an equine theme started with the P-51 Mustang. However, men of the 1st Fighter Group organized a naming contest in February 1949 and, of seventy-eight entries, 'Sabre' was considered the winner. The Air Force immediately accepted the name, making it official on 4 March, although the media began to use the term 'Sabrejet'.

Further expansion of the Sabre units began on 7 June 1949 with the delivery of two Sabres to the 4th Fighter Group at Langley AFB, Virginia, followed by another seven two days later. The 81st Fighter Group at Kirtland AFB in New Mexico then also began to re-equip with FY48 Sabres and was assigned five aircraft on 31 August 1949. These three Groups were assigned to several air-defence assignments; the 1st FG was tasked with covering the Los Angeles area, including many aircraft manufacturing plants such as NAA's Sabre factory at Inglewood. In turn, the 4th Fighter Group provided defence for the Washington DC area, and the 81st FG was assigned to the many research plants in the New Mexico area, including the Alamogordo nuclear research facilities.

On 23 February 1949 a further 333 F-86A-5s were ordered under contract AC-21671 as NAA model NA-161s. Serialled as FY49 aircraft, these machines were powered from the outset by the J47-GE-13 engine, now rated at 5,200lb (2,358kg) of thrust. Other changes included simplified cockpit wiring, and from the 282nd F-86A (49-1067), the wing was slightly redesigned, with a shorter-chord aileron and greater elevator boost. An AN/APX-6 radio replaced the SCR-695B from 49-1227 onwards.

Contrary to popular belief, the FY49 A-model did not introduce the conven-

Unlike many other 91st FS F-86As, 49-1063 did not deploy to England during 1951. Instead, as shown here, it was routed through NAA's Long Beach facility for upgrade in August 1951. It was subsequently assigned to 62nd FIS at O'Hare International Airport, Chicago. It was written off in a flying accident on 5 May 1952. W.T. Larkins via Marty Isham

tional machine-gun muzzle; these were fitted to all aircraft on a later upgrade.

The FY49 F-86A-5s began to be delivered in early October 1949, with the first few passing to the 81st FG. The 1st FIW received its first 49-FY Sabre in January 1950, but the majority of the new aircraft did not begin to reach the wing until June. Ten of these aircraft were then lost in November 1950 to the 4th FIW, which was just preparing to depart for the Korean theatre.

Other new Sabre wings also started to convert on to the type in 1950. The 33rd FIW at Otis AFB, Massachusetts received its first six Sabres straight from Inglewood on 20 January and the 56th FG at Selfridge, Michigan also gained its first three new F-86As in April of the same year. The final multi-squadron wing to receive the F-86A was the 23rd FIW, based at Presque Isle AFB in Maine. Its two squadrons received Sabres from 5 November 1951.

Early Upgrading

As with any new aircraft, it was inevitable that modification would be required to early model F-86As to bring them up to the standard of later machines. This upgrade began in 1949 with the fitting of J47-GE-7 engines to as many aircraft as possible, followed by a further upgrade to the GE-13 powerplant. These engines

were usually fitted in the field by USAF maintenance organizations, and by May 1950 most FY47 F-86As and all FY48 Sabres had been re-engined with the J47-GE-13. In addition to the field modifications, most FY48 F-86As were put through NAA's Long Beach plant for upgrading, starting in August 1950, and over 200 of the FY49 aircraft also passed through Long Beach until November 1951. Work carried out at Long Beach included the fitting of a conventional gun muzzle panel in place of the troublesome muzzle doors. The intake-mounted pitot probe was also relocated to the right wing tip, as it had been found that intake-air-pressure fluctuations caused unreliable airspeed readings on the early aircraft.

Training Use

With the huge increase in the operational units flying the F-86, it was logical that a dedicated training unit should be formed to cope with conversion on to the type. Therefore on 13 March 1950 the 3595th Pilot Training Wing at Las Vegas AFB in Nevada received two F-86As to begin familiarization with the Sabre. Further deliveries were made in October, when the first of twenty-four new-build F-86As arrived with the unit, Las Vegas AFB having been renamed Nellis AFB on 1 August. Eight of the newly-assigned Sabres were almost immediately lost to

Blue-trimmed squadron commander's F-86A from 60th FIS. Taken at Westover AFB during the 1950 Veterans Day, 49-1143 still has the early-style gun blast panel. Note how the lower door appears to be jammed open or, as often happened, it has been removed. R. Willet via Marty Isham

the Korean War effort, but were replaced by eight older FY48 Sabres in January/February 1951, plus one as an attrition replacement. Nellis then became the centre of Sabre flight training and also home to the highest attrition rate outside Korea; although only three Sabres were actually lost to flying accidents in 1951, a further sixteen were written off with the 3595th in the following year.

It appears that some thought was also given to the equipping of the 3525th Pilot Training Wing at Williams AFB with F-86As. In August 1950 five FY49 F-86A-5s were assigned straight off the production line to Williams AFB. They did not stay long, however, and were all reassigned to the 1st FIW by the end of October.

A few other USAF squadrons were also equipped with the F-86A, although they are often overlooked since they were not assigned to the normal '3-squadron' wing. One such unit was the 93rd Fighter Interceptor Squadron (FIS). Originally based at Kirtland AFB with the 81st Fighter Group, the 93rd FIS remained in New Mexico when the rest of the Group moved to Washington State in 1951. The 93rd then transferred to 34th Air Division control and flew the F-86A until June 1954. Another unit that briefly flew the F-86A was the 97th FIS, based at Wright Patterson AFB. Initially equipped with the later F-86E model, the 97th's aircraft were despatched to Korea in the autumn of 1951 and, as replacements, the unit then began to receive F-86As in November. These, however, remained only until March 1952, when sufficient F-86Es were available to re-equip the 97th FIS again. The two remaining squadrons to convert to the F-86A were the 15th FIS at Davis Monthan AFB and the 469th

FIS at McGhee-Tyson AFB in Tennessee. The 469th was assigned to the defence of the Alcoa aluminium plant as well as the Tennessee Valley dams.

In addition to the deployment of 4th FIW Sabres to Korea, one other Wing moved overseas with F-86As. During 1951 the 81st Fighter Interceptor Wing at Larson AFB, Washington, was alerted for a move to the United Kingdom. In addition to the Wing's assigned 91st and 92nd FISs, the 116th FIS Washington ANG was called to active duty on 1 February 1951 and attached to the 81st FIW, also for deployment overseas. Departing for Britain in squadrons, the 116th's F-86As were the first to leave, on 15 August and routed via Goose Bay, Bluie West One, Iceland and Stornoway before arriving in England on 27 August 1951. The F-86As of 92nd FIS followed next, landing at their new base on 5 September, and the whole Wing's aircraft were in place by 26 September 1951. The 81st FIW had its headquarters at RAF Bentwaters, alongside the 91st FIS, while the 92nd FIS and the 116th FIS were stationed at RAF Shepherds Grove. On completion of its active duty stint, the 116th FIS returned to state control on 1 November 1952 and, on the same day, the reactivated 78th FIS took over aircraft and personnel from the ANG squadron at Shepherds Grove. The 81st FIW would remain in England for over 40 years; it replaced the F-86As with F-84F Thunderstreaks during early 1954. The Sabres were returned to the United States by boat via Belfast.

The F-86A Weapons System

Standard armament for all F-86As was a bank of six M3 .50-calibre machine guns; 300 rounds of ammunition per gun could be carried, in removable containers fitted

Traces of Korean War i.d. bands are visible on the fuselage of this 75th FIS F-86A. It served with the unit at Suffolk County AFB, NY for only four months, from April to August 1953. Howard Levy via Mike Fox

In late 1952 all 81st Fighter Interceptor Group Sabres in England gained Korean-style wing and tail bands. At the same time, unit markings were toned down, and this 92nd FIS Sabre carries only a yellow squadron band on the nose and the 'skulls' unit badge. Sam Adams

below the machine-guns themselves. In the F-86A empty shell cases and links were retained after firing, and these were collected in containers fitted in the lower fuselage, just fore and aft of the live ammunition containers. However, the way in which the machine-guns were brought to bear varied greatly with the various production blocks.

On the XP-86 provision for an A-1A gunsight was provided, although only one aircraft carried the full armament. From the first production F-86A-1 the gun aiming was standardized with the fitting of the Mark 18 gunsight. Similar in

appearance and operation to the K-14C gunsight fitted to the P-51D Mustang, the Sabre's Mk 18 was a lead-computing sight that included both gyro and fixed sighting systems. When the pilot had identified his target he would set the span selector to correspond with that of the target and aim his aircraft to keep the target within an illuminated circle of six diamonds on the gunsight reflector. When the target had been framed within the circle for one second the gunsight then computed the lead and the guns could be fired. The Mk 18 gunsight was fitted as standard for all F-86As up to the 530th example

(49-1315). It is interesting to note that all the production F-86As had provision from manufacture to fit the A-1B gunsight and the AN/APG-5C radar ranging equipment.

The last twenty-four F-86As received the A-1CM gunsight, which was linked to an AN/APG-30 radar installed in the upper intake lip. The installation of a gunsight radar introduced the aluminium intake surround, with just a small radar-transparent panel on the upper intake lip to cover the radar transmitter/receiver aerial. This radar had a range of up to 3,000yd (2,743m) and could automatically lock on to and track a target. It would then provide an indication when lock-on had been accomplished. Alternatively, the pilot could select manual control of the gunsight. There were, however, two minor drawbacks with the radar ranging system. First, on overland targets at less than 6,000ft (1,828m) altitude radar ranging was often erratic because of ground 'clutter' – spurious radar returns from the ground. In this condition, these effects could be lessened by reducing the radar sweep range or by switching to manual. A second problem could result from the radar's locking on to the wrong point if multiple targets were within the radar sweep area. The pilot, therefore, had to be vigilant to ensure that this did not happen. On the A-1CM gunsight image information was presented on the reflector as a dot within a continuous circle, rather than as diamonds. The A-1CM system could also be used as a bombing sight, and in this condition the extinguishing of the sight circle on the reflector indicated the bomb release point.

The F-86A could carry up to 1,000lb (453kg) of bombs on each drop-tank pylon, although this configuration reduced the combat radius to a mere 50 miles (80 km). The aircraft could also mount up to sixteen 5in unguided rockets for the air-to-ground role.

On 2 April 1951 contract AF-18188 agreed the upgrading of 350 older F-86A models to this later standard through a programme of factory modification. Between January 1952 and August 1953 these aircraft passed through NAA's

USAF Service

The following USAF units received the F-86A (with the initial base assignment):

1st FG (later FIW): 27th, 71st and 94th FS, March AFB, California
4th FG (later FIW): 334th, 335th and 336th FS, Langley AFB, Virginia
23rd FG (later FIW): 74th and 75th FS, Presque Isle AFB, Maine
33rd FG (later FIW): 58th, 59th and 60th FS, Otis AFB, Massachusetts
56th FG (later FIW): 61st, 62nd and 63rd FS, Selfridge AFB, Michigan
81st FG (later FIW): 91st, 92nd and 116th FS (later 78th FIS), Kirtland AFB, New Mexico
15th FIS, Davis Monthan AFB, Arizona
93rd FIS, Kirtland AFB, New Mexico
97th FIS, Wright-Patterson AFB, Ohio
469th FIS, McGhee-Tyson AFB, Tennessee
3595th Pilot Training Wing, Las Vegas AFB (later renamed Nellis AFB)

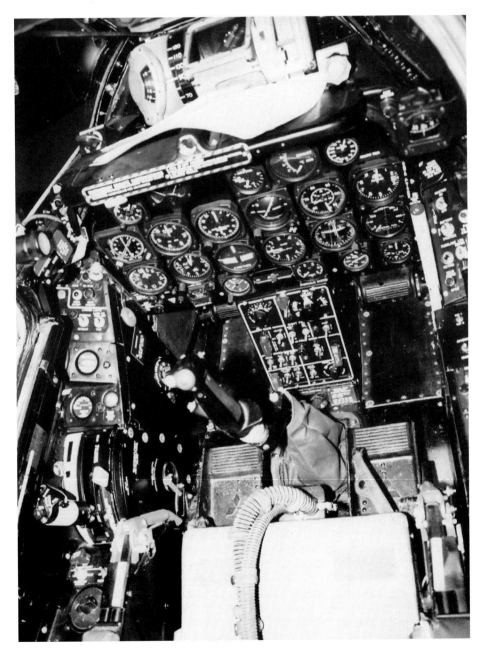

Fresno factory to have an updated gunsight and radar installed and as such they were redesignated. F-86A-5s fitted with the A-1CM sight and AN/APG-5C radar became F-86A-6s, but, more commonly, the AN/APG-30 radar was fitted with the A-1CM and these models were known as F-86A-7s. Modified aircraft could be readily distinguished by the presence of an aluminium intake ring in place of the earlier all-fibreglass item. No FY47 Sabres were brought up to the later standard.

The Korean War

The Background to the Conflict

At 0400hr local time on Sunday, 25 June 1950, the fragile post-war peace was suddenly broken as Communist North Korea launched a massive attack on the southern Republic of Korea (ROK). Although tensions had been high and the Republic had built fortifications along the 38th parallel (the line of latitude that divided North and South), the invasion came as some surprise. By 0600 North Korean columns, supported by Soviet-supplied T-34 tanks, had driven through ROK lines at Chunchon in central Korea and Kaesong in the west. Meanwhile, on the east coast Red troops were set ashore from small boats and junks at Kangnung. By 0900 Kaesong had fallen and this, along with news of the landings on the

Though this cockpit view is of restored F-86A-5 s/n 48-178, the superb stock restoration shows all the standard, early-model features, including the Mk18 gunsight. Author

east coast, graphically demonstrated that this was no skirmish.

By 0945, messages were being sent to Far East Air Forces (FEAF) units of the US armed forces, although it was not until 1130 that the acting commander of FEAF, Gen Earl E. Partridge, was located and informed. The most senior US military man in the theatre was Gen Douglas MacArthur, who held the position of Chief of US Far East Command, taking in all US forces in the area. By midnight on 25 June, only 20 hours after the invasion had started, Gen MacArthur learned that Communist tanks were only 17 miles (27km) north of Seoul. The time difference between Korea and Washington meant that news of the invasion actually broke in the US capital on the evening of 24 June.

On the afternoon of 25 June the United Nations, meeting in emergency session, ordered the North Koreans to start an immediate withdrawal, a request that was predictably ignored. Furthermore, the UN resolution called for all member nations to render assistance in its execution. On 27 June President Truman authorized American units to oppose the invasion, and Gen MacArthur committed FEAF to action against the attacking forces. Gen Partridge then ordered US units into action to support an air and sea evacuation of US citizens from the Republic at 1130hr.

At this point, the Republic of Korea Air Force (ROKAF) possessed only eight Piper L-4s, five Stinson L-5s and three NAA T-6 Texans – all propeller-driven, liaison and training machines. However, Japan-based FEAF units were far better equipped. In the theatre 8th Fighter Bomber and 35th Fighter Interceptor Wings were flying F-80 Shooting Stars, two Fighter All-Weather Squadrons (the 68th and the 339th) were operating F-82 Twin Mustangs and the 3rd Bombardment Wing was equipped with Douglas B-26 light attack bombers. Finally, the 8th Tactical Reconnaissance Squadron carried out its mission with RF-80C Shooting Stars.

On Okinawa further units of FEAF were based, including 51st FIW with F-80Cs, 4th Fighter (All Weather) [F(AW)] Wing flying F-82Cs and a number of RB-29 reconnaissance bombers of 31st Photo Reconnaissance Squadron, Very Long Range. Guam was the base for B-29 heavy bombers of 19th Bombardment Wing,

while in the Philippines 18th FBW operated F-80Cs. Finally, a number of F-51 Mustang fighters, on the point of being turned over to the South Koreans, were used in the early stages of the war. As UN member states entered the fray, further aircraft arrived in the area from the US Navy, the South African Air Force, the Royal Navy and the Royal Australian Air Force.

In support of the evacuation, 339th and 68th FIS, plus 4th F(AW)W F-82s, were deployed to Itazuke in Japan, from where they flew top cover in the Inchon harbour area. More F-80 aircraft from 9th FBS and 8th FBW also supported this mission. Initially, North Korean Air Force (NKAF) operations were light, but at noon on 27 June, five Yak fighters swept in over Seoul at 10,000ft (3,048m), heading for the main evacuation base at Kimpo. Five F-82s of 68th and 339th FISs then intercepted the intruders, shooting down three NKAF aircraft. Lt William G. Hudson of 68th FIS was later credited with the first kill of the Korean War.

The early days of the conflict showed that UN forces were able to keep the NKAF at bay during the evacuation, mainly as a result of the latter's obsolete inventory. On the day the war began the NKAF was able to deploy one Air Division, comprising one Ground Attack Regiment with ninety-three IL-10s, one Fighter Regiment – the 56th, with seventy-nine propeller-driven Yak-9s, one Training Regiment with sixty-seven training and liaison aircraft (including twenty-two Yak-16 transports and eight Polikarpov Po-2 trainers). The Air Division was supported by two maintenance battalions, the total strength being 2,829 servicemen. A number of Lavochkin La-11 fighters were also possessed, again propeller-driven. Having first suppressed the forces of North Korea, FEAF and UN Forces then turned to the task of halting the rapid North Korean advance on the ground. Despite repeated attacks on the Communist troops, however, by early September the UN armies had been squeezed down into a small area south of the Naktong River, known as the Pusan perimeter. There was now a real fear that UN troops would be forced to evacuate the peninsula altogether.

However, Gen MacArthur's inspired counter-invasion at Inchon on 15 September 1950 suddenly turned the tables in the Allies' favour, and, by the

end of the month, the Communist forces had been driven completely out of South Korea. With this success, and in spite of President Truman's reluctance, MacArthur then decided to enforce his desire to see Korea reunited under one flag and ordered UN troops to advance north across the 38th parallel. This brought Chinese troops to full alert and marked the beginning of that country's involvement in the conflict. At the end of October UN forces were nearing the Chinese frontier and some ROK units actually reached the Yalu River on 26 October. Ten days previously Chinese flak positions on the northern banks of the Yalu had shown their intent by shooting down an F-51D Mustang. But more sinister events would soon unfold.

At 1345 on 1 November 1950 a flight of F-51 Mustangs, supported by a T-6 'Mosquito' forward air controller, were fired upon by a flight of six swept-wing jets just south of the river. The American pilots all managed to escape, but the T-6 returned to Pyongyang to report a close-range look at the aircraft. The MiG-15 had arrived in Korea.

The MiGs were committed to the fray by the Chinese, they having signed an agreement with the Soviets in February 1950 for a supply of the fighters. More would then begin to flow into the NKAF's hands. On 8 November USAF F-80Cs tangled with four MiGs in history's first jet versus jet battle. Results were difficult to assess, for although Lt Russell J. Brown claimed a MiG shot down, Communist counter claims state that this aircraft managed to recover back to base. It thus seems therefore that the credit for the first kill of one jet by another probably falls to a MiG pilot. These early jet skirmishes showed that, mainly because of pilot inexperience and a lack of aggression, the UN fighters could just about hold their own. However, there was no doubt that the MiG itself was a far better fighter than any UN held in theatre, and, when the Communist fighters began to attack B-29 bombers near the Yalu, their F-80 escorts could do little to catch the much faster Red jets. Clearly, the United Nations required a better fighter aircraft in Korea. There was only one choice.

Enter the Sabre

On 8 November 1950 USAF Chief of Staff Gen Hoyt Vandenberg offered to deploy an F-86A Wing to FEAF, provided that Gen Partridge could make airfields ready for the unit in the theatre. Moving quickly, Partridge and Gen Stratemeyer at FEAF accepted the offer and, in response, the USAF issued movement orders that same day for 4th FIW to prepare its Sabres for immediate overseas movement under Operation *Straw Boss*.

Having begun equipping with the F-86A at Langley AFB in June 1949, at the time of their movement notification the 4th Fighter Interceptor Wing and its combat Group, commanded by Col John C. Meyer, was assigned to Eastern Air Defense Force. Further, the three squadrons had been dispersed during August, 334th FIS to New Castle County Airport in Delaware, 335th FIS to Andrews AFB in Maryland, with the third squadron, the 336th FIS, moving into Dover AFB, Delaware. With just four days to prepare for departure, 4th FIW commander, Col George F. Smith, was

given a 'red ball' priority by Gen Vandenberg to requisition aircraft, equipment and personnel as necessary to complete the move; all would be ready to go at 1100hr on 11 November. The Wing took off in a snowstorm, bound for McLellan AFB in California. From there the aircraft were prepared for transport by ship to Japan. Advance echelon personnel deployed by air to Japan at this time.

One of George Smith's first priorities had been to unload as many of the Wing's FY48 Sabres as possible and, with this in mind, at least thirty-six FY49 Sabres were diverted to 4th FIW from other US-based units. These aircraft were reassigned on 12 November, from the 1st, 33rd and 56th Fighter Interceptor Wings and made up the seventy-five aircraft required for Wing strength. They arrived at McLellan AFB just in time to be readied for deployment aboard the escort carrier USS *Cape Esperance* at San Diego along with the

other assigned Sabres. John Henderson, NAA's technical representative for the deployment, remembers one Sabre arriving for 335th FIS: 'One of the F-86s was delivered to Andrews from Selfridge by then 1st Lt 'Hoot' Gibson, the third American jet ace. He expressed his wish to join the 4th deployment and the Red Ball magic granted his wish and he returned to Selfridge and packed his bag.'

Further personnel and equipment, mainly from 336th FIS, was loaded on to a tanker at San Francisco. On 1 December 1950 the *Cape Esperance* arrived at Yokosuka in Japan, and the Sabres were unloaded and taken to Kisarazu for air testing.

Gen Partridge had planned to base the 4th FIW at Pyongyang, but by the time of their arrival in Korea the Wing's intended base was back in Communist hands following the Chinese counterpunch on 26 November. It quickly became clear that Kimpo was the only option, and even then its crowded state meant that only a partial deployment would be possible. With this in mind, Col Smith took Detachment 'A' to Kimpo on 13 December, comprising a small number of Sabres and pilots, mainly from 336th FIS.

Grease-protected F-86As aboard the USS Cape Esperance **for deployment to Korea, November 1950. With the acquisition of many FY49 F-86As from other units in the United States, a number of unit markings are visible here besides the 4th FG examples. In particular, 33rd FG Sabres (tapered tail flashes) and those from 56th FG are visible.** John Henderson

On 17 December 1950 Bruce Hinton scored the Sabre's first MiG-15 kill. Here, his crew chief is seen applying the 'kill' marking to the side of Hinton's Sabre, 49-1236. This historic machine was lost to enemy action during a combat mission on 24 October 1951, though the pilot on that occasion was Lt Bradley Irish. He became a PoW. John Henderson

In 1948 Smith had been assigned as USAF project officer to the XP-86 test programme; he was no stranger to the Sabre, along with many others in the Wing who also had World War II combat records. The Kimpo detachment flew its first area orientation sortie during 15 December and was immediately committed to action. The unit's mission was simple: to fly combat air patrols over North Korea and to destroy MiGs. Tactics to deal with the MiGs were discussed and it was here that the combat experience of the Wing's pilots came to good use. A procedure was adopted that would become standard practice throughout the conflict. Flights of four aircraft would take off at 5min intervals, flying in 'fingertip' formation to give a defensive posture against surprise attack. When enemy fighters were engaged, the flight would drop their wing tanks and break into two-ship elements, with the element leader protected during engagement by his number 2 or wingman. To ensure that this tactic worked, it was imperative that the wingman covered his leader by constantly checking his tail. This left the leader to concentrate on the kill without worrying whether he was in turn being engaged

from behind. To further enhance the effectiveness of this method, Sabres would arrive in the combat area at altitudes ranging from 27,000 to 33,000ft (8,229 to 10,058m). This was slightly below the level that contrails formed and gave the Sabre pilots the ability to spot their higher-flying prey from some distance.

Delayed in resuming their flying commitment by bad weather at Kimpo, a mission was finally flown on 17 December with the 336th FIS commander Col Bruce Hinton leading the four Sabres of 'Baker' Flight north towards the Yalu for a fighter sweep. On this sortie a flight of four MiG-15s, apparently presuming on an easy F-80 kill, were surprised to find that the odds were out of their favour. Hinton, flying 49-1236, succeeded in shooting down one MiG, the remaining aircraft returning to safety across the Yalu. But Hinton's flight had been lucky. They had not adopted the intercept tactics described above; instead they arrived near the Yalu at low speed and ordinarily would not have been able to engage a MiG effectively. However, luck had been on their side as the enemy aircraft were spotted below and climbing. The Sabres managed to gather speed in the dive and

the rest, as they say, is history. A lesson had been learnt.

Two days later, Hinton led another sweep up to the Yalu, where they were engaged by six MiGs, although this time the Communist aircraft merely flew through the Sabre formation before turning back north with not a shot fired. It seemed that news of the Sabres' arrival in Korea had spread quickly.

The Soviets Join In

Almost coinciding with the 4th FIW's arrival in Korea, the Soviet Union had in November committed its 64th Fighter Aviation Corps to battle. Igor Gordelianow recently interviewed one of those involved – Alexandr Smortzkov – who commanded the 18th Aircraft Regiment, equipped with MiG-15s:

In June 1950 I was flying a MiG-15 out of Moscow when the commander of the Moscow Air Defence, Gen Col K. Moscalenko, informed me of the arrival of top-secret orders concerning the conflict in Korea. The signal to initiate the orders, 'Polikarpov Po-2 in flight', had been received and we were to board a secret train at night to travel to the Far East. When we arrived in the Far East we found the weather to be very bad; heavy tropical downpours such as I have never experienced in my lifetime. Many ducks were swimming on our airfield. First we operated from Mukden airbase, but after a few days our eighteen-aircraft regiment was transferred to Antung airbase. Our first flights were in formation with MiG-15s from other regiments: twenty-four MiG-15s in three groups of eight aircraft. We were dressed in Chinese uniforms and our aircraft carried Chinese insignia. Initially, we were ordered to speak only Korean over the radio. Since most Russian pilots did not know Korean and we had to use Korean dictionaries for even the simplest words necessary for fighting and flying, as you can imagine, this order was soon abolished.

The Soviets had good reason to be in Korea; not only were they acting to protect a fellow Communist nation, they were also using the war to initiate the battlefield testing of MiG-15s (and later, in small numbers, Lavochkin La-15s). Headquartered at Antung in November 1950, the unit was tasked with three main objectives: air defence of the area north of the 38th Parallel, protection of the trans-Yalu bridges and the training of North Korean and Chinese pilots. Further to this, a more sinister mission became a priority – the management of overt and covert human intelligence (HUMINT) targeted against the USAF. Soviet pilots were directed to employ a variety of tactics to capture Sabre pilots and their aircraft. This mission was a partial success, as will later become apparent.

much; in the Korean War, 68 per cent of MiG killers were aged 28 or over, with an average of eighteen World War II missions each.

First Sabre Losses

Quickly gaining experience in the combat arena, 4th FIW pilots further developed their tactics for patrolling the area now known as 'MiG Alley'. Whenever there

dogfight lasted for about 20min and took the protagonists from 30,000ft (9,144m) down to the deck. The final score was six MiGs claimed killed for one Sabre loss. That aircraft, 49-1176, the first Sabre to be shot down was flown by Capt L.V. Bach who was killed in the action.

However, the Sabres appeared to have the upper hand, and further MiG engagements were not made until 30 December. Even then, when thirty-six of the Red fighters engaged a flight of Sabres, they were notably cautious and no kills were made on either side. And so ended 1950, at which point 4th FIW Sabres had flown 234 sorties, during which the seventy-five Sabres had claimed eight MiGs for just one loss. This was only partially true, of course, as another F-86A had been lost by this time in a non-combat flying accident in Korea. By the end of the year the Communist forces had managed to push further south and reluctantly the Sabres were pulled back to Johnson AB in Japan, out of reach of MiG Alley. It was not until 10 February 1951 that Kimpo airfield was regained by UN forces, allowing Sabres back into the fray.

A small detachment of six Sabres (49-1210, -1225, -1227, -1272, -1307 plus one other) was sent to Taegu in Korea on 14 January, however. The idea had been to evaluate the F-86A in the fighter-bomber role and at least three Sabres were assigned to 8th FBW for this purpose on 17 January; but in practice they were ill-suited to the mission after it was realized that, with bombs on their wing pylons instead of fuel, the Sabre had only minimal range and endurance. Further attacks were made using 5in rockets, but with drop tanks fitted only two projectiles could be carried; again the results were inconclusive. In early February the detachment was recalled to Japan, marking the end of the trial.

With the Sabres temporarily out of the action, the MiG forces became bolder, having shot down an F-80 near Sinuiju on 21 January and an F-84 on a bombing mission over the Chongchon River bridge the same day. The story was not one-sided though; one of the MiGs was in turn shot down by a Thunderjet piloted by Lt Col William E. Bertram, CO of 523rd FBS. Further MiGs were downed by Thunderjets on 23 January, but the withdrawal of more aircraft to Japan meant that the cover afforded to FEAF's

In the early days in Korea, maintenance personnel had to contend with primitive working conditions. Here, 336th FIS Sabre 49-1147 is undergoing an engine change at Kimpo. This aircraft was lost on 16 October 1951, when its pilot ran out of fuel on a combat mission. He ejected safely. John Henderson

It is interesting to note that the Russian pilots, many of whom had flown as allies with the USAF airmen during the Great Patriotic War, thought of their adversaries not as enemies but as opponents in a duel.

Similarly, although the USAF Sabre pilots did not know of the Soviet involvement at the time, they quickly gained respect for MiG pilots who were clearly more skilled than the Chinese or the Korean airmen they usually encountered. Plainly, in the game of dogfighting experience counted for

was the risk of attack, the Sabres would be flown at speeds above 0.85 Mach, to the detriment of patrol time, which fell to just 20min. However, this enabled the USAF aircraft to improve their odds in combat with the MiGs. In addition, standard Sabre patrols would consist of sixteen aircraft or four flights of four, arriving at slightly different altitudes at 5min intervals. The worth of this new tactic was amply demonstrated on 22 December when a mission led by Group commander John Meyer encountered more than fifteen MiGs. The ensuing

bombers was less than adequate. The situation came to a head on 1 March when B-29s from the 98th Bombardment Group were ordered back into action against targets in MiG Alley. On that day eighteen bombers ran into strong headwinds and missed their fighter-escort rendezvous. Just after the B-29s had dropped their bombs on the Kogunyong bridge they were attacked by nine MiG-15s. Ten of the bombers were damaged and three had to make emergency landings at Taegu. This crippling attack provided the impetus to get the Sabres back into Korea.

Back to MiG Alley

On 26 January UN forces managed to recapture Suwon airfield, and on 10 February US I Corps took Kimpo. Gen Partridge then informed his staff that he wanted the 4th FIW to begin using these airfields as soon as possible, although 5th Air Force aviation engineers were spread thinly and the repairing of the bomb-cratered runways took longer than expected. By the beginning of March Suwon was still little more than a barely repaired runway in a waterlogged terrain. Sabres using the base would have to land in trail and backtrack along the runway edge after landing since no taxiways were yet available. Nonetheless, on 6 March 334th FIS began to stage Sabre patrols

through Suwon, and with the completion of basic parking areas and tented accommodation, the squadron moved in four days later. Concurrently 336th FIS also started to stage patrols from Taegu through Suwon.

The mission for these units was simple: to fly combat air patrols over north-western Korea at any time UN aircraft were attacking targets in the areas where MiGs were prevalent. Utilizing tactics honed during late 1950, the 4th FIW's Sabres were hobbled by flying from separate airfields far from the target area, although it was fortunate that the MiGs initially avoided engagement. On 23 March forty-five F-86As engaged MiG-15s over the Yalu, providing a diversion while B-29s bombed the bridges at Kogunyong and Chongju. No kills were made on either side.

With the need to begin the bombing of the Yalu bridges near Sinuiju (just across the river from the main MiG base at Antung), it soon became apparent that a change in tactics was required. Thus, when the first attacks on the bridges took place on 30 March, 4th FIW Sabres were detailed to provide top cover. Eight flights of F-86As covered three bomber formations and, unusually, the MiGs did not heavily engage these aircraft. In the event, the only losses were in favour of the UN: B-29 gunners claimed two MiG-15s. Bad weather delayed further bombing

missions, but action was rejoined on 3 April. In one dogfight that day Capt James Jabara of 334th FIS claimed his first MiG kill; three other Red jets were posted as kills on the same day. One Sabre was lost during these engagements: 49-1173 piloted by Maj Ronald D. Shirlaw. He was at first posted as missing in action, but in fact he had run out of fuel and crash-landed near the Yalu River. Taken prisoner, Shirlaw was not released until 2 September 1953.

The first two weeks of April showed a marked increase in the proficiency and confidence of the MiG pilots. Not only were they aggressive in pressing home attacks, they also proved to be well organized, using their four-ship flights to good effect. With this in mind, 4th FIW began to increase its presence in MiG Alley by moving 336th FIS up to Suwon beginning on 6 April, a move completed on the 22nd. In addition, Sabre flights were increased to six aircraft in order to engage the MiG flights effectively as they broke for combat. These tactics proved to be sound almost immediately; on 22 April, twelve Sabres were attacked by thirty-six MiGs just as the F-86s began to turn for home. Jabara was again in the thick of things and, with Capt Norbert Chalwick flying his wing, managed to shoot down a MiG – his fourth – before a second group of Sabres arrived to claim a further three aircraft plus four damaged. No Sabres were lost on this mission.

In late April Communist forces began to build up the airfield at Sinuiju, dispersing Yak-9, Il-10 and La-11 propeller-driven aircraft as well as building up fuel and ammunition storage areas on the base. Reconnaissance

Before revetments were built at Suwon, the best protection afforded to the Sabres was the camouflage net. When Harrison Thyng took over 4th FIW in 1951, these nets were thrown away and an intense programme of revetment building was begun. This aircraft, 49-1298, 'The Bearded Clam', was shot down by an MiG-15 30km (19 miles) south-east of Sinuiju on 19 June 1951. Its pilot Capt Robert H. Laier is still listed as MIA.
John Henderson

photographs revealed the activity in early May, but UN commanders were initially reluctant to move, curious to know the reason for such reckless action. Gen Partridge, not ready to wait any longer, decided that the airfield should be targeted and on 9 May USAF and Marine fighter-bombers attacked the base while relays of 4th FIW Sabres provided high cover. But although many MiGs were seen taking off from Antung, only the briefest engagements were made and only two MiGs were slightly damaged in the air, for one Thunderjet damaged. Crucially, the damage inflicted on Sinuiju was highly effective: all aircraft on the airfield were claimed as destroyed along with over a hundred buildings, a fuel dump and twenty-six supply dumps.

Following the attack, the MiGs remained north of the Yalu for some days, a move that frustrated the Sabre pilots, especially Jabara. Although 334th FIS rotated back to Japan on 7 May, 'Jabby' transferred over to the 335th to remain in Korea and hoping get his fifth MiG kill for 'ace' status. This move had the full backing of Jabara's Group Commander, Col Meyer, who had been asked Gen Partridge to provide an ace. Jabara had been Meyer's choice and, so that he could rack up more kills, Jabby was put on as many missions as possible where MiGs might be encountered.

Finally, on 20 May Jabara's luck turned. As two flights of Sabres approached MiG Alley they found Red fighters ready and waiting for a fight, although the twelve Sabres soon realized that against the fifty-odd MiGs their work was cut out. Radioing for help, two following Sabre patrols, with Jabara in one, arrived on the scene within 15min and joined the dogfight. But things began badly for Jabara, whose Sabre refused to drop one of its wing tanks. In such a situation a pilot with a 'hung' fuel tank should have returned to base accompanied by his element companion. However, no doubt fearing that the opportunity to get a further kill would be lost, such thoughts were far from Jabara's mind; he pitched his Sabre into action, engaging a group of three MiGs at 35,000ft (10,668m). Registering hits in the fuselage and left wing of the last MiG, he followed the aircraft down to 10,000ft (3,048m) where the pilot ejected. Jabara had made ace – and not just that – he was history's first jet-versus-jet ace. Not content with this,

On 20 May 1951 the USAF crowned its first jet ace: Capt James Jabara of 334th FIS, seen here in the company of his flight members. Standing L-R: Lt Bill Yancey, Jabara, Lt Bill Carrington, Richard S. Becker (soon to become the second jet ace). Kneeling L-R: unknown, Lt T. Booth Hooker, unknown. John Henderson

he climbed back into action and soon locked on to another jet, scoring hits on a MiG at 20,000ft (6,096m). The aircraft began to smoke and then caught fire, spinning rapidly earthward. With two kills in one mission and six in total, Jabara managed to shake off another MiG from his tail and return safely to base for a hero's welcome. The drop tank episode was quietly forgotten; Partridge had his ace at last.

One fact that had not been missed in these early encounters with the MiGs was that the Sabre's machine-gun armament often proved feeble in comparison with the MiGs' cannons. Early in 1951 John Meyer wrote a paper to Col Benjamin O. Davis at the Pentagon detailing the problem, and although not easily solved, Meyer's letter contributed to the formation of a Pentagon armament-evaluation team, which later initiated Project *GunVal*. This team looked into the use of more effective weapons systems on a variety of fighter types for use in future combat aircraft. Lessons learnt in Korea then had a direct bearing on the fitting of 20mm cannon into the F-86H and 'Century Series' fighters.

On the same day that Jabara made ace, the FEAF Commander Gen Stratemeyer suffered a severe heart attack, following which he needed a long period of recuperation. Initially, Gen Partridge took over at FEAF Headquarters, with Gen Edward Timberlake as acting 5th Air Force Commander. With the rotation of both men back to the USA, however, their posts were taken over by Lt Gen Otto Weyland and Maj Gen Frank Everest, respectively.

For the last days of May the MiGs were generally quiet, and it was not until 31 May that they got back into the fight. On that day twelve MiG-15s surprised a pair of B-29s that were awaiting a Sabre escort 75 miles (120km) south-east of Sinuiju. The MiGs' actions were strange though; far from their usual Yalu hunting ground, they seemed unable to press a successful attack against the bombers. B-29 gunners claimed one kill and, when the Sabre escort finally arrived, they claimed a further two. But the relative inactivity on the Communists' part was the prelude to their redoubled efforts to regain air superiority over the peninsula. In mid May an International Communist

On 25 June 1951 Lt Col Glenn Eagleston was leading a 334th FIS MiG sweep over the Yalu. In an engagement with the Red fighters, Eagleston became separated from his wing man and took two 23mm cannon hits in the aft fuselage and a 37mm round in the left gun bay. Those three 0.50-calibres and the fuselage top longeron (seen here) stopped the round and saved Eagleston's life. However, the shots collapsed 3ft of engine intake, damaged the engine and rendered the hydraulic system inoperative. Shepherded into K-13 Suwon, Eagleston bellied the Sabre in and escaped serious injury. The Sabre, 49-1281 was a write-off. John Henderson

Nuisance attacks by the NKAF's Po-2 biplanes rarely caused much damage, but on the night of 14 June 1951 a 'Bedcheck Charlie' raid managed to destroy this Sabre, 49-1334, at K-13 Suwon. Four other Sabres – 49-1070, 1113, 1217 and 1318 – received major damage. John Henderson

Volunteer Force was formed to provide MiG cover for renewed efforts on the ground to recover airfields in North Korea. With Chinese and North Korean troops in retreat across the 38th Parallel, the revised organization was put into action in mid June. As soon as the airfields were reclaimed, the NKAF began to mount night nuisance missions with light aircraft, such as the Polikarpov Po-2 biplane. Although antique, the Po-2s began to demoralize UN troops in 'Bedcheck Charlie' raids. In the early hours of 14 June one of these aircraft managed to drop bombs on Suwon airfield while a partner attacked a motor park at Inchon. No casualties were recorded and both aircraft escaped. However, on 17 June an early morning strike by a pair of Po-2s wreaked havoc on Suwon. Each aircraft dropped a pair of small bombs, one

The MiG-15

The Russian-built MiG-15 was a product of the Mikoyan-Gurevich design bureau, and was originally designed as a high-altitude interceptor to counter American US B-29 and later, B-36 long-range bombers. The prototype, designated I-310, made its first flight on 30 December 1947, powered by an imported Rolls-Royce Nene-1 centrifugal flow turbojet. The Nene turbojet was placed into production in the Soviet Union as the RD-45, and the first production MiG-15s reached operational units in early 1949. The RD-45 engine was not very reliable, possessing an excessively high fuel consumption, but it was none the less quite a rugged design, capable of sustaining damage. In later production batches this engine was replaced by the Klimov VK-1, which was an improved version of the RD-45 offering 5,957lb (2,701kg) thrust. Versions of the MiG-15 powered by the VK-1 became known as MiG-15bis. These entered operational service in early 1950 and eventually became the most widely produced MiG version. Their appearance in Korea made life more difficult for the Sabre pilots, although Sabre improvements generally kept the balance. MiG-15 armament consisted of one Nudelmann NS-37 or N-37 37mm cannon with forty rounds and two NS-23 23mm machine-guns with eighty rounds per gun. Although this sounds a small payload, the MiG's firepower was devastating; just one round could bring a Sabre down.

damaging a motor pool and another scoring a bull's eye on the 335th FIS Sabre parking area. One F-86A, 49-1334, was completely destroyed and eight others were damaged.

Back in MiG Alley, the Communists showed their renewed aggressiveness on 17 June when 4th FIW Sabres met twenty-five MiG-15s. Although the Sabres managed to claim a MiG, it was obvious that the Reds had raised their game; highly competent Soviet pilots were heavily involved in the new Volunteer Force. On 18 June a Sabre, 49-1307, piloted by Capt William Crone, was shot down. Part of a four-ship Sabre formation, Crone's group was attacked by eight MiG-15s at 25,000ft (7,620m). Crone's aircraft was last seen in a 360-degree turn; he is still listed as missing in action. The following day a further Sabre was lost when Capt Robert Laier was shot down. Again part of a four-aircraft Sabre formation on a fighter sweep in the Sinuiju area, Laier's Sabre, 49-1298, was last seen trailing smoke in a steep dive following a MiG attack. Laier is also still held as MIA. Other Sabres were lost in action on 22 June (49-1276 to unknown cause during an F-80 attack on Sinuiju) and 25 June (49-1281), with eight MiGs being claimed in the early to mid June period.

During July FEAF continued the bombing of North Korean airfields, often as a co-ordinated strike force. On one such raid on 3 July thirty-two F-84s flew flak suppression over Pyongyang while a group of six B-29s bombed the airfield. Thirty-three Sabres escorted this mission and successfully deterred MiG attacks. In response, the Communist effort consisted of sporadic Ilyushin Il-10 attacks in support of the ground offensive. However, on 12 July the Red air offensive abruptly came to a halt. No more 'Bedcheck Charlie' missions were flown over the Seoul area after this date and the repairing of FEAF-damaged NKAF airfields also stopped. At the same time, both the UN and the Communist leaders seemed to realize that the unification of Korea under their differing political regimes was unlikely; truce talks began at Keasong on 10 July and a front was stabilized at the 38th Parallel.

At the end of June the Chinese possessed a total of 1,050 combat aircraft, of which 690 were fighters, mainly based at airfields around the existing Antung complex. The NKAF at the same time had 136 aircraft on strength, for just sixty pilots. The whole force, augmented by Russian pilots and equipment, carried slightly more than 440 MiG-15s, ranged against about forty-four F-86As available in Korea of a theatre total of eighty-nine. With this foremost in his mind and also looking to the defence of rear echelon facilities, Gen Weyland had requested on 10 June a further two wings of fighters to be stationed in Japan. In response, Gen Nathan Twining, USAF vice-chief of staff in Washington, informed Weyland that any further Communist build-up was considered to be purely defensive, although another F-84 wing was alerted for a move to the Far East at this time. By 12 July Weyland was getting more concerned and requested another wing of jets for Japanese defence and two more jet fighter wings for Korea.

Unfortunately, the USAF's ADC commitments were severely stretched and Washington responded that it was unable to help. For now, the best that could be achieved was to begin the replacement of the 4th FIW's 'A'-model Sabres with new F-86Es, an operation that was set in motion on 29 June 1951. Rather than rotate a whole wing of F-86Es to Korea, the early FY48 F-86As were replaced on a 'one-for-one' basis, these aircraft returning to 601st Air Repair Squadron at Kisarazu beginning in September. During October 1951, four F-86As were lost; one aircraft, 49-1267, due to a flying accident in combat on 7 October, another, 49-1147, to MiG action on 16 October, and another pair, 49-1109 and 1236, on 24 October. The latter were piloted by 1st Lts Bradley Irish and Fred T. Wicks, both of whom were taken prisoner. These FY49 aircraft remained in Korea for some time longer; the last F-86A was not returned to the United States until October 1952.

RF-86A and Photoreconnaissance F-86As

Photographic reconnaissance during the Korean War initially fell to RB-17, RB-26C, RF-51D and RF-80A aircraft. The last three were operated by the constituent squadrons of the 67th Tactical Reconnaissance Wing (TRW), the 12th Tactical Reconnaissance Squadron (TRS), the 45th TRS and the 15th TRS, respectively. Later, the North American RB-45C Tornado was used on photo-reconnaissance missions over Korea. These aircraft proved that they could rarely operate unescorted in North Korean airspace where MiGs were active. Thus it became obvious that a faster reconnaissance aircraft was needed, and this fact was brought to the attention of Far East Materiel Command (FEAMCOM). The pilots in the field felt that the Sabre would be the only reasonable answer, especially those from the 15th TRS. However, FEAMCOM originally resisted such suggestions and it fell to the 15th TRS personnel to try their own solution.

They began by inspecting 4th FIW F-86As on their airfield at Kimpo, looking for places where they might fit a camera. Irritated by constantly finding 15th TRS personnel in his hangar, the CO of the 4th FIW, Col Harrison Thyng, agreed to let the squadron have a salvaged airframe to experiment with. Working in their own time, men from the 15th TRS soon realized that it was possible to mount a small camera in the right-hand gun bay by removing the lower pair of machine-guns and the ammunition containers. In their place, the camera was fitted horizontally, and shot down through the nose, courtesy of a 45-degree angled mirror. Fuselage form was preserved by an optical glass panel. The salvaged airframe thus became

After the Korean War, a small number of Ashtray RF-86As were passed to 121st FBS DC ANG and the 115th and 196th FBS CA ANG. With ample baggage space by virtue of their stripped-out camera equipment, they made perfect 'hacks' for overnight stops. Lionel N. Paul via Mike Fox

the mock-up for what would be known as the 'Honeybucket' conversion. Soon after inspecting the airframe, Col Edwin Chickering authorized FEAMCOM to modify two early F-86As (48-187 and 48-217) to the Honeybucket specification and they passed to FEAMCOM in the fall of 1951.

The camera used in this conversion was the K-25, mounted exactly as in the mock-up. However, testing proved that vibration caused blurred photographs and it became apparent that a more radical solution would be required if the Sabre were to be used as a photoreconnaissance platform. Nevertheless, the Honeybucket Sabres flew recce missions into North Korea alongside 'regular' F-86As of the 4th FIW. These missions usually started as normal fighter sweeps and on the ground the Honeybucket aircraft were parked among the standard Sabres to preserve their anonymity.

Following on from the relative success of early Sabre recce operations, 5th AF and FEAMCOM authorized a further batch of five 48-FY Sabres for conversion, under Project Ashtray. The conversion of

this later batch began in October 1951 and the completed aircraft were redesignated RF-86A. In addition, the two Honeybucket aircraft received the RF-86A designation. The Ashtray aircraft were individually converted, and thus each was different from the last. In general, the compartment below the cockpit was enlarged and fitted with constant temperature air-conditioning for a forward oblique 24in K-11 camera and two 20in K-24 cameras mounted lengthways with a mirror arrangement to

provide vertical coverage. The RF-86As could be distinguished by the presence of camera-bay fairings underneath the forward fuselage just forward of the wings. Most RF-86As were unarmed, although some retained a pair of .50in machine-guns with limited ammunition capacity. The following aircraft were converted to the RF-86A configuration: 48-183, 48-195, 48-196, 48-246 and 48-257.

The seven RF-86A aircraft went to the 67th Wing's 15th Tactical Reconnaissance Squadron from April 1952. On combat missions they were usually able to evade interception and perform missions that were more hazardous than the typical reconnaissance flight. Only one RF-86A was lost in combat: 48-217, which was hit by ground fire on a mission over a hydroelectric plant at Wonsan. The pilot, Maj Jack Williams, the Squadron CO, managed to bail out but was found dead by the rescue helicopter crew. A further two RF-86As were written off in routine flying accidents in Korea and another example was authorized for reclamation following combat damage. The three surviving RF-86As were replaced by RF-86Fs in Korea and passed through 6400th Air Depot Wing, FEAMCOM in early 1953 for return to the United States.

The Air National Guard

From the summer of 1951 the F-86A

The second production P-86A, 47-606 was originally delivered to 2759th Experimental Wing at Muroc as a Bell X-1 chase plane. In March 1955 it was reassigned to 194th FBS California ANG at Fresno for ground instructional use and is seen here in that unit's smart yellow colour scheme. Years later, the remains of this Sabre were recovered for use in the restoration of airworthy F-86A 48-178. J.M.G. Gradidge

Following the Korean War activation and deployment to the UK with F-86As, the 116th FIS Washington ANG returned to state control in November 1952 and flew the F-51 Mustang. In late 1953 the unit acquired F-86As at Spokane. 48-281, a Korean War veteran, was assigned to the unit after overhaul at McLellan AFB in September 1953. Washington ANG

began to be replaced in front-line units by the improved F-86E Sabre, and the 'A' models began to be released for service with Air National Guard (ANG) units. The first ANG unit to receive F-86As was the 116th FIS, Washington ANG. This squadron had been called to active duty during the Korean War, before deployment to the United Kingdom with the 81st FIW. Similarly activated units, such as the 148th FIS Pennsylvania ANG, received F-86As in February 1951, followed by the 142nd FIS Delaware ANG in May and the 123rd FIS Oregon ANG in October. All these units were

returned to state control within 18 months and, in the case of the 116th FIS, many of its personnel and all its Sabres were transferred to the newly activated 78th FIS. Other ANG units received single F-86As for training use in July 1950, but it was not until late 1953 that F-86As began to arrive for service in regular ANG squadrons.

The first of these squadrons was the 190th FIS Idaho ANG at Gowen Field, which was assigned 48-240 on 30 September. By the end of 1953 five other National Guard squadrons had received at least half a dozen aircraft each, including

the 116th FIS, Washington ANG, back in the Sabre fold after its return to state control in November 1952 and a brief period with the F-51D Mustang.

As the Korean War raged on and surviving F-86As were rotated home in favour of late model Sabres, these aircraft were also routed through overhaul at NAA's Fresno plant and on to ANG squadrons. By the start of 1958 the major-ity of ANG F-86A units had either converted to more modern aircraft (often with later versions of the Sabre) or were in the course of disposing of their old Sabres. Most F-86As went to the massive storage and disposition facility at Davis Monthan AFB in Arizona, and the first of the type arrived there during October 1957. The last three ANG F-86A units were the 165th FIS Kentucky, the 192nd FIS Nevada and the 196th FIS California.

Organized for Air National Guard pilots, the second Earl T. Ricks Memorial Trophy Race was flown on 2 July 1955 from Ontario, California, finishing 1,960 miles later at Detroit. This was Maj Bob Love's 196th FBS Sabre for the race – hence the fuselage letter. 48-313 was lost in a midair collision with F-86A 49-1336 over Mount Pacifico, California on 4 September 1956. J.M.G. Gradidge

They all sent their last 'A' models to Davis Monthan in early 1959. A few managed to escape the cutting torch, but for most the end was near; by December 1960 all F-86As at Davis Monthan had been authorized for reclamation and were soon scrapped.

Other F-86A Sub-types

DF-86A

During the late 1940s and the early 1950s the trend towards research into missiles began. The notion of a pilotless jet bomber was one idea considered, and the first cruise missiles were thus born. The Glenn L. Martin Company became the main contractor for short-range, surface-to-surface missiles and the B-61 Matador was the first such missile to go into production. Powered by a J33 turbojet (the same engine powered the Lockheed F-80 and T-33), the Matador could carry a 3,000lb (1,360kg) warhead. However, during its development phase the

Air National Guard F-86A Squadrons (home bases in parentheses)
113th FIS Indiana (Hulman Field)
115th FIS California (Van Nuys Airport)
116th FIS Washington (Spokane and RAF Bentwaters, UK)
121st FIS District of Columbia (Andrews AFB, MD)
123rd FIS Oregon (Portland and O'Hare, IL)
126th FIS Wisconsin (Truax AFB)
141st FIS New Jersey (Mercer Airport)
142nd FIS Delaware (New Castle County Airport)
148th FIS Pennsylvania (Dover AFB, DE)
156th FIS North Carolina (Douglas Municipal Airport)
157th FIS South Carolina (Congaree)
176th FIS Wisconsin (Truax AFB)
186th FIS Montana (Great Falls)
190th FIS Idaho (Gowen Field)
191st FIS Utah (Salt Lake City)
192nd FIS Nevada (Reno)
194th FIS California (Fresno)
195th FIS California (Van Nuys)
196th FIS California (Ontario)
197th FIS Arizona (Phoenix Skyharbor)

Many of these units received their first F-86As as fighter bomber squadrons, although all were redesignated as fighter interceptor units on 1 August 1955.

Matador would need a fast chase aircraft to accompany it on these unmanned test flights, and this job would eventually fall to the F-86A Sabre.

To begin with, two F-86A-5s were sent

to Wright-Patterson AFB for modification to DF-86A specification, the 'D' prefix indicating the missile director role. The first aircraft arrived on 17 August 1949 and emerged from conversion on 31 August as an EDF-86A, the 'E' further identifying that, as a temporary test aircraft, it was exempt from all but urgent Technical Order modifications. Two further EDF-86As were converted at Wright-Patterson in May 1950. The DF-86 modification included the installation of a command radio system, which enabled the missile director to control the Matador's throttle, rudder and other control surfaces. Thus, despite the fact that Matador test flights would be primarily controlled from a ground station, the DF-86 pilot could take over control of the missile to guide it around populated areas in case of ground-station malfunction. The system also gave the director pilot the capability to override the missile's automatic control system and destroy the missile. Conversely, the Sabre pilot could also override the destruct system to save the missile. All DF-86As had their machine-guns removed and a flush panel was fitted in place of the gun muzzles.

The first DF-86As were assigned to the 2754th Air Base Group at Holloman AFB in New Mexico during September 1949. Lawrence Biehunko recalled the delivery of the first aircraft:

I remember the delivery date because Chuck Yeager brought it to Holloman AFB from

Wright-Patterson AFB. Before this date we were using T-33s, but they were not fast enough to keep up with the Matador missile we were radio controlling, so we requested three F-86s. [At Holloman] we had three pilots that flew chase in the Matador programme; Maj John A. Evans (now deceased), Capt Donald J. Young and myself.

These three Sabres were immediately involved in the Martin company's early testing of the B-61, aided by a detachment of forty-five airmen and twenty-five officers from the USAF's 550th Guided Missile Wing (GMW). When the 550th GMW was inactivated on 29 December 1950 the four DF-86As then available were transferred to the 4802nd Guided Missile Squadron (GMS), under the command of Lt Col John C. Reardon, also at Holloman. This squadron trained USAF personnel on the Matador, alongside Martin's test programme. Twenty-two Matadors would be launched at Holloman.

In March 1951 orders were posted to relocate the whole Matador project to Patrick AFB in Florida, alongside Cape Canaveral. This movement was completed on 12 April and the DF-86As began shepherding flights again on 20 June when the first launch from Cape Canaveral was successfully completed. Matador testing involved many aircraft, quite apart from the DF-86A. On a typical mission a B-29 simulated missile aircraft was always on station, as was a C-47 for guidance synchronization. Two B-17s served as airborne radar-surveillance aircraft, with another B-29 also in the air for interference control duties. Finally, another C-47 would be used to ensure range clearance. On 4 September 1951 all these support aircraft were placed under the control of the newly activated 6555th Test Support Squadron, again commanded by John Reardon. During 1951 and 1952 the parent 6555th GMW helped to train personnel from the first USAF cruise missile units: the 1st and the 69th Pilotless Bomber Squadron.

One of the DF-86As (49-1144) was written off on 28 January 1952, following an engine flameout. The pilot Donald Young escaped without injury. '1144 was replaced by another aircraft, which was apparently converted to DF-86A specification on site. In addition, a further 'standard' F-86A was assigned to Patrick AFB, presumably for pilot-proficiency training.

In 1955 Martin began to phase out the Matador testing operation, all subsequent launches being fully USAF-operated. In 1957 the 6555th GMW involvement in the Matador was passed to Tactical Air Command and the surviving DF-86As were converted back to F-86A configuration before going on to serve with the Air National Guard. Further missile director missions were flown by DF-89 Scorpion aircraft.

F-86J

A one-off variant of the F-86A was used as a testbed for the Canadian-built Orenda engine, later to power many licence-built Canadair Sabres. First flown in October 1950 by the former airspeed record holder Maj Richard L. Johnson, this machine, 49-1069, was given the new USAF designation F-86J and the NAA number NA-167. The F-86J was delivered to the USAF on 24 January 1951 and assigned to 2759th Experimental Wing at Edwards AFB in California. It was then transferred to Toronto for testing in Canada, although still under

Seen at Mitchell Field, Wisconsin on 28 November 1953, 48-201 was en route to assignment with 126th FBS Wisconsin ANG at Truax. Previously assigned to 3595th CCTW at Nellis, remnants of the unit's checkered tail can be seen at the top of the rudder. Leo J. Kohn via J.M.G. Gradidge

Specifications: F-86A-5-NA

WEIGHTS

empty weight:	10,093lb (4,578kg)
design gross weight:	13,395lb (6,074kg)
maximum take-off weight:	16,438lb (7,454kg)
internal fuel capacity:	435gall (1,631l)
external fuel capacity:	2 x 120gall (450l) drop tanks

DIMENSIONS

wingspan:	37ft 1in (11.3m)
length:	37ft 6in (11.43m)
height:	14ft 9in. (4.49m)
wing area:	274sq ft (25.48sq m)
aileron range:	14 degrees up and 14 degrees down
horizontal stabilizer range:	1 degrees up and 10 degrees down

PERFORMANCE

(J47-GE-7 engine of 5,340lb thrust)

maximum speed at sea level:	590mph (949mph)
service ceiling:	47,600ft (14,508m)
maximum rate of climb:	7,300ft/min (2,225 m/min)
combat range (with drop tanks):	1,044 miles (1,679 km)
combat radius (with drop tanks):	374 miles (601 km)
limiting flight loads :	+7.33g, -3.00g

ARMAMENT

6 x 0.50-calibre M-3 machine-guns capable of 1,200 rounds/min

2 x 1,000lb bombs

16 x 5in unguided rockets

2759th Experimental Wing ownership. Canadian test flying of the F-86J was mainly carried out at Avro Canada's Malton airfield, where it was known as the F-86AO. These trials highlighted the need for improved airflow around the slightly larger and more powerful engine.

By 1954 the Orenda trials were being carried out on Canadair-produced Sabres, and Bob Christie flew the F-86J back to Mobile Air Materiel Area from Malton via Wright-Patterson AFB and Nashville on 11 February 1954. Redundant for any other use, the aircraft was authorized for reclamation at Brookley AFB on 25 March that year.

XP-86 and F-86A Production

Serial	Block No.	Construction No.
45-59597 to 599	XP-86	38424 to 38426
47-605 to 637	F-86A-1-NA	38432 to 38464
48-129 to 316	F-86A-5-NA	43498 to 43685
49-1007 to 1339	F-86A-5-NA	161-1 to 161-333

49-1069 was the only F-86J; it was fitted with an Orenda engine for tests in conjunction with the Canadian Sabre programme. Howard Levy via Mike Fox

Unarmed DF-86A 49-1247 was used as a Martin Matador missile controller at Patrick AFB. Author

CHAPTER TWO

The Heavyweights

The F-86C/YF-93A Penetration Fighter

On 28 August 1945 the USAF Air Materiel Command (AMC) issued a number of requirements to industry for new pursuit (fighter) aircraft designs. In particular, the Air Technical Service Center at Wright-Patterson desired proposals for a penetration fighter and an interceptor fighter, and these two requirements led North American Aviation to design two vastly different aircraft, but both based upon the F-86 Sabre.

The penetration fighter was basically a long-range bomber escort, a requirement originally met by Republic's F-84 Thunderjet. By January 1946 a number of proposals had been received, including a tailless design from the independent engineer John Abbeman and a prone-piloted machine put forward by Northrop. Originally just two designs were recommended for prototype production –

a vee-tailed, twin-engine aircraft from McDonnell and a proposal from Vultee for a three-engined fighter. A Lockheed proposal was eliminated because, in the view of AMC, its L-1000 engine was merely a 'paper' design. However, in what was largely a political decision to keep Lockheed in Air Force (rather than Navy) business, the decision was revoked on 1 April, AMC stating that, 'Consideration of Vultee in the penetration proposal has been abandoned in favor of the Lockheed proposal.' McDonnell's aircraft became the XP-88 and Lockheed went back to the drawing board to put together a twin Westinghouse 24-C-powered aircraft, which was funded into prototype form as the XP-90. Contracts for two prototypes each were awarded in 1946.

Originally, the penetration fighter requirement stipulated a top speed of 550mph (884km/h) at 35,000ft (10,668m), and 600mph (965km/h) at sea level. Climb to 35,000ft should take 10min, for a combat radius of 900 miles (1,448km).

Armament would be six forward-firing, fixed guns of either .60-calibre or 20mm bore. Over the following months the characteristics of the requirement changed, and on 22 August 1947 they were revised such that the aircraft would need to operate at 50,000ft (15,240m) with a top speed of 600 knots (1,110km/h), climb to that height in ten minutes, and have a combat radius of 1,300 nautical miles (2,406km).

It was this revision to which North American addressed their efforts, submitting their design in December 1947, and thus already at somewhat of a disadvantage to the competition. In addition, although the AMC penetration fighter specifications had established the need for two turbojet engines, NAA felt that a single, high-power engine would benefit their design. In effect, they were proved correct, as the Westinghouse J34 engines originally fitted to the XP-88 and XP-91 produced only 3,000lb (1,360kg) of thrust apiece. North American, on the other hand, decided to use the new Pratt & Whitney J48-P6, which produced 8,500lb (3,854kg) thrust with afterburner for a total weight of only 2,080lb (943kg). The J48 was actually a licence-produced, Rolls-Royce Tay engine, and utilized a single-stage centrifugal compressor and a single axial-flow turbine. However, one downside of the J48 was its immense girth. Therefore, in order to accommodate the engine's 50in (1.27m) diameter (versus 39in (0.99m) for the J47 fitted in the P-86A), North American's designers came up with an entirely new fuselage to be mated to the P-86A wing and tail unit. The increased weight of the design then led to a redesigned undercarriage, and increased armament also ruled out a nose-mounted, engine intake at an early stage. With this design configuration finalized, NAA proposed its model NA-157 as the P-86C to the USAF on 20 September 1947 and also put forward the design to fulfil the all-weather interceptor requirement. No doubt in an effort to sway

Seen on an early test flight, the first YF-93A suffered from the poor performance of its NACA-ducted engine intakes. This machine was damaged following an afterburner explosion on 5 June 1950 and taken back to NAA for repairs. At the same time, more conventional side-mounted intakes were fitted. NAA

Following modification and repair at North American, the no.1 YF-93A, with new intake configuration, was passed to NACA Ames in September 1951. Used to compare intake performance, NACA 139 was withdrawn from use in 1956. Note the two ventral brake panels. NASA Ames via Mike O'Conner/Fox

USAF decision-making, on 1 December NAA proposed that 190 P-86Bs, on order under contract W33-038ac-16013, should be cancelled in favour of continued P-86A production and two P-86Cs under the same contract. After a period of consideration, the USAF issued an order for two prototypes (48-317 and 318) on 17 December as contract AC-21672. Crucially, the Air Force ordered the F-86C into production solely as a penetration fighter; the all-weather interceptor requirement proved difficult to satisfy and eventually a number of designs took up this role in USAF service, notably another F-86 derivative. On 22 March 1948 a revision to the contract finalized side-mounted engine intakes, and a further change on 29 March reflected the deletion of external fuel tanks.

The design of the F-86C was frozen at this time, and, in order to minimize the effects of the increased frontal area of the aircraft, NAA decided to use flush-fitting, NACA air intakes. Engineered by the National Advisory Committee for Aero-

nautics, these promised to provide an improved airflow for jet engines (through the venturi effect) and to decrease drag. However, in practice they proved a disappointment. When fitted to an experimental XP-80R, Lockheed had discovered that the in-flight ram characteristics of the intakes were poor and, despite this being known to NAA as early as October 1946, the design of their machine had progressed too far to permit modification. This proved a mistake. It is also worth noting at this point that the F-86C did not encompass 'area rule' in its design, as is often stated. Richard Whitcomb's area rule or 'wasp waisting' theory was not released by NACA to the aviation industry until September 1952. By that time the F-86C had been designed, built and flown.

Other aspects of the F-86C prototype included greatly increased firepower and far more fuel capacity than its distant F-86A relative. The armament would comprise six 20mm cannon, linked to an AN/APG-3 radar mounted in the nose,

and an A-1B gunsight (later an AN/APG-30 was installed). Additionally, two 1,000lb bombs could be carried. The range for the F-86C was stated to be an incredible 2,000 miles (3,218km), courtesy of a 1,581gall (5,298l) internal fuel capacity, representing more than three times as much as the F-86A carried. The side-mounted air brakes of the F-86A were replaced on the F-86C by two large brake panels fitted under the mid fuselage. These would be important pieces of equipment, for, despite the increase in size of the airframe, North American declared a top speed of over 700mph (1,126km/h) for the F-86C.

NAA then proposed a contract on 9 April 1948 for the two P-86C prototypes at a fixed price of $6,811,449, plus 118 additional P-86C production aircraft. The Air Force, obviously impressed by the claims being put forward for the aircraft, agreed with this proposal and authorized North American to proceed on 29 May, to include spares and production tooling to cater for an ultimate production rate of 180 aircraft per month. At this time, it was decided that there was so little commonality between the F-86C and the production Sabre that the aircraft should be assigned a new designation; thus in October 1948 the design became known as the F-93, with the two prototypes being designated YF-93As. At this time it seemed that the F-93 was assured of a long and distinguished Air Force career, but the production contract (including a static test airframe) was cancelled on 11 January 1949. In a renegotiation of the contract, the two YF-93As were retained, but this time at a price of $7,329,816 for the aircraft and a further $4,167,568 to cover spares, data and support equipment. The Air Force stated that no production order for further penetration fighters would be awarded until a competitive fly-off

between the three contenders had taken place. Despite this, the USAF placed a further order on 5 May for one F-93A as an all-weather fighter. Given the contract number AC-21672 and the NAA designation NA-166, this anomaly came to nought shortly afterwards when the contract was cancelled, no doubt as a result of the plethora of other designs by then coming into production.

The first YF-93A was completed at Inglewood in late 1949 and trucked to Edwards AFB in December for maiden-flight preparations. It is worth noting that the two competing aircraft, the XF-88 and the XF-90, had made their first flights on

20 October 1948 and 3 June 1949, respectively. With the future looking bleak, George Welch took the YF-93A (48-317) on its first flight on 24 January 1950.

Flight testing of the first YF-93A soon showed that the flush intakes of the aircraft starved the engine of air, especially at high angles of attack. This would then often cause compressor stall and engine flame-out. It was later decided to modify the number two machine to incorporate conventional, side-mounted engine intakes, and this solved the air starvation problem. This configuration was not used in the fly-off evaluation, however. Further difficulties centred around the wheel and the brake assemblies, which had been contracted originally to the Bendix Aviation

Not often seen, the YF-93As were equipped for JATO assisted take-off. Note also the red wing-tips on the no.1 machine. NASA Ames via Mike O'Conner/Fox

Corporation in October 1948. A subsequent award of the contract to B.F. Goodrich only served to complicate matters, and, despite being superior in all respects, the Goodrich equipment was never fitted to the YF-93, although NAA modified the aircraft's hydraulic system to accept either item. Problems with the aircraft were tempered by the knowledge that both McDonnell and Lockheed were also experiencing flight test headaches with their competing aircraft.

Phase II flight tests of the YF-93A with Air Force pilots began in April 1950 and were not without incident. On 5 June, following a 1hr 13min flight, the aircraft experienced an afterburner fuel-drain leak during a roller landing. The fuel leak subsequently caused an explosion and the pilot was lucky to escape with his life. Though recovered to land, the rear fuselage of the YF-93A was severely damaged and the aircraft needed to be removed to Inglewood for repairs. It was then decided to modify the aircraft to the conventional, side-mounted intake configuration, following advice from NACA.

The second YF-93A flew in May 1950 and its test programme was also incident-packed. In June, while completing test flight 23 at Edwards, the aircraft suffered an engine fire which resulted in turbine damage and an inevitable engine change.

Though the USAF penetration fighter fly-off officially took place between 29 June and 7 July 1950, it was not until 23 August that the Air Force Evaluation Board released their verdict. And what a bombshell it was, for, despite the XF-88's being declared the winner of the contest, the Air Force announced that none of the penetration fighters would be funded into production. The YF-93 design was ignominiously placed third and last. Largely as a result of a budget ceiling imposed by President Truman, AMC had revised their requirements to procure further B-36 bombers ñ crucially, designed to operate without an escort. Of the penetration fighters, only the XF-88, in heavily modified form as the F-101 Voodoo, ever got into production.

In evaluating the YF-93A, Air Proving Ground Command pilots cited numerous inadequacies. They felt that the aircraft had insufficient range [1,708 miles (2,748km) with no payload, and a mere 700 nautical miles (1,296km) combat radius] and endurance (less than 4hr), and

also noted that it could not adequately operate above 25,000ft (7,600m) without afterburner. In turn, they also felt that the afterburner consumed too much fuel at low altitudes. Evaluation flights also revealed that the airspeed degraded too quickly in manoeuvres, even with the engine at full thrust. With a limiting Mach of 0.94, the aircraft was difficult to keep on track above 0.70 Mach due to snaking. Finally, in simulated pull-outs from bombing runs evaluation pilots reported wing-tip stalls and mild stick force reversals.

Despite the failure of the aircraft during the fly-off, the flight-test programme was briefly resumed, the second aircraft being returned to NAA for the removal of radar, gunsight and radio equipment. At this

time, an all-moving tailplane was also installed in the number two machine, and both aircraft were returned to Edwards AFB in October 1950. At this juncture NAA proposed that a modified tail be installed on 48-317, in which the horizontal stabilizer would be lowered 10nin and moved slightly forward to increase manoeuvrability; the decision was referred to Washington but not approved. The flight-test phase was completed in December and the two YF-93As were then officially accepted on to USAF charge in February 1951, almost immediately being bailed back to North American for further flight tests. Released from North American, following the contract termination on 28 March, the first and the second prototype were delivered to NACA's Ames research facility on 1 September and 6 May 1951, respectively. Both then flew comparison tests between the two intake designs until retired for salvage in 1956.

F-86D Interceptor

North America's response to the second Air Materiel Command request – for an interceptor fighter – took longer to develop. Indeed, developments of existing designs, such as Lockheed's F-94 Starfire and the NAA F-82 Twin Mustang, originally filled the requirements, and AMC further favoured Republic's AP-31 project (eventually funded as the XP-91) and another from Convair (later the XP-92). Eventually these designs fell by the wayside, Convair's because of its substantial backlog in B-36, XB-46 and XC-99 production, and Republic's apparently for a similar reason. Both machines were built and served in several testing roles. Northrop's F-89 Scorpion, although built for the all-weather fighter requirement, also eventually became the front runner in the interceptor competition. Problems with the latter in its early stages left the door open for an enterprising North American design team. And Soviet progress with nuclear research meant that much emphasis was now put on the interceptor requirement.

Specifications: YF-93A

POWERPLANT
Pratt & Whitney J48-P-6 rated at 6,000lb (2,721kg) thrust dry and 8,750lb (3,968kg) thrust with afterburner

WEIGHTS
empty weight:	14,035lb (6,364kg)
gross weight:	25,000lb (11,337kg)
fuel capacity:	1,581gall (5,928l)

DIMENSIONS
wingspan:	38ft 9in (11.8m)
length:	44ft 1in (13.4m)
height:	15ft 8in (4.7m)
wing area:	306sq ft (28.4sq m)

PERFORMANCE
maximum speed:	708mph (1,139km/h)
cruising speed:	530mph (852km/h)
climb rate:	11,960ft/min (3645m/min)
range:	2,000 miles (3,218km)
service ceiling:	46,800ft (14,264m)

ARMAMENT (proposed)
6 x 20mm cannon with 1,380 rounds total
2 x 1,000lb bombs
16 x 5in T-38 High Velocity Aircraft Rockets
or 8 x 5in T-200 rockets

YF-93 Production		
Serial No.	Model	Construction No.
48-317 and 318	YF-93	157-1 and 2

Design of NAA's F-86-based interceptor started on 28 March 1949 as company project NA-164. Despite being a single-seat design and heading into a strong wind of opposing two-seaters, USAF showed immediate interest. The Air Force Senior Officers Board had earlier stated that its reluctance to grant the production of penetration fighters was due in part to the need to fund an F-86-based interceptor within FY49 and FY50 budgets. At NAA engineering work on an NA-165 production version started on 7 April and construction of a full-scale mock-up was begun on 1 June. The NA-165 would be known in USAF service as the F-86D.

To fulfil its all-weather requirement, the new fighter was to be equipped with an 18in-diameter Westinghouse AN/APG-36 radar dish in the nose, originally controlled by the 50kW Hughes E-3 fire control system (FCS), and later by the 250kW E-4 FCS. The pilot would carry out most of his interception by viewing a cathode-ray-tube screen positioned in his lower instrument panel. Crucially, the E-3 and the E-4 FCS allowed the F-86D to make attacks on a target from any angle. Before this, the intercept pattern had necessitated an attack from astern. Additionally, Hughes made the interception phase semi-automatic, which meant that more of the work was done by the aircraft. This was theoretically a clever move since, up until that point, only 5 per cent of pilots had accounted for 40 per cent of kills in combat. Of the remaining crews, nearly 50 per cent often achieved no kill at all. Thus, if the pilot could not be better trained, the aircraft and its intercept system had to be improved. The F-86D was the answer to that problem.

The positioning of the F-86D's radar dish dictated a repositioned engine air intake, which was relocated below the nose. To assist in ejection, a clamshell canopy was fitted and the machine utilized F-86A wings, undercarriage and tail fin in all production versions. The 'all-flying tail', developed for the F-86E, was used, but, on the F-86D, the tailplane area was increased and no dihedral was required. Internal fuel was increased to 608gall (2,760l), and the F-86A's dual 120gall (546l) drop-tank capability was retained.

The armament for this bomber hunter would be confined to twenty-four 2.75in (70mm) rockets, fitted in a retractable

Pictured devoid of markings at Inglewood before its first flight, the no.1 YF-86D 50-577 also apprears to be sans engine, judging by the length of the undercarriage oleos. The F-86A-style sliding canopy and vee-shaped windshield are apparent here. NAA

tray beneath the forward fuselage. Some design work was also carried out into the incorporation of four 20mm cannon, but this idea was dropped in February 1950, before the start of full-scale production. To cope with the increased weight of extra internal fuel plus the considerable amount of electrics and electronics in the new design, the thrust of the J47 engine was upped to 6,650lb (3,015kg) by fitting an afterburner, and was redesignated J47 GE-17. This further led to an increase in the rear fuselage length to accommodate the afterburner section.

One of the major developmental problems for the new fighter was in the engine electronic fuel-control system. There would be no physical link between the pilot's throttle lever and the engine, all fuel metering and throttle variation would be performed by an electronic selector, which controlled and correlated engine and afterburner operation. Many years of effort were put into the resolution of the afterburning J47's electronic fuel-control system, and even when it entered operational service the engine still gave problems in this area.

The rocket armament of the F-86D was often claimed to be a 'first', although in truth that honour goes to the Messerschmitt Me 262 of World War II. The irony is that the Me 262's unguided R4M rocket design was developed after the war into the same unguided rocket

fitted to the F-86D. The Sabre's 2.75in unguided folding fin aircraft rockets (FFAR), dubbed 'Mighty Mouse', weighed 18lb (8.2kg) each and could be fired in salvos of six, twelve or twenty-four. As the rockets left the aircraft, they fanned out to give a 'shot-gun' effect, increasing the chances of a kill; each rocket had the explosive power of a 75mm artillery shell, and travelled at a speed of 2,600ft/sec (792m/s). Optimum range for the Mighty Mouse was around 4,500ft (1,371m), with a theoretical maximum effective range of 9,000ft (2,743m). In tests it was soon discovered that anything but the firing of all twenty-four rockets at a target was less than adequate, and, even with all rockets fired, the kill probability was still only 60 per cent. Other fighters which used the Mighty Mouse, such as the F-94C Starfire (with Hughes E-5 FCS) and the F-89D Scorpion (Hughes E-6) had the capacity for forty-eight and 104 rockets, respectively. In the F-86D the rockets were mounted in a retractable tray, fitted under the forward fuselage.

But what really set the D-model apart from other all-weather fighters was that it was a single-seater. All previous designs, such as the F-82 Twin Mustang and the P-61 Black Widow, had been two-seaters, with the second crewman dealing with the radar interception. Indeed, the other two contemporary USAF all-weather interceptor designs, the Lockheed F-94

514th FIS pilot Dave Roberson gives some scale to the diminutive 'Mighty Mouse' rocket. Before installation in the F-86D, the rocket's folding fins were protected by the metal foil cap seen here. This shot was taken at the 1956 Yuma Worldwide Gunnery Meet. Dave Roberson

Seen in flight near Edwards AFB in early 1950, the no.2 YF-86D was transferred to Hughes for fire-control system testing during October. Note that this machine has an F-86A-type tailplane with conventional elevator arrangement. The rear fuselage was remodelled for production aircraft and vortex generators added to the engine cooling ducts. NAA

Starfire and the Northrop F-89 Scorpion, were also two-seaters. Much was expected of the new Sabre but teething troubles put its service debut back for some time. It was not until 13 July 1952 that the first 'definitive' aircraft with the E-4 FCS was ready for trials.

By the time of its first flight in December 1949 the new aircraft had been redesignated F-95A, as there was only a 25 per cent parts commonality with the earlier Sabres. In a political move the designation reverted to F-86D in July 1950, however, as a result of the Congress's need to approve budgets for new aircraft types. As the F-86D, the aircraft would be seen as merely an F-86 development and required less strict monetary control. In addition, contractors on the project were restricted to costing outlined in F-86 contracts, whereas an F-95 would require new contracts to be drawn up, no doubt at increased prices. As it was, the fixed price for the first thirty-seven F-86Ds came out at $380,232 each.

Contract AF-9211 for two NA-164 prototypes and 122 NA-165 production aircraft was agreed on 7 October 1949. The NA-164s would be known as YF-86Ds, with the remaining NA-165s

The no.1 YF-86D prototype was assigned to Inyokern for 'Mighty Mouse' rocket testing, where the first firing took place in February 1951. For these tests the whole forward fuselage was painted Dayglo orange.
San Diego Aerospace Museum/Ray Wagner

becoming F-86Ds and were assigned dash-1, 5, 10 and 15 block numbers. These aircraft were given serial numbers 50-455 to -578, although it is interesting to note that the YF-86Ds were assigned the final two serial numbers in this block rather than the first two, as might have been expected. Specification for both the E-3 and the E-4 fire-control system was approved by Air Materiel Command on 17 February 1950, and the F-86D contract was amended on 2 June to include a further thirty-one F-86D-15 production aircraft (serials 50-704 to -734), bringing the initial total to 153. To expedite the development and flight testing of the aircraft both prototypes would not at first be fitted with any fire-control system and, furthermore, the thirty-seven F-86D-1 machines would be fitted with the E-3 FCS.

The first prototype (50-577, still designated YF-95A) was rolled out at Inglewood in September 1949 and was taken to Muroc on 28 November for flight testing. The first flight was made on 27 December, with George Welch at the controls. This and the second prototype differed from the production models in retaining the F-86A's sliding canopy and vee-shaped windshield, and the rear fuselage was much more voluminous to accommodate the thus-far unproved afterburner section. Additionally, the first prototypes featured the F-86A's tailplane arrangement; the all-flying tail would be fitted later in the first production aircraft. Throughout 1950 NAA test pilots made seventy-four test flights on the YF-86D to evaluate the afterburner and engine electronic controls. The second YF-86D, 50-578, became available in early March 1950 and was fitted with the E-3 FCS, although this was not actually received from Hughes until 26 May; it was finally tested on the second YF-86D in September. On 17 October this aircraft was bailed back to Hughes for two years of development testing and it was not until 31 May 1952 that this machine was officially accepted by the USAF. Even then, it was almost immediately passed on, to NACA's Ames test facility for control sensitivity research.

The retractable rocket pack was originally fitted to the first prototype, which went to Inyokern, the Navy's rocket range at China Lake in California for firing tests. First airborne firing was accomplished in February 1951, the programme transferring to Edwards AFB in May. On 12 March 1952 this machine was finally delivered to the USAF. It then returned to NAA's Inglewood plant in June and was fitted with a low-set tailplane to test the stability advantages of such a design. These tests were a success and later served as a starting point for the F-100's tailplane design aspects. In addition, the YF-86D was fitted with inboard ailerons; but flight testing of these was not proceeded with after mid-span ailerons were shown to be more effective.

At the end of June 1952, with the low-set tailplane still fitted, the No.1 YF-86D was disposed of to NACA at Ames. It was then employed on control sensitivity research and in 1955 a J34 engine was fitted along with the high-set tailplane for a series of wind-tunnel tests to prove the blown-flap concept. The J34 engine provided high-pressure air, which was then exhausted over the extended wing flap to increase boundary layer adhesion and lower the theoretical stalling speed for a set flap selection.

The No.1 YF-86D was modified by NAA to incorporate a low-set tailplane and re-sited speed brake. It was then transferred to NACA Ames in June 1952 for control sensitivity tests. Here, a NACA engineer checks wing-mounted vortex generators, designed to improve airflow over the wing trailing edge during tests of the lowered tailplane. NASA Ames, 3 December 1953

Though it was accepted by the USAF in March 1951, the first F-86D-1, 50-455, did not make its first flight until 8 June and became the aerodynamic prototype for production aircraft, although it flew originally without any fire-control system equipment. This aircraft featured the standard clamshell canopy, flat windshield and redesigned rear fuselage. Aerodynamic problems in this area soon led to the fitting of fuselage and tailplane-mounted vortex generators to reduce the effects of parasitic drag. Thus, the new design could reach a top speed of 614 knots (1,136km/h) and a service ceiling of 55,400ft (16,885m). In order to better cope with high-altitude operations, the F-86D introduced an anti-icing provision, utilizing engine air to heat the wing, fin, tail and intake leading edges. The F-86D-1 tipped the scales at 12,470lb (5,655kg) empty and possessed a 17,150lb (7,777kg) maximum take-off weight, representing an increase of 2,400lb (1,088kg) over the F-86A. Despite the higher weight of this variant, the F-86D-1 had a 17,750ft/min

In 1957 50-462 was assigned to Patrick AFB in Florida and redesignated as the only JDF-86D; it was heavily involved in the Navajo missile programme until March 1959. The nose, boom and tail trim is red. Author

These tests were completed on 9 September and, though highly successful, the system was not adopted for F-86 use. The aircraft was not flown in this configuration but enjoyed a particularly long test life. It was finally dropped from the NASA inventory on 15 February 1960.

(5,410m/min) maximum rate of climb – more than twice as quick as an F-86A.

As production at Inglewood geared up alongside F-86E construction, further early F-86Ds began to join the test programme, the first four D-1s being bailed back to NAA for this purpose. The first production E-3 fire control was received for installation in a D-1 airframe

The Air Force finally received its first F-86D on 12 March 1952, when aircraft 50-560 was assigned to the Air Force Flight Test Center at Edwards AFB. New-build aircraft were then assigned further to Edwards as well as 3200th Proof Test Group at Eglin AFB from 19 March 1952. Problems in equipping production aircraft continued to hound their delivery and it was not for some time that any were assigned to active duty squadrons. In order to start the training of F-86D crews the 3625th Flying Training Wing at Tyndall AFB in Florida began to gear up, accepting its first F-86D in July 1952, and by the end of the year the unit had been assigned seventeen F-86D-1s under Project TRC-1PF-869. Ground training units also received F-86D-1s at this time, including the 3345th Technical Training Wing at Chanute AFB, Illinois.

The next block of aircraft on the production line was the F-86D-5, which introduced the production standard E-4 fire-control system. In addition, the twenty-six D-5s featured an additional oxygen cylinder for the pilot, a redesigned instrument panel, an engine-driven alternator for the FCS and repositioned the main electrical battery from the left-hand nose area to the lower rear fuselage. Again, the first deliveries were bailed back to NAA for testing and the remaining -5s were assigned to the 3200th Proof Test Group at Eglin and the 3625th FTW at Tyndall. Supply difficulties again emerged and many aircraft in this batch were delivered after those in subsequent blocks. The final F-86D-5s were delivered in January 1953, despite having been available since July the previous year.

Cockpit view of the second production F-86D-1, s/n 50-456. The radar scope dominates the instrument panel. The handle at the bottom left is the radar antenna control. San Diego Aerospace Museum/Ray Wagner

in July 1951. Other F-86D-1 aircraft were assigned to various test programmes, including 50-462 with NAA's Electromechanical Division at Downey, California, 50-480 with General Electric and 50-473 with Hughes at Culver City. Cold-weather testing was carried out by 50-472 at Ladd AFB in Alaska, starting in November 1952.

Fears engendered by the Korean War of a Soviet attack on the US mainland were largely responsible for a further F-86D

contract, AF-19056, and this order for 188 F-86D-20 (NA-177) aircraft was approved on 11 April 1951. Another contract (AF-14800) for 638 F-86D-25 to -35 aircraft was approved on 18 July, under NAA designation NA-173. Thus a total of 979 production F-86Ds were now on order, barely a month after the first flight of the first production aircraft. A further contract, AF-6202 for 901 NA-190s, was approved on 6 March 1952 and covered 300 F-86D-40s, 300 D-45s and 301 -50 models.

F-86D Interception

The interception of enemy aircraft had been the main reason for the F-86D's existence, so it is worth explaining the pilot's end of an intercept. First, the interceptor aircraft relied heavily upon a string of Ground Controlled Intercept (GCI) sites, which were ground-based radar stations manned by USAF (and later in England by Royal Air Force) personnel. At the GCI sites a controller would pick up unidentified aircraft on his scope and vector an interceptor on to it. F-86D pilot Richard White explains the procedure, once the controller had vectored the aircraft:

Prominent in this F-86D cockpit view is the hood of the radar scope. Taken on 5 April 1954, this aircraft is an F-86D-40. NAA

In the F-86D the pilot had to do the work of the radar operator, as well as the flying. After the pilot, with the help of the ground controller, located the target on his radar scope (up to 30 nautical miles – 55km) he closed to within 15 miles (27km), where he could 'lock on' the target, that is, lock his radar on the target for automatic tracking. He then received steering information on his scope and could concentrate on flying the aircraft to follow the steering signals (represented as a dot on the 8in screen). At 20sec to go, a circle began shrinking on the screen and the pilot had to increase his precision to keep the dot centred in the circle, while keeping the trigger depressed. If the dot was in the circle when the circle was down to ½in (diameter), the rockets fired, and when they reached a point 2,000ft (610m) in front of the F-86D, the target plane would cross in front on a course 90 degrees to the F-86D.

With 4 sec to go, Phase III of the fire-control-system operation came into effect, during which the computer corrected for any movement of the aircraft about the vertical axis; the pilot then had just to attend to the attitude of the aircraft. If the pilot were still flying on to his 'target', at 2 sec to go, the circuits in the firing section of the computer were readied for the target to be shot down. 'Of course,' remembers White, 'we did not fire

but we still had strict rules to avoid collision on these training missions.'

At North American the next production F-86D was the -10 block, comprising thirty-six aircraft, and incorporated design changes over the D-5, including the addition of a power rudder with no trim tab in place of the cable-operated trim tab. In addition, the engine featured a modified afterburner fuel pump, and a gun camera was introduced, installed in the left wing root. Starting in February 1953, the 3555th Flying Training Wing at Perrin AFB in Texas began to receive its first F-86Ds and was assigned the first pair of new-build D-10s on 4 February, with further aircraft arriving at Perrin during the month and through June.

Starting with 50-554, the fifty-four F-86D-15s introduced a single-point refuelling capability. Thus aircraft could be pressure refuelled via a quick-release coupling on the left-hand fuselage side, just to the rear of the wing trailing edge. This saved a considerable amount of time when compared with the gravity refuelling of individual tanks. Again, many of this production batch were assigned straight to flying training units, though at last, with the D-15, active USAF squadrons began to receive the F-86D. From 10 February 1953 94th FIS at George AFB received seven 'Dogs' under

ADC Project 3F213, comprising five D-15s and two D-20s, presumably for accelerated service tests. These aircraft departed for Norton AFB at the beginning of March, but the 94th began to receive replacement F-86D-25s later that month. 323rd FIS at Larson AFB in Washington received its first F-86Ds in April 1953, followed in May by 62nd FIS at O'Hare International, 95th FIS at Andrews AFB and 60th FIS at Westover AFB.

Few other FY50 F-86Ds were delivered to the squadrons, however, and most that did were reassigned to the two Flying Training Wings operating the aircraft. As the E-3 FCS fitted in the F-86D-1s was of limited use, many of those at Tyndall were converted to 'Pacer' aircraft. Work carried out included the replacing of the radome with a metal version, removing the rocket package, related hydraulic equipment, the fire-control system, the autopilot, the engine-driven alternator, and the glide path, localizer and marker-beacon equipment. Though an amount of ballast was installed to provide a satisfactory centre of gravity, these aircraft still tipped the scales 750lb (340kg) lighter than their standard contemporaries. Thus performance was improved overall, and redesignated TF-86D, they were used as chase aircraft during F-86D training. The first aircraft to be converted was 50-479, the work being carried out at Tyndall. This machine emerged as a TF-86D on 27 July 1954, and thirteen further Sabres were converted to TF-86D specification at Tyndall by early February 1955. Beginning in May 1955, another twenty-five F-86D-1 and -5 airframes were converted to TF-86D configuration for use at Yuma AFB, Arizona during rocket-firing training missions. Many of these conversions were done at North American's Fresno, California facility.

As crews began to be fed into the F-86D conversion process, it quickly became apparent that the F-86D would require more pilot training than any other USAF aircraft of the time, owing to the many operations carried out by its pilot. Fresh F-86D aircrews were trained at the Interceptor Training Schools at Perrin AFB, Texas and Tyndall AFB, Florida. The prospective F-86D pilot would begin in the Erco MB-18 flight simulator, which was a ¼-ton contraption that included a replica of the F-86D cockpit. As the pilot sat in this $150,000 machine, his progress

The fifth F-86D-5, 50-496, was delivered to 3200th Proof Test Group at Eglin AFB on 29 July 1952 for armament testing, and this photograph was taken then. In February 1956 it was converted to TF-86D configuration and assigned to 4750th Air Defense Wing at Yuma AFB. J.M.G. Gradidge

was monitored by an instructor and a technician seated at a control panel in an adjoining room. From this room, 'targets' and flying situations such as emergency procedures could be fed into the simulation. The then Capt Duane E. 'Bud' Biteman recalled his time at Perrin:

I was scheduled for the F-86D All-Weather Interceptor School at Perrin AFB, reporting not later than 23 September 1954. My school, a four-and-one-half-month course, was designed to qualify me as an F-86D all-weather interceptor pilot, with logical assignment to follow in the Air Defense Command (though things would turn out differently). For the first two weeks we were to be totally involved with ground school, no flying whatsoever. Weather and instrument principles; the second month we would fine-tune instrument flying techniques in the air. Only then would we finally check out in the F-86D... the 'Dawg' and learn the latest air-defense combat techniques.

Those first two weeks turned out to be a real challenge; primarily devoted to review of weather phenomena, with special effort

devoted to the codes and symbols used by the weather service, and coming as close as possible to making us certified weather observers/forecasters. As we started F-86 systems training we simultaneously went into the T-33 instrument practise portion of the training... not especially difficult for me since I had been instructing students in the same basic techniques for the past three years.

Although we began our F-86D ground training shortly after commencing the course at Perrin, it was to be almost five weeks before I would be able to 'light the fire' and take off. Instead, we divided our time between the classrooms and the exotic flight simulator... a new million-dollar computerized device which almost exactly duplicated every system and action of the airplane. We learned and practised every emergency procedure which might befall us in the airplane, and learned to manipulate the radar controls while 'flying' in thunderstorm instrument conditions. We would fly in-trail formation (follow the leader, line astern) behind a flight of simulated F-86s, then, when directed on to a 'collision course' attack pattern by the ground controller and locked-on to an 'enemy' aircraft, we would

maneuver in to 'rocket release' and pitch-out break-away to avoid falling 'debris' from the destroyed enemy. Then, inevitably, the controller would give us a simulated flame-out to see if we were still alert enough to restart the engine, or to glide down to a safe instrument landing!

With 30hr in the simulator before climbing into the F-86D for my first flight, I was completely familiar with the single-place machine and all of its systems – even the sounds! It was the first single-seat fighter that I ever checked out (on 23 November 1954) for a first flight with complete familiarity and confidence.

Upon return to duty following the Christmas holidays, I flew just a few more flights in the '86, beginning a long association with GCI [ground-controlled interception] controllers, as we learned the positioning tactics the ground controllers would use to maneuver our flights of attacking fighters on to the 'lead-collision' intercept line, where our short-range, airborne radar sets could be locked on allowing the onboard computers to display the track necessary for successful attack.

These attacks consisted of firing rockets at a target towed 6,000ft (1,828m) behind a converted B-45 bomber. The banner was a mere 6ft by 30ft (1.8x9.1m) plastic-mesh panel with spinning metal discs on it to

Above: These 5th FIS Sabres at McGuire AFB have yet to be modified to incorporate the brake parachute. Note the curved base to the vertical fin and the position of the rear identification lights. On 'Pull Out' aircraft these were relocated to the base of the drag chute fairing. A.J. Jackson

Below: This F-86D-25 was pictured on delivery to 95th FIS at Andrews AFB in May 1953. It was lost in a crash a year later. Note the lack of a 'Pull Out' drag chute. Howard Levy via Mike Fox

provide a radar signature. Following the 'daylight' phase came a period of intensive night/adverse weather training, as Biteman related:

On January 10th the training curriculum put me on the night-flying schedule, where I remained for two solid months... straight through to the end of the course, I flew the '86 only at night, practising GCI tactics and intercepts. The 36hr of night F-86D time acquired during that time eliminated any apprehension I might possibly have retained about flying at night (and a good thing, it was a precursor of things to come... lots of night and solid-weather instrument flying). On February 22nd I finally received word of my over-due transfer orders following completion of the course at Perrin and, typically, rather than being sent to the West Coast, as I'd been led to believe, we were to be sent [to] the 406th Fighter Interceptor Wing at RAF Station Manston, England.

Though the first FY51 F-86D-20s were not accepted by the Air Force until December 1952, the USAF and North American were anxious to show off their

stated that the record-breaking machine had been fully equipped for this flight, but the poor state of spares availability, especially as regards the E-4 FCS, makes this claim look shaky. 51-2945 was the first D-20 delivered to the USAF, at Edwards AFB on 6 December 1952. The record stood for just seven months, being bettered on 16 July 1953 by Lt Col William Barnes flying the first F-86D-35 over the same Salton Sea course. Barnes averaged 715.697mph (1,151km/h) at this attempt.

As with previous blocks, the F-86D-20 contained numerous changes over previous models. Chief among these was the relocation of the aircraft's external power receptacles to an external position under the rear fuselage. This meant that D-20 and later models could operate from alert barns. The relocation of the external power receptacle gave the pilot the ability to start up and taxi away with minimal ground crew assistance. The power lead would then pull out automatically as the aircraft moved off.

Another item introduced with the dash-20 was an engine-fuel-filter de-

On the D model at [an] altitude such as 40–45,000ft (12,192 to 13,716m) the slats would pop out in a high turn and would degrade the performance significantly. The airplane at that time was a good flying machine. The big problem, and I might say the only problem, with the airplane was its electronic fuel-control system. I was a maintenance officer and test pilot at Moody [AFB, Georgia] and if I had over 50 per cent in-commission, I considered we were doing good. All the problems were either fuel control or radar.

Nevertheless, the F-86D was appreciably faster than its contemporaries. The Northrop F-89C Scorpion, although possessing a far greater combat range, could achieve a top speed of only 650mph (1,045km/h), Lockheed's F-94C Starfire faring even worse at 640mph (1,029km/h). Thus the F-86D was chosen for two-thirds of the Air Defense Command's wings and became the dominant ADC interceptor during the late 1950s.

Subsequent F-86D batches rolled off the Inglewood lines with no break between each block of aircraft. The F-86D-25 was the first model to have provision for

Though sharing the same designation as earlier versions of the engine, General Electric's J47-GE-17 was more than just a GE-13 with an afterburner. The complex electronic fuel-control system was a key feature and gave many problems throughout the life of the engine. The variable exhaust nozzle 'eyelid' is also visible here. General Electric/Eric Falk

new hot rod interceptor to the public. Thus, in November 1952, the second F-86D-20, 51-2945, was prepared for an attempt on the world's airspeed record, held by an F-86A since 1948 (see Chapter 1). The 1952 attempt was flown over a 3km FAI instrumented course at Salton Sea, California by Capt J. Slade Nash. Flying at only 125ft (38m) above sea level, Nash successfully broke the record on 18 November, pegging the new record at 698.505mph (1,123km/h). It has been

icing system. Although many F-86D-20 aircraft were assigned to the still expanding flying training commitment, further examples did start to trickle out to the active squadrons, beginning with the 2nd FIS at McGuire AFB, New Jersey.

In squadron use the F-86D did present maintenance problems as well as imposing certain limitations on its combat crews. Bill Plunk had mixed feelings about the aircraft:

jettisonable drop tanks, and the D-30 introduced an automatic-approach control system. The D-35s incorporated an AN/ARN-14 omnidirectional range set (VOR) and an external receptacle for inverter ground power in the right-hand nose area. Additionally, the rudder trim tab system was reintroduced in favour of the power boost of the D-10 to -30 production blocks. On the F-86D-40 a fuel-flow meter replaced the earlier engine fuel-pressure gauge, and further cockpit refinements included the addition of an electrical face-mask defrost. All D-40s except 52-3598 to -3847 deleted the wing-root gun camera, and the model introduced the AN/ARN-18 glide-path receiver in place of the earlier AN/ARN-5B item.

In order to carry out live firing training, Air Defense Command F-86D and L aircraft undertook an annual month-long deployment to Yuma AFB (later renamed Vincent AFB) in Arizona. Here, F-86D-41s of 37th FIS are seen at the Squadron's 1956 detachment *Jim Thompson via Green and Isham*

Project Pull Out

These relatively small batches of aircraft marked minor refinements in the basic F-86D design; but it was not until the arrival of the F-86D-45 that a definitive 'Dog' rolled off North American's production line. It had been known for some time that the F-86D's landing run presented a limitation when it operated from airfields with short runways. In an effort to reduce this problem, a tail-mounted, drag parachute was fitted to a modified F-86D-15 aircraft, 50-457 in January 1953. This and another D-15, 50-554, were bailed to North American for the programme and testing proved that the deployment of such a parachute on landing reduced the run from 2,550ft (777m) to 1,600ft (487m). The success of these tests led to the installation of drag parachutes on all aircraft beginning with the F-86D-45 batch, and externally these aircraft could be recognized by a flattened drag parachute housing at the base of the rudder. Engine improvements were also slotted into D-45 production, the first 238 D-45s introducing the J47-GE-17B with 7,500lb (4,301kg) thrust, while remaining F-86D-45 and subsequent models were equipped with the J47-GE-33 (originally known as GE-X17) with a dry thrust of 5,500lb (2,494kg) and 7,650lb (3,469kg) with afterburner. The F-86D-50 model differed only slightly from the previous model, only modified engine-oil drains, brake parachute (52-

10026 and on) and the addition of a ceramic aspirator liner (52-4198 to -10025) setting them apart.

Thus, by 1953, there were already a number of different production blocks of F-86Ds in service, differing from each other in respect of spare parts, instruction manuals and maintenance procedures. This made maintenance and repair of the F-86D a logistics nightmare, and Air Defense Command initiated Project Lock On to verify the effectiveness of ADC's several weapons systems, including the F-86D. In order to make the several production blocks of the F-86D standard throughout the USAF, a decision was made in late 1953 to initiate Project Pull Out, which withdrew all pre-F-86D-45 models from service and upgraded them to F-86D-45 standard. Work was centred at North American's Fresno, California plant, with other conversions carried out at the McLellan AFB Sacramento Air Material Area. The pre-D-45 models were fitted with braking parachutes (standard on the F-86D-45), and all models had uncompleted Technical Orders and modifications completed before their dispatch to operational units. In total 1,128 F-86Ds went through 'Pull Out', which was completed in September 1955. In order to differentiate the modified aircraft, their block numbers were changed, so that D-10 to D-40 airframes became dash-11, 16, 21, 26, 31, 36 and 41 machines, respectively. It is thought that few, if any, F-86D-1 or -5 Sabres were subjected to Project Pull Out.

There were many ramifications of Project Pull Out, but the main result was that, with a generally standardized Sabre interceptor force, the USAF could now begin to deploy F-86Ds overseas, in many cases replacing earlier day fighter Sabres. This process brought some upheaval as personnel became accustomed to flying and maintaining the more complex aircraft. Pilots in particular received the F-86D with mixed emotions, many feeling aggrieved at losing their MiG-killing dogfighters to a less agile interceptor. That said, the Dog pilots generally came to respect their new machine. The 514th FIS pilot Dave Roberson was quick to defend the F-86D's apparent shortcomings:

I take exception to the statement that the Dog wasn't suited to the alert mission. You could start it as fast as any other. In fact, with the electronic fuel control you could hit the starter and put the throttle in afterburner position and it would automatically start and accelerate to full power. I think it was well under a minute. The radar may have taken longer to warm up, but you didn't use it until you were in the target's vicinity and it had more than ample time to warm up. There were glitches with the electronic fuel control. As I recall, there was an 'auto' position for take-off. When this switch was on, the fuel system would automatically go to emergency fuel as it detected trouble with the electronic system. After take-off you were supposed to move this switch to the normal position. The problem was that if it had automatically changed to 'emergency' it also drove the normal fuel control to the idle position. So when you moved the switch to normal it felt like a flame-out, in that you were at idle and it took several seconds for the thing to catch up to the throttle position. Therefore a lot of folks did go ahead and use the emergency fuel [position] for take-off. For its day it was a pretty good system, but did have lots of glitches. For instance, in normal flight, it would sometimes lock up, that is the power stayed at the last setting regardless of what you did with the throttle. The only way out was to manually switch to emergency fuel. This was always thrilling when you were on someone's wing in the weather.

Overseas deployment began in 1954 with USAF Europe (USAFE) and Far East Air Forces (FEAF) squadrons equipping with post-Pullout F-86D-26, 31, 36, 41 and 45 aircraft, although it seems that only FEAF deployed F-86D-26s. In Europe the 86th and the 406th Fighter Interceptor Wing replaced their F-86Fs during 1954, the former having five squadrons in France and Germany, the latter with three squadrons based in England. Further single squadrons also gained F-86Ds at around the same time, beginning with the 357th Fighter Interceptor Squadron (FIS) at Nouasseur Air Base (AB), Morocco and the 431st FIS at Wheelus AB, Libya in 1955.

In 1958 the 324th FIS moved from the USA to a new base a Sidi Slimane, Morocco, thus completing USAFE's F-86D equipment. The first F-86Ds assigned to the Far East arrived by sea at Kisarazu in Japan in early 1954. On 20 January the first FEAF F-86D flew at Kisarazu, with the Korean War ace Robert Baldwin at the helm. It is interesting to note that this particular machine, 51-8345, an F-86D-35,

52-4304, an F-86D-50 of 514th FIS seen here at RAF Manston, England in May 1955. All European-deployed F-86Ds were drag-chute equipped 'Pull Out' D-36s, -41s or later standard D-45s and -50s. Larry Brooks

In July 1958 324th FIS deployed from Westover AFB, MA to Sidi Slimane Air Depot in French Morocco. Unusually, the unit had previously flown the F-86L, but received F-86Ds from Mobile Air Materiel Area upon arrival in Europe. The unit's first Sabres initially carried this scheme, with red lightning flashes on drop tanks and tail fin plus the squadron badge on the nose. Candid Aero-Files

had not been through Project Pull Out and was one of few assigned overseas without a drag parachute. FEAF F-86D assignment took in a number of units, 26th FIS being one of the first, when it received Dogs at Naha AB, Okinawa in 1954. The unit was assigned to 51st FIW but attached to

6351st Air Base Wing and subsequently to 13th Air Force during this period. 68th FIS at Itazuke AB, Japan re-equipped at about the same time, and next to receive F-86Ds was 4th FIS at Misawa AB in Japan, converting from F-94Bs to F-86Ds in August 1954 upon its assignment to 39th

Air Division and the Japanese Air Self Defense Force. Another Wing to receive F-86Ds was the 35th FIW, again re-equipping with this model in August 1954 at Yokota AB in Japan. The 51st FIW of Korean War fame also received F-86Ds in December 1954, with two squadrons at Naha AB. The wing then almost immediately began regular deployments to Taiwan in support of the Quemoy and Matsu operations. One squadron originally flew to Chiayi Air Base on Formosa in mid-April 1955, being relieved by another

Above: **These are some of the last F-86Ds accepted by the USAF on 30 September 1955. Personnel L-R are: Lt Mason Anderson, Lt John Clark, unknown NAA representative, Lt Thomas Dobbs, Lt Col Robert 'Pappy' Myers (pointing), Lt Jack Gresham, unknown NAA representative, Lt John Brown. All were from 332nd FIS at McGuire AFB, NJ.** NAA

Below: **In the Far East a number of units operated the F-86D until the late 1950s. This F-86D-36 is from 4th FIS at Misawa AB in Japan during October 1956. It was scrapped at Kisarazu in 1960.** Marty Isham

F-86D squadron at the end of the month. These missions tailed off at the end of the year with the cessation of open hostility between China and Taiwan; but in 1957 the F-86Ds of 51st FIW again returned to Taiwan and to give support in the renewed Quemoy crisis. At this time several F-86D flights were shadowed by Chinese MiGs, and, on occasion, flak bursts warned the Sabres that they were straying too close to

China. This is probably the closest that any F-86D got to combat. The final FEAF Sabre deployment to Taiwan ended on 24 November 1958.

North American won the F-86D one further order, AF-22303, which was placed on 12 June 1953 for 624 machines, comprising 225 F-86D-55s and 399 D-60s. This final batch was given NAA designation NA-201 and aircraft in these blocks were primarily purchased to equip and upgrade Air Defense Command wings in the continental United States. The F-86D-55 introduced an alternate hydraulic system accumulator dump valve (53-707 and on), the inverter external power receptacle was relocated to the right-hand aft fuselage area, AN/ARC-34 UHF command radio replaced the AN/ARC-27, and lap belts were fitted that opened automatically after ejection. The first F-86D-55s were delivered in November 1954 and assigned to 60th FIS at Westover AFB, 83rd FIS at Paine AFB and 97th FIS at Wright-Patterson. The D-60 began delivery in March 1955 and further relocated the inverter external power receptacle, this time to the underside of fuselage from 53-857 onwards. All D-60s featured modified wing attachment fittings and incorporated provision for an AN/APX-25 identification radar (IFF) set. These machines went to squadrons including 94th FIS at George AFB and 325th FIS at Hamilton AFB. The final F-86D, 53-4090, was delivered to the Air Force in September 1955.

In USAF service the F-86D eventually equipped seventy-five operational squadrons, far outnumbering those of the F-94 and the F-89. That fact was largely due to the F-86D's ability to react quickly to intruders. However, it is worth noting that in its standard ADC guise with two 120gall drop tanks fitted, it was severely compromised as an interceptor. This fact was not lost on the combat squadrons operating the aircraft, and, in June 1954, Maj Vince Gordon, commander of 325th FIS, made his feelings known to his superiors. In a detailed letter to Brig-Gen Munro MacCloskey, commander of 78th Air Division, Gordon highlighted the following points:

a. That an afterburner climb to 45,000ft (13,716m) could be accomplished without drop tanks in 7.6min. With drop tanks fitted this rose to 12min.
b. At 35,000ft (10,668m) at 100 per cent

52-3598, the first F-86D-40, was bailed to North American for testing these twelve-shot underwing rocket packs during 1953. San Diego Aerospace Museum/Ray Wagner

Artist's impression of a GAR-1 Falcon missile-armed F-86D interceptor. Believed to have been proposed in 1953, this design was not put into production. Instead, the Northrop F-89H Scorpion was chosen as an expedient measure to carry the GAR-1. USAFM

military power and with drop tanks fitted, maximum speed was 0.79 Mach. At the same height in 'clean' configuration, top speed was 0.89 Mac
c. Airborne duration for similar flight profiles was just 12–15min more for an aircraft with drop tanks fitted.
d. Combat radius of an F-86D operating without external tanks was only 75 miles (120km) less than an aircraft with external tanks.

These points had been raised at various times by other Sabre pilots, and even by other air forces, but ADC stood firm that F-86Ds would operate with drop tanks

fitted. It can only by conjectured that the slight increase in combat radius was seen as a worthwhile trade-off for the multitude of valid points raised above.

Not Quite a Dead End – the 1954 Interceptor

During 1953 a number of aircraft were put forward as carriers for the new Hughes GAR-1 (later to become the AIM-1 Falcon) air-to-air guided missile. North American proposed a modified F-86D design, featuring four of these rockets,

Project Arrow

In 1955 the USAF initiated Project Arrow, a major realignment under which dispersed squadrons would be returned to the parent groups or wings to which they were assigned during World War II and before. This immense project was considerably simplified by transferring these units 'less personnel and equipment'. Thus, instead of moving a squadron bodily to the home base of its traditional parent wing, in most cases a squadron on that particular base would change its designation. Most squadrons affected were in Air Defense Command, and of the Sabre squadrons involved all were US-based F-86D units. The date chosen was 18 August 1955 and, overnight, tens of squadrons gained new identities. In some cases units were inactivated to make way for historically important organizations to be concurrently reactivated. There follows a listing of all F-86D squadrons involved in Project Arrow. In order to try and simplify what is inherently complex, squadrons are shown as 'taking over' and 'transferring' aircraft and personnel. Note that all such transfers were on paper only.

94th FIS at George AFB took over 56th FIS F-86Ds at Selfridge, reassigning from 27th Air Division (AD) to 1st FIW. The 94th FIS F-86Ds left at George were then reassigned to 327th FIS, which was activated at the base on 18 August under 27th AD. 56th FIS then took over 97th FIS F-86Ds at Wright-Patterson AFB, being reassigned from 575th Air Defense Group (ADG) to 4706th Air Defense Wing (ADW). 97th FIS then re-equipped with F-94Cs under 82nd FG.

2nd FIS at McGuire AFB took over F-86Ds from 75th FIS at Suffolk County AFB, reassigning from 4709th ADW to 52nd FIW. The ex-2nd FIS F-86Ds at McGuire were then transferred to 332nd FIS, converting on paper from F-94Cs. 75th FIS in turn took over on F-89 Scorpions at Presque Isle AFB.

5th FIS at McGuire took over 331st FIS F-86Ds at Suffolk County AFB, reassigning from 4709th ADW to 52nd FIW. 5th FIS then transferred its old F-86Ds at McGuire to 539th FIS, which, in turn, reassigned from 4700th to 4709th ADW, in turn transferring its F-86Ds to 331st FIS at Stewart AFB. 331st FIS was then reassigned from 519th ADG to 329th FG.

83rd FIS at Paine AFB took over 325th FIS F-86Ds at Hamilton, reassigning from 529th ADG to 78th FG; 83rd FIS then transferred their previous F-86Ds to 321st FIS at Paine originally, but most then transferred to 329th at George, which had activated under 27th AD on 18 August. 321st instead re-equipped with F-89Ds. 325th FIS then took over 432nd FIS F-86Ds at Truax AFB, assigning from 566th ADG to 327th FIW. Finally, 432nd FIS converted to F-89 Scorpions at Minneapolis-St. Paul. Moving back to 329th FIS, the Squadron activated on 18 August under 27th AD at George AFB, and took over 518th FIS aircraft at the same base, 518th inactivating concurrently.

71st FIS at Greater Pittsburgh took over 13th FIS F-86Ds at Selfridge, reassigning from 500th ADG to 1st FIW; 71st FIS then transferred the F-86Ds at Pittsburgh to 42nd FIS, which was reassigned in turn from 501st ADG to 54th FIW. 42nd FIS then handed

its F-86Ds to 63rd FIS at Oscoda AFB, which converted from F-89Ds. 13th FIS then took over 519th FIS F-86Ds at Sioux City, assigning from 575th ADG to 53rd FG. The similarly F-86D-equipped 14th FIS remained at Sioux City throughout, but was reassigned from 521st ADG to 53rd also on 18 August.

354th FIS at Oxnard took over F-86Ds from 460th FIS at McGhee-Tyson AFB, reassigning to 355th FIW and losing their F-89Cs in the process. This allowed 460th FIS to take over 497th FIS F-86Ds at Portland International Airport under 53rd FIW. 497th FIS then moved (on paper) to Geiger AFB, gaining F-86Ds from 445th FIS under 412th FG. Finally, 445th FIS converted to F-89Ds at Wurtsmith AFB.

337th FIS at Minneapolis-St. Paul converted from F-89Ds, taking over 60th FIS F-86Ds at Westover AFB, reassigning from 514th ADG to 4707th ADW. 60th FIS then converted to F-94C Starfires.

82nd FIS at Presque Isle converted from F-89Ds, taking over F-86Ds from 413th FIS at Travis AFB, reassigning in turn to 78th FG. 413th FIS was inactivated the same day.

538th FIS activated at Larson AFB under 9th AD, gaining F-86Ds from 323rd FIS. 323rd in turn moved to Truax AFB and 327th FG, also gaining some ex-432nd FIS aircraft as well as those from 325th FIS at the same base. This allowed 432nd FIS to convert to F-89Ds.

A number of squadrons were not moved on paper, merely reassigning to new wings and groups in order to make Project Arrow's rationalization easier. 11th FIS remained at Duluth Municipal with F-86Ds, but was reassigned from 515th ADG to 343rd FIW control. Likewise, 62nd FIS remained based at O'Hare International Airport, but reassigned from 501st ADG to its traditional parent wing, the 56th FIW. 86th FIS at Youngstown Municipal also retained base and personnel, but reassigned its F-86Ds from 502nd ADG to 79th FIW control. The F-86Ds of 317th FIW stayed at McChord AFB, though it was placed under 325th FIW control instead of the previous assignment, 567th ADG. 465th FIS, also at McChord, was inactivated on 18 August, but personnel and F-86Ds remained at McChord, reactivating concurrently as 318th FIS, which was also placed under 325th FIW. 37th FIS at Ethan Allen AFB reassigned to 14th FG from 517th ADG, but remained with F-86Ds. 322nd FIS activated under 9th AD at Larson AFB, gaining F-86Ds from 31st FIS, which inactivated the same day. The famed 'Geiger Tigers', 498th FIS at Geiger AFB, took over F-86Ds from 520th, also at Geiger, having reactivated under 84th FG on 18th August. 520th FIS was then inactivated on the same day.

Finally, in order to make way for squadron reactivation, inevitably a few units were also closed down, notably 456th FIS at George AFB. However, in a quirky twist to this tale, the unit reformed at Castle AFB one month later with F-86Ds.

Despite the best intents of Project Arrow, it is ironic that within a few years these hastily drawn up plans came to nought. With changing air-defence requirements, the parent wings soon lost their squadrons, sometimes for good.

This F-86D-60 was bailed to North American in 1955 for GAR-1B Falcon missile testing. The four pylons look more like a service installation than a pure test configuration. No Sabres were equipped with this missile, however. San Diego Aerospace Museum/Ray Wagner

which would be mounted in place of the Mighty Mouse belly pack. However, although the Air Force decided to turn down the F-86D proposal, choosing instead to wait until the advent of the '1954 Interceptor', Northrop's F-89 Scorpion was chosen as a stop-gap to carry the GAR-1 and this went into production as the F-89H.

Undaunted, NAA undertook a further review of the F-86D design to take part in the subsequent '1954 Interceptor' competition. With the inclusion of the low-set tailplane, previously tested on the YF-86D, Hugh Elkin and a small team came up with a wing with a 7 per cent thickness ratio, incorporating an aft-swept F-86D wing box, giving a wing area of 385sq ft (35.81sq m). Called the

Following the success of the 'sugar scoop' cooling intakes fitted to the F-86L, a number of overseas-based F-86Ds were also modified from 1957 onwards. This 526th FIS F-86D-36, based at Landstuhl AB in Germany, was thus configured. It later passed to the Greek Air Force. Author

Advanced F-86D, this design, with its 45-degree swept wing, updated fire-control system and J57 engine, was taken up by Ray Rice and submitted as NAA's 1954 Interceptor. Although it lost the competition to Convair's F-102, the USAF was sufficiently impressed by NAA's proposal that a parallel contract was agreed for a day fighter variant, which eventually became the F-100 Super Sabre.

By the mid-1950s the F-86D was already being replaced by more modern interceptors, including the Convair F-102A, which entered USAF service with 327th FIS in April 1956. However, a comprehensive F-86D upgrade and conversion programme breathed new life into the Sabre. In addition, standard F-86Ds served with the Air Force in Europe and the Far East until the end of 1960. Some of the last Dog Sabres in Air Force service were flown by 513th FIS at Phalsbourg AB, France and the 4th FIS at Misawa AB in Japan. By this time, the US-based units had already re-equipped with newer types. Many of these F-86Ds then passed into

the Military Assistance Program for use by foreign air forces.

F-86L – Semi-Automatic Interceptor

Despite the relative success of the F-86D and GCI intercept team, there remained numerous problems with this type of operation. Critically, there was a delay in relaying GCI site intercept data vocally to the interceptor. Therefore in the early 1950s the US government authorized research into a better system of relaying intercept data. The Massachusetts Institute of Technology (MIT) Lincoln Laboratory, which had been set up in 1951, was chosen to lead the project. The Lincoln Laboratory team, led by Dr Albert G. Hill, quickly formulated an idea which became known as Semi Automatic Ground Environment (SAGE). The SAGE system, accepted by the USAF in 1953, would use upgraded GCI sites to relay radar data to

the interceptors at the exact moment it was received at the ground site, enabling the aircraft to be steered on to an intercept course automatically by the autopilot. The interceptor would in turn be modified to carry the datalink equipment, so that the pilot could now receive range, heading and altitude information for a target without speaking direct to a GCI site. The F-86D, in upgraded form, would figure large in the early days of SAGE, where GCI sites would be controlled by the AN/FSQ-7 Combat Direction Central.

A small-scale SAGE demonstration network was built on the north-east coast of the USA, and this 'Cape Cod system', utilized, among others, F-86Ds from 331st FIS at Suffolk County AFB to act as interceptors for the trial period. At the same time, Strategic Air Command B-47s were detailed to act as intruders. Series II of the Cape Cod System Operations Test (SOT) took place from November 1955 to January 1956, when B-29s flew dummy raids against Boston, with sixty-two interceptors directed from Hanscom AFB and South Weymouth NAS against them. Just over one-third of the intercepts were successful. Series II SOT started on 14 February 1956 with up to thirty-two B-47 bombers attacking Boston, Martha's

Vineyard and Portsmouth. The Series II tests were completed on 25 April and a further series was run from 6 July to 7 November, Boston again being the target for B-47s, with F-86Ds included in the interceptor force from Otis, Westover and Hanscom AFBs. It was not until 1957 that the final tests on the Cape Cod system were completed, but the time spent on perfecting the system had been worthwhile: the interceptors demonstrated almost 100 per cent interception success rates, with up to 70 per cent permitting successful firing passes.

In theory, the SAGE system was a sound concept but, in practice, it took a long time to iron out numerous bugs in the project. Dr Hill led the SAGE team from 1952 until 1955, and it was only after four years of solid toil that the system really showed signs of promise. Testing of the SAGE system was started to include F-89C Scorpion aircraft of 6520th Test Wing at Hanscom AFB, Massachusetts, and, from March 1953, the unit also gained its first F-86Ds for use in conjunction with the Cambridge Research Center project team from nearby MIT. Even with the proof of the Cape Cod system it was not until July 1958, with the setting up of the MIT offshoot Mitre Corporation, that the full-scale, nationwide system began to be perfected.

In order to upgrade F-86Ds for the operational SAGE mission, the USAF initiated Project Follow-On (Air Materiel Command Project 6F375) to convert existing airframes. Low-time aircraft were routed through North American's Inglewood and Fresno plants for this work to be carried out, and further conversion was accomplished at Sacramento Air Materiel Area, McLellan AFB. Project Follow-On started in May 1956 and SAGE-converted machines emerged with a new designation – F-86L. These aircraft received an AN/ARR-39 datalink receiver, which featured a small blade antenna on the fuselage just forward of the left wing. In addition, the AN/ARC-27 command radio was replaced by an AN/ARC-34 set, and an AN/APX-25 identification radar was added in place of the earlier AN/APX-6. To complete the system upgrade an AN/ARN-31 glide slope receiver was also installed. The total weight of this equipment was around 100lb (45kg).

To improve the flying characteristics of

The first ADC unit to receive F-86Ls was the 49th FIS at Hanscom AFB, MA. The Squadron markings on this F-86L-60 are unusual in employing green as the primary colour. Don Bennett

the aircraft, the so-called 'F-40' wing configuration was incorporated into the conversion, with 12in (0.3m) wing-tip extensions and the '6-3' slatted wing leading edge. The new wing improved handling and provided better turning at high altitudes. The reconditioned F-86Ls retained the armament of twenty-four rockets of the F-86D. Finally, the NACA-ducted engine compartment cooling inlets on the mid fuselage were replaced by protruding scoops on either side. The NACA intakes had given less than satisfactory performance in the F-86D and the modified intakes (known by ground crews as 'sugar scoops') resulted in such improved cooling properties that they were also retrofitted to many non-SAGE F-86Ds during the late 1950s.

All F-86Ls were modified to incorporate the J47-GE-33 engine, and it has been reported that they also received the drag parachute modification, if necessary. However, as most, if not all, of the affected machines had earlier passed through Project Pull Out, this seems likely to have been unnecessary. In any case, post-Pull Out F-86Ds retained their modified block numbers after conversion to F-86L, and thus an F-86D-36

(converted from F-86D-35 under Project Pull Out) would now become an F-86L-36. It is worth noting here that SAGE was designed for use only in the continental United States and there was therefore no requirement to convert USAF F-86Ds assigned to USAF Europe and Far East Air Forces.

The first flight of a SAGE-modified aircraft reportedly took place on 27 December 1955, though this machine did not incorporate the airframe structural modifications, and the first full conversion was carried out in May 1956, though it was not until October 1956 that the first aircraft began to be assigned to USAF units. As F-86Ls began to emerge from the conversion process, they supplanted and began to replace earlier F-86Ds, freeing many of the latter to undergo F-86L conversion. The first F-86L conversions were assigned to ADC under project 6F674, 49th FIS at Hanscom AFB getting the first aircraft on 23 October. It appears that this unit was then used in further SAGE testing and proving programmes with the Mitre Corporation. By the end of that year further squadrons had also received F-86Ls, including the 62nd FIS at O'Hare

Many of the early-model F-86Ds that were brought up to F-86L standard served with training units. This F-86L-21 is in the markings of 3555th Combat Crew Training Wing at Perrin AFB in Texas. via Mike Fox

This immaculate F-86L belonged to 95th FIS at Andrews AFB. Howard Levy via Mike Fox

International Airport, 94th FIS at Selfridge AFB and 331st FIS at Stewart AFB.

In total, 981 F-86Ds were modified to the F-86L configuration and, although 575 F-86Ds were received at Inglewood, a large number were transferred to and from Fresno in October 1957 for the work to be completed. It is thought that 452 F-86L conversions were undertaken at Fresno and a further fifty-two at McLellan AFB. Finally, it appears that many of the 49th FIS aircraft, although converted at Fresno, did not receive their F-86L designation until they were assigned to the unit at Hanscom AFB. The reason for this is not known.

Originally, many early aircraft were modified, with progressively newer machines going through as conversion progressed. However, many F-86D-10, 15 and 20s were placed into storage at McLellan AFB in 1955, apparently as reserves for F-86L conversion. Some of these aircraft were then the last F-86L modifications to be completed, though large numbers of these early model F-86Ds were declared surplus to requirements and scrapped in 1957. The last F-86L

conversions were assigned to their new units in early 1958, and eventually equipped thirty front-line squadrons.

In line with the active-duty units, the flying training squadrons also began to re-equip with the F-86L, under Air Training Command Project 7F205, starting with 3625th Combat Crew Training Wing (CCTW) at Tyndall AFB in July 1957. The other two main F-86D/L training units, 3550th CCTW at Moody AFB and 3555th CCTW at Perrin AFB, received their first F-86Ls in December 1957. Tyndall's F-86L training ceased in late

1957 and, during August 1958, the remaining CCTW's became Flying Training Wings (FTW). With the drawdown in F-86L operations, the remaining training units relinquished their Sabres in 1960, the 3555th FTW in April and the 3550th FTW in November.

A few exceptions to the rule of F-86Ls replacing F-86Ds within the same unit are worth mentioning at this point. For reasons unknown, the 37th FIS at Ethan Allen AFB in Vermont did not convert to the F-86L, instead choosing to keep its F-86Ds until December 1957, when

USAF F-86D/L Sabre Squadrons

2nd FIS, McGuire AFB, NJ and Suffolk County AFB, NY	322nd FIS, Larson AFB, WA (+ F-86L)
4th FIS, Misawa Air Base (AB), Japan	323rd FIS, Larson AFB, WA
5th FIS, McGuire AFB, NJ and Suffolk County AFB, NY	324th FIS, Westover AFB, MA; Sidi Slimane AB, Morocco (+ F-86L)
11th FIS, Duluth Municipal Airport, MN	325th FIS, Travis AFB, CA
13th FIS, Selfridge AFB in MI, moving to Sioux City Municipal (+ F-86L)	326th FIS, Fairfax AFB, KS; Grandview AFB, MT
14th FIS, Sioux City Municipal Airport IA (+ F-86L)	327th FIS, George AFB, CA
15th FIS, Davis Monthan AFB (+ F-86L)	329th FIS, George AFB, CA
16th FIS, Misawa AB, Japan and Naha AB, Okinawa (1st August 1954)	330th FIS, Stewart AFB, NY
18th FIS, Minneapolis-St. Paul	331st FIS, Suffolk County AFB, NY; Stewart AFB, NY; Webb AFB, TX
25th FIS, Naha AB, Okinawa	332nd FIS, McGuire AFB, NJ
26th FIS, Naha AB, Okinawa and Clark AB, Philippines	337th FIS, Westover AFB, MA
31st FIS, Larson AFB, WA	339th FIS, Chitose AB, Japan
37th FIS, Ethan Allen AFB, VT	354th FIS, McGhee-Tyson AFB, TN
39th FIS, Johnson AB, Japan; Yokota AB, Japan; Komaki AB	357th FIS, Portland International Airport, OR; Nouasseur AB Morocco
40th FIS, Johnson AB, Japan; Yokota AB, Japan	413th FIS, Travis AFB, CA
41st FIS, Johnson AB, Japan, Yokota AB, Japan, Andersen AFB, Guam	431st FIS, Wheelus AB, Libya and Zaragosa AB, Spain
42nd FIS, O'Hare IAP, IL; Greater Pittsburgh Airport, PA (+ F-86L)	432nd FIS activated, Truax AFB
47th FIS, Niagara Falls Municipal Airport, NY (+ F-86L)	440th FIS, Geiger AFB and Landstuhl AB, West Germany; Erding Air Base, West Germany
49th FIS,†Dow AFB, ME; Hanscom AFB, MA (+ F-86L)	444th FIS, Charleston AFB†(+ F-86L)
54th FIS, Rapid City AFB, SD	445th FIS, Geiger AFB WA
56th FIS, Selfridge AFB, MI; Wright-Patterson AFB, OH (+ F-86L)	456th FIS, Castle AFB (+ F-86L)
62nd FIS, O'Hare International Airport, IL; K.I Sawyer AFB, MI (+ F-86L)	460th FIS, McGhee-Tyson AFB, Portland International Airport
63rd FIS, Oscoda AFB, MI (+ F-86L)	465th FIS, McChord AFB, WA; Hanscom AFB (+ F-86L)
68th FIS, Itazuke AFB, Japan	469th FIS, McGhee-Tyson AFB
71st FIS, Greater Pittsburgh Airport, PA; Selfridge AFB, MI (+ F-86L)	496th FIS, Hamilton AFB, Landstuhl AB, West Germany; Hahn AB
75th FIS, Suffolk County, AFB	497th FIS, Geiger AFB, WA; Torrejon AFB, Spain
82nd FIS, Travis AFB, CA	498th FIS, Geiger AFB, WA
83rd FIS, Paine AFB, WA, Hamilton AFB, CA (+ F-86L)	509th FIS, Luzon, Philippines
85th FIS, Scott AFB, IL (+ F-86L)	512th FIS, RAF Bentwaters, England; Sembach AB, West Germany
86th FIS, Youngstown Municipal Airport (+ F-86L)	513th FIS, RAF Manston, England; Phalsbourg AB, France
87th FIS, Sioux City AFB, IA; RAF Bentwaters; Lockbourne AFB, OH (+ F-86L)	514th FIS, RAF Manston, England; Landstuhl AB, West Germany
93rd FIS, Kirtland AFB, NM (+ F-86L)	518th FIS, George AFB, CA
94th FIS, George AFB, CA; Selfridge AFB, MI (+ F-86L)	519th FIS, Sioux City Municipal Airport, IA
95th FIS, Andrews AFB, MD (+ F-86L)	520th FIS, Geiger AFB, WA
97th FIS, Wright-Patterson, AFB	525th FIS, Landstuhl AB, West Germany; Bitburg AB
317th FIS, McChord AFB, WA	526th FIS, Landstuhl AB, West Germany
318th FIS, McChord AFB, WA	538th FIS, Larson AFB, WA (+ F-86L)
	539th FIS, Stewart AFB, NY; McGuire AFB NJ (+ F-86L)

Convair F-102As became the mission aircraft. This is despite a number other USAF F-86L squadrons having re-equipped with other aircraft types by this time. Another anomaly was the 324th FIS, flying from Westover AFB in Massachusetts. This unit received F-86Ls in August 1957, but, upon being notified of a permanent overseas movement to Sidi Slimane AB in Morocco, 324th FIS relinquished all its L-models. Upon arriving overseas in July 1958, the Squadron began operating F-86Ds again, as there was no overseas SAGE facility. The Geiger AFB, Washington-based, 497th FIS also received an overseas deployment notice in 1958, but this unit did not gain any F-86Ls, choosing instead to retain its F-86Ds and take them direct to Torrejon AB in Spain during July 1958. The last USAF squadron to convert fully from the F-86D to the F-86L was 93rd FIS at Kirtland AFB in New Mexico. Though the unit had received F-86Ls during August 1957, the last F-86Ds did not depart until February 1958. The 93rd then flew the F-86L until June 1960 as the last active USAF squadron flying the type.

Guard Dogs – F-86D/L in ANG Service

As Convair F-102A, and later F-106A interceptors, became available to Air Defense Command, USAF F-86Ds began to filter down to the Air National Guard (ANG) units; but it was not until 1957 that sufficient surplus aircraft were available to begin the process. The first unit to receive F-86Ds was the 173rd FIS Nebraska ANG, based at Lincoln Municipal Airport. The Squadron received F-86Ds starting in May 1957, converting from F-80C Shooting Stars. Also during 1957, the 111th and the 181st FIS Texas ANG Squadron received F-86Ds, along with the 125th and the 185th FIS Oklahoma ANG. Ten ANG squadrons had received F-86Ds by May 1958, but, by this time, F-86Ls had also become available and a number of other Guard squadrons converted straight on to this aircraft without receiving any D-models. The first ANG F-86L unit was the 108th FIS Illinois ANG, based at O'Hare International Airport. The Squadron gained its first aircraft in December 1957, having previously flown the F-84F. National Guard F-86Ds were gradually phased out in 1960, the 196th FIS California ANG flying on with the 'Dog' until March 1961, having received F-86Ls in the previous month. Flying only F-86Ds, the 198th FIS Puerto Rico ANG re-equipped with the type in February 1959 and flew these until November 1960. Conversely, the 199th FIS Hawaii ANG operated only F-86Ls, and gained aircraft specially converted for the

An element of 456th F-86Ls out of Castle AFB, CA. Coincidentally, 52-4197 was the last F-86D-45 built and 52-10176 was the last D-50. Brig Gen K.W. Bell via Marty Isham

The 196th FIS California ANG at Ontario was the last National Guard unit to operate the F-86L. Retiring its last Sabre in 1965, the unit then converted to F-102 Delta Daggers. This F-86L-55, like so many of the 196th's Sabres, was stored briefly at Davis Monthan AFB and then acquired by the New Mexico Institute of Mining and Technology at Socorro. MAP

Specifications: F-86L

POWERPLANT
General Electric J47-GE-33 with 5,550lb (2,516kg) thrust dry and 7,650lb (3,469kg) with afterburner

WEIGHTS
empty:	13,822lb (6,268kg)
gross:	18,484lb (8,382kg)

DIMENSIONS
wingspan:	39ft 1in (11.9m)
length:	40ft 3in (12.26m)
height:	15ft (4.5m)
wing area:	313sq ft (29.11sq m)

PERFORMANCE
maximum speed:	
at sea level:	693mph (1,115km/h)
at 40,000ft:	616mph (991km/h at 12,192m)
initial climb rate:	12,200ft/min (3,718m/min)
service ceiling:	49,600ft (15,118m)

Squadron from December 1957. Like their Air Force counterparts, the ANG F-86Ls were ultimately replaced by the F-102A Delta Dagger, and in 1960-61 many squadrons finally lost their Sabres for good. By early 1962 only six F-86L units remained in ANG service: 124th FIS Iowa ANG, 173rd FIS Nebraska ANG, 181st FIS Texas ANG, 190th FIS Idaho ANG,

Following their withdrawal, large numbers of Sabres were presented to towns across the United States. This proved a mixed blessing, as many were heavily vandalized and subsequently scrapped. This F-86L 53-809 for many years languished at Provo Airport, Utah. Its fate is not known. Author

194th FIS California ANG and 196th FIS California ANG. The 196th became the last unit to operate the type, converting to F-102s in the summer of 1965.

The only foreign air force to use the F-86L was Thailand, gaining ex-ANG aircraft in 1962; that country's use of the Sabre is told in another chapter.

ANG F-86D/L Sabre Squadrons

108th FIS Illinois ANG, O'Hare International Airport (F-86L)

111th FIS Texas ANG, Ellington Field (F-86D and L)

120th FIS Colorado ANG, NAS Denver (F-86D and L)

122nd FIS Louisiana ANG, New Orleans Airport, NAS New Orleans (F-86D and L)

124th FIS Iowa ANG, Des Moines (F-86L)

125th FIS Oklahoma ANG, Tulsa (F-86D)

127th FIS Kansas ANG, Wichita Municipal Airport (F-86L)

128th FIS Georgia ANG, Dobbins AFB (F-86L)

133rd FIS New Hampshire ANG, Grenier Field (F-86L)

146th FIS Pennsylvania ANG, Greater Pittburgh Airport (F-86L)

147th FIS Pennsylvania ANG, Greater Pittburgh Airport (F-86L)

151st FIS Tennessee ANG, McGhee-Tyson AFB (F-86D and L)

156th FIS North Carolina ANG, Douglas Municipal Airport (F-86L)

157th FIS South Carolina ANG, Congaree (F-86L)

159th FIS Florida ANG, Imeson Field (F-86D and L)

173rd FIS Nebraska ANG, Lincoln Municipal Airport (F-86D and L)

181st FIS Texas ANG, Hensley ANG Base, Dallas (F-86D)

182nd FIS Texas ANG, Kelly AFB (F-86D and L)

185th FIS Oklahoma ANG, Will Rogers ANG Base, Oklahoma City (F-86D and L)

187th FIS Wyoming ANG, Cheyenne Municipal Airport (F-86L)

190th FIS Idaho ANG, Gowen Field, Boise (F86L)

191st FIS Utah ANG, Salt Lake City (F-86L)

192nd FIS Nevada ANG, Reno Municipal Airport (F-86L)

194th FIS California ANG, Fresno (F-86L)

196th FIS California ANG, Ontario (F-86D and L)

197th FIS Arizona ANG, Phoenix Skyharbor (86L)

198th FIS Puerto Rico ANG, San Juan International Airport (F-86D)

199th FIS, Hawaii ANG, Hickam AFB (F-86L)

F-86D Production

Serial	Block No.	Construction Nos
50-577 to 578	YF-86D-NA	164-1 and 2
50-455 to 491	F-86D-1-NA	165-1 to 37
50-492 to 517	F-86D-5-NA	165-38 to 63
50-518 to 553	F-86D-10-NA	165-64 to 99
50-554 to 576	F-86D-15-NA	165-100 to 122
50-704 to 734	F-86D-15-NA	165-123 to 153
51-2944 to 3131	F-86D-20-NA	177-1 to 188
51-5857 to 5944	F-86D-25-NA	173-1 to 88
51-5945 to 6144	F-86D-30-NA	173-89 to 288
51-6145 to 6262	F-86D-35-NA	173-289 to 406
51-8274 to 8505	F-86D-35-NA	173-407 to 638
52-3598 to 3897	F-86D-40-NA	190-1 to 300
52-3898 to 4197	F-86D-45-NA	190-301 to 600
52-4198 to 4304	F-86D-50-NA	190-601 to 707
52-9983 to 10176	F-86D-50-NA	190-708 to 901
53-557 to 781	F-86D-55-NA	201-1 to 225
53-782 to 1071	F-86D-60-NA	201-226 to 515
53-3675 to 3710	F-86D-60-NA	201-516 to 551
53-4018 to 4090	F-86D-60-NA	201-552 to 624

CHAPTER THREE

Day Fighters: the F-86E and F

F-86E: Rebirth of the All-Flying Tail

In early 1948 testing of the XP-86 prototype showed notable instability at high speeds, a trait that was soon pinned down to the aircraft's elevator assembly. Despite numerous modifications to this area, notably the addition of an elevator trailing-edge extension, the problem was not fully solved on the XP-86 and the system therefore went into production with the F-86A. However, it was known by this time that, if the whole tailplane assembly acted as one movable control surface, such high-speed instability was considerably reduced and control effectiveness was increased. Known as the 'all-flying tail', this idea had been tested by NACA at Langley on a Curtiss XP-42

from 1943, and subsequently was used for the first time in a high-speed aircraft when fitted to the Bell X-1. Also, in 1943-44 the still-born British Miles M.52 supersonic research aircraft had featured an all-flying tail in its design.

North American decided that an all-flying tail would be the ideal solution to their problems and introduced the modification into the next incarnation of the Sabre, the F-86E day fighter. The all-flying tail proved an immediate success, and all subsequent Sabre sub-types featured this aerodynamic tweak. Concurrent with the F-86E, the F-86C/YF-93 and the F-86D design also incorporated all-flying tails into their airframes.

Initial work on the F-86E, as NAA model NA-170, began at Inglewood on 15 November 1949 and an initial contract,

AF-9456 for sixty F-86E-1s and fifty-one F-86E-5s was finalized on 17 January 1950. The E-model had much in common with its F-86A stable mate, and only the addition of two tailplane strakes on the F-86E readily distinguished the two aircraft. The strakes were installed on the E-model to clean up airflow around the tail area, and not, as has been often asserted, to accommodate the tailplane actuator. The latter item was in any case installed in the F-86E's vertical fin and actuated the tail assembly by attaching to a crossbeam near the leading edge, while the whole assembly pivoted around a point at roughly mid-chord. The F-86E also introduced hydraulically-powered flying controls, whereby the pilot's stick input was used to displace a pilot valve on the control actuator. This then metered hydraulic pressure to whichever side of the actuating piston was required, thus moving the control surface. Check valves in the hydraulic system prevented external air loads from affecting the control's position. The incorporation of

This F-86E, 50-583, was assigned to 3200th Proof Test Wing at Eglin AFB in May 1951 and used for various tests, including gunsight development. Another project involved these probed in-flight refuelling drop tanks and, though they represented a good idea, the system was never taken up in service. A.J. Jackson

50-682, the fourth F-86E, was assigned straight to Edwards AFB in May 1951. Note the lack of armament.
Howard Levy via Mike Fox

Little is known of the early research into rocket boost on Sabres. This aircraft, 51-2773, was assigned to Inglewood for conversion on 25 August 1955 and redesignated a JF-86E temporary test aircraft. It was then fitted with an Aerojet rocket motor and tested at Palmdale in July 1956. The photo caption states that an altitude of 59,000ft (17,983m) was reached. John Henderson

irreversible, hydraulically-actuated tail-plane surfaces left only the F-86E's rudder as a manual primary control. The F-86E's all-flying tail had a range of movement 6 degrees up and 10 down at the leading edge, while the geared elevator could move 3 degrees down and 10 up, respectively, in relation to the horizontal plane. Artificial feel was incorporated to give the pilot an effective indication of control forces, and consisted of sprung preload on the control column, which increased as the stick was moved. Simple but effective, the system was first flight tested on a modified F-86A airframe as a company-sponsored project in mid-1949.

Powerplant for the F-86E-1 was the J47-GE-13, rated at 5,450lb (2,741kg) thrust, and in line with the last F-86As, the A-1CM gunsight and AN/APG-30 radar set-up was retained, as was the six 0.50-calibre weapon fit and fibreglass intake ring. The empty weight of the aircraft rose to 10,555lb (4,786kg), more than 400lb (181kg) greater than the F-86A, though the service ceiling, range and initial climb were all marginally improved. With relatively small design differences, the F-86E soon began to roll off the production

Left: **The majority of F-86E-15s were assigned straight to 3595th CCTW at Nellis AFB. Accident rates for the training unit were high; 51-13019 was lost in a crash just south of Las Vegas on 30 January 1954.** Howard Levy via Mike Fox

Below: **This Edwards-based 6510th Air Base Wing F-86E was one of a pair briefly assigned in August 1951 for a speed record attempt by Col Fred Ascani. He flew a sister F-86E at the 1951 National Air Races, establishing a new world speed record of 635.686mph (1,022.82km/h) over a 100km closed course. Nose trim is Dayglo. Like so many other F-86Es, this machine was lost in Korea.** A.J. Jackson

lines, and the first aircraft, 50-579, made its maiden flight on 23 September 1950, flown by George Welch. The first aircraft were then delivered to the USAF in February 1951, barely two months after the last F-86As.

In common with previous Sabre variants, the first production aircraft filled a variety of test functions in their early days. As there was no F-86E prototype, the first two machines were bailed straight back to North American for manufacturer's appraisal. Other aircraft also underwent Air Force testing under the guise of Air Materiel Command Project 1PF-169, notably 50-582 and 50-588 at 2759th Experimental Wing, Edwards

AFB. Later machines were further assigned to Eglin AFB's 3200th Proof Test Wing under Air Proving Ground Project 1F-172 from early 1952. One important aspect of Eglin's test programme was the cold-weather evaluation of the F-86E. This was successfully accomplished at Ladd AFB, Alaska beginning in October 1951.

Air Defense Command gained its first F-86Es in April 1951, the first deliveries being divided between 97th FIS at Wright Patterson AFB and 23rd FIW at Presque Isle AFB. In November the first F-86Es for 60th FIS at Otis AFB in Massachusetts were delivered, the Squadron being unique in the parent 33rd FIW

by being thus equipped. These aircraft were assigned under ADC Project 1PF-497, with delivery of F-86E-1s completed in March 1951, and followed immediately by further F-86E-5s to the same units. The E-5 differed only in minor changes to the cockpit instruments arrangement. Many other F-86Es were at this point assigned straight from the factory to the Korean theatre, where 4th FIW would exchange their F-86As on a one-for-one basis, starting in July 1951. When, on 22 October, Gen Hoyt Vandenberg authorized the re-equipping of a second Korean Wing, the 51st FIW, there was no more factory capacity to cope. As a result, many of the seventy-five F-86Es

63

required for this operation were requisitioned from the 23rd FIW and the 97th FIS. The situation was so bad for the ADC squadrons that the 97th was forced to temporarily revert to F-86As as its main equipment.

NAA had originally planned to follow the short run of F-86Es with a further improved version of the aircraft, the F-86F. However, this design, known as NA-172 by the company, was experiencing problems with its intended J47-GE-27 engine, and the first 132 NA-172s were instead fitted with the GE-13 and delivered to the USAF as F-86E-10-NAs from August 1951. These aircraft had provision for the installation of the -27 engine once it became available, and could be distinguished from the earlier F-86Es by the introduction of a flat windshield, which replaced the vee-shaped screen of other F-86A and E models. Further delays in delivery of -27 engines led to the last ninety-three aircraft on the NA-172 contract also being completed as F-86E-15-NAs, with deliveries beginning in August 1952. As fully equipped F-86Fs were by that time beginning to come into service, the F-86E-15s were generally assigned only to training units.

In common with earlier F-86 variants, the F-86E also became a record breaker. In August 1951 two new F-86E-10s were temporarily assigned to 6510th Air Base Wing at Edwards AFB for an attempt on the closed-course world speed record. Col Fred Ascani was the pilot who would attempt the record:

The flight was conducted at Detroit, Michigan in conjunction with the National Air Races held every year. I had [the aircraft] numbered '2' and '4' purposely so there would be no mistaking the aircraft in flight by the official observers at each pylon. The observers were there to insure that I did not cut inside of any pylons. Only one aircraft flew in the official race [51-2721 – '2']. The other was a spare [51-2724 – '4'].

The F-86E was a standard, combat-equipped aircraft, carrying 50 cal ammo in six 'cans' for the 50 cal guns. It was not carrying bombs or other external stores. The record was set around a six-pylon closed course, the total being the requisite 100km. The speed was 635.68mph [1,022.81km/h], and the flight was made in August of 1951. This record eclipsed the 100km closed-course record held by John Derry, who set the record in a stripped-down

One of sixty Canadair Sabre 2s supplied to the USAF in Korea, 52-2857 was the personal mount of Lt Peter 'Freddie' Frederick of 336th FIS. Note Misawa drop tanks. Sommerich via Levy

De Havilland aircraft. His record, set in 1948, was 605.23mph [973.89km/h].

One final F-86E variant entered USAF service; but this time the aircraft was not actually built by NAA. With the increase in MiG activity in Korea allied to the introduction of the improved MiG-15bis, the USAF wished to place further Sabres in combat. As the Inglewood factory was already working at peak capacity, the Air Force instead looked to Canadair in Canada for more F-86Es. Canadair had been licence-producing F-86Es for some months already (see Chapter 5), and, despite producing aircraft for the Royal Canadian Air Force, the government agreed to supply sixty Canadair Sabre Mk 2s to the USAF. These machines were flown to NAA's Fresno plant in California beginning in April 1952, where specific USAF equipment was installed, before the aircraft were shipped to Korea. In USAF service these aircraft were known as F-86E-CANs. Following their use in Korea, many of these Canadian-built Sabres were passed to the Air Force Academy at Colorado Springs.

Concurrent with the Korean assignment of F-86Es, further ADC squadrons and wings also began to receive the aircraft. The 94th FIS at George AFB was assigned a number of F-86E-15s beginning in early September 1951 but, by the end of October, these had been flown out for duty in Korea. At Wright-

Patterson the 97th FIS began to receive F-86E-15s in February 1952, finally allowing the Squadron to dispense with its F-86A aircraft. Activated in April 1953, 325th FIS at Travis AFB in California began to receive F-86Es shortly thereafter, and also formed an aerobatic team known as the Sabre Knights. This quickly became acknowledged as the finest in the USAF. The Squadron moved to Hamilton AFB during February 1954. In Korea the ceasefire meant that many F-86Es could be put through overhaul, and these machines were then transferred to 35th FIW in late 1953. The aircraft were then returned to the United States in early 1955 and, after further maintenance at McLellan AFB, passed into Air National Guard service.

Korea: the First F-86Es Arrive

The 4th FIW received its first F-86Es on 26 August 1951, these being brand-new F-86E-5s, which were followed by a number of similar machines and F-86E-1s transferred from home-based ADC units, such as the 97th FIS and the 23rd FIW. The latter models began to come into 4th FIW service during early December. On the Communist side, deliveries of MiG-15bis aircraft began around the time that the first F-86Es appeared in Korea. This new MiG variant had a higher thrust engine, which increased the top speed and the ceiling of the 'bis' or Mk 2 aircraft. The arrival of this jet raised the Red inventory of all marks of the MiG-15 to 525. With the breakdown in the Kaesong peace talks on 23 August, it was only a matter of time before these forces were once again in action. On a positive note, 4th FIW's pilots had continued to rack-up MiG kills, and when a renewed Communist air offensive was launched on 1 September these same pilots had the opportunity to add to their scores.

MiG formations in the new onslaught varied considerably; some aircraft attacked in trail and, on one occasion, sixteen MiGs approached in line abreast, all firing on one Sabre. A very effective tactic took advantage of the MiG-15's superior climb and ceiling performance. Formations of these aircraft would orbit at great height, awaiting the approach of UN aircraft below. When the time was right, the MiGs would then dive at great speed, make an attack and quickly climb to altitude again. Even the Sabres could not catch the MiGs when they employed this tactic, and F-86s were lost on 2 and 26 September to this type of action.

In a large dogfight on the afternoon of 9 September, twenty-eight Sabres encountered some seventy MiGs near the Yalu, an action that resulted in two MiG kills and two more aces: Capt Richard Becker of 334th FIS and Capt Ralph 'Hoot' Gibson of 335th FIS. Sabres claimed fourteen MiGs in the entire month, though often these aircraft avoided the Sabres in favour of attacks on UN fighter bombers. With the Communists' burgeoning air armada showing signs of overcoming the UN bombing offensive, Gen Weyland frankly informed Gen Vandenberg on 15 September that the MiGs were becoming a serious threat to the whole air campaign. Weyland pleaded for a further wing of FEAF Sabres, or, if this were not possible,

for one of the existing F-80 wings to convert to the Sabre. Five days later came Vandenberg's reply: the USAF simply could not provide, much less support, any additional Sabre squadrons in Korea without compromising the security of the United States itself.

Fortunately, the air campaign generally went well for the UN, and, by a stroke of luck, on 25 September a 67th TRW recce mission revealed that the Chinese were building a new MiG base near Saamcham, well to the south of the Yalu. Further searches on 14 October revealed another two airfields also under construction at Taechon and Namsi, within 30 miles (48km) of Sinanju. B-29 missions were launched to destroy these bases, which, if completed, would have extended MiG Alley as far south as Pyongyang. Sabre patrols were also intensified, and the kill rate increased: two MiGs on 1 October, six the next day, one each on 5 and 12 October, and nine on 16 October. The last was the biggest daily claim yet, but the Sabres were not invincible – especially the F-86As, with four lost during the month.

51-2719 was modified by NAA during late 1951 for testing a gloved wing and modified canopy. Bailed to North American in January 1952, the purpose of this modification is not known. Note the NACA duct on the rear fuselage. San Diego Aerospace Museum/Ray Wagner

During October the Reds moved a number of MiGs across the Yalu into the airfields at Sinuiju and Uiju, but continued bombing of the new bases further south prevented their use at this time. The FEAF bombing of these airfields led to high B-29 losses, and this in turn showed all too clearly that the USAF could no longer ignore Weyland's requests for more F-86s in Korea. Thus, on 22 October, Vandenberg ordered ADC to dispatch seventy-five F-86Es and pilots to Alameda in California for deck loading and transfer to Japan. In effect, however, these aircraft did not form a new wing in the theatre; they went to re-equip the 51st FIW's two squadrons of F-80s – the 16th and the 25th Fighter Squadron. A further positive note was the move of 335th FIS into Korea on 2 November, placing the whole 4th FIW in the country. One of the more unusual formations encountered by the 4th FIW's Sabres on 30 November was a group of twelve Tupolev Tu-2 propeller-driven bombers heading for Taehwa-Do. They were escorted by twelve La-11s and covered by twelve more MiG-15s. In the ensuing battle four La-11s, three Tu-2s and a MiG-15 were claimed by the Sabres, elevating Maj George Davis and Maj Winton Marshal to 'ace' status.

Enter the 51st

Loaded at Alameda aboard the USS *Cape Esperance* and the USS *Sitkoh Bay*, a mixture of new and requisitioned F-86Es was shipped to Japan on 1 and 9 November. Col Gabreski took over as 51st FIW commanding officer on 6 November, moving in from the 4th FIW, and Lt Col George Jones took over command of the group. On 19 November 51st FIW transferred its F-80s to 8th FBW and three days later received its first Sabres, to begin conversion training. In only a short time the wing qualified its pilots and flew the first combat mission on 1 December.

51st FIW pilots scored their first MiG kill on 2 December, followed by another on 4 December, and 4th FIW Sabres claimed thirteen MiGs on 13 December. But the end of 1951 and the early days of 1952 marked a change in the effectiveness of the Communist fighter pilots. Apparently the Chinese had rotated a number of air divisions back from the front line, replacing them with relatively

This 51st FIW F-86E, 51-2732, took a single 23mm hit from a MiG-15. Presumably as a result of this damage, the aircraft was shipped to FEAMCOM in April 1952 and returned to the US. *John Henderson*

F-86Es of 51st FIW at Suwon, 1952. 51-2786, a 25th FIS aircraft, was lost in combat on 1 May 1952. The pilot Col Albert Schmitz, of 25th FIS evaded capture and his story is covered in the book *Beyond Courage*. *Leroy Bain via Warren Thompson*

inexperienced MiG pilots. There then began a phase of fluctuating aggressiveness and capability of these pilots in combat, reflecting their initial inexperience, then a gain in confidence and ability, followed by rotation home again, at which point the cycle repeated. Sabre pilots were frustrated

in the early phases of these cycles by the unwillingness of the MiG crews to fight, and, in addition, many Sabre pilots newly assigned to Korea in early 1952 had little previous jet time. Later in 1952 a number of young pilots were assigned to Korea straight from F-86 training in the United

Specifications: F-86E-5-NA

POWERPLANT

General Electric J47-GE-13 of 5,200lb
(2,358kg) thrust

WEIGHTS

empty:	10,555lb (4,786kg)
take-off (clean):	14,578lb (6,611kg)
take-off (drop tanks):	16,346lb (7,412kg)

DIMENSIONS

wingspan:	37ft 1in (11.3m)
length:	37ft 6in (11.43m)
height:	14ft 9in (4.49m)
wing area:	287.9sq ft (26.78sq m)

PERFORMANCE:

maximum speed:

at sea level:	679mph (1,092km/h)
at 35,000ft:	601mph (967km/h at 10,668m)
initial climb rate:	7,250ft/min (2,209m/min)
service ceiling:	47,200ft (14,386m)
combat radius:	321 miles (516 km)
ferry range:	1,022 miles (1,644 km)

F-86F: the Definitive Day Fighter

The ultimate production day-fighter Sabre was the F-86F. In essence, it was simply a more powerful version of the F-86E and was powered by the 5,970lb-thrust J47-GE-27, giving more than 400lb of thrust over the F-86E. Work on the new aircraft began on 31 July 1950 as the NA-172, and it was originally planned to begin production as the F-86F in October 1950. Contract AF-14801 for 109 F-86Fs was approved on 11 April 1951 and was increased to 360 on 30 June.

Serious delays in the J47-GE-27 programme began to have a knock-on effect with the F-86F production line. It took GE some time to gain the extra thrust from the engine reliably, which also came out nearly 80lb (36kg) heavier, and the first 132 aircraft of the NA-172 contract had to be delivered with the -13 engine as F-86Es. The first production J47-GE-27 engine finally became available in December 1951 and the first of seventy-eight F-86F-1 aircraft, 51-2850, took to the air on 19 March 1952,

F-86E Production

Serial No.	Model	Construction Nos
50-579 to 638	F-86E-1-NA	170-1 to 60
50-639 to 689	F-86E-5-NA	170-61 to 111
51-2718 to 2849	F-86E-10-NA	172-1 to 132
51-12977 to 13069	F-86E-15-NA	172-268 to 360
52-2833 to 2892	F-86E-6-CAN, ex-RCAF Sabre Mk 2	various

a few subsequent days, but not again thereafter. It appears that the Soviets may well have been testing the machine in combat in the ground-attack role, but further information is not forthcoming.

Although the first F-86Fs arrived in Korea during mid-1952, the F-86Es remained in Korea to serve alongside the 'F' models in 4th and 51st FIW until long after the conflict had ended. Many of the F-86Es remained with these wings until mid-1955 when they finally returned to the US for ANG service.

The Air National Guard

First entering ANG service in early 1954, many units operated the F-86E as a stop-gap aircraft, pending the assignment of later machines. 115th and 195th FBS California ANG were two such squadrons, initially operating the E models alongside their previous F-86As, and then moving on to full conversion to F-86Hs in 1957.

Other squadrons, such as the 165th FIS Kentucky ANG, received less than half a dozen aircraft and held them for only a short period without being operational on the type. Those squadrons that did operate the F-86E for longer periods found it to be a safe and practical aircraft to fly. The last Air Guard F-86Es were retired to Davis Monthan AFB in early 1959.

piloted by J. Pearce. The F-1 model introduced a flat windscreen, although this feature had actually first appeared on the F-86E-10s, as they owed their basic airframe to the F-86F project. Other detail refinements included a gunsight-mounted gun camera and provision to carry AN-M10 chemical tanks on the external pylons. Otherwise the F-86F-1 was equipped structurally, electrically and mechanically as the earlier F-86E had been. First deliveries of the F-86F were slated for 94th FIS under ADC Project 2PF-550, but these machines were immediately redirected to 126th FIS Wisconsin Air National Guard at Madison, which had been called to active duty for the Korean War. Deliveries to the 126th FIS began on 1 April 1952, and further F-86F-1s were also allotted to the

The General Electric J47-GE-27 engine. Standard fitment on the F-86F, the GE-27 featured a compressor with increased pressure ratio (5.45:1 vs. 5.05:1 of the GE-13) and gave more power. The first production engine was completed in December 1951. General Electric/Eric Falk

similarly activated 123rd FIS Oregon ANG at Portland. The 123rd received its first F-86F on 2 May, and it appears that these squadrons served as accelerated service test units, as well as training Korean-bound Sabre pilots on the new model. Both units returned to state control in November, passing their Sabres to Far East Air Forces squadrons. By June 1952 F-86Fs were in service with 84th FIS at Hamilton AFB and 63rd FIS at Oscoda AFB, though the latter also relinquished its aircraft for the war effort in late July.

During April 1952 the majority of new-production F-86Fs were assigned to FEAF Project 2F-544 and flown to McLellan AFB before embarking for Korea. The first of these aircraft arrived in Japan during June and were assigned to 51st FIW in the same month. The F-86F was assigned to 4th FIW in September.

Illustrating the unsung heroes of the Korean War, this F-86F served with 3595th CCTW at Nellis AFB in the training role. via Mike Fox

Production Begins at Columbus

Meanwhile, the concurrent production of F-86D, E and F models at Inglewood was causing serious problems and NAA looked to its Columbus, Ohio plant to meet the need. During 1950 NAA had received permission to take over the old Curtiss factory in Columbus for further aircraft production. Built during World War II for the production of Navy SB2C Helldiver dive bombers, the Curtiss Aeronautical Division experienced numerous problems post-war in gaining defence contracts and, with the failure of the XF-87 fighter, was

51-13070 was the first Columbus-built Sabre, an F-86F-20. It flew for the first time in May 1952. These Sabres were assigned to Stateside training units rather than to Korea. NAA

One of only sixteen F-86F-5s, 51-2936 was assigned to 126th FIS Wisconsin ANG on 12 June 1952. The unit had been called to active duty for pilot training on the F-86F. The aircraft then saw service in Korea with 39th FIS and was lost in a flying accident there on 23 February 1953. MAP

forced to undergo a major downsizing. It closed down its Columbus factory and all assets there were turned over to North American. NAA's Columbus plant was refurbished and opened for F-86F production in December 1950, though it would be some time before the first machine rolled out. Columbus-built F-86Fs were designated NA-176 and the project was initiated on 29 September 1950. The initial Columbus contract, AF-18988 dated 6 September 1951, was for 441 aircraft.

Back at Inglewood, the F-86F-5 appeared in June 1952. This model differed in having the capability to carry new 200gall (750l) drop tanks or the earlier 120gall (450l) tanks. These increased the combat radius from 330 to 463 miles (530 to 744km). Further changes involved the electrical system and resulted in a redesigned engine-starting circuit. Only sixteen F-86F-5s were built and these were delivered in June 1952.

The F-86F-10-NA introduced a new gunsight, the A-4 replacing the earlier A-1CM sight. On the A-4 gunsight, aside from improved performance and maintenance aspects, the projected reticle or 'pipper' was represented as ten diamonds arranged in a circle around the central dot. The gunsight-mounted gun camera was also relocated into the lower intake lip. Thirty four F-10s were built with most being assigned straight to Korea.

The last hundred aircraft of the NA-172 contract were to have been F-86F-15s with repositioned control systems. However, in April 1952, further delays in the delivery of J47-GE-27 engines forced NAA to revert again to GE-13 power for ninety-three more aircraft, which were then redesignated F-86E-15, as indicated above. This allowed a mere seven F-86F-15s to be produced after GE-27 engines again became available. The F-15s repositioned and redesigned control systems were designed to improve battle-damage tolerance.

At this point the Columbus plant began to complete its first F-86Fs, and the first Sabre built in Ohio flew during May 1952. To differentiate between factory production blocks, Columbus-built Sabres gained an 'NH' suffix, Inglewood-built Sabres having previously been assigned the suffix 'NA'. Columbus initially built a hundred F-86F-20-NHs, which introduced AN/ARC-33 VHF command radio in place of the earlier AN/ARC-3. The gun camera on these Sabres was also resited to the gunsight itself and, from the sixtieth machine, the cockpit canopy manual operation was modified. Delivery of these aircraft was slow, the final F-86F-20-NH being completed in January 1953; all Sabres in this batch were delivered to US-based units, such as the 84th and the 63rd FIS, as well as the 3595th Combat Crew Training Wing at Nellis AFB.

The next version of the Sabre was designed to fill a USAF fighter-bomber requirement and detailed work on this NA-191 project began on 26 October 1951. The requirement called for the capability to carry two stores under each wing rather than just one, addressing a problem inherent in the design from its inception: when bombs were carried on the external pylons no drop tanks could be fitted, and the combat radius was barely 50 miles (80km). Therefore NAA designers came up with a further under-wing pylon attachment, inboard of the existing fixture, which could accommodate a 120gall drop tank or a 1,000lb bomb. If the maximum fuel load of two 200gall and two 120gall drop tanks was carried, the ferry range was increased to 1,600 miles (2,574 km) and the combat radius was 568 miles (914km). To cope with the fighter-bomber role of these aircraft, the flight-control system was modified to give improved longitudinal stability and stick forces were also reduced. An AN/ARC-27 VHF command radio was also installed.

On 5 August 1952 Contract AF-6517 was approved for 907 Inglewood-built NA-191 aircraft. The same configuration was used on 341 further NA-176 aircraft already on order from Columbus, following on directly from the F-86F-20s built there. Another 259 Columbus-built NA-193 aircraft were added to this contract on 17 October. Fighter-bomber F-86Fs built at Inglewood under this contract were known as F-86F-30 and 35-NA; the Columbus machines were built as

F-86F-25-NHs. The Inglewood F-30 and the Columbus F-25 were basically the same aircraft and, when improvements emerged from the NAA design office, they were slotted into both production lines, though sometimes there was a delay. Thus, when the Alternate Hydraulic

Above: **This F-86F-30 was assigned to 390th FBS at Alexandria AFB in Louisiana during 1955. Trim colours are blue and white.** Howard Levy via Mike Fox

Below: **This F-86F-25 was assigned to 401st FBGp at Alexandria AFB, Louisiana in 1955. The yellow trim is the 613th FBS squadron colour.** MAP

System was redesigned to incorporate one accumulator instead of two, this improvement was installed on the sixtieth Inglewood F-86F-30 but not on the Columbus line until the four-hundred and fifty-seventh F-86F-25.

The first Sabres built to the fighter-bomber specification were the F-86F-30-NAs, which started to come off the production lines at Inglewood in October 1952. These aircraft were then mostly sent to Korea in order that fighter-bomber units could begin to convert on to the type. In January 1953 the first Columbus-built F-25 version appeared, though, again, these aircraft were not deployed to Korea; instead they began to further equip US-based squadrons and from early 1953 many of these machines began to be assigned to USAF Europe under AFE Project 3F-220.

In an attempt to improve the performance of the Sabre, a new wing was tested on three aircraft during August 1952. This wing design had its leading edge extended by 6in (152mm) at the root and 3in (76mm) at the tip, and this became known as the '6-3 wing'. The wing area was increased from 287.9sq ft (26.78sq m) to 302.3sq ft (28.12sq m), and the automatic slats of earlier Sabres were deleted. In order to decrease the effects of spanwise airflow over the wing, a 5in-high (127mm) wing fence was installed at 70 per cent span on the leading edge. Tests with this wing showed an increased maximum speed, from 688 to 695mph (1,106 to 1,118 km/h) at sea level and from 604 to 608mph (972 to 978km/h) at 35,000ft (10,668m). However, the most important improvement was in the manoeuvrability at high altitudes and Mach numbers, the new wing enabling tighter turns to be made at high altitudes. The one major drawback was that the stalling speed increased from 128 to 144mph (205 to 231km/h), and the stall was also more violent, with a noticeable yaw and roll component. This required a faster approach speed and therefore gave a longer landing roll. Crucially, when the leading edge extension began to be fitted to Sabres in service, it was found with tragic consequences that many pilots failed to appreciate the degraded stall properties of the 6-3 wing.

In September 1952 fifty 6-3 wing conversion kits were shipped to Korea so that F-86Fs in theatre could be converted

52-5434, a red-trimmed F-86F from 721st FDS at Foster AFB, Texas in 1955. This machine was the personal mount of Squadron commander Maj A.D. Donavan and was lost in a crash on 9 April 1957. J.M.G. Gradidge

An unsung USAFE unit, the 7272nd Air Gunnery Group at Wheelus AB in Libya, provided chase planes for European-based fighters on weapons training. This 7272nd AGG F-86F wears the unit's red and yellow scheme. Pete Hutting

to the new configuration. It was soon discovered that, although the MiGs still held an altitude advantage, the '6-3'-equipped Sabres could out-turn and match the MiGs for speed. In time, enough sets of '6-3' kits were supplied to convert all Korean-based F-86Fs and, by this time, the NAA factories were installing the wings on the production line, beginning with the 171st F-86F-25 (51-13341) and the 200th F-86F-30 (52-4505). As a rule, only post-modification aircraft were assigned to USAFE, beginning with the 86th FBW in April 1953, followed by the 36th and the 406th FBW in August. All these units converted from F-84 Thunderjets. Before this, the 45th Fighter Day Squadron (FDS) had deployed with F-86Fs from its base at

Suffolk County AFB in New York state to Sidi Slimane AB in Morocco. 45th FDS brought with them their slatted F-86F-25s, which were converted to '6-3' configuration after arrival. A further interesting exception to the rule was the 81st FIW, which was assigned a number of slatted F-86F-25s for a short time in 1953, before converting to F-84F Thunderstreaks.

The F-86F Arrives in Korea

The first brand-new F-86Fs reached Korea in June 1952 and were issued to 51st FIW from 21 June, equipping the 16th and the 25th FIS, as well as the 39th FIS, which had been attached to the Wing on 1 June

1952 from 35th Fighter Wing. Further 'F' models then began to pour into 4th FIW during September and, in addition to these new aircraft, a number of early-model F-86Fs arrived which had been requisitioned from home-based units, such as the 94th FIS and the activated 126th FIS Wisconsin ANG. The arrival of the new aircraft finally allowed the 4th FIW to relinquish its last FY49 F-86As, although MiG kills in these aircraft were registered until as late as June 1952. In turn, the F-86Es would remain in service alongside the F-86Fs until the end of the conflict. The impact of the new models was soon felt and, not long after the arrival of the F-86Fs in Korea, a further improvement – the '6-3' wing modification, was made available. The UN now had an aircraft that could outrun and outmanoeuvre the MiG-15, though the Sabre's ceiling and rate of climb would never match that of the Russian fighter. Enough modification kits were ordered to convert many of the Korean-based F-86Fs to the '6-3' configuration.

But it would be wrong to think that all was rosy with the Sabre pilots, far from it. For some time, returning crews had been expressing their concerns of the MiG's superiority over the F-86. On 5 February 1953 nine Korean veterans met the Air Force Chief of Staff Gen Vandenberg and Lt Gen Jimmy Doolittle to voice their opinions. Among their number was Col Francis Gabreski and Capt Frederick Blesse, a nine-kill ace from 334th FIS. Blesse, in particular, was outspoken in his concerns, declaring that, 'The current combat ratio over Russian interceptor planes in Korea is being gained with what is unquestionably an inferior piece of equipment. [The situation] could change overnight if the Russians moved their first combat team into the MiG-15 squadrons there.' Of course, Blesse could not know that the Russians had been in Korea as long as the Sabres, but, if their involvement had been greater, undoubtedly the situation would have been quite different. Vandenberg and Doolittle heard that their pilots considered many of the Sabre's systems and equipment to be superfluous, unnecessarily increasing weight, with detrimental effects on its performance. Among these items parking brakes, frontal armour plate, self-sealing fuel tanks and electric canopy retraction were seen as luxuries not required on a fighter.

This Sabre wreck was dumped off the runway at K-14 Kimpo Air Base in early 1953 as a decoy. However, all is not what it seems, as this machine comprises an F-86A forward fuselage, F-86F wings and an F-80 tail unit. Royce Raven

Ultimately, none of these items was removed, the USAF Generals arguing with some justification that, though the equipment was of questionable use to a seasoned veteran, it most definitely was useful for a younger or less experienced pilot. But the effects of this meeting cannot be underestimated; many features designed into the F-100 Super Sabre originated as a result of lessons learnt in Korea.

Back in MiG Alley, January 1953 had heralded two new aces – Dolph Overton and Harold Fischer, who became the twenty-fourth and the twenty-fifth jet ace, respectively. In addition, Capt Joseph McConnell started an amazing run, reaching ace status on 16 February, double ace on 24 April and downed his fifteenth MiG on 18 May 1953. In between, McConnell had been forced to eject into the Yellow Sea on 12 April, but was rescued and soon back into combat. He ended the war with sixteen kills, the highest scoring ace on the UN side. But it should be remembered at this point that the Russians claim two higher-scoring pilots in the same conflict: Yevgeni Pepelyaev with twenty-three kills and Nikolai Sutyagin with twenty-one.

Losses to the Sabres were still being sustained though. On 7 April Harold Fischer, by then a double ace, was shot down over Manchuria and taken prisoner. He was not released until May 1955, more

A flight of red-trimmed 36th FBS F-86Fs over Kunsan, Korea during summer 1955. The first three aircraft later passed to the Republic of China Air Force, while 52-4796 went to the Philippines. Les Sundt via Marty Isham

than two years later. Fischer was shot down by Han Decai, at the time claimed to be the youngest MiG pilot in the Chinese Air Force. On the day that Fischer was downed, Lt Col Edwin Heller of 16th FIS was lost over China. He also spent two years in captivity. But the Sabres were managing to even up the score. In the period from 8 to 31 May 1953, F-86Fs with '6-3' wings claimed fifty-six MiG kills for only one loss. On 20 June Sabres accounted for sixteen victories, their biggest daily score of the war.

With greater numbers of Sabres available to FEAF, it next fell upon the fighter-bomber units to re-equip with the type, and it was planned that this process would begin during November 1952. However, delays led to this timetable's slipping, and the first three F-86F-30 fighter-bombers did not arrive in Korea until 28 January. These aircraft initially began re-equipping the 18th Fighter Bomber Wing at the new Osan Air Base, finally relinquishing its last F-51D Mustangs and moving from Chinhae to begin Sabre training flights on 3 February. Gen Barcuss, the Commander of 5th Air Force, decreed that these units should gain proficiency in fighter interception before starting their fighter-bomber conversion, and thus the Wing flew its

first combat mission as a fighter sweep in MiG Alley on 25 February, scoring its first MiG kill on the same day. By the end of March there were enough F-86F-30s to equip the 12th FBS and the attached No.2 Squadron, South African Air Force. 67th FBS flew F-51Ds until 23 January and then stood down as the last squadron within 18th FBW to convert. They gained full operational strength with Sabres on 7

April. Having begun flying missions before this, however, Maj James Hagerstrom of the 67th shot down two MiGs on 27 March to raise his score to five. He ended the conflict with eight-and-a-half kills, the only Sabre fighter-bomber pilot to make ace.

The 8th Fighter Bomber Wing based at Suwon began trading in its F-80C Shooting Stars for F-86F-30 Sabres on 22 February 1953, though the conversion was much smoother, aided by their not having to move base. The conversion was finally completed at the end of June.

52-4366, 'Laura Ann', a bombed-up F-86F-30 of 67th FBS at K-55 Osan AB, 1953. This aircraft also carries a pair of 200gall Misawa drop tanks. R. McNeil via Marty Isham

Above: **These two 335th FIS F-86F-10s were seen at Kimpo in early 1953. They display a large number of kill markings, especially 51-12953 nearest, with thirteen. However, kills painted on the right side of a Sabre reflected those accrued by the aircraft itself rather than an individual pilot.** Royce Raven

Below: **52-4778 was the personal F-86F of double ace Capt Ralph Parr, 334th FIS. In this shot, taken during 1953, the aircraft appears to carry nine kill markings. Parr got his last kill – an IL-12 transport – on 27 July; it was the last kill of the war.** Royce Raven

The last squadron to convert, 80th FBS, had been delayed while UHF radios were removed from their intended aircraft. Finally standing down on 1 May for conversion, the first missions were flown within two weeks. The 8th FBW took their Sabres into action in a MiG sweep on 8 April. Gen Barcuss, having earlier ordered the Sabres to qualify in fighter-interceptor tactics, was forced to think again. With the transition programme slipping, interceptor and fighter-bomber training was integrated and 8th FBW flew its first air-to-ground mission on 13 April, with 18th FBW making its debut the following day. By the end of July FEAF possessed 132 F-86F fighter-bombers and five jet fighter-bomber wings in total, three with F-84G

but fourteen F-86Fs were lost to ground fire.

By mid-1953 the ground offensive in Korea had reached a stalemate and a negotiated truce brought hostilities to an end on 27 July. The peninsula would be divided into north and south about the 38th Parallel. Sabre losses continued almost until the last day of the war. On 20 July 2nd Lt Gerald Knott was lost during a rescue combat-air patrol mission along the west coast of northern Korea. As Knott and his flight leader patrolled the rescue area, they spotted an enemy boat and peeled off to take a look. Knott failed to pull out of the dive and his F-86E, 51-2756, crashed on the shoreline. Soviet anti-aircraft batteries claimed the kill, also stating that Knott was captured alive

truce saw 67th TRW RF-86Fs flying recce missions over as many Red airfields as possible to gain last-minute intelligence.

The Sabre in Korea: Analysis of Combat Effectiveness

With the end of hostilities in Korea many bold claims were made of the Sabre's complete mastery of the skies above the combat area. Such figures as a fourteen to one kill ratio in favour of the Sabre were bandied about, and even more considered opinion revised this only as far as a ten to one ratio. Added to this, the reluctance of the Communists to reveal their version of events for many years led to the

On 21 September 1953 Lt Kom Suk Ro of the North Korean Air Force defected to the South along with his MiG-15bis. This unofficial shot was taken that day as amazed USAF personnel survey the Red jet. The MiG is now preserved in the USAF Museum. Royce Raven

Thunderjets and two with F-86F-30s. The Thunderjets had a superior range, but the Sabres proved themselves in this configuration, especially as they could also carry out fighter sweeps in MiG Alley and fend for themselves better than the 'plank wings'. However, the danger came not from the MiGs but from flak. During June 1953 more Sabres were lost in ground-attack missions than in air-to-air combat. They delivered 3,044 tons of bombs during that month,

by Chinese volunteers. He is still listed as MIA.

The last Sabre versus MiG dogfight of the conflict took place on 22 July, when Lt Sam P. Young of the 51st FIW scored his first and only victory. The final kill of the Korean War took place on 27 July, Capt Ralph S. Parr flying an F-86F-30 to shoot down an Il-12 twin-engined transport aircraft while flying an escort mission to Chunggangjin. He thus made double ace. The final hours before the

persistence of unsubstantiated arguments that the Sabre was a superior fighter. However, information from behind the now fallen Iron Curtain seems to contradict this belief, and even first-hand reports from USAF Sabre pilots in April 1953 rated the F-86 as inferior in many respects to the MiG-15. One revealing fact was disclosed by no less than then Maj James Jabara in the spring of 1952. In a lecture on fighter operations in Korea, on 10 March, Jabara stated that, 'Losses to date average one American jet for every two MiG-15s destroyed.' This would seem to back up a best-case argument that the Sabre/pilot combination enjoyed only a two to one kill

An interview with Jim Low, seventeenth Jet Ace, with nine MiGs

James F. Low began his USAF flight training at Perrin AFB in Texas during November 1950, moving up to F-51 Mustangs. He then went to Williams AFB in Arizona for jet conversion, before gunnery training at Nellis, where he checked out in the F-86. Assigned to the Korean theatre, Low (nicknamed 'Dad' because he was slightly older than his contemporaries) arrived at Tachikawa AB in Japan during April 1952. He was eager to fight:

When I first went over, I found out the squadron which was getting most MiGs, which was the 335th, so I signed up for that, and I was lucky to get in 'D' Flight, because the other three flights in the Squadron weren't doing very much. It'd just depend on who the leaders were. The guys [in D Flight] were aggressive; they were street smart. And the other people just kinda toured around there and diddled this and diddled that, got a little action here, a little action there. But we, the 335th, did a yeoman's job.

Our Flight – D Flight – in the 335th got more MiGs than the whole squadron did in one month. We knew how to hunt them, we had Kasler in there and Bob Love and Casey Colman and myself. Everybody in the Flight had a MiG or two and there were about five or six aces that came out of D Flight. You had to go up there [MiG Alley], you had to want to go up and hunt them. We were the first in and the last out. These other guys would go up there and they'd make one big swing at Mach 0.95 and swing back and come back and land and log a mission. We'd go up there and hang and wait until they started flying and then we'd be in there and we'd get some action.

I was a balloon – I was a second lieutenant and I flew wing, but I could see the airplanes – I had 20/10 eyes and I saw them before these other guys did, and they said, 'Well, OK, you take the bounce.' And I'd say, 'Are you sure now?' and they'd say, 'Yeah, you take the bounce' and we'd drop the tanks and go and get 'em.

My first kill was on 2 May, and I did a barrel roll around this guy, and he had a leather helmet on and he was an oriental, so I actually saw his face. [On] my first mission, I was flying with Jim Kasler on his wing and we're just hosing around up there and all of a sudden we get jumped by some MiGs, and he saw them and he says, 'Break right', and then he says, 'Break left, break right' and 'Break left.' And I broke right again and I didn't see him any more – I don't know where the hell he went. And I'm at 85 per cent power, I've still got my tanks on – I'd never dropped tanks before – it's my first mission. And all of a sudden these three MiGs come down on my ass and I dropped my tanks and I got around on one of them and I got my first MiG.

Of course, I lost him [Kasler], but I came back, and Harry Thyng was the Wing Commander. He says, 'God bless him, he got a MiG!', and he said, 'What happened to the other guy? You know he didn't get one.' And I said, 'I didn't leave him – on the fourth break I lost him.' I was on untenable ground there for a while. Kasler left, and another commander came in, and he said, 'Well, they're talking about you, you know about leaving your leader.' And I said, 'You don't have to worry about me

Cockpit shot of Jim Low in Korea. Aircraft is his personal mount, F-86E s/n 50-680, named 'Dad'.
Jim Low

leaving you if we get in a fight and something happens. I'm not going to bust off.' I said, 'I got lost and I got screwed up. I knocked an airplane down, I guess that vindicated me, but it wasn't my choice.'

Low received a fair share of criticism for a single mistake. Most vicious was Capt James Horowitz, who under the pseudonym Salter wrote the novel *The Hunters*. His character Pell is by both Salter's and Low's admission based on the latter. Not until *The Hunters* was made into a movie did the wrongs of the book get righted to some extent. Jim Low has his own views about Horowitz:

I was precocious and he was a Hudson High boy, you know. He didn't want to fight – he wasn't in the clique. He was the kind of guy who says, 'I think I've got MiGs over here', and it was the 51st [FIW] coming up from down below. But he got out of there and got home and he was a good writer. The first book he wrote was *The Hunters*. I was at Command & Staff School and Harry Thyng, he was a Wing Commander. He called me from California – he was CO at Western Air Defense Force, and he said, 'Hell, they're coming out with a book and a movie, you'd better sue them if you want.' Because all he [Salter] did was take a pot shot at the aces. But then Dick Powell [the film director] took care of it and everybody was a hero. Bob Wagner played my part.

But everybody had an agenda – some people wanted to go over there and do their tour, some guys were recalled; they had families. They just wanted to get their missions over and come home. Hell, I was a young

buck and I loved the action. I enjoyed it – I've been a hunter all my life. I knew how to lead in firing a gun, I'd always hunted ducks and deer.

On his fourth mission Low got his second MiG, this time flying an F-86A. Much has been said of the area north of the Yalu being forbidden to UN pilots. Not so, says Low:

It was called 'hot pursuit' – if you were on his tail before you crossed the Yalu River then it was legal to go after him. We were tooling at 30,000; this was around the time they were tackling me for leaving my leader, so the guy's wing I was flying was Bob Ronca. He was the flight leader then. We're flying up there and my eyes are damn good, and I caught these guys on the deck. They were flying about 2,000ft above the ground, and we were at 30 [thousand]. They flew right across the Yalu, across Sinuiju and they were heading east. I said, 'Bob, I got two, they're on the deck and I don't want to lose them.' He says, 'You take the bounce', and I says, 'Could you repeat that?' He says, 'You take the bounce.' I says, 'OK, I'm dropping tanks and just follow me on down.' So I went on down there and I got, I guess, about 2500ft and my gunsight wasn't working. So I had to kind of aim and use tracers and what have you, and I hit him and then he broke. He really broke and I had a tangle with him. I scissored with him a couple of times and I got back and got so close to him that when I hit him the debris came back and broke my windshield. And then he flipped over and then he bailed out. And when he bailed out, I saw [he had a] red beard. But then Bob turned around and he knocked the other airplane down.

The two MiGs were camouflaged, the first time Low had seen such markings. The red beard of his adversary proved he was not oriental.

When I got my 3rd and 4th MiG I was just getting wing jobs as a wingman, so I volunteered to be on the alert pad. And I'd got a couple of MiGs before, and I talked to the radar set-up there on Radar Hill. I took a couple of cases of beer up there and let them know that we appreciated their help. So these guys called in and said, 'We've got a bandit train that just took off from Antung and it's heading across the Suiho – would you guys like some action?' And I said, 'My God, yeah, we've been sitting here all day.' So they scrambled us. And by the time we got up there these guys were at 55,000ft, and it was what we called a 'jackpot flight' – in other words, they were North Koreans, so they weren't too adept at flying. And I was with a guy named Smiley and he says, 'I don't see anything, I'll go down to the end of the Yalu.' And I said, 'Well I'll stay around here.' The radar site were still 'painting' these guys but we couldn't see them – they were at 55,000. So all of a sudden, they let down a little bit, and they made short contrails – 'short cons'. So I said, 'There they are – they're in the cons.' and the other two guys are down there [at the mouth of the Yalu] and said, 'Where are they?' I said, 'They're in the cons, we're up here at the Mizu.' But these [MiGs] came down, and I turned around this guy and he flipped over and spun out, and bailed out at 40,000ft – I don't know how he ever survived. And another one came by and I barrel-rolled on him and shot his engine up and came back on him and got him again. So I got two [MiGs] in one mission.

Low made ace on 15 June 1952, scoring a further kill before he rotated back to the United States for some months to lecture on the virtues of the Sabre's gunsight. He was one of a new breed of pilots who managed to master the F-86's system, unlike many earlier jet aces, who got kills by the 'chewing gum on the windscreen' technique. But when Low returned to Korea, things had changed:

I got six MiGs six months after I got out of flying school – I was an ace. And there were all captains and majors and colonels leading every mission. I wasn't leading any missions until I got three MiGs and then I got upgraded to element leader and then I got my other three. And then when I came back from my three-month tour ordered by Gen Vandenberg (I left [Korea] in July and went back in October) – there was a whole new deal. I had forty-four missions before I left, and when I went

back the new regime kind of sat on my ass, and I was a wingman for forty more missions before I got a chance to lead again. And I was an ace! But I still got them anyway because these older guys couldn't see as well as I could. I'd be flying wing, and we're looking and searching, and I'd say, 'OK, I've got a bogey at ten o'clock, now he's moving to twelve, and now he's moving to one.' And I'd say, 'It's a MiG', and these guys, I could see them straining, looking for him. And I'd say, 'We're going to lose him', and they'd have to say, 'Well, you take the bounce.' And then they'd fly my wing and then I'd go shoot them down.

Low's most memorable kill was his seventh:

We were up there tooling around the Suiho Reservoir over North Korea, and we got bounced. This guy overshot, and my wingman says, 'I got him Yellow 3, I got him Yellow 3.' And he starts firing at him, and I could see he wasn't pulling any lead at all, and I could see the damn tracers were going behind. I says, 'Stop shooting, stop shooting – get some lead, get some lead!' and he just went off on his own you know. Well, I didn't care, I said, 'Well, let's see what happens.' He finally went around and around with this guy and he fired out – he didn't have any more ammunition. And he said, 'Yellow

Lead, you'd better take over, I don't have any more ammunition.' I said, 'Well thanks for talking to me.' Anyhow, I slid in there and knocked off a little burst, and I wasn't pulling any lead, so we went around and around, back and forth. And then I got a little lead on him, and I hit him in the wing roots and the engine, and then I got a pretty good shot on the side of the engine and he lost his power. So this guy drops down, and of course, we're up around Mach 0.9 and we're running around trying to stay behind him and he goes back down. And all of a sudden, this guy pulls up right into my line of flight and fires all his guns – his 37 and 20mm right in my face, you know. And I yanked away and he pulled back down and I hit him again, and he went into the mountain. That guy had a lot of guts.

[On] my eighth kill, I was flying Col Baker's airplane over there, and it had the A-4C gunsight, and man, I locked that on – it was out at max range. I got him about 4,800ft, and I fired and got him right on the nose. I hit him right in the engine section.

Low's final kill was on 18 December 1952 – he knocked down a MiG that had been tailing his element; a 'trailer'. The kill was at 30,000ft over Sinanju. Jim Low returned to the United States soon after and later flew with the highly-rated Sabre Knights aerobatic team.

Following his ninth MiG kill on 18 December 1952, Jim Low celebrates with his ground crew at K-14 Kimpo AB. Low was flying F-86E s/n 51-2870. Jim Low

ratio over the Communist jet and pilot in Korea.

Though the figures mean little, it is interesting to note that the USAF claims account for 792 MiGs destroyed by F-86s for seventy-eight Sabre losses in air-to-air combat. In comparison, the Soviets alone claim 1,097 UN aircraft 'kills' for 335 losses on their own side (source: *Mir Aviatsiyi* magazine). The Chinese air force claim 271 shot down for 231 lost, and the NKAF make the somewhat ambitious claim for 5,729 aircraft shot down, but will not divulge losses on their side. In any case it is difficult and pointless to try and evaluate the Sabre's performance in the conflict on statistics alone.

However, after the war had ended, the USAF finally got the opportunity to evaluate the MiG's flying qualities against the Sabre. On 21 September 1953 Lt Kom Suk Ro of the North Korean Air Force defected to the South along with his MiG-15bis, landing at Kimpo amid a flurry of confused and amazed Sabre

Basic Comparison: MiG and Sabre		
	MiG-15bis	F-86F-30 (6-3 wing)
Wingspan	33ft 3in (10.13m)	37ft 1in (11.31m)
Wing area	221.8sq ft (20.6sq m)	303sq ft (28.1sq m)
Length	33ft 4in (10.16m)	37ft 6in (11.44m)
Height	11ft 1in (3.39m)	14ft 9in (4.5m)
Engine thrust	5,950lb (2,698kg)	5,910lb (2,680kg)
Initial rate of climb	10,100ft/min (3,078m/min)	9,300ft/min (2,835m/min)
Service ceiling	50,855ft (15,500m)	48,000ft (14,630m)
Max. speed	518kt (958km/h) at sea level	604kt at sea level (1,118km/h)
Max. speed	565kt (1,046km/h) at 10,000ft	530kt at 35,000ft (981km/h)
Empty weight	8,115lb (3,681kg)	10,950lb (4,967kg)
Max. weight	13,327lb (6,045kg)	20,357lb (9,234kg)

personnel. Lt. Kom was given a $100,000 reward and a new life in the West and, in return, the USAF had its first airworthy example of its main fighter opponent. The MiG was dismantled and flown to Okinawa aboard a C-124 Globemaster. There it was reassembled and flown by a

crew of experienced test pilots including Maj Gen Albert B. Boyd, Maj Charles E. 'Chuck' Yeager and Capt H.E. Collins.

Flight testing at Kadena AFB showed that the impressions of combat pilots in Korea were indeed accurate. The MiG-15bis was faster than the F-86A and F-86E at altitudes above 20,000ft (6,096m), and only marginally slower at lower altitudes. The first F-86Fs were superior in speed to the MiG up to

52-4330, a FEAMCOM-modified RF-86F, is characterized by the lack of 'cheek' fairings. Also note the blanked-off lower gun port. This machine was the mount of 67th TRW's Lt Col R. Newman. Royce Raven

35,000ft (10,668m), whereas the '6-3'-winged F-86Fs were faster than their opponent all the way up to the Sabre's service ceiling. But therein lay another MiG advantage: the Russian jet could operate some 4,000ft (1,220m) higher than even the best F-86Fs. On many occasions during the war formations of Sabres flying at 46,000ft (14,000m) had noted MiG-15 flights patrolling at ease 5,000ft (1,524m) above them.

The lighter weight of the MiG for a similar engine output to the Sabre's meant that the Red jet was also far superior in the climb. In a dogfight the MiG-15 pilot could easily evade his opponent by performing a zoom climb to altitude, out of reach of the Sabres. Of course, he could also make for the sanctuary of his airfields north of the Yalu.

Where the Sabre did score was in the dive. With a higher weight than the MiG, as well as a cleaner design aerodynamically, an F-86 pilot could shake off a MiG by opening his throttle and pulling over into a dive, and at lower altitudes the Sabre could then easily out-turn the MiG. Above Mach 0.86 the MiG-15 suffered from severe directional instability, which made the aircraft a poor gun platform at high speeds, and Communist pilots were restricted to a maximum of Mach 0.92. The tests on Okinawa took the captured machine to Mach 0.93, where a nose-up tendency was noted, and higher speeds were not attempted. In contrast, the all-flying tailed F-86E and Fs were truly transonic aircraft, easily capable of safe manoeuvring at these high speeds.

The difference in armament between the two aircraft has often caused debate; the MiG-15's suite of one 37mm cannon and two 23mm guns reflected its original use as an interceptor designed for attacking bombers. Forty rounds of 37mm ammunition and 160 rounds of 23mm ammunition were carried, the 37mm cannon firing at 450 rounds per minute, the 23mm guns firing at 650 rpm. The MiG's cannon shells were highly destructive, though the slow rate of fire was considered a disadvantage in a dogfight. But experience had shown that it took only one cannon hit to down a Sabre.

On the other hand, the Sabre was proposed from the outset as a dogfighter, the F-86's armament of six 0.50in machine-guns having a rapid firing rate but lacking the stopping power of the MiG's cannon. Russian pilots in Korea often joked about the Sabre's guns as 'peashooters'. Though the argument was that the six 0.50-calibres provided a similar weight of fire on a target, the positive results of the GunVal project would seem to indicate that a combination of both systems, that is, a rapid-firing cannon, was the best option.

The MiG-15's gunsight was of a simple gyro design, similar to that of the early F-86A, and was thought to have been copied from the RAF's GGS Mk 2 sight. It lacked any radar ranging capability, and the Sabre's superior gunsight was probably the single item that the Communists envied most. The radar ranging A-1CM gunsight of the later Sabres made the aircraft a far better gun platform than the MiG, once reliability and spares problems in Korea had been overcome.

Overall, each aircraft had its strengths and weaknesses, but it certainly seems that the MiG-15bis was the equal of the '6-3'-winged F-86F and maybe even superior to it. Ultimately, though, it was the quality of USAF and Allied airmen that tipped the balance in favour of the Sabre in Korea.

Korean War Aces: UN Forces

Name	Date of 5th Kill	Date of 10th Kill	Date of 15th Kill	Total
Capt James Jabara	20 May 51	10 June 53	15 July 53	15
Capt Richard S. Becker	9 Sept 51	-	-	5
Capt Ralph D. Gibson	9 Sept 51	-	-	5
Maj Richard D. Creighton	27 Nov 51	-	-	5
Maj George A. Davis	30 Nov 51	13 Dec 51	-	14
Maj Winton W. Marshall	30 Nov 51	-	-	6.5
Maj William Whisner	23 Feb 52	-	-	5.5
Col. Francis S. Gabreski	1 April 52	-	-	6.5
Capt Robert H. Moore	3 April 52	-	-	5
Capt Iven C. Kincheloe	6 April 52	-	-	9
Capt Robert J. Love	21 April 52	-	-	6
Maj William H. Wescott	26 April 52	-	-	5
Capt Robert T. Latshaw	3 May 52	-	-	5
Maj Donald E. Adams	3 May 52	-	-	6.5
1st Lt James H. Kasler	15 May 52	-	-	6
Col Harrison R. Thyng	20 May 52	-	-	5
2nd Lt TJames F. Low	15 June 52	-	-	9
Capt Clifford D. Jolley	8 Aug 52	-	-	7
Maj Frederick C. Blesse	4 Sept 52	?	-	10
Capt Robinson Risner	21 Sept 52	-	-	8
Capt Royal N. Baker	17 Nov 52	?	-	13
Capt Leonard W. Lilley	18 Nov 52	-	-	7
1st Lt Cecil G. Foster	22 Nov 52	-	-	9
Capt Dolphin W. Overton III	24 Jan 53	-	-	5
Capt Harold E Fischer	24 Jan 53	? April 53	-	10
Capt J.D. McConnell, Jr	16 Feb 53	24 April 53	18 May 53	16
Capt Manuel J. Fernandez	18 Feb 53	21 Mar 53	-	14.5
Maj James P. Hagerstrom	27 Mar 53	-	-	8.5
Col. James K. Johnson	28 Mar 53	?	-	10
Lt Col George L. Jones	29 Mar 53	-	-	6.5
Lt Col George I. Ruddell	18 May 53	-	-	8
Lt Col Vermont Garrison	5 June 53	?	-	10
Capt Lonnie R. Moore	18 June 53	?	-	10
Capt Ralph S. Parr	18 June 53	27 July 53	-	10
Col Robert P. Baldwin	22 June 53	-	-	5
1st Lt Henry Buttleman	30 June 53	-	-	7
Maj John F.Bolt	11 July 53	-	-	6
Lt Guy Bordelon*	16 July 53	-	-	5
Capt Clyde A. Curtin	19 July 53	-	-	5
Maj Stephen L. Bettinger	20 July 53	-	-	5

*USN, kills in F4U-5N, all others are F-86 pilots

fuselage bottom. The conversion removed the lower pair of machine-guns and the camera ports in the lower fuselage necessitated the addition of small fairings in that area. It is thought that three RF-86Fs were converted in this way – 52-4330, -4357 and -4529. These machines were turned over to 15th TRS in early 1953 and flew with the remaining RF-86As, again with similar markings to the standard 4th FIW F-86Fs.

Further to this, North American converted eight RF-86Fs, though this time they managed to mount the cameras vertically, and NAA-converted RF-86Fs thus gained the 'cheek' fairings to account for the more awkward (but better photographically) camera installation. The NAA-built RF-86Fs used two K-22s and a single K-17 camera. These NAA machines arrived in Korea on 21 March 1954 and were thus too late to see action in the war; at least fifteen further Sabres were converted to a similar RF-86F specification. Most of the RF-86Fs had a ballasted panel fitted to the forward fuselage in place of the gun-blast panel and, to preserve the looks of a 'standard' F-86F, fake gun muzzles were painted on.

67th TRW's RF-86Fs continued in service until they were replaced by RF-84F Thunderflashes from 1956; they took part in many detachments, notably to Taiwan during September/October 1955. All surviving RF-86Fs were 'on paper' transferred to 21st TRS in July 1957 and were forwarded to 2723rd Air Base Squadron at Kisarazu before the end of the year, most going on to see further service with Taiwan and Korea under the Military Assistance Plan. The three original REMCO-modified RF-86Fs were scrapped in December 1957.

Project Haymaker: the RF-86F Photo Ship

The relative success of earlier photo-reconnaissance RF-86A aircraft in Korea led in late 1952 to the conversion of F-86Fs to a similar role. In fact, NAA had already instigated an RF-86F design study based on the lessons learnt from the Honeybucket and Ashtray RF-86As, but this would take some time to reach the production stage. Thus it was again down to 15th Tactical Reconnaissance Squadron (TRS) personnel to seek authority for

the field conversion of Sabres to meet this requirement. In effect, this was only a matter of protocol, for it was obvious that there was still a need for high-speed missions to be flown over North Korea. Therefore in early 1953 several F-86F-30s were put through the Tsuiki Rear Echelon Maintenance Combined Operations (REMCO) depot for conversion as part of Project *Haymaker*. The RF-86Fs were fitted with two K-14 cameras mounted horizontally and took photographs again through an arrangement of mirrors so that the camera opening was located in the

Further Sabre Production

At North American, the next Sabre model was the F-86F-35, an Inglewood-built, nuclear-capable fighter-bomber. The F-35 had the capability to carry a Mk 12 nuclear weapon under its inner left-hand wing pylon; the remaining positions would be available for drop tanks on a typical mission. The quaintly-titled Mk 12 'Special Store' was a 20kt device, which would be delivered using the low-altitude bombing system (LABS), in which the pilot approached the target at low altitude, pulled up into a loop and

Korean War Aces: Communist Forces

Name	Kills	Notes
Yevgeni G. Pepelyaev	23	2 F-86s, 6 F-80s, 4 F-84s, 1 F-94s
Nikolai V. Sutyagin	21	plus 2 shared kills
L.K. Schukin	15	
D.P. Oskin	14	
M.S. Ponomaryov	14	
S.M. Kramarenko	13	
N.K. Sheberotov	12	
Alexandr P. Smortzkow	12	5 B-29s, 2 F-86s, 5 Meteors
Sutzkow	12	
S.A. Bakhayev	11	
N.G. Dokashenko	11	
G.U. Ohay	11	
Pomaz	11	
G. Ipulov	10	
M.S. Milaushkin	10	
D.A. Samoylov	10	
G.I. Ges	9	
Anatoly M. Karelin	9	all B-29s
Mikhail I. Mihin	9	all F-86s
S.P. Subbotin	9	
N.V. Zabelin	9	
N.N. Babonin	7	
S.A. Fedorets•	7	
Nikolai M. Ivanov	7	includes 6 F-86s
I.M. Zaplavnev	7	
A.S. Boitsov	6	
B.V. Bokatz	6	
V.M. Hvostontsev	6	
Kim Gi Ok*	6	
A.P. Nikolayev	6	
P.F. Nikulin	6	
S.F. Vishnyakov	6	
N.M. Zameskin	6	
B.S. Abakumov	5	
A.T. Bashman	5	
V.I. Belousov	5	
G.N. Berelidze	5	
G.I. Bogdanov	5	
S.D. Danilov	5	
G.F. Dmitryuk	5	
N.I. Gerasimenko	5	
A.M. Kochegarov	5	
N.L. Korniyenko	5	
V.L. Lepikov	5	
S.I. Naumenko	5	
B.A. Obraztsov	5	
Olenitsa	5	
Prudnikov	5	
B.N. Siskov	5	
N.K. Shelamanov	5	
Nikolai I. Shkodin	5	4 F-86s, 1 F-8

• plus one unconfirmed kill: JosephMcConnell, 12 April 1953
* denotes NKAF pilot

released the bomb as he reached the top of the loop. This action would then toss the bomb away from the flight path while the pilot executed an Immlemann turn to escape the shock wave's effects. The F-86F-35 was fitted with an M-1 LABS computer, and also featured a redesigned instrument panel to reflect the new mission capability. Deliveries began in October 1952 with the last 108 aircraft of the NA-191 order, and a further contract, AF-22304, was placed for 157 NA-202s which were completed in June 1954. Most of these aircraft went straight to the 48th and the 388th FBW for deployment to Europe. These should have been the last F-86Fs off the production line at Inglewood.

By mid-1954 it became apparent that there was a significant requirement for Sabres to be supplied under the Military Assistance Program (MAP), and, beginning in late 1954, that requirement could not be met unless further Sabres were produced ñ and quickly. Two solutions were provided to overcome this shortfall. First, in Japan, Mitsubishi was granted a licence to produce F-86Fs for the Japanese Air Self Defense Force, and this agreement was signed on 13 July 1954. It was obvious, however, that such an agreement would take some time to reach a point where real aircraft were produced in Japan and, therefore, it was decided to reopen the production line at Inglewood for one last batch of F-86Fs. The designing of the new model was started on 28 October 1954 and given the NA-227 designation. Contract AF-29371 for 215 aircraft was approved for this design on 27 June 1955, with a further sixty-five aircraft being added to the order on 27 March 1956. As F-86F-40 aircraft, this final block incorporated all the best features of previous models, such as the dual-store wing, and also brought some new ones. Aerodynamically, wing slats were introduced on the 6-3 wing, but this time a 12in (0.3m) wing-tip extension further improved the Sabre's flying ability. The gunsight radar was now the AN/APG-30A, and revisions to the parking brake, compass and emergency undercarriage system were also undertaken. Finally, a trim impulse system was installed, whereby instantaneous trim adjustment was provided without the lag or overshoot associated with earlier F-86Fs. The F-86F-40 modifications, especially the wing-tip extensions, were such a success that many remaining F-86Fs in the USAF inventory were retrofitted to this standard. In addition, early model F-86Fs for delivery to foreign countries through the MAP system were brought up to F-86F-40 standard before delivery.

The first Inglewood-produced F-86F-40, 55-3816, was delivered in October 1955 and initially bailed to NAA for

Rarely seen, export F-86F-40s carried USAF markings for delivery to MAP nations. This aircraft, 55-3977, was on its way to the Spanish AF in October 1956. Routing through Prestwick in Scotland, the aircraft carries insignia red Arctic markings for the ferry flight. MAP

testing, though all aircraft in this final batch soon passed into foreign hands, at first to Japan, but further aircraft went to the air forces of Spain and Pakistan.

Two little-known episodes in history, the Quemoy and Matsu crises of 1954 and 1955, almost sparked off another conflict and involved the mobilization of numerous Sabre and other USAF units in the Far East. The crisis began in August 1954, when Chinese Nationalist troops under the leadership of Generalissimo Chiang Kai-shek were moved to the islands of Quemoy and Matsu, just off the coast of Communist China. In total, 58,000 troops moved into the first and 15,000 into the second. Such blatant aggression then sparked off the shelling of the islands by Communist Chinese forces on the mainland during the following month. Almost immediately, the US Joint Chiefs of Staff mobilized US forces to bolster Taiwan, although it was not until early 1955 that the Sabre units became involved. On 1 February F-86Fs of the 18th FBW deployed into Formosa on a two-week temporary duty (TDY) assignment, flying top cover to Nationalist Chinese aircraft attacking the mainland.

From 20 February the 58th FBW from Taegu AB in Korea took over, rotating a squadron at a time through Chiayi AB, starting with the 69th FBS. Jack Brauckmann, a Sabre pilot with one of the next two 58th FBW squadrons to deploy, the 311th FBS, recalls this episode:

In early 1955 we were informed that we would soon be moving north to Osan-Ni, not far from Seoul. However, in between Taegu and Osan-Ni, each of the three squadrons went to Formosa for about a month. We flew high altitude top cover to scare off the MiG-15s as the Nationalist Chinese Air Force, commanded by Gen 'Tiger' Wong, flew bombing missions to China. Now I never saw them drop a bomb, but their single-tailed Liberators would take off from our joint base at Chiayi in fine shape, then stagger home all shot up. Author Richard Tregaskis (*Guadalcanal Diary*, etc.) and his photographer wife spent a few days with us there, incidentally, doing a story for *Look* or *Colliers*, but they sent him away when he began asking questions about this totally unknown action, which, of course, is still almost unknown. Dick never did publish a story, to my knowledge.

The crisis subsided somewhat on 23 April, when China declared that it was ready to negotiate with Taiwan, the shelling of Quemoy and Matsu stopping on 1 May. However, tensions remained in the area and regular deployments of USAF Sabres to Taiwan continued until 1958 when the aircraft passed from the FEAF inventory. In that time 4th FDW Sabres also took up TDY duties at Tainan AB and, beginning

in March 1955, small numbers of RF-86Fs were deployed to the island to provide tactical reconnaissance. There were a number of engagements during this period and F-86 did register MiG kills, for no Sabre losses.

The majority of USAF squadron F-86Fs were phased out in 1955 and few went into Air National Guard use. The only two non-activated ANG units to operate the F-86F were the 115th and the 195th FIS, California ANG. Based at Van Nuys, these two squadrons flew the 'F-20' from December 1957 until July 1959, alongside a number of F-86E-10s that had been brought up to F-86F standard.

The heavy requirements of the Military Assistance Program dictated that any available F-86Fs were refurbished in-theatre and passed on to foreign nations in that area. A number of training units, notably at Williams and Nellis AFBs, retained F-86Fs into the 1960s, ostensibly to train foreign pilots under the MAP scheme. Those F-86Fs that did remain in the United States upon their withdrawal from service were overhauled and sent overseas, many to South American countries.

F-86F Sub-types

GunVal F-86Fs

On 3 April 1951 Air Materiel Command initiated Project GunVal, under the heading 'Evaluation of Aircraft Armament'. Under this project AMC would appraise a number of weapons with a view to incorporating them into contemporary fighters, as well as developing such systems for use on the forthcoming Century Series of aircraft, such as the F-100. Aircraft to be utilized in GunVal included the F-94B, F-89C, F-84F and F-86F.

At North American four F-86E-10s and six F-86F-1s were modified under AMC project 2F-543 to accommodate four T-160 20mm cannon in place of the standard six 0.50-calibres. The six-gun blast panel was extended on the converted aircraft, the muzzle openings being much larger than the normal item. The T-160 guns were belt-fed and capable of firing 1,400 rounds per minute, with 100 rounds per gun fitted in the modified aircraft. Such was the increased recoil of the gun that after ground tests further strengthening was required in the nose area to prevent structural damage when the guns were fired. In the course of completing this cannon installation, NAA engineers identified and corrected many system problems, led by engineering supervisor Paul Peterson and armament engineer Jim Robertson. The aircraft conversions were completed in March 1952 and all aircraft involved were then redesignated F-86F-2-NAs, with an A-4 gunsight, J47-GE-27 engines and '6-3' wings. The first GunVal F-86F-2 was flown by George Welch during March 1952 and live firing was carried out in 51-2803 at altitudes of 10 to 25,000ft (3,000 to 7,600m) over the Pacific near Catalina Island. These tests were satisfactory, and during October the GunVal F-86F-2s were assigned to 6510th Air Base Wing at Edwards AFB for USAF trials. At this point all four guns were wired to fire simultaneously, and, in order to purge gas from the gun bays, NAA had designed small doors that opened into the engine intake. It appears that all firing tests up to late 1952 were carried out at relatively low altitudes; this would later present a problem.

In December 1952 eight of the F-86F-2s were assigned to FEAF for combat evaluation in Korea and embarked from San Diego aboard the escort carrier USS *Windham Bay*, bound for Kisarazu in Japan. The two remaining GunVal F-86Fs, 51-2884 and 2900, were assigned to Eglin AFB in Florida for further evaluation. Following their arrival in Japan, the eight F-86F-2s were assigned to 335th FIS during January under the command of Col Vermont Garrison. To support the GunVal detachment's F-86Fs, spares, armament technicians, five assigned pilots and four contractor technicians (including Paul Peterson) were relocated with the aircraft. It was at this point that the gun gas problem emerged. In Korea combat missions were generally flown at around 40,000ft (12,200m), and in one of the first encounters with MiGs, Maj John Moorehead fired his 20mm guns in a fairly long burst, at which point the engine stopped. Although he was able to relight his engine, the problem occurred again soon after.

On 25 January 1953 Capt Murray Winslow was on a GunVal combat mission. Winslow managed to engage a MiG-15 at around 45,000ft (13,700m) with his four cannon, and again, after a short burst, his engine flamed out. This time the pilot was not so lucky and was unable to restart his engine; Winslow was forced to eject over the Yellow Sea. His Sabre, 51-2861, was lost.

Following the grounding of the GunVal aircraft, it soon became apparent that the purging of gun gas into the intake at altitude was starving the engine of oxygen, causing a flame-out. When testing had been carried out in the United States this problem had not been encountered as the air density at lower altitude had managed to sustain combustion when the guns were fired. A number of solutions were found to overcome this, starting with the intake doors, which were fixed closed. The guns were then wired to fire either in pairs or all four at once and, finally, holes were let into the gun bay doors to get rid of the gas overboard.

These modifications seemed to provide a solution, and in forty-one engagements six MiGs were claimed destroyed and thirteen damaged. Two F-86F-2s were damaged, Maj Ray Evans being hit in the intake by a 37mm round and Lt Col Don Rodewald took two hits in the wing from 23mm MiG cannon. Both aircraft (51-2836 and 2868) were recovered successfully and repaired at Kimpo.

These two 67th FBS F-86Fs were pictured on 14 June 1955 while taking part in a FEAF gunnery meet at the Suwon range in Korea. These aircraft carry small practice bomb dispensers on the left wing pylon. 52-4351 had just returned from a two-week deployment to Formosa, and, three days after this shot was taken, 52-4396, 'The Destroying Angel' was off to Taiwan for three weeks at Chiayi AB. USAF via Jon Lake

However, all was not well. On 30 April 1953 Capt Lonnie Moore flying 51-2803, suffered a flame-out followed by turbine failure, forcing him to eject over the Yellow Sea. The following day the Korean GunVal test was concluded.

Further testing of the F-86F-2's gun installation revealed that gun gas was now building up in front of the gun muzzles and then being ingested by the engine. NAA engineers next devised a C-shaped plate, which, when fitted into the blast panel's gun trough, dissipated the gun gas very effectively. Though this solution had no effect on the Korean GunVal F-86Fs, in later years, when the T-160 (as the M-39) was adopted for use in the F-86H, those same C-shaped fittings proved invaluable.

Upon their return from Korea in June 1953, the GunVal F-86F-2s saw further use at Eglin AFB; then the survivors spent short periods assigned to 3595th CCTW at Nellis and 3515th Support Sqn at Randolph AFB. In May 1957 six of these machines were sent to McLellan AFB for removal of their armament and, after the gun muzzles had been welded up, they were assigned to the 120th FIS Colorado ANG's Minutemen aerobatic team.

Two further F-86Fs were assigned to the GunVal programme. Fitted with four Oerlikon 206 RK 20mm cannon, these aircraft were modified in a similar fashion to the F-86F-2s, but the installation took some time longer. The guns were installed in the aircraft, two on each side of the fuselage, but their bulk and the length of the barrel adapter meant that instead of a flush blast panel at the muzzle end, four pronounced fairings had to be fitted. Provision was made for 100 rounds for each gun in linked ammunition. Expended links were retained in the

aircraft to preserve the centre of gravity, but spent shell cases were ejected overboard via ejection chutes in the lower fuselage. Each gun bay featured a gun-gas purging system whereby a pneumatically-operated, electrically-actuated, air-inlet door opened into the engine intake duct to act as a ram air scoop. These doors were set to open upon trigger depression and remain open for 5sec after trigger release. To purge the compartment gas, six vertical slots were cut in each gun bay door, with further ventilation holes in each expended-link access door.

The 206 RK gun itself was a revolver gun, designed to fire electrically-primed ammunition automatically with a muzzle velocity of 3,500ft/sec (1,066m/sec) at a cyclic rate of 1,600 to 1,800 rounds per minute. A five-chambered drum at the rear of the weapon then rotated upon firing to align each chamber with the barrel, the round being fired at the 12 o'clock position. A novel feature of the F-86F installation was the use of a mounting yoke at the forward end of the gun whereby the barrel could be withdrawn, allowing the weapon to be

After their Korean deployment, many of the GunVal F-86F-2s were assigned to training units throughout the United States. In early 1957 they were sent to McLellan AFB where their cannon armament was removed and they were reassigned to 120th FIS Colorado ANG. They then flew with the Minute Men aerobatic team for two years. via Mike Fox

More famous for the Korean-based F-86Fs, the GunVal project also generated two F-86F-3 aircraft. This shot taken at Inglewood on 16 November 1953 shows one of two Oerlikon cannon-equipped F-86F-3s. John Henderson

Close-up of the Oerlikon 206 RK 20mm cannon installation. The gun barrel could be detached, allowing the whole breech assembly to be swung out for maintenance. NAA technicians John Deslierres (L) and Henry Juul demonstrate this feature. John Henderson

swung out at the rear to aid servicing.

Initially tested by NAA, the two modified aircraft were not delivered to the USAF until April 1954. They were redesignated F-86F-3-NA and sent to the Air Force Armament Center at Eglin AFB in Florida. GunVal testing of this weapon covered three areas: rigid ground-mounted firing, aircraft-mounted on the ground, and finally in a nineteen-mission flight phase. The programme was overseen by Project Officer 2nd Lt Charles Heins, Jr with Operational Test Officer 1st Lt W.S. Snyder undertaking the flight testing.

The ground-mounted phase was used to determine barrel life, projectile velocity and cyclic rate. 304 rounds were fired in total in this test. The static aircraft test was used to evaluate installation reliability, dispersion and cyclic rate, with 1,835 rounds being expended. Finally, the aerial firing of the guns was used to show the effectiveness of the bay ventilating systems at several altitudes. In this phase vacuum bottles were fitted to collect gun gas for ground analysis, while electrical 'fire-eyes' would indicate whether gun-bay fires had occurred during firing.

The aerial phase quickly highlighted installation problems. On Mission 2, conducted at 10,000ft (3,000m), a dent appeared in the right-hand nose of the aircraft immediately forward of the upper muzzle. This was attributed to excessive muzzle blast, and further flights at altitudes up to 40,000ft (12,200m) reinforced the conclusion. Additionally, on Missions 15 and 19, compressor stall was encountered.

The conclusion of this programme in February 1955 showed the Oerlikon to be generally unsatisfactory for a variety of reasons. The installation failed to meet GunVal standard stoppage rates of 2.8 per 1,000 rounds, though the installation was deemed to be 'marginally satisfactory'. However, what was not acceptable was the poor round dispersion of the gun, the unsuitability of the 20mm, steel-cased SS/K rounds and ammunition links and the low component life. Furthermore, the F-86F-3 installation also required additional modification to rectify compressor stall and muzzle-blast problems.

Not surprisingly, the Oerlikon gun was not adopted for USAF service, though it has to be said that manufacturer-based modification would have rectified many of the problems outlined above. At the end of the evaluation, one of the F-86F-3s remained at Eglin for test support work until January 1958.

TF-86F Two-seat Sabre

On 3 February 1953 NAA began design of a two-seat F-86F, to meet a USAF requirement for a high-speed T-33 trainer replacement. Initial construction as the NA-204 began on 8 April, the company proposing that modification of an F-86F-30 aircraft could meet the needs of this project by splicing in a 63in (160cm) forward fuselage extension to accommodate the second cockpit. The change in the centre of gravity then necessitated the whole wing's being moved forward 8in (20.3cm). Instead of a sliding canopy, as used on the F-86F, the trainer would use a large, one-piece, clamshell item, with just one bracing frame at its midpoint.

The first TF-86F 52-5016 carried no armament. It first flew on 14 December 1953 and crashed at Nellis on 17th March 1954, killing the NAA test pilot Joe Lynch. NAA

Armament would not be fitted on this aircraft, but in most other ways the conversion would use standard F-86F-30 components. One exception was in the wing area, for, despite the availability of the '6-3' wing with fence, it was decided to use a standard slatted mainplane on the trainer. NAA's design and modification proposal were forwarded to Air Materiel Command on 9 July 1953.

On 9 September the USAF authorized the conversion of an F-86F-30 to the tandem two-seat configuration. The aircraft, 52-5016, was completed in December 1953 and designated TF-86F. The TF-86F made its maiden flight on 14 December with Ray Morris at the controls, and the aircraft generally performed on a par with the F-86F, having a similar top speed, climb rate and ceiling. On 17 March 1954 the NAA test pilot Joe Lynch took the TF-86F out to Nellis AFB to demonstrate the aircraft on what

First flight of the no.2 TF-86F, 53-1228, on 5 August 1954. It differed from the first machine in having twin-0.50-calibre machine-gun armament. In order to improve longitudinal stability, it also featured increased vertical tail area and a small additional ventral fin. NAA

would be its ninth flight. While pulling into a slow roll on take-off from Nellis, Lynch lost control, the aircraft crashed and exploded and Lynch was killed, apparently because the fuel tanks had been filled by the Nellis personnel, rather than left partially full, as would have been required for the demonstration flight. The extra weight meant that Lynch had far less margin for error.

Less than a week after this crash, on 23 March, the Air Force authorized conversion of a further F-86F to trainer configuration, under the NAA designation NA-216. The last F-86F-35 was therefore pulled from the production line and modified to the two-seat TF-86F configuration, although lessons learnt in the brief test career of the first aircraft were put to good effect in the second

With no orders forthcoming for the TF-86F, the second prototype was assigned to the Air Force Flight Test Center at Edwards AFB. It served as a chase plane until November 1958 when it was flown to McLellan AFB for storage and scrapping. Lionel N. Paul via Mike Fox

TF-86 Production		
Serial	Model	Construction No.
52-5016	TF-86F	204-1(conversion from 191-712)
53-1228	TF-86F	216-1(conversion from 202-157)

Specifications: TF-86F

POWERPLANT
General Electric J47-GE-27 of 5,910lb (2,680kg) thrust)

WEIGHTS
take-off (clean):	14,836lb (6,728kg)
take-off (drop tanks):	18,040lb (8,181kg)
combat weight:	12,980lb (5,886kg)

DIMENSIONS
wingspan:	37ft 1in (11.3m)
length:	42ft 9in (13m)
height:	14ft 9in (4.5m)
wing area:	287.9sq ft (26.78sq m)

PERFORMANCE
maximum speed (clean):
at sea level:	692mph (1,113km/h)
at 35,000ft:	611mph (983km/h at 10,668 m)
initial climb rate:	10,300ft/min (3,139m/min)
service ceiling:	50,500ft (15,392m)
maximum ferry range:	1,293 miles (2,080km)

ARMAMENT
2 x 0.50in calibre machine-guns (second aircraft only)

machine. This time, to counter the aerodynamic effects of the lengthened forward fuselage, an extension to the vertical tail was installed, as was a new ventral fin, situated under the rear fuselage. Armament was also fitted in this aircraft, comprising a pair of 0.50-calibre machine-guns, fitted in a position corresponding to the lowest gun position on the standard F-86F. Underwing pylons were also fitted, to carry drop tanks or bombs, and the slatted wing was again fitted.

Delivered on 24 June 1954, the second TF-86F (53-1228) made its maiden flight on 5 August and was initially demonstrated by Bob Hoover. On 31 January 1955 the aircraft was assigned to 3595th Combat Crew Training Wing at Nellis AFB, but the Air Force announced on 7 February that no production orders for the trainer would be forthcoming. In future, two-seat F-100s would fill this requirement and, as a result, on 10 March the TF-86F was transferred to 6515th Maintenance Group at Edwards AFB for use as a chase plane. Following a successful career at Edwards, the aircraft was flown to McLellan AFB for depot work on 20 November 1958. It was then reclassified for storage on 21 July 1959,

declared excess one month later and finally scrapped in March 1961.

Test Programmes

During the 1950s several Sabre airframes were assigned for test programmes, either within the USAF itself or by bailment of certain aircraft to military contractors and other research establishments. Notably, a number of F-86A and F aircraft were bailed to Boeing for use as chase aircraft in the B-47 and later B-52 flight-test programmes. The F-86F, in particular, also saw varied use in many esoteric projects and a few initiated by NAA itself are worthy of note.

Under company project NA-210, two new F-86F-30 aircraft, 52-5143 and -5163, were modified to incorporate internal rocket-projectile packs in much the same manner as on the F-86D. On 13 July 1953 Contract Supplement 3 to AF-6517 agreed the conversion of these machines for assignment under Air Research and Development Command Project 6F-119. Conversion was carried out at Inglewood and consisted of the installation of three retractable rocket packs, one on either side of the fuselage, situated roughly in the space vacated by deleted machine-gun armament, and a further one in the lower fuselage, just aft of the nose undercarriage.

These packs were designed to house 2.5in air-to-air rockets, a total of 200 being carried; these could be salvoed in groups of 24, 48, 96 or all 200. Both aircraft were bailed to NAA upon delivery on 12 September 1955 for flight testing, though it appears that only 52-5143 actually took part in rocket firing trials, being equipped with camera-modified drop tanks for the purpose. USAF pilot Capt James Roberts was assigned project pilot for this phase of testing. On 21 February 1956 both aircraft were assigned JF temporary test prefixes and delivered to the USAF at Hanscom AFB on 5 July. The programme eventually came to naught, however, and it appears that the impressive firepower was let down badly when the excessive flash caused by firing the side pods affected the pilot's vision. At the end of 1956 both airframes were reassigned to other roles, 52-5143 to Boeing at Wichita on 10 December 1956 and the second machine to ground training duties with 3320th Technical Training Wing at Amarillo AFB in Texas.

In 1960 a joint NAA/USAF project developed an experimental Sabre which became the highest-flying and fastest of all F-86s. Believed to have been the result of a request for the development of an interim interceptor pending delivery of further F-104 Starfighters, this premise seems unlikely: the time (1960) would render the F-86 unsuitable and other types were readily available by then. It seems more likely that this aircraft was a proof-of-concept testbed following a Japanese proposal to extend the useful life of its Sabres by fitting a rocket motor or motors. Such a suggestion had been made by the Japanese in 1959. What is beyond doubt is that one F-86F was fitted with a Rocketdyne AR2-3 rocket motor and used in a series of tests that implied the engine's use on an operational Sabre. To undertake the project, F-86F-30 serial no. 52-4608 was ferried from 4530th CCTW at Williams AFB to NAA's Inglewood plant on 5 October 1959 for modification. The rocket motor was installed under the rear fuselage in a faired external structure, weighing 225lb (102kg) for a throttleable thrust of between 3,000lb (1,360kg) and 6,000lb (2,720kg). The AR2-3 was capable of a 190sec burn and could be used at up to 80,000ft (24,400m) altitude. Fuel for the engine was standard JP-4 jet fuel, mixed with hydrogen peroxide, the latter being housed in modified and enlarged 200gall drop tanks fitted on the outer wing pylons. Each tank could hold 165gall

(618l) of oxidant. Though machine-guns were deleted from this machine, pylons and dummy Sidewinder missiles were fitted, and for many flights in the programme 120gall drop tanks were also installed on the inner pylons. In the cockpit, rocket-motor selectors and switches were mounted on the drop-tank release panel, just forward of the

standard throttle box, while the rocket gained its own throttle just aft of the standard item.

In early 1960 flight testing began from North American's Palmdale test area, with Jay Hanks assigned as project test pilot. Further flights were centred on Edwards AFB, NAA pilots Jim Brooks and J.O. Roberts also being involved

USAF F-86F Units

4th FIW (334th, 335th, 336th FIS, FDS), Kimpo AB, Korea, Chitose and Misawa AB, Japan and Kadena AB, Okinawa

8th FBW (35th, 36th, 80th FBS), Suwon AB, Korea, Kadena AB, Okinawa and Itazuke AB, Japan

15th TRS, Kimpo AB, Korea, Komaki and Yokota AB, Japan and Kadena AB, Okinawa

18th FIS, Minneapolis-St. Paul Airport, MN and Ladd AFB, AK

18th FBW (12th, 44th, 67th FBS), Clark AB, Philippines, Osan AB, Korea and Kadena AB, Okinawa

21st FBW (72nd 416th, 531st FBS), George AFB, CA, Chateauroux AB and Chambley AB, France

35th FIW (39th FIS), Suwon AB, Korea, attached to 18th FBW and 51st FIW

36th FBW, FDW (22nd, 23rd, 32nd, 53rd FBS, FDS), Bitburg and Landstuhl AB, Germany, Soesterburg AB, Holland

45th FDS, Suffolk County AFB, NY and Sidi Slimane AB, Morocco

48th FBW (492nd, 493rd, 494th FBS), Chaumont AB, France

50th FBW (10th, 81st, 417th FBS), Clovis AFB, NM, Toul AB, France and Hahn AB, Germany

51st FIW (16th, and 25th FIS), Suwon AB, Korea, Misawa AB, Japan and Naha AB, Okinawa

56th FIS, Selfridge AFB

58th FBW (69th, 310th, 311th FBS), Taegu and Osan AB, Korea

63rd FIS, Oscoda AFB, MI

81st FIW (78th, 91st, 92nd FIS), RAF Shepherds Grove and Bentwaters, England

84th FIS, Hamilton AFB, CA

86th FBW (461st FDS, 525th, 526th and 527th FBS), Landstuhl and Hahn AB, Germany

94th FIS, George AFB, CA

322nd FDW (450th, 451st, 452nd FDS), Foster AFB, TX

323rd FBW (453rd, 454th, 455th FBS), Eilson AFB, AK and Bunker Hill AFB, IN

357th FIS, Portland International Airport, OR and Nouasseur AB, French Morocco

366th FBW (389th, 390th, 391st FBS), Alexandria AFB. LA

386th FBW (552nd, 553rd and 554th FBS), Bunker Hill AFB, IN

388th FBW (561st, 562nd, 563rd FBS), Clovis AFB, NM, Bitburg, Spangdahlem and Hahn ABs, Germany, Etain AB, France

401st FBW (612th, 613th and 614th FBS), Alexandria AFB, LA

406th FBW (512th, 513th, and 514th FBS), RAF Manston, England and Soesterburg AB, Holland

431st FIS, Wheelus AB, Libya

450th FBW, FDW (721st, 722nd, 723rd FBS, FDS), Foster AFB, TX

474th FBW (428th, 429th, 430th FBS), Clovis AFB, NM

479th FBW, FDW (434th, 435th and 436th FBS, FDS), George AFB, CA

720th FBS, Ladd and Eilson AFB, AK

1708th Ferry Wing, Kelly AFB TX.

3525th Combat Crew Training Wing, Williams AFB, AZ

3595th CCTW, Nellis AFB, NV

4510th Combat Crew Training Wing, Luke AFB, AZ

4520th Combat Crew Training Wing, Nellis AFB, NV

4530th Combat Crew Training Wing, Williams AFB, AZ

6024th Flying Training Wing, Hamamatsu, Japan

6146th Flying Training Wing, Sach'On and Seoul, Korea

7272nd Air Gunnery Group, Wheelus AB, Libya

7330th Flying Training Wing, Furstenfeldbruck AB, West Germany

F-86F Production

Serial No.	Model	Construction Nos
51-2850 to 2927	F-86F-1-NA	172-133 to 210
51-2928 to 2943	F-86F-5-NA	172-211 to 226
51-12936 to 12969	F-86F-10-NA	172-227 to 260
51-12970 to 12976	F-86F-15-NA	172-261 to 267
51-13070 to 13169	F-86F-20-NH	176-1 to 100
51-13170 to 13510	F-86F-25-NH	176-101 to 441
52-4305 to 5163	F-86F-30-NA	191-1 to 859
52-5164 to 5271	F-86F-35-NA	191-860 to 967
52-5272 to 5530	F-86F-25-NH	193-1 to 259
53-1072 to 1228	F-86F-35-NA	202-1 to 157
55-3816 to 4030	F-86F-40-NA	227-1 to 215
55-4983 to 5047	F-86F-40-NA	227-216 to 280
55-5048 to 5117	F-86F-40	231-1 to 70*
56-2773 to 2882	F-86F-40	238-1 to 110*
57-6338 to 6457	F-86F-40	256-1 to 120*

* licence-built by Mitsubishi

at this time. Immediate positive results were gained from these flights, including an altitude of 70,840ft (21,592m) being achieved and a top speed of Mach 1.22 at 60,000ft (18,300m) in level flight.

These quoted figures were in the 'clean' configuration, but with the oxidant tanks fitted.

Further flights demonstrated a climb to 60,000ft in 2.4min and a Mach 1.03 top speed in level flight at 45,000ft (13,700m) with the rocket running in addition to the aircraft's J47. During one flight in November 1960 the aircraft managed to climb up to 40,000ft (12,200m) in only 66sec.

52-4608 was redesignated as a JF-86F (Special Test, Temporary) on 1 July 1960, the AR2-3 programme being generally deemed a success, though further Sabre development was not forthcoming. However, these same AR2 rocket systems were fitted into three NF-104A Starfighters during 1963 for use in NASA and USAF research projects, including astronaut training programmes.

As late as 1963, NAA Los Angeles were still expending time and money in the investigation of yet further extension of the Sabre's useful life. In that year the company proposed an 'expedient' F-86F to be used in the counterinsurgency role. The idea centred around a heavily-modified aircraft which would have the J47 engine removed and the fuselage space left vacant filled with bag-type fuel tanks. Power instead would come from two General Electric J85 engines, mounted in pods beneath the wings. Further details are sketchy, but NAA stated that the range of such a machine would be 'several times' that of a standard Sabre. The project came to nothing.

The rocket-boosted JF-86F at Palmdale. The Rocketdyne pack can be seen under the fuselage; note also the modified drop tanks. This aircraft still exists, owned by Robert Scott of San Martin, CA.
Howard Levy, May 1960

CHAPTER FOUR

Last of the Sport Models

The F-86H

Many lessons were learned during the Korean War, and chief among these was that the days of pure air superiority fighters were numbered. The USAF's experience had shown that Tactical Air Command's aircraft would in future be required to cope with both air superiority and close-support bombing. The fighter-bomber F-86Fs initially covered this eventuality, but it was clear that in the longer term a purpose-built F-86 development could better fill the role until the arrival of the Century Series fighters, notably the F-100 and the F-105.

North American began the design of this fighter-bomber variant on 16 March 1951 under NAA designation NA-187, a mock-up being available for inspection by 24 July. This design retained a standard F-86 undercarriage and wing assembly, coupled to the nose intake configuration, but there the similarity ended. In order to increase performance and carry the proposed external stores load, the NA-187 would use General Electric's J73 engine, which developed upwards of 8,000lb (3,628kg) of thrust. This in turn required a larger air intake to cope with up to 142lb of air per second at maximum thrust, and this was achieved by designing the fuselage to be 6in (15.2cm) deeper. The continued knock-on effect was that more internal space was created within the airframe, which allowed internal fuel capacity to be increased from 435gall (1,631l) to 562gall (2,107l).

Though armament for the NA-187 was to have been four 20mm T-160 cannon, development and production problems with these (as experienced in the F-86F GunVal experiment) required an alternative to be fitted on the first aircraft off the production lines. Instead, the tried and tested installation of six 0.50-calibre Browning machine-guns was chosen, and this would eventually be fitted to 115 aircraft, including the second prototype. Other salient features of the design included a wing with four underwing hard points for bombs or drop tanks and an F-86D-type clamshell cockpit canopy to go with the F-86D-type ejector seat. Horizontal tail surfaces were of the 'all flying' type, but with increased area, no dihedral and no separate trim surface.

The J73 Engine

The J73 engine resulted from General Electric's desire to develop a high-power J47 engine for the F-86H. In order to do this, a major redesign was required, including the use of a two-stage turbine, cannular combustion chambers and a maximum pressure ratio of 7:1 (compared with 5.45:1 for the J47-GE-27). Thirty-six variable incidence, steel inlet guide vanes gave the engine better efficiency below maximum power.

Though it would eventually tip the scales at around 3,895lb (1,766kg) dry – more than 1,000lb (453kg) heavier than the J47 – the new engine was both shorter and narrower than the previous design and considerably more powerful. Initially designated XJ47-GE-29, the mock-up was inspected by the USAF on 17 July 1951, and further defined for installation in the F-86H mock-up during August. The first experimental engine went on test in April 1952, passing its 50hr preliminary rating test in January 1953. By the time of its installation in the prototype F-86H, the J73 was capable of

reaching 8,920lb (4,045kg) thrust with ice and FOD debris screens retracted and 8,740lb (3,693kg) with them in operation. The Air Force signed contract AF-28881 for 720 J73-GE-3 production engines, increasing this order later by a further 150.

No other aircraft used the J73, which at first proved troublesome in service. However, problems with inlet guide vanes were solved in later variants and it eventually powered some of the last Sabres in US military service.

Though it started life as the XJ47-GE-29, General Electric's J73 engine was an entirely new design. In particular, the variable inlet guide vanes and the annular cased combustion chamber gave it a more advanced look, which was matched by its performance. General Electric/Eric Falk

From the second prototype, provision was made for the carriage of the 1,200lb 'special store', a Mk 12, 20kt nuclear device, which would be delivered using the low altitude bombing system (LABS) previously mounted in the F-86F fighter bombers. Like their close cousin, nuclear-capable F-86Hs also utilized the M-1 LABS computer. All F-86Hs were equipped with the A-4 gun-bomb-rocket sight, linked to an AN/APG-30 radar in the intake lip. Ancillary equipment included an AN/ARC-27 UHF radio and an AN/ARC-6 radio compass. Aircraft modified to TO 1F86H-638 standard carried a TACAN system, by which the pilot obtained line-of-sight distance and bearing information from a ground station. These machines had a prominent blade aerial atop the nose intake. The second prototype also introduced a single-point refuelling capability.

On 3 November 1952 Contract AF-27681 was signed, which covered the production of 175 NA-187s, to be known as the F-86H-1 in USAF service. This order included two Inglewood-built, pre-production aircraft and a static test airframe, with the balance of the F-86H order to be manufactured at Columbus, as would all subsequent F-86Hs.

On 30 April 1953 the prototype F-86H, 52-1975 took to the air, piloted by Joseph Lynch. This and the second machine carried no armament and were both accepted and then bailed to NAA at Inglewood for further testing. The first prototype was assigned to Edwards AFB in October for Phase II testing, by which time the '6-3' wing modification had been carried out. The first Columbus-built F-86H-1 flew on 4 September 1953,

The first YF-86H 52-1975 pictured around the time of its first flight in April 1953. NAA test pilot Joe Lynch is about to board the aircraft. Later, an instrumented nose boom was fitted. NAA

though deliveries did not begin to take off until April 1954, when the last Columbus-built F-86Fs rolled off the line. Continued J73 engine development meant that the slightly improved J73-GE-3A could be installed from the sixty-first aircraft.

In common with previous Sabre models, many of the early production aircraft were assigned to test roles, mainly in connection with the aircraft's entry into service. Eight of the first twenty-three production aircraft were delivered to 6510th Test Group at Edwards AFB, with others going to Eglin and Wright-Patterson. By the end of June 1954 Columbus had delivered thirteen F-86Hs, including the first machine to feature the improved '6-3' wing so successfully tested and used in service by F-86Fs. The F-86H

installation also featured 12in (0.3m) wing-tip extensions, similar to those being developed for the F-86F-40. The first aircraft to be factory fitted with the '6-3' wing was 52-1991, which was assigned straight to Edwards AFB on 21 June. This aircraft also marked the deletion of the electric cockpit heater fitted to all previous H-models. However, deliveries of further aircraft were held at the factory because of a series of accidents, one of which involved the loss of the sixth production aircraft, 52-1982, at Edwards AFB on 24 May. Deliveries began again on 2 August, but, almost immediately, a further accident occurred which cast a shadow over the whole programme. On 25 August 1954 the famed Korean War ace Capt Joseph McConnell was killed while flying 52-1981 from

52-1977, the first Columbus-built F-86H, took to the air on 4 September 1953. It was bailed straight back to NAA at Columbus for testing. Note that the aircraft is painted in primer here. Jon Lake

52-1980, the sixth F-86H, was assigned to 6510th Test Wing at Edwards AFB on 7 April 1954. In this shot it has bomb racks fitted. J.M.G. Gradidge

This 3595th CCTW F-86H is still fitted with the early '6-3' wing. In service, most F-86Hs were retrofitted with a slatted 'F-40' wing. Howard Levy via Mike Fox

At this time there were no simulators, no two-cockpit aircraft and no real training program. Check out consisted of a Mobile Training Detachment that came to our Wing and gave about a week of classes on how the F-86F differed from the F-86H, which really had a lot of meaning to the F-84E pilots. The next step being to go back to the squadron for your check out. You got a quick briefing from someone that had 'checked out' on the Columbus trip, had the crew chief help you start the airplane, taxi out and meet your instructor at the end of the runway. As I recall, the instructor took off on the student's wing ñ my log book shows 18 January 1955 as my first flight in the F-86H.

Edwards. McConnell had experienced a complete hydraulic failure and decided to try and recover to base, using just the throttle and rudder. He nearly made it, but turbulence on his approach lifted one wing and he had no way to correct it. At low altitude he ejected, but his parachute was unable to deploy fully.

At the September 1954 National Air Races at Dayton Airport, Maj John L. Armstrong, flying an F-86H set a world 500km closed-circuit speed record of 649mph (1,044km/h). Another F-86H, flown by Capt Eugene P. Sonnenberg set a 100km closed course record of 692.8mph (1,114km/h). Sadly, Armstrong was killed on 5 September while trying to beat this record. He was flying 52-1988, the twelfth production aircraft, which had been assigned to the Wright Air Research & Development Center.

It was not until November 1954 that the first aircraft began to equip the operational squadrons, starting with the newly-activated 312th FBW at Clovis AFB, New Mexico. The first aircraft planned for the 312th was the F-84F, but the field elevation was too high for it to operate well in hot weather. Concurrently, 3595th Combat Crew Training Wing at Nellis AFB began to receive F-86H-1s; the final aircraft in this block were assigned in late January 1955, completing the equipping of 312th FBW. This unit had been assigned up to ninety newly-qualified second lieutenants, who had either completed F-84E or F-86F short courses; few had seen an F-86H and none had flown it. Facilities were basic, the hangars and maintenance buildings being occupied

by 388th FBG and their F-86Fs. It was not until late 1954, with the departure of that unit to Europe, that 312th FBW managed to take over these facilities; at that time there were no F-86Hs with the Wing, however. Wayne Heise, one of the new officers, recalls that when it came to picking up their new F-86Hs, things became interesting:

Our well-qualified short course F-86F pilots were loaded on the local civilian air liner with parachutes and helmets and flown to Columbus to check out – 'one trip around the pattern' and fly as a group back to Clovis. Some of the airplanes arrived as planned; however, the majority of them were scattered at various Air Force bases along the route with various maintenance problems and hairy stories on how they got that way.

The one-hundred-and-fifteenth F-86H, 52-2090, introduced the four-cannon armament of definitive H-models; these aircraft were known as F-86H-5s to differentiate them. Previously known as the T-160, the production M-39/M-39A gun of the F-86H-5 had a 20mm bore and in total weighed 286lb (129kg) more than the 0.50-calibre machine-gun installation. However, the cannon was far superior as a weapon, and proved devastating in practice. Lessons learned in the F-86F GunVal programme were put to good use in the F-86H's cannon installation; chief among these was the use of the C-shaped muzzle fittings to dispel gas during firing. The first F-86H-5 was retained on bailment at Columbus and Inglewood and five early models were assigned to Eglin AFB's 3200th Proof Test Group for armament testing. From November 1954 413th FDW at George AFB also began to

In April 1956 430th FBS deployed from Clovis AFB, New Mexico to Chaumont AB in France. The unit's aircraft are seen here at Thule AB in Greenland on the way over. In 1957 these aircraft were replaced at Clovis by F-100s and those Sabres still in France were scrapped. Lee Gollwitzer

Seen stored at Davis Monthan, this 413th FDW F-86H still shows the gaudy Dayglo markings associated with the unit. As Frosty Sheridan puts it, 'Most pilots I know hated the colors because we looked like a flock of parrots being flushed when we took off.' MAP

receive the aircraft following activation, and in January 1955 the first F-86H-5s began to equip a third 'H' wing, the 474th FBW at Clovis AFB.

On 11 June 1953 the USAF had approved an additional contract AF-22305 for 300 F-86H-10s, known as NA-203. These aircraft would differ only in minor detail from the H-5, though the empty weight was reduced by 187lb (84kg). Aircraft 53-1439, the two-hundred-and-eleventh H-10 introduced an external AC power receptacle, and other small electronic equipment changes were made. The first H-10, 53-1229, was delivered on 9 February 1955, the final aircraft of this order being assigned during the summer. The last ten H-10s had wing slats installed as standard, which considerably improved low-speed handling and reduced the number of F-86H landing accidents. The slatted, extended span wing was then retrofitted on to most in-service F-86Hs.

Many F-86H-10s were assigned to 50th FBW in Europe beginning in June 1955,

replacing fighter-bomber F-86Fs in the three squadrons at Hahn AB. These aircraft arrived by ship at Brindisi and were then ferried initially to the 10th FBS, with the other squadrons within the Wing converting by the end of the year. In April 1956 the Wing began to move across to Toul AB in France, finishing the relocation in July. French objections to the assignment of nuclear weapons in their country often led to strange situations in daily life: should an F-86H require the fitting of a Mk 12 weapon it had to fly over to a German USAF base to be armed. Despite the objections, the unit remained in France and underwent heavy air-to-air gunnery training on the Cazaux range.

The fifth USAF F-86H wing was activated at Seymour Johnson AFB, North Carolina in July 1956, the 83rd Fighter Day Wing flying the cannon-armed F-86H for just over a year before converting on to F-100 Super Sabres. The final unit to equip was the famed

4th Fighter Day Wing. Reformed at Seymour Johnson AFB after its return from the Far East on 8 December 1957, the unit took over all 83rd FDW's Sabres on the same day. 4th FDW then flew the F-86H until early 1958 when it also received F-100s.

An Interlude: the US Air Force Reserve

For a brief period in 1957 the Air Force Reserve (AFRES) gained large numbers of F-86Hs with a view to finally equipping the service with relatively modern fighter jets. In the past, and for a long time, AFRES had been a poor cousin to the Air National Guard and units of the former had been flying obsolete F-80 Shooting Stars.

Tasked with AFRES F-86H training, the 2584th Reserve Flying Center (RFC) at Memphis received its first F-86H in May 1957 and by the end of June had seventy-five Sabres on strength. Further aircraft were then allotted to parent wings, enabling the conversion process to begin. Thus, in mid-July, 2234th RFC at Hanscom AFB,

The aftermath of Lt. Ron Crozier's wheels-up landing at Wheelus. His F86H, 52-5748, is seen here receiving replacement flaps, speed brakes, etc., prior to recovery back to Hahn AB for more permanent repairs. Lee Gollwitzer

A young Lee Gollwitzer in the cockpit of F-86H 53-1243. The red fuselage band denoted that it was assigned to 430th FBS flight commander Capt. Blunenstein. Lee Gollwitzer

Massachusetts, 2589th RFC at Dobbins AFB, Georgia, and the NAS Dallas-based 2596th RFC started to receive Sabres. These aircraft began conversion from F-80s, allowing the 89th FBW at Hanscom, 482nd FBW at Dobbins and 448th FBW at Dallas to start Sabre flying, in addition to the 26th FBS at Youngstown, Ohio and the 439th FBW at Selfridge, Michigan. These units should not be confused with regular USAF squadrons and wings. However, in the autumn of 1957 a change in policy led to the withdrawal of all F-86Hs from the AFRES; for the foreseeable future the Reserve would be assigned transport aircraft instead. The last AFRES F-86H left Memphis in mid-November 1957.

Final Days with the USAF

The USAF's use of the F-86Hs was relatively short; 413th FDW received F-100s at George AFB in 1956, and the 312th and the 474th FBW at Clovis went the same way that year. In April 1956 one of the 474th's squadrons, the 430th FBS, deployed to Europe in the first F-86H flight across the Atlantic. The Squadron's aircraft were originally based at Chaumont AB in France, moving to Toul in mid-April. Gunnery missions were then flown at Wheelus AB in Libya, and, when the parent wing began to convert to

F-100s back at Clovis in autumn 1957, the 430th FBS's F-86Hs were ferried to Bordeaux for scrapping.

The French-based 50th FBW received F-100Ds in 1957 and chose to scrap their aircraft rather than have them shipped home. They were reclaimed at Bordeaux in late 1957. That low point effectively marked the end of USAF F-86H service, apart from THE 4th FDW which continued flying the type into early 1958. However, the F-86H went on to see much greater use with the Air National Guard, with which the type became synonymous.

The Accident Record

Over the years some negative opinions have been expressed concerning the F-86H's 'poor' accident record. However, while it is true that the early 'hard edge' aircraft did account for a number of accidents in the landing pattern, it is equally true that there were a higher than average number of junior pilots flying the aircraft. Lee Gollwitzer, a pilot with 430th FBS at Clovis AFB remembers that some accidents were just bizarre:

One anecdote I recall is when Lt Col Davis was returning from the factory with a brand-new 'H' to Clovis AFB. He entered initial and when he pulled back and started his pitch-out, the

next thing he knew he was outside of the plane, automatically ejected. He pulled his 'D' ring, the chute opened and he landed safely on the airbase. The plane continued on for about 52 miles [84km] before crashing near Hearford, Texas. The cause was a faulty ejection-seat system.

Another interesting story took place in Tripoli [Wheelus], North Africa. Lt Ron Crozier, part of a flight of four 'H' models flying south from Europe, pitched out for his landing, but, unknown to him, his landing gear failed to extend. He probably did not hear the warning from the tower because of the noise the warning horn was making in the cockpit. Upon rounding out, he settled down on the drop tanks which exploded like two napalm bombs. He threw the coal to the engine and skidded 3,200ft [980m] down the runway before – lucky him – he became airborne again. As he was turning back on downwind, he heard the tower alert all aircraft that the runway was closed due to a crash. Ron radioed the tower that he was the crash, and, turning base, he put the gear down, got three 'safe' indicators and continued to a normal landing. The plane was scraped pretty thin on the bottom, but it was flown back to Germany to full service.

One problem that did occur with the early F-86Hs was that the J73 engine's inlet guide vanes would freeze open after the throttle was pulled back, normally in the landing pattern. The problem was caused by differential expansion of the blade and

Above: **This ex-Japanese Sabre '56-2827' was converted to QF-86F target configuration for the US Navy. It was received at China Lake NAS in California on 13 March 1986 and stricken on 2 November 1987, presumably shot down.**

This picture was taken on 6 August 1987 and shows the black destruct-system status-panel on the fuselage, a red light marked 'A' signifying that the system was armed, and the green 'S' light indicating 'safe'. USN

Above: **This WS10 Sabre 5 (c/n 880) was photographed from a sister ship in summer 1958. BB-120 was piloted on this occasion by Uffz. Dieter Runz. Runz was killed on 7 November 1958 in the crash of another WS10 Sabre.** E. Witfer via Peter Sickinger

Right: **Reloading the bottom pair of 0.50-calibres on a 512th FIS F-86F-25, at Nouasseur AB in May 1954. Like many USAFE F-86F units, the 512th took its Sabres to French Morocco for gunnery training.** Richard T. Grace

Above: **These F-86E(M) aircraft of 4° Aerobrigata, Italian AF are painted in the standard 'delivery' camouflage.** Stato Maggiore Aeronautica via Mike Fox

Below: **The Berlin crisis saw the 101st TFS, Massachusetts ANG, called to active duty and deploy to Phalsbourg AB, France on 1 November 1961. This shot, taken at Phalsbourg, shows a 101st TFS F-86H on that 'Stair Step' deployment.** George Getchell

Above: **53-4078, a new F-86D-60, is seen here in 331st FIS colours at Yuma in 1955. The unit had just traded in their older F-86D-45s for these, some of the last 'Dogs' built. Note the B-29 target tug in the background.** Master Sgt D. Cleeton via Marty Isham

Below: **Based at Wright-Patterson AFB, the 97th FIS operated some of the first F-86Ds delivered. However, in late 1954 these were traded in for later D-55 and -60 models, seen here. This view, taken in early 1955, shows the unit's stylized 'Devil Cat' fuselage flash.** D.N. Drew via Marty Isham

Right: **On 25 June 1951 Lt Col Glenn Eagleston's Sabre took just three MiG hits – two 23mm in the rear fuselage and one 37mm round in the gun bay. Though Eagleston recovered to Suwon for a belly landing, the damage was enough to write off the Sabre, 49-1281.** John Henderson

Below: **Registered N98279 for delivery to the US Army, this newly-converted QF-86E was previously RCAF 23323. Note that the gun blast panel has been faired over and a warning light panel fitted on the fuselage side.** Author

Below: **Sailing to Korea aboard the USS** Cape Esperance **in November 1950, these aircraft are some of the many that were requisitioned by 4th FIW for Korea. Protective grease has been applied to stop the effects of salt water** corrosion; it did not. Many aircraft had to be repaired on arrival in Japan. The Sabre in the foreground, 49-1128, had previously served with 60th FIS of 33rd Fighter Group. John Henderson

Above: **Mitsubishi converted eighteen early-model F-86Fs to RF-86F configuration for the Japanese Air Self-Defense Force in the early 1960s. These aircraft are from 501st Hikotai, a recce unit formed specifically for Sabre operations in December 1961.** MAP

Below: **One of the first privately-owned Sabres in America, red and white-trimmed N231X was owned by Banker's Leasing of Washington, DC from 1972. A Canadair Sabre 5, this aircraft was bought by Flight Systems in 1982 and reregistered as N91FS.** MAP

Above: **C5-2 was the second Sabre delivered to Spain in June 1955, an F-86F-25, 51-13239.** Mike Fox

Below: **55-3822 was one of a number of QF-86Fs to serve with the Pacific Missile Test Center at Point Mugu, Ca. Ex-Japanese, the aircraft was received from conversion at Inyokern on 6 November 1989 and survived the Navy's drone programme, only to be placed on the China Lake gunnery ranges.** Michael Anselmo, October 1990

Above: **51-2805, an F-86E-10 of 191st FIS Utah ANG, at Salt Lake City. This machine was assigned only briefly, from March to August 1958, when the unit converted to F-86Ls.** via Mike Fox

Below: **One of a number of F-86As originally slated for 31st Fighter Escort Wing at Turner AFB, 48-152 was instead assigned to 1st Fighter Group at March AFB. In August 1951 it was reassigned to 93rd FIS at Kirtland AFB in New Mexico, whose markings it wears here.** Richard Escola

Above: **Not often photographed, this blue-trimmed F-86A from 75th FIS at Suffolk County AFB was assigned to the Squadron in January 1953. Like so many other F-86As, it ended its days at Davis Monthan AFB, being authorized for reclamation there in September 1958.** Marty Isham

Below: **The last Royal Thai AF unit to fly the F-86F, 43 Squadron at Takhli AB, retired its last aircraft in 1972. The machine in the foreground, 52-5017, had previously served with 4530th CCTW at Nellis AFB in Nevada.** Jon Lake

Above: **This F-86A was flown by Lt J.W. 'Whip' Leatherbee of 334th FIS. The unit markings are unusual; soon after their arrival in Korea the Sabres gained less nondescript squadron badges. This aircraft, heavily damaged in the 14 June 1951 'Bedcheck Charlie' raid on Suwon, survived and is today preserved by the Planes of Fame Museum at Chino, CA.** Leatherbee via John Henderson

Left: **In addition to converting Canadair Sabre 5s to drone configuration for the US Army, Mojave-based Flight Systems Incorporated was also contracted to tow aerial gunnery targets for the US Air Force in the early 1980s. N89FS was one of five ex-Luftwaffe Sabre 6s acquired from the defunct Haydon-Baillie aircraft collection in 1979. The aircraft has been retrofitted with a '6-3' wing.** Melvyn Hiscock

Below: **94th FIS moved to George AFB in California during July 1950, before the three 1st FIW squadrons dispersed across the United States. 49-1207 was photographed at George in June 1953 just weeks before it was reassigned to McLellan AFB for maintenance.** B. Butcher via Marty Isham

This F-86H was the originally the personal mount of Maj 'Moon' Mullins, commander of the 1st Fighter Day Squadron at George AFB. When Mullins departed for a Korean assignment, he passed the plane to 1st Lt 'Frosty' Sheridan, who flew it in these colours until the heavy maintenance workload allowed a repaint. *Frosty Sheridan*

housing in the engine, and caused the engine to stall and flame-out. Many aircraft were lost in this way; 1st Lt Edward Kowalczyk of 428th FBS was fortunate; he survived. Kowalczyk was flying 53-1256 in a group of two aircraft from Foster AFB to Clovis on 18 February 1956. Though he had encountered engine problems *en route*, he had switched to emergency fuel and continued smoothly. However, as he turned into the traffic pattern at Clovis and retarded the engine through the 'take-off' position, the engine flamed-out. With no chance to restart, pilot and aircraft parted company to the tune of $680,000.

Other similar problems were encountered by 1st Lt Gerald Lewis of 534th FDS, whose Sabre, 52-5752, flamed-out during a go-around at Seymour Johnson AFB on 5 December 1957. Again the pilot ejected successfully. 1st Lt Lawrence Johnson of 312th FBW also had a lucky escape on 6 December 1956 as he neared Goodfellow AFB on a flight from Clovis. The engine in Johnson's aircraft, 53-1254, suddenly exploded and amid a shower of sparks and fire; the pilot ejected to safety. The F-86H's safety record is best summed up by Lee Gollwitzer: 'I don't think it was any better or worse than any other fighter that would be put into the hands of low-time second lieutenants. Safety comes with seasoning and experience.'

F-86H – a Pilot's View, by 'Frosty' Sheridan, 1st FDS, 413th FDW George AFB

I can say the F-86H was as safe as the guy flying it. It had some nasty little tricks but on the whole it was a very straightforward flying machine and a dream after the F-84. I flew the 'H' from the summer of '54 to early '56. During that time it never gave me a bad time, with the exception of a fire-warning light and reported smoke and possible fire from my squadron Operations Officer, who I didn't have a lot of faith in. Upon reporting this to me, he immediately departed from sight. My feelings proved correct. No fire.

It's my belief the primary reasons for most F-86H accidents were human. If you look back at the experience level of most pilots who initially flew the plane you will find it was 'zero' in the operational arena. Approximately 80 per cent of the pilots were just out of Gunnery School and flight training. In addition, we were almost all straight wing F-80 and F-84 pilots before moving into our first swept-wing jet. I can't remember one pilot who had been to F-86 Gunnery School. Training in the plane consisted of taking the Technical Order home and reading it. We did have a maintenance school on the plane (Clovis Air Force Base, New Mexico) and many of us attended that, but it was well after we had flown the plane for some time and covered nothing about

flying. Truthfully, we taught each other how to fly it by trial and error.

Acceptance of the jet by our upper ranks was not that much of a problem. In fact, we had an ace or two at Wing HQ. In our case we initially had a great squadron commander who loved the jet. He gave me his 'H' when he got his orders to Korea. When he departed they gave the squadron to a base HQ paper-pusher because he had done an outstanding job walking the soon-to-be-general's dog. He refused to fly at night and out of sight of the field. Although he had the squadron for almost a year he never completed his check out in the 86 or the F-100. Eventually, he was returned to a less hazardous position as Base Operations Officer, by an inspecting general, at some out-of-the-way podunk airfield, thank God. During his reign we were restricted to fields we had already made at least one landing at. This some of us solved by declaring an emergency in flight and landing wherever we found a new airfield to add to our approved list. Then we were usually told to await an escort home when the plane was 'fixed'. If you held out long enough the ops officer would get exasperated and order you to fly home alone. Where there is a will...

Our transition into the 'H' was a bit haphazard. First, some of the pilots had not actually flown in several months. Most had been getting time in L-20s and C-47s, which consisted of sleeping in the back end. Putting fifteen to twenty pilots in the back end of a C-47 and flying all over the US was a normal procedure and I doubt if half ever made it to the cockpit. From this we went into checking-out, which consisted of getting four hours a month in four flights a week apart. Not enough to stay proficient in a new plane. Our instructors were seldom the same person so there was little continuity in the training. The guys maintaining them were as new as we were. My crew chief had 6hr experience on F-86s. Zero on 'H's. We learned the plane together, during which time I saw some terrible things done to the planes. I was 'high time', I think, as far as experience being a crew chief, aircraft and engine (three years).

Our Group and my Squadron were provided with pilots from another Group who served as our flight commanders. These pilots had just arrived from Korea but had missed combat in that theater and were pretty low-time pilots themselves (mostly new 1st lieutenants) and in many cases were not of the quality a flight commander should have been. In my Squadron we initially had a commander with a solid, positive attitude, but he was transferred to Korea and we received an individual who had little experience and whose only love for the jet was when his name was painted on its side. He preferred to get his flying time in the C-47 transport and refused to fly jet fighters at night. Several of the flight commanders openly expressed reservations about the 'H' and jets in general and ended up departing for airline jobs. Good riddance. Within a short period of time I was up-graded to flight leader and this was when I really learned how to fly the F-86.

I had a very good friend, Lt Jimmy Goode (now deceased) who had the same 'let's go do it' attitude as I did, and we slowly became proficient enough to where we could hold our own against some of the combat-experienced pilots within the Wing. After the F-84 – underpowered, heavy but with a big, straight wing – the '86H' was a dream. Power and performance made you forget that you could not bend the 86 around the landing pattern and slip the hell out of it if you screwed up. You could cross control the heck out of the 84 to bleed off altitude and airspeed on final approach. I personally would bend the 86 around the corner, final turn, slip and slide until one day when another more experienced pilot took me aside and explained the facts of life to me. It was just a matter of time until I pulled it too tight because there was never anything mentioned in the training I got that examined the difference between the wings. The hard-winged 'H' couldn't match a straight-winged 84 in the pattern. I think this may have been a factor in a few mishaps that we experienced.

Flying time was another problem. With nothing like a simulator around, hands-on experience was slow in coming. During the time I flew the 'H' I had to attend three schools, not including the 'H' ground school. A tour with the Army as a forward air controller for four months didn't help much either. Grounding for up to a month for aircraft problems added to our low flying hours.

F-86H-1 52-2074 ended its life as an F-104 chase plane for Lockheed, hence the semi-obliterated 'shooting star' emblem on the forward fuselage. It was last seen here, at Riverside, CA in the early 1970s. MAP

Aircraft maintenance deliveries for flying were dismal. Since I was an ex-crew chief (F-80s), I helped maintain my own plane but that did not mean I got to fly it when it was ready. My check-out took four months to complete due to availability of aircraft, averaging a flight a week until the very end, when I was given a plane and told to complete my own check-out. Surviving that I became an operational pilot.

During this period we experienced a problem with 'inadvertent ejections'. Initial cause was suggested to be accidentally pulling the ejection handle during flight. I believe Clovis AFB had the brunt of this problem but it affected all the 'Hs'. After many stupid statements about accidentally pulling handles during flight, the problem was traced to the canopy external release handle, which was held in place by a small, clip-like device. Evidently, the clip size was reduced to save weight or something to that affect and during flight the

vibrations allowed it to slip, releasing the handle into the airstream. When there was enough force to rotate the handle 90 degrees into the air, the canopy fired, followed by the seat, depending upon how tight the tolerances of the ejection system were. 'The pilot may or not hear the ejection seat fire', became the statement of the month. Evidently a few souls were rather surprised to see their plane flying away as they sat in their ejection seats. I did have a handle come loose; however, I was able to 'safe' the seat and land. After that they informed us that safing the seat would not stop the sequence of ejection after the handle opened. Oops!

Another problem early on was the engine quitting. While at Clovis they lost a commander when his plane flamed-out. Asking a wing man the best glide speed (something I found very strange, not knowing the best glide speed), he proceeded to deploy the speed brakes to slow to best glide speed rather than trading speed for altitude as he headed for home. He eventually crashed just short of the runway killing himself.

Fires with no indications in the cockpit, the problem my operations officer suspected I had, was a problem that we had at George AFB. It killed my Flight Commander, Lt Ray Fogle. With no indications, the tail burned off as he was turning final. It was briefed to us that there had been other cases of this happening. Here the saying became, 'The pilot may or may not hear the explosion.' This actually later appeared in the tech manual but I can't remember if it was for the F-100 or -86. While flying the 'H' I loved the time, but, as said, there was just not enough. During that two

Relatively few F-86H-1s went to the Air National Guard, and many of those that did flew with the 167th FIS West Virginia ANG at Martinsburg Municipal Airport. This aircraft survives and is being restored. MAP

years I also checked out in the L-20, C-47, B-26, T-33 and H-19 in an attempt to get some serious flying time. I wish the 'H' had had a slatted wing [later, of course, it did] and there were rumors of a 'poor man's afterburner', which would have provided another dimension to our dog-fighting ability which was pretty good. Our best fights were with the Navy which had their 'H' model [the FJ-3]. The Palmdale beacon was the gathering place for all (AF, Navy and Marines) who wanted to stretch the envelope and I spent some of my most joyful minutes there learning my trade.

Because of the sudden build-up of the USAF during these years, priorities would change from day to day. The reason we F-84 pilots were sent to a base getting F-86s was because the F-86 people (class just before ours) going through training at Nellis AFB were pulled out just before completing training and sent to C-119s. (A reason for suicide right there.) We were the next out of the training pipeline to fill the void at George AFB and Clovis AFB, all the time expecting to go to F-84s. Their loss our gain. I had some every good friends in the F-86 class at Nellis and they were devastated. Upon arrival at George we were assigned to the 413 TFG. For months we had something of the order of seventy-five 2nd lieutenants, one colonel (referred to as 'Ravin' Lavin', a strange duck) and one T.Sergeant in the Group. It was a pretty good mob and consisted of perhaps a little more than half ex-enlisted men. Slowly we were assigned commanders and operations officers. Finally, when they realized we needed some experience in F-86s they rounded up the boys who had just finished·their tour in Korea (non-combat). Many of these guys were just waiting to get out of the AF and return to civilian life. A couple were less than enthusiastic about flying the 86. After Lt Fogle got killed we received an F-84 (combat-

experienced) pilot who, while lacking the 86 experience, had a good attitude about flying. This situation did not hold for each squadron. The 22nd and 34th (I believe) both had combat-experienced commanders. Several of their Flt Cos, while lacking combat, were very aggressive pilots and great fun to be with.

Considering all these factors, I think we did damn well with the 'H'. Another consideration in the feeling that things were not safe is that we were experiencing approximately a fatality a month at George but not all in the 'H'. We had another group that was preparing to deploy to Europe. Another had just received the first F-100As. We did a good job scattering plane parts around California. Of the guys I hung around with we had three fatalities and three major accidents. Of course, we also had two

fatalities in automobile accidents and five other wrecks so the attitude was kind of devil-may-care. Once we got into the F-100 it actually got worse and made the 'H' look like a loving grandmother. I won't mention the F-105.

The Air National Guard

Beginning with the withdrawal of USAF F-86H-1s in mid-1957, many Air National Guard squadrons began to re-equip with the type during the late summer of that year. One of the first units to receive the H model was 167th FBW, West Virginia ANG. Based at Martinsburg, the squadron began to receive

Air National Guard units took great pride in the appearance of their aircraft, as exemplified by this 121st FIS DC ANG F-86H. This machine is now displayed at Shortsville, NY. Howard Levy via Mike Fox

The Berlin crisis saw the 101st TFS Massachusetts ANG called to active duty and deploy to Phalsbourg AB, France on 1 November 1961. This shot, taken at Phalsbourg, shows a 101st TFS F-86H on that 'Stair Step' deployment. MAP

USAF F-86H Units

4th FDW (334th, 335th and 336th FDS), Seymour Johnson AFB, NC

50th FBW (10th, 81st and 417th FBS), Hahn AB, Germany and Toul AB, France

83rd FDW (532nd, 533rd and 534th FDS), Seymour Johnson AFB, NC

312th FBW (386th, 387th and 388th FBS), Clovis AFB, NM

413th FDW (1st, 21st and 34th FDS), George AFB, CA

474th FBW (428th, 429th and 430th FBS), Clovis AFB, NM

3595th CCTW, Nellis AFB, NV

The 136th FIS New York ANG converted from F-94Bs to F-86Hs in October 1957 at Niagara Falls Municipal Airport. The Sabres left the squadron in favour of F-100s during August 1960. Larry Milberry via Mike Fox

F-86H-1s in favour of F-86Es during August 1957. F-86H-5 and -10s soon followed into ANG service.

On the night of 12/13 August 1961 the sudden construction of the Berlin Wall signified the start of the so-called 'Berlin crisis'. As a result, numerous USAF units were called upon to strengthen European forces and, in addition, a number of ANG squadrons were called to active duty. Significantly, three ANG F-86H squadrons were called up and sent to Europe. The 101st and the 131st Tactical Fighter Squadrons (TFS), Massachusetts ANG and 138th TFS New York ANG were activated on 1 October under Operation Stair Step, deploying their F-86Hs to Phalsbourg AB in France under Tactical Air Command (TAC). The three squadrons were further assigned to 102nd Tactical Fighter Wing, under the command of Maj Gen Walter Sweeney, who had been on the Hiroshima B-29

raid. The three squadrons deployed from Loring AFB, Maine through Goose Bay in Canada, to Sondrestrom in Greenland and on to Keflavik in Iceland. Staging from there to Prestwick in Scotland, the Wing's aircraft officially arrived in France on 11 November. Into 1962 the Stair Step augmentation of USAFE remained, and, despite protests from the West, the Berlin Wall stood firm. To maintain proficiency the three squadrons rotated through Wheelus AB in Libya for gunnery practice and also flew regular, simulated tactical missions throughout Europe. Typical of the sorties was a three-ship, close-support, practice mission against armoured vehicles near Kirm in Germany on 17 April. The three Sabres, all from 138th TFS, were directed on to the target by a forward air controller, but one of the aircraft hit trees on the third pass. The pilot Capt William Kelly and his F-86H, 53-1234 were lost.

On a lighter note, 18 May 1962 marked 'Sabre Night', a strictly unofficial letting-off steam at Phalsbourg. Before this, 102nd TFW Sabres had flown throughout Europe dropping leaflets on NATO Sabre bases, inviting all and sundry to the gathering. The guest speaker on the occasion was the Luftwaffe ace Adolph Galland.

By the end of the summer it was clear that there would be no response from the Soviets, and in August many of the ANG units flew their aircraft back to the United States. The three F-86H squadrons returned in that month, reverting to state control on 20 August. During the Stair Step deployment, four Sabres and two pilots were lost.

Further activations were carried out as a result of the USS *Pueblo* crisis from January 1968, and on 13 May two ANG F-86H squadrons – the 104th TFS, Maryland and the 138th TFS, New York – were called to active duty and deployed to Cannon AFB, New Mexico. The idea was that the F-86H squadrons would serve as a Forward Air Control and Air Liaison

Air National Guard F-86H Units

101st FIS, TFS Massachusetts ANG, Logan Airport, Boston

102nd FIS New York ANG, Floyd Bennett NAS (June-September 1958 only)

104th FIS, TFS Maryland ANG, Andrews AFB and Glenn L. Martin Airport, Baltimore

115th FIS California ANG, Van Nuys

118th FIS Connecticut ANG, Bradley Field

119th TFS New Jersey ANG, Atlantic City

121st FIS, TFS District of Columbia ANG, Andrews AFB

131st FIS, TFS Massachusetts ANG, Barnes Field

136th FIS, TFS New York ANG, Niagara Falls Municipal Airport

137th FIS, TFS New York ANG, Westchester

138th FIS, TFS New York ANG, Hancock Field, Syracuse

139th FIS, TFS New York ANG, Schenectady Airport

141st TFS New Jersey ANG, McGuire AFB

142nd FIS, TFS Delaware ANG, New Castle County Airport

167th FIS, TFS West Virginia ANG, Martinsburg Municipal Airport

195th FIS California ANG, Van Nuys

198th FIS Puerto Rico ANG, San Juan International Airport

Officer Tactical Training Wing, but, after six months in New Mexico the idea was scrapped. In that time the F-86Hs had towed targets for the F-4s at George AFB in California. Both squadrons returned to state control on 20 December 1968. However, the Vietnam War had one major effect on the National Guard's F-86H squadrons. By the beginning of 1967 it was becoming clear that significant USAF losses over the war zone would mean that ANG squadrons would

Not often photographed, the California ANG's two Van Nuys-based squadrons, the 115th and the 195th FIS both flew the F-86H for a time in 1959. Equally rarely seen, two of the 195th's outgoing F-86Fs and an F-86E are seen in the background. J.M.G. Gradidge

Rarely depicted, this US Navy F-86H aggressor aircraft was operated by VX-4 out of China Lake. The F-86H helped to develop tactics and training for Vietnam-bound pilots. MAP

have to wait to be equipped with newer types. Thus F-86H (and F-89J Scorpion) squadrons would continue to operate their ageing aircraft. In line with the south-east Asia-based fighters, many ANG F-86Hs were repainted in camouflage colours in 1966.

By 1970 the final F-86H squadrons began to be assigned the A-37B Dragonfly, and the last military Sabre flight was carried out on 4 August when 104th TFS F-86H 53-1370 was flown in to Seymour Johnson AFB for preservation.

MiG Simulator

After their withdrawal from ANG service a number of F-86Hs were turned over to the Navy for use in aggressor training. It had not gone unnoticed that the F-86H's similar performance to those of the MiG-17 and -19 could prove useful in training pilots for Vietnam duty. During 16-20 August 1966 'Feather Duster II' missions were flown against a number of USAF types at Nellis AFB. As the F-86H was deemed to be the closest to the Vietnamese MiG-19, ANG Sabres were used to simulate this type. In thirty-three sorties the F-86Hs tangled with F-4, F-5, F-100, F-104 and F-105 aircraft to evaluate fighter tactics for the USAF machines and, crucially, highlighted that in low-speed dogfights the F-86H (and the MiG) had a distinct advantage.

By 1969 the US Navy had managed to capture its own MiG-19 and in November the Navy loaned two 104th TFS F-86Hs for use in a top-secret programme called 'Have Drill' at Nellis AFB. Using the captured MiG-19, the two Sabres were flown by ANG pilots Lt Cols Joe Maisch and Les Waltman to gain details of the MiG's weaknesses in combat. The three-day flight evaluation also proved that the Sabre had a higher rate of roll, but that the MiG turned tighter and slowed down quicker; it is thought that the Sabres gained the Navy serial numbers Bu.158436 and 158437 for this programme.

In 1970 Navy squadron VX-4 at NAS

F-86H Production		
Serial	Block No.	Construction Nos
52-1975 and 1976	F-86H-1-NA	187-1 and 2
52-1977 to 2089	F-86H-1-NH	187-3 to 115
52-2090 to 2124	F-86H-5-NH	187-116 to 150
52-5729 to 5753	F-86H-5-NH	187-151 to 175
53-1229 to 1528	F-86H-10-NH	203-1 to 300

Specifications: F-86H-10

POWERPLANT
General Electric J73-GE-3D or -3E of 8,920lb (4,045kg) static thrust

WEIGHTS
empty weight:	13,836lb (6,276kg)
gross weight:	24,296lb (11,021kg)

DIMENSIONS
wingspan:	39ft 1in (11.92m)
length:	38ft 10in (11.83m)
height:	14ft 11in (4.56m)
wing area:	313.4sq ft (29.15sq m)

PERFORMANCE
maximum speed (clean):
at sea level:	692mph (1,113km/h)
at 30,000ft:	617mph (992km/h at 9,144m)
initial climb rate:	12,900ft/min (3,931m/min)
service ceiling:	50,800ft (15,483m)
combat radius:	519 miles (835km)
maximum ferry range:	1,810 miles (2,912km)

One of up to thirty QF-86H radio-controlled target conversions for the US Navy, this aircraft had previously flown with 1st FDS at George AFB. Note the datalink aerials on the nose and fuselage. All QF-86Hs carried the red and white, high visibility bands seen here, though most often the aircraft retained their camouflage schemes until withdrawn in 1979. Author

Point Mugu in California began to receive ex-ANG Sabres to continue the 'aggressor' role, with up to thirty-two being assigned. At about the same time, the usefulness of the F-86H as a high-speed, unmanned, target drone became apparent, and most of the surviving Navy Sabres were converted for use in this role. Following conversion, the F-86H target aircraft could be flown either 'live' by a pilot, or in a 'no onboard live operator' (NOLO) configuration from a ground station. Based at the Pacific Missile Test Center at Point Mugu, and also at the Naval Weapons Center, China Lake, the redesignated QF-86H drone aircraft flew until 1979 when the last flying aircraft was shot down. The QF-86Hs contributed significantly to the Navy's missile programmes, notably the AIM-54 Phoenix.

CHAPTER FIVE

Development and Export

Mitsubishi F-86F-40

Following on from North American's build of 280 export F-86F-40s, NAA and Mitsubishi in Japan signed a licence-production agreement on 13 July 1954 for a significant number of Sabres to be assembled in Japan. To begin production, NAA began project NA-231 on 19 August 1955, and built seventy sets of parts under contract AF-31077, which was signed on 28 June 1956. These aircraft were assigned USAF serials 55-5048 to -5117, but upon their assembly at Mitsubishi's Nagoya plant the aircraft gained Japanese Air Self Defense Force (JASDF) serials. The first Mitsubishi-assembled F-86F-40 was flown on 9 August 1956 and by the end of the year four had been accepted by JASDF.

In total, 300 F-86Fs were assembled by Mitsubishi, the remaining batches being for 110 aircraft (contract AF-31748, signed on 28 September 1956) and a further 120 (contract AF-35431, signed on 24 April 1958) to complete the run. Severe typhoon damage at the Nagoya plant in September 1959 caused upheaval in the assembly process, and the final three aircraft were not completed until 25 February 1961. They were then accepted into JASDF service two days later.

Mitsubishi also converted eighteen Sabres to RF-86F specification, using modification kits supplied by NAA. All aircraft for modification came from the US-supplied batch of F-86F-25 and -30s originally taken over by the Japanese in 1955. Similar in configuration to the 'Haymaker' RF-86Fs, the Japanese-converted aircraft featured a pair of oblique-

This unremarkable-looking F-86F seen at China Lake was in fact the first Mitsubishi-assembled aircraft and entered Japanese Air Self-Defense Force service on 20 September 1956 as 62-7701. MAP

Specifications: Mitsubishi RF-86F

Weights, dimensions and performance as for the F-86E/F except:

WEIGHTS
empty weight:	11,464lb (5,198kg)
loaded weight:	19,599lb (8,888kg)
max take-off weight:	20,194lb (9,157kg)

PERFORMANCE
maximum speed:	656mph (1,055km/h) at sea level
cruising speed:	506mph (814km/h)
initial climb rate:	9,320ft/min (2,840m/min)
range:	890 miles (1,432 km)

mounted K-22 cameras in the gun bay positions and a single downward-pointing K-17 in the centre forward fuselage. Conversion was carried out by Mitsubishi Heavy Industries at Nagoya, starting in 1961. The converted aircraft were delivered from August 1961, the last being taken over by the JASDF in January 1962.

F-86K Interceptor for Export

On 22 January 1953 Air Materiel Command (AMC) issued a request for a Mutual Defense Assistance Program (MDAP) interceptor, in order to begin equipping NATO countries. Despite firm stipulations that the aircraft would have a two-man crew, NAA looked to the designing of a simplified version of the F-86D, which would also incorporate fire-control equipment in place of the still-secret Hughes E-4 system. This equipment, known as the MG-4 fire-control system, was designed and built by NAA's Electro-Mechanical Division at Downey. It was linked to an AN/APA-84 computer, which would provide intercept

Mitsubishi F-86F Licence Production		
Serial	Type	Construction Nos
55-5048 to 5117	F-86F-40	231-1 to 70
56-2773 to 2882	F-86F-40	238-1 to 110
57-6338 to 6457	F-86F-40	256-1 to 120

The first YF-86K 52-3630 on the ramp at Inglewood in 1954. The aircraft initially flew without the cannon armament installed. NAA

information to a cockpit-mounted scope in the same manner as the F-86D. To give a back-up to this system, the aircraft would also mount an A-4 gunsight for manual control. North American's designers had no problems in modifying the design to accept the specified four 20mm cannon armament in place of the rocket system, but differences in weight between the two installations required an 8in (203mm) forward fuselage extension to regain the position of the centre of

gravity. In most other respects the new aircraft, accepted by AMC as the F-86K, differed little from the F-86D and was fitted with an afterburning J47-GE-33 engine of 7,650lb (3,469kg) thrust.

In order to furnish two prototypes of the F-86K, contract AF-25402 was signed on 14 May 1953 and allotted two F-86D-40 aircraft from the Inglewood production line to be converted to YF-86K prototypes. As NA-205s, the first of these machines, 52-3630, was flown at Los Angeles on 15 July 1954. The NAA test pilot Raymond Morris flew the aircraft on this occasion, it then being unarmed and powered by a J47-GE-17B. Armament for

production versions would be a group of four 20mm M-24A1 cannon with 132 rounds per gun, firing at 700 rounds per minute. The second prototype, 52-3804, was completed initially with just the lower pair of cannon, but later in the test programme both sets were fitted. It is interesting to note that the upper pair of cannon, which had their gun muzzles adjacent to the engine air intake, were fitted with the gas-dispersing C-shaped fitting as seen on GunVal F-86Fs and cannon-armed F-86Hs. The lower and thus rearmost cannon, with its muzzle a good 30in (762mm) aft of the intake, was not configured in this way. However, to further purge gas from the gun compartment, five prominent ducts were cut into the main access panel. Both prototypes were retained for testing by North American, eventually being scrapped at McLellan AFB in 1957.

FIAT in Italy signed a licence-production agreement on 16 May 1953, under which F-86Ks would be built at the company's Turin-Caselle plant from US-supplied components. Further to this agreement, on 18 May MDAP funds were committed for NAA to supply fifty sets of F-86K parts under contract AF-25402, signed on 28 June 1954. These aircraft would be assigned USAF serials, but after assembly they would wear Italian Matricola Militare (MM) serial numbers. Meanwhile, NAA was contracted under AF-26479 on 18 December 1953 to begin the construction of 120 NA-213 F-86Ks for delivery to Norway and the Netherlands. FIAT-assembled machines would then equip the French and the German air force, as well as the Italian.

The first NAA-built F-86K, 54-1231, was flown on 8 March 1955, and this aircraft was also retained by North Amer-

The first NAA-built F-86K was detached to Nellis AFB for cannon firing tests during 1955. It was finally delivered to the Norwegian AF in 1960. Howard Levy via Mike Fox

ican as the production-standard model. Deliveries were completed in December 1955, with sixty being shipped to the Royal Norwegian Air Force and fifty-nine to the Royal Netherlands Air Force. On 23 May, just over two months after the first NAA-built production model flew, the NAA representative Col Arthur DeBolt took FIAT's first machine into the air from Turin. Further contracts were subsequently signed with FIAT for F-86K assembly: seventy under NA-221 (con-

tract AF-28086, signed on 8 September 1955), fifty-six NA-232s (contract AF-30742, signed on 31 May 1956) and forty-five NA-242s (amended contract AF-30742, signed on 4 September 1956). Significantly, the last forty-five aircraft were fitted with the extended-span wing as used on the F-86F-40 and the F-86L model.

FIAT-assembled F-86Ks began to be assigned to Italian AF units in November 1955, and the last Turin-built Sabre was

YF-86K 52-3804 at NAA's Palmdale facility on 19 May 1956. The aircraft carries wing and tail-mounted cameras for recording cannon firing. This aircraft passed to McLellan AFB in December 1956 and was scrapped. Doug Olson via J.M.G. Gradidge

Specifications: F-86K

POWERPLANT
General Electric J47-GE-17B of 7,650lb (3,469kg) thrust with afterburner

WEIGHTS
empty weight:	13,367lb (6,061kg)
combat weight:	16,252lb (7,370kg)
maximum take-off weight: 20,171lb (9,147kg)	

DIMENSIONS
wingspan:	37ft 1in (11.3m); 39ft 1in (11.92m) for extended wing
length:	40ft 11in (12.49m)
height:	15ft (4.5m)
wing area:	287.9sq ft (26.78sq m); 313.4sq ft (29.15sq m) for extended wing

PERFORMANCE
maximum speed:	
at sea level:	692mph (1,113km/h)
at 40,000ft:	612 mph (984km/h at 12,192m)
initial climb rate:	12,000ft/min (3,657m/min)
service ceiling:	49,600ft (15,118m)
combat range:	272 miles (437km)
ferry range:	744 miles (1,197km)

F-86K Production		
Serial No.	Model	Construction Nos
52-3630	YF-86K	NA-205-1 (NAA)
52-3804	YF-86K	NA-205-2 (NAA)
53-8273 to 8322	F-86K	NA-207-1 to 50 (FIAT)
54-1231 to 1350	F-86K	NA-213-1 to 120 (NAA)
55-4811 to 4880	F-86K	NA-221-1 to 70 (FIAT)
55-4881 to 4936	F-86K	NA-232-1 to 56 (FIAT)
56-4116 to 4160	F-86K	NA-242-1 to 50 (FIAT)

received by the German Luftwaffe in June 1958. Ironically, by this time, it had been agreed that the F-86D and its fire-control system were suitable for export. Service details of the F-86K are covered in a subsequent chapter.

Canada's Sabre

Canada's desire to licence-build the Sabre can be traced back to 4 April 1949. On that date the country, along with eleven others, signed the agreement that marked the formation of NATO. The Canadian contribution to the Organization was, among other things, the commitment of a full air division to the defence of Europe.

With only obsolete Vampire jets on the Royal Canadian Air Force (RCAF) strength, it was decided to begin an upgrade programme, with both home and overseas defence in mind; it soon became clear that the F-86 was the best choice to fill the RCAF fighter requirement. Therefore, in early 1949, the Canadian Government began talks with North

53-8273 was the first FIAT-built F-86K, and is seen taxiing out for its first flight from Turin/Caselle on 23 May 1955. Note the short-span wing and lack of 'sugar scoop' cooling intakes. Howard Levy via Mike Fox

Rarely seen, FIAT-built F-86Ks for delivery overseas carried USAF ferry markings. 55-4881 was the first NA-232 aircraft and was delivered to Dornier for the Luftwaffe on 26 November 1957. Like so many German F-86Ks, it never entered active service.
Peter Sickinger

American to procure a number of Sabres. With NAA working flat out to meet USAF contracts, however, it became obvious that the company would not be able to produce additional aircraft for the Canadians. The answer was simple: Canada would obtain a licence to build them itself, and by April 1949 the deal had been made public. For an initial payment of just $1 million licence-production of the aircraft would be undertaken by the Canadair company of Montreal. The first payment on the agreement was made to NAA on 14 May and in August a contract was signed for Canadair to produce a hundred F-86As. The contract specified delivery to begin twelve months later and the company proved its capability by living up to this. It is interesting to note that Canadair's licence agreement covered all F-86 derivatives and thus the company could well have taken up the manufacture of F-86Ds had not the Avro CF-100 design come to fruition as the RCAF's interceptor.

Canadair's first Sabre 191-010 was in essence a licence-built F-86A. Subsequent aircraft were based on the F-86E. Howard Levy via Mike Fox

Based at Cartierville, the Canadair complex comprised several factories; Plant 1 was where Sabre production began. An already large building, it was soon extended by 200,000sq.ft (18,604sq.m) to cope with the increased production. The plant contained a number of heavy machine tools for F-86 manufacture, including 4,000 and 5,000-ton hydraulic presses and a 150-ton Hufford stretch former. The latter could grip a 66x144in (1.67x3.65m) sheet of aluminium and form it over a die. This machine, along with a wing-skin miller, were bought specifically for the Sabre programme.

The actual assembly of these manu-factured components was accomplished inside Plant 2, from where the first Canadian-built F-86 – officially the Canadair CL-13 Mk 1 – rolled out in August 1950. Though this aircraft was in essence an F-86A-5, developments at North American had overtaken the

Pictured on predelivery flight test in August 1954, Canadair Sabre 5 c/n 1113 shows off the '6-3' wing and leading-edge fence typical of the 'hard edge five'. As 23323, this aircraft passed through the RCAF and ended its days as a QF-86E target drone with the US Army. Jon Lake

The last 'military' Sabre flight took place on 22 January 1970 when Maj Bob Ayers took this Mk 5, 23102, to the storage depot at Trenton. The aircraft had been Canadair's chase plane. The aircraft later became a QF-86E target drone at White Sands, NM. Canadair

design and all subsequent Canadair Sabres were based on the all-flying tailed F-86E.

Serialled 191-010, the Sabre 1 flew for the first time on 8 August 1950 from Dorval. Canadair's chief test pilot Al Lilly flew the aircraft on a 30min check flight, followed by a further 15min the next day. This flight was curtailed by an electrical failure, but the aircraft was so on back in the air again. The Sabre 1 was heavily involved in Canadair's Sabre test programme and the J47-GE-13-engined machine was finally struck off on 7 September 1965. It is preserved in Canada. The early Sabre flights continued for a short time at Dorval, as the Cartierville runways were originally too short for jet operations. This was quickly remedied and early in 1951 Canadair started test flying from its home base.

Meanwhile, on 31 January 1951 the first production Canadair Sabre, the CL-13 Mk 2, had flown, this machine being based on the F-86E-1, again with J47-GE-13 power. Three hundred and fifty Sabre 2s were ordered for the RCAF, the first 149 featuring the full fibreglass nose ring of the early F-86Es. On subsequent aircraft the aluminium nose ring with a small

dielectric panel in the upper intake lip was fitted. Another modification introduced with the 70 aircraft was the deletion of the drop-tank inboard sway brace, at the same time the cockpit fuel-level indication was changed from gallons to pounds. To begin RCAF Sabre training, a number of pilots were detached to Larson AFB in Washington in November 1950 for one month for F-86A conversion. Other groups were sent to Langley and Kirtland AFBs. The first Sabre 2s were delivered to the RCAF in April 1951and the last of the 350 flew on 16 October 1952 with delivery being accomplished on 13 November.

Concurrently with Sabre 2 production, Canadair was planning a CL-13 to be fitted with the new indigenous 6,000lb (2,721kg) thrust Orenda 3 jet engine. The Orenda had earlier been tested in a modified F-86A airframe (as the F-86J: see Chapter 1), the engine showing great promise. Canadair followed this up with a single modified Sabre 2 to serve as its test bed and, redesignated CL-13 Mk 3, this aircraft took to the air from Cartierville on 25 September 1952 with Scotty McLean as pilot. This particular Sabre was the aircraft that Jacqueline Cochran used to set a new women's air speed record. Flying from Edwards AFB in California on 18 May 1953, Cochran pegged the new 100km mark at 652.552mph (1,050km/h), and on 3 June she set a 15km closed-circuit record at 670mph (1,078km/h). Finally, flying the same aircraft she became the first woman to break the sound barrier.

With the Orenda programme coming on satisfactorily, Canadair received an order for more than 400 Sabres from the Royal Air Force. Updating its design to F-86E-10 specification, Canadair came up with the CL-13 Mk 4, the first aircraft flying on 28 August 1952, even before the last Sabre 2s had been delivered. Some of the Sabre 4s saw limited RCAF service before being delivered to the RAF and in total 438 were built. The F-86E-10's flat windshield was incorporated into the Sabre 4 and other improvements included the relocation of the oxygen filler from the lower left nose area to the upper right and the hydraulic system fillers were moved from the left-hand speed brake well to the underside of the rear fuselage. The tail fin-mounted IFF antenna was also relocated to a position under the wing centre section. The fourteenth Sabre 4 introduced the A-4 gunsight, the A-1C having previously been the

standard item. Finally, on the forty-ninth aircraft target-towing provisions were installed. The final Sabre 4 flew from Cartierville on 21 October 1953, being delivered straight to the RAF.

Into Production with the Orenda

When the Orenda engine was finally suitable for production, it was slotted into the Canadair line starting on the seven-

hundred-and-ninety-first aircraft. Powered by an Orenda 10 of 6,500lb (2,947kg) thrust, the new model, designated CL-13A Mk 5, also featured the latest '6-3' wing with fence that had proved itself in Korea. The first Sabre 5, 23001 flew on 30 June 1953 with Bill Longhurst as pilot. With more than 1,000lb (453kg) of extra thrust compared with the standard F-86E, it was a hot performer. The top speed increased by up to 20mph (32km/h) and the ceiling from 42,500ft (12,954m) in the Sabre 4 to 50,700ft (15,453m) in the Sabre 5.

The Orenda installation required a

The Orenda Engine

During 1945 Hawker Siddeley bought the Victory Aircraft factory at Malton, Ontario and formed Avro Canada, later to manufacture the CF-100 Canuck interceptor. In 1946 the company took over Turbo Research, a government-run, gas-turbine laboratory, and under the designer Winnett Boyd built the Chinook axial-flow turbojet, which ran for the first time in March 1948. The Chinook engine had nine compressor stages, a single-stage turbine and six can-type combustion chambers, producing 2,600lb (1,179kg) thrust. This engine essentially paved the way for the later Orenda engine, the development of which was supervised by engineers Paul Dilworth and C.A. Grinyer.

The Orenda 1, with a ten-stage compressor, ran in February 1949 and, by June 1950, was flying in a Lancaster test-bed aircraft. Refinement of the design led eventually to the Orenda 10, which retained the ten-stage compressor and single-stage turbine arrangement, but produced a pressure ratio of 5.5:1 and an air mass flow rate of 106lb/sec (48kg/sec). Engine starting was provided by an intake bullet-mounted Jack and Heintz electric starter. The 6,500lb (2,947kg) thrust Orenda 10 powered the Sabre 5, the similar Orenda 9 being modified for use in the CF-100 aircraft.

The Orenda installation of the Sabre 3, 5 and 6 required modification to the standard aircraft's firewall area. This shot clearly shows the vee-shaped cutout in the lower fuselage required to clear the Orenda's bottom-mounted oil pumps and temperature regulator. The engine mountings were also pushed forward by 4in (102mm). This aircraft, Sabre 5 s/n 23293/N4689H, was under restoration. Warbird Images

Continued development of the basic design led to the addition of a second turbine stage, and compressor modifications also raised the pressure ratio to 6.6:1. This engine entered production as the Orenda 14 (Orenda 11 in the CF-100), and was fitted into the Sabre 6 as standard equipment. With a dry weight of only 2,430lb (1,102kg), the Orenda 14 possessed an enviable power to weight ratio of 0.32lb per pound of thrust.

In 1956 the engine department became a company in its own right, taking the Orenda name from its highly successful powerplant.

---

number of internal airframe modifications to be made. The Orenda was slightly heavier than the J47 but 22in (0.57m) shorter and, to maintain the aircraft's centre of gravity, the main engine mounting trunnion was moved forward by 4in (102mm), via a specially-designed casting, to fuselage station 231.869. The 3in (76mm) diameter increase of the Orenda also resulted in modifications to the firewall, which had a large vee cut into its lower edge to accommodate the engine's oil pumps and temperature regulator. Sabre 5 production ran to 370 aircraft, the last being delivered on 13 December 1954.

The final Canadair Sabre was the CL-13B Mk 6, in many eyes the ultimate F-86 model. By installing the Orenda 14 engine in the Sabre 6, Canadair gave the aircraft a climb rate of 12,000ft (3,657m) per minute, nearly twice that of an F-86A. The increased cooling requirements of the Orenda 14 led to the previously flush-mounted cooling ducts at the wing trailing edge being replaced by prominently scooped items.

These were then retrofitted on to many Sabre 5s.

The first Sabre 6 flew on 19 October 1954 and production ran to 655 aircraft. The first 160 Sabre 6s continued with the 'hard edge' 6-3 wing of the Sabre 5, but thereafter a slatted version of the 6-3 wing was fitted to the Sabre 6. Aside from RCAF requirements, the Sabre 6 attracted a number orders from other countries, including Colombia (six aircraft), South Africa (thirty-four) and Israel (six, order later cancelled). The final 225 Mk 6 Sabres were built for the Luftwaffe and c/n 1815, the last Canadian-built Sabre, its construction number reflecting the total production run, flew on 21 November 1958. Canadair retained a number of Sabres for test purposes, notably Sabre 5 serial 23102 as a chase plane. This aircraft marked the last active Sabre flight in Canada on 22 January 1970, when it was ferried into Trenton for storage.

Canadair undertook a number of design studies during the Sabre days. Though none actually went into production, they show that Canadair was

Previously in use with Boeing as a chase plane, N74170 was the first QF-86E target drone converted by Bob Laidlaw of Flight Systems, Inc. It was shot down over the White Sands Missile Range on 29 August 1980.
MAP

This Sabre 6, serial 23544, was assigned to the National Aeronautic Establishment as part of the CL-13C project. It was fitted with an afterburning Orenda engine, as evidenced by the extra cooling ducts on the rear fuselage. Jon Lake

far from being just another Sabre factory. The CL-13C was proposed as a more advanced version of the Sabre utilizing an afterburner. Although an afterburner was actually fitted to Sabre 6 serial 23559 for tests, the installation did not enter production. It was was proposed to equip the CL-13D with a 2,000lb (907kg) thrust Armstrong-Siddeley Snarler rocket motor. The CL-13E was actually an area-rule test aircraft, and the twenty-first Sabre 5, 23021, had fuselage fairings installed to complete these tests. At the end of the programme the aircraft reverted to standard configuration, eventually ending its life as a Flight Systems QF-86E target drone. The CL-13G was put forward as a two-seat, training version similar in concept to the TF-86F. The CL-13H was to have been fitted with all-weather radar, in the same way as the F-86D. Finally, the CL-13J was to have incorporated a simplified Bristol afterburner.

Flight Systems, Inc. and the QF-86E

Founded in 1968 by Bob Laidlaw at Mojave in California, Flight Systems, Inc. (FSI) began its involvement with the Sabre in the mid-1970s. At that time the company signed a contract to supply remotely-piloted Sabres to the US Army for use as high-speed targets. Laidlaw had demonstrated two such aircraft to the Army in 1975.

In order to fulfil this contract, ex-RCAF Canadair Sabres were overhauled and converted to drone configuration at a plant in Moncton, Canada, which was run by David McEwen. After modification, the Sabres were then dismantled and trucked in crates to Mojave for flight testing. The Moncton plant opened on 30 September 1976 and the first deliveries to the US Army began from Mojave in mid-1977. Converted aircraft became known as QF-86Es, and

by 1 January 1980 thirty-six had been ordered.

A remote destruct system was fitted to QF-86Es so that the aircraft could be destroyed if control were lost. Two lights installed on a panel in the fuselage side indicated whether this system was 'safe' or 'armed'. Many QF-86Es were also equipped with a smoke system, similar to that fitted to the Golden Hawks aerobatic team's aircraft.

The QF Sabres were placed on the US civil register by FSI for flight testing, but often carried 'US Army' titles on the tail fin before delivery to the Army at the White Sands Missile Range in New Mexico. Around fifteen FSI personnel (pilots and technicians) were deployed to Holloman AFB NM for QF-86E operations. Each drone flew on average about twenty-five hours before being shot down, as destruction of the QF-86E was usually avoided. By October 1984 fifty QF-86Es had been delivered to the Army, from a final total of fifty-six. Further Canadair Sabre airframes were obtained from South Africa in 1981, but most of these aircraft were never converted for use

Specifications: QF-86E

POWERPLANT

Orenda 10 engine, rated at 6,325lb (2,868kg)
thrust

FUEL CAPACITY

415 US gall (1,556l), plus 2 x 120 or 200gall
drop tanks

LAUNCH

conventional; aircraft programmed to come to
a halt and make a safe take-off and climb out
if control lost on take-off

GUIDANCE

radar command guidance system, primary
mode: NoLO (No Local Operator) over full
range of preprogrammed manoeuvres, including take-off and landing, but provision for
pilot control retained; control: from one fixed
and one mobile station manufactured by Vega
Precision Laboratories or a Drone Control
System made by IBM

SPECIAL EQUIPMENT

Vega Precision Laboratories command/teleme-
try data system and FSI interface computer for
processing uplink command and downlink
telemetry data to and from aircraft; a fourth
installation, the IBM Drone Function Control
System, is optional. Other options include
radar altimeter (for simulated low-level
attacks), scoring gear, infra-red flare dispenser,
chaff dispenser, ECM pods and TV (used as a
take-off and landing aid)

WEIGHTS

empty: 10,850lb (4,920kg)
clean, take-off: 13,500lb (6,122kg)
take off + 2 x 120gall drop tanks:
                          15,200lb (6,893kg)

PERFORMANCE

maximum speed: 607mph (976 km/h)
ceiling: 45,000ft (1,3716m)
stress limit: +7.0

Canadair Sabre Production

Serial	Type	Construction Nos
19101	CL-13 Sabre Mk 1	1
19102 to 19199	CL-13 Sabre Mk 2	2 to 99
19200	CL-13 Sabre Mk 3	100
19201 to 19452	CL-13 Sabre Mk 2	101 to 352
19453 to 19890	CL-13 Sabre Mk 4	353 to 790
23001 to 23370	CL-13A Sabre Mk 5	791 to 1160
23371 to 23752	CL-13B Sabre Mk 6	1161 to 1815

Specifications: Canadair Sabre Mk 6

POWERPLANT

Orenda 14 of 7,275lb (32,99kg) thrust

WEIGHTS

empty: 11,143lb (5,053kg)
normal, loaded: 16,426lb (7,449kg)
maximum take-off: 17,611lb (7,986kg)

DIMENSIONS

wingspan: 37ft 1in (11.3m)
length: 37ft 6in (11.44m)
height: 14ft 7in (4.44m)
wing area: 303sq ft (28.1sq m)

PERFORMANCE

maximum speed:
at sea level: 710mph (1,142 km/h)
at 10,000ft: 680mph (1094km/h
                      at 3,048m)
at 36,000ft: 630 mph (1,013
                      km/h at 10,972m)
initial climb rate: 11,800ft/min (3,596
                      m/min)
combat radius (clean): 363 miles (584 km)
maximum range, 2 x 200 gall drop tanks:
                      1,495 miles (2,405 km)

ARMAMENT

6 x 0.50-calibre Colt-Browning machine-guns
2 x 100lb, 500lb, or 1000lb bombs
750lb napalm tanks
500lb fragmentation clusters
16 x 5in rocket clusters

by FSI or the Army. The US Army QF-86E drone programme finished in June 1996 and, fortunately, a few Sabres survived to see another day. The drone requirement was then filled by the QF-100, the first arriving at Mojave in early 1985 for conversion.

Further to the target drone requirement, FSI was awarded a contract to tow aerial-gunnery targets for the USAF in the early 1980s, and thus began another era in FSI Sabre operations. To fulfil this need, further Canadair Sabres (mainly Sabre 6s) were converted to enable Dart targets to be carried.

Conventionally piloted, these aircraft differed from the QF-86Es in wearing FSI's smart blue and white corporate colour scheme. These aircraft spent much of their time away from Mojave and could often be found towing targets at USAF Bases. One FSI Sabre target tug was also deployed to Kadena AFB, Okinawa to serve PACAF requirements and an FSI team would annually travel to Kadena to service the aircraft. Many of these target

tugs were purchased from the defunct Haydon-Baillie collection in Britain. In addition to the Sabres, FSI F-100s also towed targets for the USAF. Surviving FSI Sabres were transferred 'on paper' to the parent company Tracor, based in Austin, Texas during 1989.

Commonwealth Sabre

Following World War II, Australia, as a Commonwealth member, began to equip its air force with a number of British-built or designed types, notably the Vampire and the Meteor fighter. These aircraft were first-generation jets and the pace of fighter development post-war quickly rendered them obsolete. Looking to update its forces, the Australian Government focused on a number of fighter types, initially favouring the Commonwealth Aircraft Company (CAC) CA-23. This design, a tailed delta with a Mach 1.5 top speed, was inexplicably dropped in February 1950 when the government announced that it had instead placed an order for seventy-two of the British-designed Hawker P.1081, a swept-wing, single-seater designed for Rolls-Royce reheated Nene power. The assembly of the P.1081 for the Royal Australian Air Force (RAAF) was to be carried out by CAC and the new contract stipulated a somewhat ambitious delivery date for the first machine of July 1951. This became academic when, later in 1950, the project was cancelled in Britain. Unable to supply the Australians without its own government's support, Hawker reluctantly also withdrew from the RAAF bid.

This left the Australians in a dilemma and quick decisions were made. Evaluations of the Hawker Hunter and North American F-86 Sabre were made, with the Hunter's being quickly eliminated as its development period would mean a long wait for deliveries. As an off-the-shelf design, the Sabre ideally suited the RAAF requirement and on 22 February 1951 the F-86 was selected for licence-production by CAC. Fortunately, Commonwealth's managing director Lawrence Wackett had begun talks with North American Aviation even before the P.1081 cancellation with a view to gaining a licence to manufacture F-86s in Australia. During 1950 the government itself had also approached NAA for US-built Sabres to be supplied for the RAAF in Korea. Numerous factors conspired to prevent this happening, not least the lack of available Sabres at that time, but Wackett realized that home production in Australia would overcome the problem. To improve the Sabre's performance, he also proposed that the Australian-built aircraft should be powered by a Rolls-Royce Avon engine. This not only made sense from an engineering point of view but it would also help to pacify the 'Buy British' school within the government. Thus, thanks to Wackett, when the Sabre was selected in 1951 much background work had already been accomplished.

For production by CAC at the Fisherman's Bend, Victoria plant, the initial Sabre contract called for one prototype and seventy production aircraft, with Commonwealth also taking up the manufacture of the Avon engine. CAC-built Avons eventually powered all except the first twenty-two Australian-built F-86s. In April 1951 a number of designers and engineers from Fisherman's Bend were sent to NAA's factory in Los Angeles to begin the process of gathering information and experience of Sabre manufacture. The licence contract also agreed that North American would supply drawings, data and manufacturing machinery for the project, as well as finished components for assembly. Though the prototype was begun in 1952, series production of the fighter did not start until 1954, but, based upon a hundred sets of F-86F components, the CAC Sabre manufacturing process was considerably eased by the 75 per cent NAA content in the first few aircraft.

Though based on the F-86F, Commonwealth's Sabre differed in two main regards, which resulted in an aircraft that shared little with its American cousin. First, the installation of the Avon engine also brought numerous airframe modi-

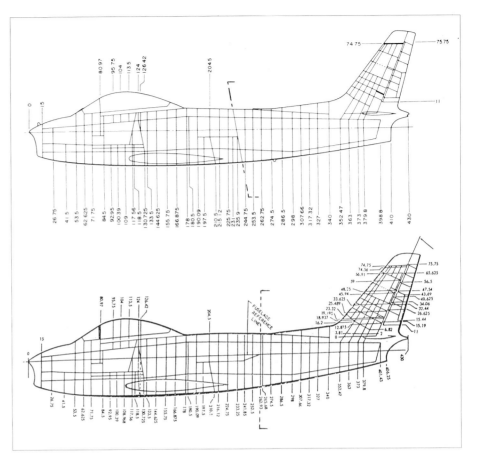

Comparative schematics of F-86F (top) and CA-27 reveal bulkhead modifications, especially the vertical fuselage break of the CA-27 at Station 262.5 (dotted line).

fications and, secondly, the standard six, 0.50-calibre machine-gun armament of the F-86F was dropped in favour of a pair of Aden 30mm cannon. The CAC-built Rolls-Royce Avon RA.7 was not only more powerful than the J47, it was also shorter at 102in (2.59m) and lighter, tipping the scales at 2,460lb (1,115kg). With a slightly greater diameter of 42.2in (1.07m) and a compressor mass flow of 120lb/sec (54.4kg/sec) at 7,950 rpm, the engine also required a major redesign of the forward fuselage. In order to cater for the Avon's greater need for air. CAC redesigned the Sabre intake by lowering the lip 3.73in (94mm), which in turn increased the inlet duct area to 435sq. in (2,800sq. cm). This then led to a recontouring of the fuselage, which was faired back into the standard contour at fuselage station 178, just in line with the cockpit canopy's rear edge. Yet further engine installation modifications were necessitated by the need to preserve the aircraft's centre of gravity, the lighter

Avon's main trunnions being relocated rearwards at station 264.5, which was 28in (717mm) behind those of the F-86F. The engine removal fuselage break point was then also relocated vertically at station 262.5. Detailed refinement of the redesign involved the installation of a number of external cooling ducts for the engine, both fore and aft of the firewall bulkhead. The Avon engine used an isopropyl nitrate starter, in which the liquid monofuel was ignited to rotate a small turbine which then engaged with the engine to initiate rotation. A small, 1gall starter fuel tank was installed in the Avon Sabre and this provided enough propellant for at least three starts, independent of external electrical power.

The Aden cannon installation also required localized strengthening of the forward fuselage as well as redesigned blast panels. The twin 30mm cannons were designed to carry 180 rounds per weapon, though in service 150 to 160 was more the norm. The rate of fire was between 1,200 and 1,400 round per minute, and in the CAC Sabre the guns were staggered relative to each other, the right-hand cannon being mounted 8in (203mm) further forward of its companion to provide a straight feed path for the weapon's ammunition. Ejected links and cases were retained in a belly compartment in the forward fuselage; but on later production aircraft the cases were ejected overboard. The F-86F's armament access-door aperture was retained, but the door itself was strengthened to act as a structural member. In all, this design process resulted in 268 engineering changes, with only 40 per cent of the fuselage structure remaining unchanged.

The first CAC Sabre, designated CA-26, was completed in July 1953, the original target date of April 1952 having slipped somewhat. Fitted with a British-built, Avon RA.7 Mk 20, the first engine run was accomplished on 20 July and a taxi run was made three days later. As the Fisherman's Bend runway was considered too short, the prototype, serial A94-101, was then dismantled and trucked to the nearby Avalon airfield for flight testing. With reassembly and further engine runs complete at Avalon, the Sabre finally flew on 3 August. RAAF pilot Flt Lt W. Scott flew this 30min sortie. Following a successful flying programme, the prototype was delivered in August 1954 for RAAF evaluation at the Aircraft Research and Development Unit (ARDU) at Laverton.

Production aircraft then began to roll off the line at Fisherman's Bend and these machines also required dismantling and test flying at Avalon. The first twenty-two Sabres were designated CA-27 Mk 30, the first aircraft flying on 13 July 1954. It was then handed over to the RAAF on 18 August, but subsequent deliveries were slow with only four further Sabres being accepted during the remainder of the year; the final Mk 30 was not delivered until July 1955.

Specifications:
Commonwealth Sabre Mk 32

POWERPLANT
CAC-built Rolls-Royce Avon 26 of 7,500lb (3,401kg) thrust

WEIGHTS
empty:	12,120lb (5,496kg)
loaded, clean:	15,990lb (7,251kg)
maximum take-off:	18,650lb (8,457kg)

DIMENSIONS
wingspan:	37ft 1in (11.3m)
length:	37ft 6in (11.43m)
height:	14ft 4in (4.4m)
wing area:	303 or 326sq ft (28.1 or 30.3sq m)

PERFORMANCE
maximum speed:
at sea level:	700mph (1,126km/h)
at 10,000ft:	672mph (1,081km/h at 3,048m)
at 38,000ft:	607mph (976km/h at 11,582m)
initial climb rate:	12,000ft/min (3,657m/min)
service ceiling:	55,000ft (16,764m)

tactical radius:
clean:	290 miles (466km)
with 2 drop tanks and two Sidewinder AAMs:	400 miles (644 km)
maximum range with 2 x 200gall drop tanks:	1,150 miles (1,850 km)

ARMAMENT
2 x 30mm Aden cannon
2 x AIM-9 Sidewinder infra-red-homing air-to-air missiles
2 x 500lb bombs and 2 x 100gall drop tanks

CAC Sabre Production

Serial	Type	Construction Nos
A94-101	CA-26 Sabre	1428
A94-901 to 922	CA-27 Sabre Mk 30	CA-27-1 to 22
A94-923 to 942	CA-27 Sabre Mk 31	CA-27-23 to 42
A94-943 to 990	CA-27 Sabre Mk 32	CA-27-43 to 90
A94-351 to 371	CA-27 Sabre Mk 32	CA-27-91 to 111

Logically, the next CAC Sabre variant was the Mk 31, and this model introduced the '6-3' wing. Twenty Sabre 31s were built, with delivery ending in September 1956. The 6-3 wing was then retrofitted on to Sabre 30s as well as the prototype during overhaul. The sole CA-26 then saw regular squadron use with the RAAF. Two Sabre 31s, A94-938 and -942, were modified on the production line to permit the carriage of 35gall (157l) of fuel in each wing leading edge, and this successful improvement formed the basis of the next model, the CA-27 Mk 32.

Twenty-eight Mk 32s completed the initial production order, delivery beginning in March of 1956, but a second order for twenty more of this type had been placed in May 1954 and this was followed by a final batch of twenty-one ordered in 1957. The so-called 'wet wing' Sabre 32s featured an internal fuel capacity of 422 imperial gall (1899 litres), and ultimately, with maximum external tankage, possessed a ferry range of 1,150 miles (1850 km). Top speed for the Sabre 32 was 700 mph (1126 km/h) at sea level with a 12,000ft per minute (3657 m/min) initial rate of climb. The final Sabre Mk. 32 was flown in August 1961 and delivered to the RAAF in December.

Further Sabre 32 improvements included the installation of the Avon RA.7 Mk 26 engine, which incorporated improvements designed to overcome engine surge when the cannons were fired. Chief among these was a linkage between the trigger and the throttle which briefly 'dipped' the engine during cannon firing, thus alleviating the surge problem. Modified blast panels also helped to cure the same problem and these were retrofitted to all earlier models. A dual store wing was also introduced on the Mk 32, enabling 100gall (450l) and 167gall (750l) drop tanks to be carried for a total of 946gall (4,257l) of fuel. Leading-edge fuel capacity in this configuration was reduced by 10gall (45l) because of internal structural modifications.

Missile Armament

Though the De Havilland Firestreak missile was evaluated on the CAC Sabre during 1956 and 1957 for use on RAAF aircraft, it was the Sidewinder that was eventually chosen as standard equipment. In 1959 Sabre 32 A94-946 was modified to carry AIM-9Bs and successfully performed test firings against Jindivik aerial targets over the Woomera range. In late 1959 the first RAAF Sabres in Malaya were converted to carry the missile, though the Sidewinders themselves were not delivered until February 1960.

Wallace Lien as pilot. The second and the third aircraft flew in October 1946 and February 1947, respectively, and, following completion of manufacturer's testing, were all handed over to the Navy in September 1947. It is interesting to note that the NAA constructor's numbers for these XFJ-1s immediately preceded those of the XP-86 prototypes.

In May 1945 the Navy had ordered a hundred production FJ-1s under contract Noa(s)6911, although in reality only thirty FJ-1s rolled off the production lines at Inglewood. Known by NAA as the NA-141, the first FJ-1 was delivered straight to the Naval Test Center at Patuxent River in Maryland on 5 October 1947. Along with six other NATC

39054, the second XFJ-1 fitted with 170gall tip tanks. Note that this machine lacks the prominent engine cooling ducts which were a feature of the first XFJ-1 and production aircraft. A fin-mounted pitot probe was later adopted on the XP-86. MAP

XFJ-1 and FJ-1 Production

Bureau Nos	Type	Construction Nos
Bu.39053 to 39055	XFJ-1	55996 to 55998
Bu.120342 to 120371	FJ-1	38394 to 38423

Specifications: FJ-1

POWERPLANT
Allison J35-A-2 of 4,000lb (1,814kg) thrust

WEIGHTS
empty:	8,843lb (4,010kg)
take-off with 2 x 170gall wing-tip tanks:	15,115lb (6,854kg)
internal fuel capacity:	465gall (1,743l)
total fuel capacity:	805gall (3,018l)

DIMENSIONS
wingspan:	38ft 2in (11.63m)
length:	34ft 5in (10.48m)
height:	14ft 10in (4.52m)
wing area:	221sq ft (20.5sq m)

PERFORMANCE
Maximum speed:	547mph at 9,000ft (880km/h at 2,743m)
Stalling speed:	121mph (194km/h)
Initial rate of climb:	3,300ft/min (1,005m/min)
Service ceiling:	32,000ft (9,753m)
Range with external tanks:	1,496 miles (2,407 km)

ARMAMENT
6 x 0.50-calibre machine-guns with 1,500 rounds total

machines, this aircraft began the service testing of the type, though with just thirty aircraft large-scale squadron assignment was never on the cards. The last of the FJ-1s was delivered on 30 April 1948, just one month before the first P-86A Sabre was delivered to the Air Force. The production version differed little from the XFJ, the main difference being the deletion of the wing-mounted, dive brakes in favour of more conventional, fuselage-mounted panels. It is interesting to note that the FJ-1 retained the tailfin-mounted pitot probe – a location initially chosen for the P-86.

The only US Navy squadron to receive the FJ-1 was VF-5A, based at NAS North Island near San Diego. Commanded by Cdr Evan 'Pete' Aurand, the squadron received its first FJ-1 on 15 November 1947 and VF-5A eventually operated twenty-four of the type. Alongside VF-17, which flew the FH-1 Phantom, VF-5A was tasked with proving the suitability of jet operations at sea and the unit began an exhaustive familiarization programme which took in many landings aboard a simulated carrier deck painted on the runway at North Island. Aurand had the distinction of carrying out the first carrier landing of an FJ-1 when on 16 March 1948 he brought his aircraft aboard the USS Boxer, CV-21. The squadron

executive officer, Lt Cdr Robert Elder, followed him. Aurand then just managed to take off from the Boxer without catapult assistance, but the poor engine acceleration proved too much of a risk and thereafter catapult assistance was considered obligatory for FJ-1 carrier operations. It is not known when the name 'Fury' was assigned to the FJ-1, but by early 1948 the name was in regular use.

However, the aircraft did not really demonstrate much suitability for carrier landings, the undercarriage in particular being a weak spot. In August 1948 VF-5A was redesignated VF-51 and was ordered to deploy up to eight FJ-1s aboard the USS Princeton, CV-37. Four aircraft were loaded aboard at San Diego and the remaining machines were to arrive while the carrier was at sea. Which was fine in principle, but the pilot of one FJ-1, Bu No. 120371, the last aircraft built, landed hard, broke the whole left wing off and went over the side. Luckily he was rescued, but the cruise did not proceed well, with further landing accidents occurring. Ignominiously, Aurand was ordered to take his aircraft back off the ship within two days.

However, all was not doom and gloom for VF-51. In September 1948 the unit entered seven FJ-1s in the Bendix Trophy Race for jets. Flying from Long Beach,

Following a short but eventful life with VF-51, surviving FJ-1s passed to Naval Air Reserve Squadrons. This NAR Oakland machine was struck off on 31 March 1952 with NAR Olathe. A.J. Jackson

California to Cleveland, Ohio, VF-51 aircraft took the first four places, ahead of two California ANG F-80s. First past the post was Ensign F.E. Brown, in 4hr 10min 44.4sec, followed 2min later by Cdr Aurand. Much was made of the fact that the Navy aircraft had carried all operational equipment, including ammunition.

At least one further carrier operation was accomplished by VF-51: during February 1949, again aboard USS *Boxer*. However, in May 1949 the FJ-1s were phased out in favour of the new F9F-3 Panther. Surplus FJ-1s were then overhauled at Alameda before being allotted to Naval Air Reserve units, beginning with NAR Oakland in early March 1950, though the unit received only seven aircraft. NAR Los Alamitos then received a trickle of aircraft, eventually being assigned ten models of the Fury, and further units at Dallas and Olathe then took up other machines.

NAR Dallas was assigned only three FJ-1s, operating them from 14 June to 4 October 1951. Tail codes for the NAR aircraft were as follows: 'F' for Oakland, 'L' for Los Alamitos, 'D' for Dallas and 'K' for Olathe. VF-5A/VF-51 FJ-1s wore the code 'S'. NAR Olathe retired the last of the type in June and July 1953.

FJ-2: the First Swept-wing Fury

The immense promise shown by the F-86 series soon led both North American and the Navy to look at a swept-wing Fury variant; NAA initiated design project NA-181 on 30 January 1951 with this in mind. Based upon the F-86E, a proposal was presented to the Navy on 6 February, and 300 NA-181s were ordered four days later. (This order was reduced to 200 as a result of the Korean War.) Three

preproduction aircraft were also ordered, two as NA-179s, later designated XFJ-2 by the Navy and one NA-185/XFJ-2B. Ordered on 8 and 19 March 1951, respectively, these aircraft were based on F-86E-10 airframes which were rolling off the Inglewood production line at the time. The two XFJ-2s would retain the basic F-86E features, but would incorporate a modified undercarriage with an extending nose leg and strengthened main gear legs with lateral bracing struts. A tail hook and retractable tail bumper were fitted to these machines, but no armament. The XFJ-2s were able to carry the specially-designed 'Fury' 200gall drop tanks, as would the production models.

The single XFJ-2B served as the armament test airframe and featured none of the modifications built into the XFJ-2s. Armament for this machine would be four Colt Mk 12 20mm cannon with 150 rounds per gun. As the weapon testbed, the XFJ-2B was not designed to undergo sea trials and for this reason it was built with the standard F-86 undercarriage. All three prototypes were powered by J47-GE-13 engines. The mock-up inspection for the production NA-181 was completed between 26 to 28 June 1951, with work continuing on the prototypes at Inglewood. First to fly was the XFJ-2B, on 27 December 1951, piloted by Bob Hoover. This aircraft was almost immediately detached to the Naval Ordnance Test Station at Inyokern for weapons testing and from there to the Naval Air Test Center at Patuxent River in Maryland. The first XFJ-2 flew on 14 February 1952, again with Hoover at the helm. Following NAA evaluation of this and the second machine, both were flown to Patuxent River for NATC evaluation. In December 1952 both XFJ-2s began carrier-qualification trials aboard the USS *Coral Sea*. These were less than satisfactory, the aircraft proving to be unsuited to carrier operations. In particular, the new landing gear and the arrester hook bumper were too weak for carrier landings under realistic conditions, and the aircraft handled poorly during carrier approaches and landings.

Too late to be resolved before manufacture, the FJ-2 went into production with many problems outstanding. The manufacture of the 200 aircraft was begun at Columbus, where all future FJ models would be built. The production version differed in many ways from the prototypes. First, wing folding was incorporated, and this led to one small problem – that of the splitting of the one-piece,

Bu. No.131941, an FJ-2 on pre-delivery test from Columbus. Note the slats opening separately about the wing fold line. The aircraft also carries the special Fury drop tanks of 200gall (750l) capacity. This machine later served with VMF-451 at MCAS El Toro. USMC

leading-edge slat. The solution was simple: the slat was split at the fold line and, unusually, each wing's leading-edge device operated as two separate panels. Standard powerplant for the FJ-2 was the J47-GE-2, a navalized variant of the GE-13, which produced 6,000lb (2,721kg) thrust. Armament was carried over from

the XFJ-2B, but with 720 rounds total, and utilized AN/APG-30 ranging with a Mk 16 gunsight. The undercarriage of the XFJ-2s was adopted for production, the main wheel track being increased by 8in (20cm). The dihedral tailplane of the prototypes was dispensed with, in favour of a slab tail with no dihedral. Finally, to

Marine FJ-2 Bu. No.132093 of VMF-312, MCAS Cherry Point. Checks and nose trim are black and white. This unit flew the FJ-2 for just two years, beginning in November 1954. Author

Pictured here being towed in after its first flight on 3 July 1953, the prototype FJ-3, Bu. No.131931 was actually the fifth production FJ-2, converted to J65 power. NAA

improve its suitability for carrier oper-ations, the cockpit area was heavily modified. A British-built Martin-Baker ejector seat, adjustable for height, was installed and this necessitated a modified canopy and rail mechanism to clear the seat as the canopy retracted rearwards. To further improve the pilot's view forward on take-off with the nose leg extended, the windshield was extended forward and down.

Sidelined by Sabre production for Korea, delivery of the FJ-2 was slow. The first machine was delivered in October 1952, but only twenty-five had been assigned to the Navy by January 1954. With the Columbus plant now free of F-86F production, that rate then soared and the last FJ-2 was delivered in September 1954. It had originally been planned to deploy FJ-2s in Korea, and, with this in mind, production of the variant was undertaken solely to equip Marine units. However, production delays meant that action in Korea was not an option and, though the Marines did get their aircraft, it went into service with one insurmountable fault: aiming the four cannons in a dogfight was almost impossible. This problem was caused by a basic design fault, whereby the cannon's muzzle axis was aligned significantly below that of the aircraft's longitudinal axis. It had been thought that this would make the weapons easier to aim in high-g situations, but the reality was exactly the opposite.

Nevertheless, Marine squadrons began to receive the FJ-2, starting in January 1954 with VMF-122 'Candystripers' at Marine Corps Air Station (MCAS) Cherry Point in North Carolina. In March 1955 the squadron deployed aboard the USS *Coral Sea* for a six-month Mediterranean cruise. On the West Coast, VMF-235 replaced their F4U-4 Corsairs with FJ-2s at MCAS El Toro and deployed aboard the USS *Hancock* in June 1954 before moving to NAS Atsugi in Japan. Front-line use of the type was, however, relatively short and by the end of 1956 the type had been replaced. A number of FJ-2s were then operated by Navy Reserve units at St. Louis and Columbus, but they were retired in 1957.

Trials were undertaken to incorporate the Sabre's non-slatted '6-3' wing on to the FJ-2 Fury, in the hope of increasing high-speed manoeuvrability. However, the poor low-speed handling characteristics yielded by this modification led to a study whereby the '6-3' wing's positive characteristics could be incorporated without detracting too much from the low-speed end of the spectrum. The third FJ-2, Bu. No.131929 was modified in August 1953 with a 'hard-edge, 6-3' wing, but with a full-chord wing fence at

FJ-2 Units

VMF-122, MCAS Cherry Point – tail code 'LC'

VMF-232, MCAS Kaneohe Bay – tail code 'WT'

VMF-235, MCAS El Toro and NAS Atsugi, Japan – tail code 'WU'

VMF-312, MCAS Cherry Point – tail code 'WR'

VMF-334, MCAS El Toro – tail code 'MX'–

VMF-451, MCAS El Toro and NAS Atsugi, Japan – tail code 'AM'

Fleet Air Gunnery Unit, NAAS El Centro – tail code 'TR'

US Naval Reserve Columbus – tail code '7C'

US Naval Reserve St. Louis – tail code '7U'

Specifications: FJ-2

POWERPLANT

General Electric J47-GE-2 of 6,000lb (2,721kg) thrust

WEIGHTS

empty:	12,275lb (5,566kg)
take-off with 2 x 200gall drop tanks:	
	18,882lb (8,562kg)
internal fuel capacity:	435gall (1,631l)
total fuel capacity:	835gall (3,131l)

DIMENSIONS

wingspan:	37ft 1in (11.3m)
length:	37ft 7in (11.4m)
height:	13ft 7in (4.14m)
wing area:	287.9sq ft (26.79sq m)

Performance

maximum speed at sea level:

	609mph (981km/h)
stalling speed:	91.2mph (146km/h)
initial rate of climb:	4,700ft/min
	(1,432m/min)
service ceiling:	37,000ft (11,277m)
range with external tanks:	1,040 miles (1,673 km)

ARMAMENT

4 x 20mm cannon with 720 rounds total

XFJ-2, -2B and FJ-2 Production

Bureau Nos	Type	Construction Nos
Bu. 133754 and 133755	XFJ-2	179-1 and 2
Bu. 133756	XFJ-2B	185-1
Bu. 131927 to 132126	FJ-2	181-1 to 200

This arrangement was more successful, and resulted in adequate stall warnings under most conditions. By this time, however, the configuration could not be fitted on to production FJ-2s and was instead used in the development of the next production version, the FJ-3.

FJ-3 Fury: Bigger and Better

Continuing improvements upon the FJ-2 design inevitably led to another model, and NAA began work on the NA-194 in March 1952. To be powered by a Wright J65-W-4 engine, itself a licence-built, British Armstrong-Siddeley Sapphire, the NA-194 offered improved performance and the ability to carry a heavier payload. On 18 April 1952 the Navy agreed a contract for 389 production aircraft, as the FJ-3 Fury.

NAA did not produce a prototype of the FJ-3 as such, instead converting the fifth FJ-2 to take the J65 engine, as the NA-196. The aircraft flew from Columbus on 3 July 1953, but, aside from the engine, it bore none of the other FJ-3 improvements. Principally, in order to allow more air into the new engine, NAA increased the intake size on production FJ-3s and the more voluminous front fuselage that resulted enabled 648 rounds of 20mm ammunition to be carried against 600 for the FJ-2. However, the gun-alignment problem was carried over from the FJ-2. Cockpit armour protection was also installed, to the extent of 88lb (40kg) in front of the cockpit and another 52lb (23kg) plate behind the seat, which again was a Martin-Baker item.

wing station 100. Extended wing-tips were also fitted, but this modification caused the aircraft to exhibit abrupt roll-and-yaw tendencies before the onset of sudden stall. During 1954 a thick, cambered fence was used in conjunction with another fence near the wing-tip and, although this partially cured the stall problem, stall warning was still considered unsatisfactory and yaw was experienced during the glide in to land. In October 1954 the aircraft was further modified with wing fences covering the leading edge only, at wing stations 100 and 176.

Fleet Introduction Program (FIP) FJ-3s in flight out of Patuxent River in the autumn of 1954. Aircraft Bu. No.135786 was lost during the FIP when its pilot became lost and ditched in the Patuxent. NAA

The first production FJ-3 flew from Columbus on 11 December 1953, piloted by Bill Pearce. But deliveries of the type were slow, and in August 1954 when eight FJ-3s were assigned to NATC at Patuxent River for Fleet Introduction Program (FIP) trials, this represented nearly a third of all FJ-3s in existence. Aside from the known fault with the cannon alignment, few problems were found, although the twelfth and the thirteenth production aircraft were lost during the introduction programme to non-specific aircraft faults. The carrier trials were undertaken aboard the Coral Sea, using crews from VF-173 and VC-3. They highlighted one problem

– that the engine occasionally was prone to seize during catapult launches. Though Wright did pay close attention to this and other problems, such as turbine blade failures, the engine was never really free from trouble, a problem that furthermore plagued the Republic F-84F, also powered by the J65.

The first Navy squadron to receive FJ-3s was VF-173 at NAS Jacksonville in Florida. Gaining its first Fury in September 1954, VF-173 began an intense period of training on the type before embarking on the USS Bennington. First landings aboard the Bennington were carried out by VF-173 on 8 May 1955.

Another unit to receive the new Fury was VF-51, noteworthy as the original Navy FJ-1 squadron.

While the first deliveries continued, work went on in trying to improve the FJ-3's carrier performance. Inevitably such efforts centred on wing design, and an early fix had involved fitting five small, leading-edge fences to the wing – one just inboard of the slat panels and four further more on the slats themselves. A number of early FJ-3s were manufactured in this way and low-speed handling was improved. The adoption of a '6-3' wing was then investigated, but a solution to the poor low-speed handling qualities of this wing would need to be overcome first.

Referring to NACA research into leading-edge camber and radius modifications (using F-86A 47-609), NAA engineers at Columbus came up with a

Bu. No.135776, the third production FJ-3 Fury, made the type's first carrier take-off from the USS *Coral Sea*. The extended nose landing gear is especially evident in this view. The 'FT' stencil indicated Flight Test.
NAA

Above: **VC-3 was a Navy composite unit involved with early evaluation of the FJ-3 during the Fleet Introduction Program in 1954. Trim is white on the sea blue overall scheme. Wing, tail and drop tank leading edges are treated with an aluminized lacquer to prevent rain erosion.** J.M.G. Gradidge

Below: **In February 1955 the US Navy moved to a new colour scheme, that of light gull gray upper surfaces and insignia white lower surfaces. This FJ-3, Bu. No.136011, is from VF-24 at NAS Miramar. Tail trim is red.** J.M.G. Gradidge

One of a number of FJ-3s converted to FJ-3D2 configuration; this aircraft from utility squadron VU-3 was tasked with directing F-6F-6K airborne target drones. Colour scheme is fluorescent red-orange for the tail area, engine gray fuselage and orange-yellow wing-tips. J.M.G. Gradidge

non-slatted wing to incorporate a leading edge extension with camber. One other bonus of this design, aside from overcoming the handling problems, was that 124gall (465l) of extra fuel could be carried in the wing leading edges. Considerable refinement of the design was first required though. The NAA team, led by Pete Marshall, eventually settled on a wing-fence installation which retained four of the small fences already installed, and replaced the middle item with a larger leading-edge fence, installed just outboard of the wing fold. These changes were incorporated into production during July 1955 and also retrofitted to earlier models with great success.

Further design refinements led to a six-store wing, introduced from the three hundred and forty-fifth FJ-3, Bu. No.136118. In this configuration the outboard pylons could carry 200gall (750l) drop tanks, the inners 500lb bombs or rocket pods, and the intermediate pylons either 1,000lb bombs or AAM-N-7 Sidewinder missiles. Aircraft equipped

for the Sidewinder were designated FJ-3M, with VF-211 receiving the first aircraft in 1956. FJ-3 and 3M deliveries from the first order were completed in February 1956. A further contract for FJ-3s, received on 26 March 1954, then went into manufacture, though a number of changes to the contract were required, based upon the future availability of more modern types. The contract had first been for 214 FJ-3s, but this was soon cut to just sixty-nine. Later, a further eighty aircraft were added, all going into production as NA-215s. Another order for eighty FJ-3s, NA-228, was placed on 2 November 1954 but later cancelled. The remaining FJ-3s were completed by the end of August 1956.

In contrast to the earlier aircraft, FJ-3s undertook many carrier cruises, among the first being VF-33's Mediterranean deployment aboard the USS *Lake Champlain* in September 1955. A couple of 'firsts' were also accomplished at this time. In place of the manually-controlled approach to landing on a carrier, the US

Navy had developed a mirror system to guide a pilot's approach automatically to the carrier. The first mirror landing on to a carrier was made on 22 August 1955 by Cdr Robert D. Dose, using an FJ-3 to come aboard the USS *Bennington*. On 4 January 1956 a VF-21 FJ-3 flown by Cdr Ralph L. Werner became the first aircraft to land aboard the USS *Forrestal*, the first of the new class of post-war giant carriers. Though the FJ-3 was never used in action, on at least two occasions it came close. During 1956 the US Navy's Sixth Fleet, comprising the carriers *Coral Sea* and *Randolph*, became involved in the evacuation of American nationals from Egypt during the Suez Crisis.

On a number of occasions FJ-3s from the Sixth Fleet encountered aircraft from the Anglo-French forces which were offensively targeting Egypt. On one occasion on 2 November two RAF Hunters from 34 Squadron were scrambled from Cyprus to intercept a flight of 'intruders'. It was not until the Hunters had closed to within 3,000ft (900m) that the 'targets' were discovered to be Furys. During 1958 FJ-3s were again in harm's way in the Mediterranean – supporting the American intervention in Lebanon. This time,

Furys from VF-62 landed at RAF Akrotiri in Cyprus by invitation.

FJ-3 Furys were retrofitted in service with an in-flight refuelling probe under the port wing for mid-air 'probe and drogue' refuelling. These aircraft were often refuelled from North American AJ-2 Savage tankers, but could also 'buddy refuel' from other tactical jets such as the Skyhawk and the FJ-4 Fury. The in-flight refuelling capability more than doubled the combat radius from 645 miles (1,040km) to 1,784 miles (2,870km). During 1957 a number of FJ-3s were converted as missile and drone directors. Those modified to handle the direction of the Vought Regulus surface-to-surface missile were redesignated FJ-3D, and those modified to handle radio-controlled F6F-6K drones were redesignated FJ-3D2. They served in utility and guided missile groups, often sending carrier-borne detachments to accomplish the mission at sea.

On 1 October 1962 remaining FJ-3s were redesignated F-1C under the new Tri-Service designation scheme.

FJ-3D Bu. No.136010 of Guided Missile Group 1 waits for the wave-off from USS Shangri La, **CVA-38, during 1957.** Bill Allen, Sr

Seen in flight soon after its first outing in October 1954, the first prototype FJ-4, Bu. No.139279, clearly shows the thin and highly cambered wing that made this model of the Fury such an effective machine. NAA

FJ-3 and FJ-3M Units

[CVG = assigned carrier air group as of December 1956]

VF-12 (FJ-3M) – CVG-1 (Atlantic Fleet)
VF-21 (FJ-3 and 3M) – CVG-6 (Pacific Fleet)
VF-24 (FJ-3 and 3M) – CVG-2 (Pacific Fleet)
VF-33 (FJ-3) – CVG-3 (Atlantic Fleet)
VF-51 (FJ-3M) – CVG-5 (Pacific Fleet)
VF-62 (FJ-3M) – CVG-4 (Atlantic Fleet)
VF-73 (FJ-3 and 3M) – CVG-7 (Atlantic Fleet)
VF-84 (FJ-3M) – CVG-8 (Atlantic Fleet)
VF-91 (FJ-3) – CVG-9 (Pacific Fleet)
VF-94 (FJ-3) – CVG-9 (Pacific Fleet)
VF-121 (FJ-3M) – CVG-12 (Pacific Fleet)
VF-142 (FJ-3M) – CVG-14 (Pacific Fleet)
VF-143 (FJ-3 and 3M) – CVG-14 (Pacific Fleet)
VF-154 (FJ-3) – CVG-15 (Pacific Fleet)
VF-172 (FJ-3M) – CVG-17 (Atlantic Fleet)
VF-173 (FJ-3M) – CVG-17 (Atlantic Fleet)
VF-191 (FJ-3) – CVG-19 (Pacific Fleet)
VF-211 (FJ-3 and 3M) – CVG-21 (Pacific Fleet)

Marine Units

VMF-122, MCAS Cherry Point
VMF-235, NAS Atsugi, Japan
VMF-333, MCAS Beaufort
VMF-334, MCAS El Toro

FJ-3 and FJ-3M Production

Bureau Nos	Type	Construction No.
Bu.131931	FJ-3	(converted FJ-2 with J65 engine)
Bu.135774 to 136162	FJ-3	194-1 to 389
Bu.139210 to 139278	FJ-3	215-1 to 69
Bu.141364 to 141443	FJ-3	215-70 to 149

Specifications: FJ-3 and FJ-3M

POWERPLANT
one Wright J65-W-4 or 4B of 7,650lb (3,469kg) thrust

DIMENSIONS

wingspan:	37ft 1in (11.3m)
length:	7ft 7in (11.45m)
height:	13ft 8in (4.16m)
wing area:	303sq ft (28.1sq m) or 287.9sq ft on early machines (26.79sq m)

WEIGHTS

empty:	12,205lb (5,534kg)
take-off fully loaded:	21,024lb (9,534kg)
internal fuel capacity:	559gall (2,096l)
total fuel capacity:	959gall (3,596l)

PERFORMANCE

maximum speed at sea level:	681mph (1,095km/h)
stalling speed:	133mph (213km/h)
initial rate of climb:	8,450ft/min (2,575m/min); 7,100ft/min with two Sidewinders (2,164m/min)
service ceiling:	49,000ft (14,935m)
range with external tanks:	1,784 miles (2,870 km)

ARMAMENT
4 x Colt Mk 12 20mm cannon with 648 rounds total
2 x AAM-N-7/GAR-8 Sidewinder or 2 x 1,000lb bombs
2 x 500lb bombs or four rocket packs

Although the FJ-3 was the third FJ model, the FJ-1 and the FJ-2 were not officially assigned 'F-1A' and 'F-1B' designations, having long since passed from the inventory. Subtypes of the FJ-3 were also redesignated; the FJ-3M became the MF-3C and the drone directors FJ-3D and FJ-3D2 became DF-1C and DF-1D, respectively.

Saving the Best for the Last: FJ-4 and FJ-4B

The final Fury variant was the FJ-4, arguably the finest iteration of the Sabre design concept. The FJ-4 owed little to its forebears from a design point of view and began life in February 1953 as project NA-208 in response to a Navy request, necessitated by the cancellation of the troubled McDonnell F3H Demon all-weather interceptor. The design brief was simple, the aircraft had to:

• Attain the maximum speed (Mach 0.95) and combat ceiling goals of the afterburning F3H Demon.

• Meet the endurance requirement of the F3H without drop tanks: 2hr combat-patrol time.

• Be carrier suitable.

• Be ready for delivery in two years.

On 4 June 1953 the Navy agreed a contract for two NA-208 prototypes and, sufficiently impressed with the pace of design work, the Navy then signed a contract for forty-three production NA-

209s on 16 October. These aircraft would be known as the FJ-4 Fury.

With a tight schedule it made sense for NAA designers to base their new design heavily upon the FJ-3, but the endurance requirement alone meant that 50 per cent more internal fuel would be required for an engine with no afterburner. The powerplant would be the same 7,650lb (3,496kg) thrust Wright J65-W-4 that drove the FJ-3; but the airframe was almost totally redesigned from the ground up, making the FJ-4 effectively an entirely new aircraft, rather than an evolution as with previous models. In order to carry the extra fuel the fuselage was deepened, and the tail fin featured an extended spine which faired forward into the cockpit canopy. The undercarriage was also entirely new, and wing box restrictions led to a new 'levered' design of main undercarriage leg. The main undercarriage track was increased to 11ft 7in (3.53m). The armament was again the four 20mm cannon installation, though this time with the alignment problems rectified. But the main feature that bestowed exceptional performance upon the FJ-4 was its wing.

The design brief was to develop a 6 per cent thickness ratio wing with more taper and camber for the same 35 degree sweep, while also incorporating leading-edge camber and space for integral fuel carriage. The undercarriage design, which was itself necessitated by the wing box, then predicated that, with mid-span ailerons, there was little room for conventional trailing edge flaps. Additionally, the retraction of a large-chord slotted flap into the wing would impinge on the fuel volume; clearly some radical thinking was required. The flap problem was quickly solved, and NAA's Paul Titus managed to evolve his 'gipper' slotted flap to leave the integral fuel volume relatively untouched. With lift being a crucial requirement, the cambered '6-3' wing developed specially for the later FJ-3s was used as a starting point, and

Above: **Many FJ-4s were used as target towing aircraft for the Navy. This VU-7 machine was based at NAAS Brown Field near San Diego.** J.M.G. Gradidge

Below: **The fourth FJ-4, seen here at Columbus, featured the originally designed short tail and flat rudder. Flight testing highlighted the need for a taller version, later trialled on this machine and adopted for production.** MAP

The FJ-4B was able to carry specially-designed 'buddy' refuelling tanks, which trailed a hose and drogue via a small airflow-driven turbine in the nose of the tank. This FJ-4B from development squadron VX-5 'Vampires' at China Lake has the right-hand hose trailed. J.M.G. Gradidge

enhanced by applying further camber far forward on the aerofoil along with an increase in the nose radius of the wing section. Slats were never an option for the FJ-4 as their operating tracks and mountings would have reduced fuel space. The highly tapered wing planform also caused some headaches since it was thought that this feature would lead to early tip stalling. As a result, three wind tunnel models were constructed to demonstrate three different wing arrangements: twisted but no camber, cambered but with no twist, and cambered and twisted. Testing at both the NAA and the California Tech wind tunnel showed that the twisted and cambered wing possessed tremendous stability over the whole speed range. The design went ahead with a 4-degree washout at the wing-tip, using what was later realized to be effectively a modified NACA 64A006 aerofoil.

On 26 June 1954 the NA-209 order was modified to incorporate a further 107 aircraft, bringing the total to 150. The first FJ-4, Bu. No.139279, was flown from Columbus on 28 October, piloted by Richard Wenzell. The only problem encountered during the test phase was a slight directional instability which was rectified by lengthening the vertical tail fin. The modification was first incorporated in the second production aircraft and then retrofitted to earlier machines. The first production FJ-4s came off the Columbus production line in February 1955. These were also powered by the Wright J65-W-4, but, from the thirty-third aircraft, Bu. No.139313, the J65-W-16 of 7,700lb (3,491kg) thrust was fitted. Other aircraft had W-4 engines reworked to W-16 standard and these were redesignated J65-W-4B. Further improvements led to the ability to carry 150gall (680l) fuel tanks on the outer wing pylons, a feature incorporated in the twenty-second production

aircraft. The first production run also introduced an air-driven emergency hydraulic pump, powered by a ram-air turbine. This item was fitted, in favour of a battery-driven electric pump, on the first six FJ-4s, then on the eighth aircraft and finally introduced as standard on Bu. No.139323, the forty-fifth production machine. Also installed was in-flight refuelling equipment, again using a wing-mounted probe. The system considerably increased the effective range of the aircraft, which was limited only by the engine's oil consumption. On the first aircraft a 3gall (11.25l) oil tank was mounted on the upper right-hand side of the compressor housing and this fed the engine oil system through a gear-driven pump. Oil to the centre and rear main engine bearings was 'total loss', that is, after it had lubricated these bearings the oil was vented overboard. With a maximum allowable oil loss rate of 0.4gall (1.5l) per hour, this limited the mission time, irrespective of in-flight refuelling, to 5hr. From aircraft Bu. No.139471, a 4gall (15l) oil tank was fitted, which raised the mission time to 7hr.

During 1955 seventeen FJ-4s were

completed, followed by 113 in 1956. Slated for Marine use, the FJ-4 Fleet Introduction Program was initiated at NATC, Patuxent River by Marine pilots. Carrier suitability tests were then carried out aboard the USS *Forrestal* in April 1956. The first Marine unit to receive FJ-4s was the VMF-323 in September. By the end of March 1957 all 150 FJ-4s had been delivered, passing to a total of eight Marine fighter and attack squadrons.

FJ-4B

The FJ-4B was developed as a ground-attack variant of the FJ-4 and was eventually built in greater numbers than the original FJ-4 Fury. The FJ-4B differed in having a wing strengthened to take six ordnance stations, capable of carrying up to 6,000lb (2,721kg) of fuel tanks, rockets or bombs. These included a variety of nuclear weapons or 'special stores', which were mounted on a specially-configured pylon under the left wing.

The FJ-4B was also fitted with an additional pair of speed brakes on the rear fuselage flanks and these were rigged to open with the conventional speed brakes, but on landing the additional panels retracted when the undercarriage was lowered. These additional brakes were fitted to reduce speed during low-level attacks, and an F-86H type low altitude bombing system (LABS) was also installed.

Twenty-five FJ-4Bs were ordered on 26 July 1954 and added to the original NA-209 contract. With relatively minor revisions to the FJ-4 design, production was smoothly integrated into the Columbus line and the first aircraft flew on 3 December 1956, again with George Wenzell as pilot. Forty-six more FJ-4Bs were ordered under contract NA-229 on 2 November 1954 and the last of these was delivered in August 1957. One further order was placed for 151 aircraft, as NA-244s, on 5 April 1956. These were delivered beginning in July 1957, with the last being completed in May 1958, for a total of 222 aircraft. The FJ-4B Fleet Introduction Program began at Moffett Field in California during 1957, with the emphasis being on the perfection of techniques for the LABS

FJ-4B of VA-192, piloted by Bill Allen, Sr, about to engage the barrier on USS Bonne Homme Richard, **CVA-31. The unit was on a WestPac deployment to Japan at the time.** Bill Allen, Sr

Aftermath of Bill Allen's barrier engagement, 1959. Bu. No.143569 received minor damage to its fin. Note the 'buddy' refuelling pod turbine. Bill Allen, Sr

delivery of nuclear weapons.

The FJ-4B was also equipped to deliver the Martin ASM-N-7 Bullpup air-to-surface guided missile, up to five being carried, with the starboard inner wing station carrying the missile's guidance-transmitter pod. The Bullpup was 11ft (3.4m) in length, driven by an Aerojet General solid rocket motor. The total weight of the missile was 571lb (258kg) and it was equipped with a 250lb (113kg) high-explosive warhead. The missile was guided visually by the pilot through a correlation radio link and thus flew line-of-sight to the target. Testing of the missile was begun at Point Mugu in California in 1956 to ascertain whether the 'human servo and computer' (the pilot) was able to perform this function. Flight testing began on 19 November 1956 and in total eighty-five Bullpups were launched. The evaluation squadron VX-4 used FJ-4Bs in this phase, firing forty-two missiles in total

and twenty-seven of them during the accelerated flight test phase on 5 and 6 November 1957. In two days the Bullpup showed an airborne reliability of 85.7 per cent. The ASM-N-7 initially deployed with the FJ-4Bs of VA-212 aboard the USS *Lexington* in April 1959 and, although some Marines units trained with the missile, it was never fired by them. The Bullpup was redesignated AGM-12 in 1962.

The Marine Fury units began to withdraw their aircraft in the early 1960s, with VMA-216 at Kaneohe in Hawaii being the last; their final machine departed for NAS Barbers Point on 23 January 1962. VA-216 had the distinction of undertaking the FJ-4B's final Navy cruise, when the Squadron embarked on the Lexington in February 1962. When the cruise ended in August the Furys were replaced in naval use by the A-4 Skyhawk. On 1 October 1962 the

adoption of the uniform designation system for all US military aircraft led to surviving FJ-4s being redesignated F-1Es, while FJ-4Bs became AF-1Es. However, by this time the F-1Es and AF-1Es had been assigned to Naval Reserve units, such as those at NAS Atlanta, Glenview, Glynco, New Orleans, New York, Willow Grove and Andrews AFB. AF-1E Furies and a small number of F-1Es remained with the Naval Air Reserves until 1964 when they were finally withdrawn and placed in store at the Naval Air Facility Litchfield Park in Arizona.

Though the Fury did not have cause to demonstrate its nuclear capability, it did get a chance to prove that such a mission was feasible. During the early 1960s an FJ-4B with 500gall (1,875l) of external fuel was flown from NAS Quonset Point to NAS Mayport in Florida. There it descended to near sea level, delivered a Mk 28 dummy nuclear weapon and returned to Quonset Point. It thus demonstrated a combat radius of more than 820 nautical miles (1,518km) in this role.

Above: **Dayglo-trimmed FJ-4B Bu. No.143607 served with the Navy and Marine Reserve unit at NAS Willow Grove. Some of the last Furys in service, these aircraft were redesignated AF-1Es in October 1962.** J.M.G. Gradidge

Below: **One of two rocket-augmented FJ-4F conversions, Bu. No.139282 began flight test in April 1957. The tail-mounted rocket motor powered the FJ-4Fs to speeds of Mach 1.41 and altitudes of 71,000ft (21,640m). Retired from use, they were stored at NAS Litchfield Park in Arizona.** J.M.G. Gradidge

The Rocket-augmented FJ-4F

One final Fury development that reached flight status was the FJ-4F, which began life as NAA project NA-234 on 12 August 1955. With further development, the project was amended to NA-248 on 28 May 1956 and two prototypes were ordered, to be converted from the second and the fourth production FJ-4s. This project was designed to flight test the 5,000lb (2,267kg) thrust Rocketdyne AR-1 rocket engine; for this the rocket motor was installed above the tailpipe on the two aircraft, the J65 engine being retained. The throttleable AR-1 was fuelled by a mixture of hydrogen peroxide and JP-4, the latter being held in modified underwing drop tanks. It is thought that the first flight of the FJ-4F was during early 1956, with testing centring around Patuxent River, though it appears that the rocket motor was not used for some time after this. The aircraft were first flown

For many years, Flight Systems at Mojave in California operated the world's only airworthy FJ Fury. Withdrawn from use in 1982, the FJ-4B, ex-Bu. No.143575, was purchased by Larry Mockford of T-Bird Aviation at Mojave in 1991 and restored again to airworthy condition. MAP

with an instrumented belly pack, but both FJ-4F aircraft were later configured with instrumented nose cones, similar in their location to the USAF's F-86D. One FJ-4F set an unofficial speed and altitude record of Mach 1.41 and 71,000ft (21,640m), but their primary use was in Rocketdyne testing. In 1960, with testing completed and further tests under way with a modified F-86F, the FJ-4Fs were retired to Litchfield Park.

FJ-4 and FJ-4B Units

[CVG = assigned carrier air group as of 1 July 1960]
VA-22 (FJ-4B) CVG-2
VA-23 (FJ-4B) CVG-2
VA-55 (FJ-4B) CVG-5
VA-56 (FJ-4B) CVG-5
VA-63 (FJ-4B) (became VA-22 on 1 July 1959)
VA-116 (FJ-4B) (became VA-144 on 23 February 1959)
VA-126 (FJ-4B) CVG-12
VA-144 (FJ-4B) CVG-14
VA-146 (FJ-4B) CVG-14
VA-151(FJ-4B) (became VA-23 on 1 July 1959)
VA-192 (FJ-4B) CVG-19
VA-212 (FJ-4B) CVG-21
VA-214 (FJ-4 and FJ-4B) ATG-4
VA-216 (FJ-4 and FJ-4B) CVG-21

Marine Units

VMA-212 (FJ-4), MCAS Kaneohe
VMA-214 (FJ-4), MCAS Kaneohe
VMA-223 (FJ-4), MCAS El Toro
VMF-232 (FJ-4), NAS Atsugi, Japan
VMF-235 (FJ-4), NAS Atsugi, Japan
VMF-323 (FJ-4), MCAS El Toro and NAS Atsugi, Japan
VMF-334 (FJ-4), NAS Atsugi, Japan
VMF-451 (FJ-4), NAS Atsugi, Japan

Specifications: FJ-4 and FJ-4B

POWERPLANT
Wright J65-W-4 of 7,650lb (3,469kg) thrust (early machines) or Wright J65-W-16A or ñ4B of 7,700lb (3,491kg) thrust

WEIGHTS (FJ-4)
empty: 13,210lb (5,990kg)
take-off (clean): 20,130lb (9,128kg)
maximum take-off weight: 28,000lb (12,968kg)
internal fuel capacity: 840gall (3,150l)
total fuel capacity: 1,240gall (4,650l)

WEIGHTS (FJ-4B)
empty: 13,778lb (6,248kg)
maximum take-off weight: 28,000lb (12,968kg)

DIMENSIONS
wingspan: 39ft 1in (11.91m)
length: 36ft 8in (11.17m)
height: 13ft 10in (4.21m)
wing area: 338.66sq ft (31.5sq m)

PERFORMANCE
maximum speed at sea level: 680mph (1,094 km/h)
stalling speed: 139mph (223 km/h)
initial rate of climb: 7,660ft/min (2,334m/min)
service ceiling: 46,800ft (14,264m)
range (with external tanks; no in-flight refuelling): 2,020 miles (3,250 km)

ARMAMENT
4 x Colt Mk 12 20mm cannon with 576 rounds total
2 x AAM-N-7/GAR-8 Sidewinders or 2 x 1,000lb bombs
2 x 500lb bombs or four rocket packs
5 x Bullpup air-to-surface missiles + 1 guidance pod
1 x Mk 7, Mk 12 or Mk 28 Special Store

FJ-4 and FJ-4B Production

Bureau Nos	Type	Construction No.
Bu.139279 and 139280	FJ-4	208-1 and 2 (prototypes)
Bu.139281 to 139323	FJ-4	209-1 to 43 (including 2 FJ-4Fs)
Bu.139424 to 139530	FJ-4	209-44 to 150
Bu.139531 to 139555	FJ-4B	209-151 to 175
Bu.141444 to 141489	FJ-4B	209-176 to 221
Bu.143493 to 143643	FJ-4B	244-1 to 151

CHAPTER SEVEN

Overseas F-86 Operators

Background to the Military Assistance Program/Mutual Defense Assistance Program

During World War II the American Government had provided significant military assistance to a host of countries throughout the world. With the end of the war the situation had changed somewhat, but the need to defend and rearm those same nations became perhaps even more important – now the enemy was communism.

The Lend-Lease of the war period was superseded by the Interim Allocation Program and then other similar schemes by which modern military equipment and support was provided to 'friendly' nations. The plan was put forward by the USAF Commander Gen Henry 'Hap' Arnold. He finalized this idea, and, by the early 1950s, significant numbers of US-funded, war-surplus aircraft (such as the P-47 Thunderbolt and the B-25 Mitchell) found their way to air forces around the world, in theory providing a lucrative buffer against the Communists. The scheme would eventually be known as the Military Assistance Program (MAP) or the Mutual Defense Assistance Program (MDAP). In either case the rationale behind the concept was the same. In order to also provide a good basis for trade the MAP aircraft were usually supplied at little or no cost to the user.

But the rules of MDAP/MAP were clear: all equipment was to be used in a defensive role, and at the end of its useful life all equipment supplied under the Programs had to be destroyed or returned to the United States. These basic tenets were often ignored, but the American government did, to its credit, keep a tight rein on the machinery supplied under MAP and often applied diplomatic pressure if the terms of the agreement were undermined. It is worth noting that this did indeed happen in more than one case involving MAP-supplied Sabres, notably with the Portuguese and German aircraft.

From 1954, the F-86F and the F-80C became the standard MAP fighters and both types began to equip foreign air forces, though the Sabre became the dominant aircraft, not least because there were far more of them available. Before their deployment to MAP countries, however, air and ground crews from these nations were trained in the United States, beginning at Nellis and Williams AFB. Bob Murray was at Williams in 1954, involved in such pilot training which brought some famous airmen to the base:

> We had Germans, Japanese (including two Pearl Harbor veterans), Nationalist Chinese, Danes, Norwegians, one or two Belgians, some South Americans and others. [World War II ace] Johannes Steinhof was one of my students. Needless to say, I didn't try to tell him how to shoot down planes.

Later on, when F-86Ds began to trickle into the MAP system, their pilots and ground crews were trained at Chanute and Perrin AFBs. The actual aircraft for supply to MAP countries were usually overhauled and IRAN (Inspect and Repair As Necessary) maintenance was carried out. On the F-86Fs the F-40 wing was usually installed, and in many cases TACAN and Sidewinder missile capability was incorporated before delivery. This maintenance was usually carried out by civilian contractors, such as North American itself at Inglewood and Palmdale, FIAT in Italy, Scottish Aviation at Prestwick, CASA at Madrid and Shin Meiwa at Komaki and Itami in Japan. Other significant civilian F-86F work for the MAP programme was undertaken at Tainan in the Republic of China. In addition to civilian conversion work, USAF Air Materiel Areas undertook Sabre maintenance before transfers overseas were made. In particular, Sacramento Air Materiel Area at McLellan AFB in California, Mobile Air Materiel Area at Brookley AFB in Alabama, and the Chateauroux Air Depot in France were involved in this way. It is

This unusual, silver-painted F-86F was assigned to McLellan AFB in August 1958 and used to evaluate modifications for MAP-supplied Sabres. Note that it has an F-40 wing fitted as well as Tacan nose antenna. As the last active USAF Sabre, it was retired in 1970. The extra 'zero' in the serial number was applied to differentiate between (in this case) FY52 and FY62 aircraft. MAP

also worth mentioning that, in many cases, in-theatre assets were often routed through conversion in that area and then passed to nearby countries. Thus, as an example, many USAF Europe F-86Ds were routed through FIAT and Chateauroux for conversion before being transferred to MAP customers in Europe.

The MAP/MDAP programmes outlasted the Sabre, many further deliveries of more modern aircraft being made up to the present day. The F-5 Freedom Fighter replaced the F-86F as the standard MAP fighter, though other US-supplied machines also eventually replaced F-86s in these countries.

In the remainder of this chapter the experiences of many of the world's air forces with these programmes are summarized.

Argentina

During the late 1950s the Argentine Air Force (FAA, Fuerza Aérea Argentina) came to an agreement with the American Government to purchase a quantity of F-86 Sabres, having earlier been unsuccessful in obtaining thirty-six Canadair Sabre 6s. The FAA received twenty-eight F-86Fs and, starting in May 1960, sixteen aircraft were ferried from storage at Davis Monthan AFB, Arizona to NAA's Inglewood plant for refurbishment. The remaining twelve Sabres were transferred in May from McLellan AFB to Inglewood. All were F-86F-30 models and were converted at NAA with the long-span F-40 wing modification. As they passed through North American, the FAA Sabres were assigned Argentine serials in the C-101 to C-128 range, following straight on from a batch of Gloster Meteors. The 'C' indicated Caza (fighter). It is interesting to note that in 1956 the Soviets had offered Argentina a number of MiG-15s and Il-28 bombers in exchange for raw materials.

The Argentinian Sabres were transferred to MAP between 18 August and 29 October 1960 and flown to Williams AFB, Arizona for ferrying out under the command of Col Jorge Martinez Zubiria. The first batch of twelve Sabres departed from Williams AFB on 6 September on a mission code-named Operacion *Sabre*, bound for El Plumerillo Air Base in Argentina. From Williams the

In early Fuerza Aérea Argentina (FAA) service, the F-86Fs of IV Brigada Aérea carried this rather plain natural metal finish. C-122, ex-USAF 52-4973, was among the last FAA Sabres in use and was withdrawn in July 1986. J.F.N. Padin

aircraft routed via Kelly AFB in Texas and Brookley AFB in Alabama. It was here that the formation was delayed for several days due to hurricane 'Donna'. When the weather cleared, the Sabres then flew on to Homestead AFB in Florida, Kingston in Jamaica and then to Howard AFB, Canal Zone. Here maintenance work was carried out on the aircraft before the longest leg – 825 miles – into Peru was accomplished. Landing first at Talara, the Sabres then routed via Pisco (Peru) and Antofagasta (Chile) before the formation touched down in Argentina on 26 September. However, only nine Sabres actually made it into El Plumerillo on the 26th as one aircraft (C-116) had experienced a generator failure and diverted to Talara and two more (C-109 and C-115) were temporarily grounded at Antofagasta. These Sabres arrived in Argentina on 28 and 29 September.

The first ferry flight was performed by FAA pilots, with the exception of one aircraft, piloted by USAF Maj Manuel J. 'Pete' Fernandez, the well-known Korean War ace. Fernandez was to assume the role

of adviser to the fledgling Sabre squadron, and later retired to live in Argentina. To provide logistics and rescue backup, two FAA C-54A transports and a USAF SA-16B amphibian accompanied the Sabres to Argentina. The last of the final batch of fourteen FAA Sabres were delivered on 6 December and it seems that a twenty-ninth F-86F was also assigned for instructional use. Before this, FAA personnel had undergone training in the United States, where, in late 1959, the pilots were put through 80hr of T-33 training, followed by 50hr conversion on the F-86F with the 4530th Combat Crew Training Wing at Williams AFB.

Following the delivery of the last Sabres, a hand-over ceremony was held at the end of December 1960 at Ezeiza International Airport in the presence of the Argentine President. All Argentine AF Sabres were then assigned to Grupo 1 de Caza-Bombardeo within IV Brigada Aérea.

In late 1961 the Commander in Chief of the FAA formulated plans to create aerobatic squadrons to commemorate the

FAA's Bodas de Oro (Golden Jubilee). This would eventually result in the creation of four distinct teams: Escuadrilla 46 equipped with Meteor IVs from Grupos 2 and 3 de Caza, Bodas de Oro flying T-34 Mentors from the Grupo 1 de Entrenamiento (training) and Condor with MS 760 Paris from the Escuela de Aviacion Militar. The final team was Escuadrilla Cruz del Sur (Southern Cross) from IV BA with their F-86Fs. Escuadrilla Cruz del Sur flew their first display at Tandil on 12 February 1962, followed by many other shows during the year. At the end of the season, with the drawing to a close of the FAA anniversary celebrations and the dispersal of team personnel to other assignments, the Cruz del Sur team was quietly disbanded. By November most of the team aircraft had been stripped of their colourful schemes, though it is known that C-119 retained its colours until mid-1963. The FAA never reformed a Sabre aerobatic team.

On 1 and 2 August 1962 the first Inter-American Air-Ground Gunnery Meeting was held on the Las Lajas ranges, with participating aircraft flying from El Plumerillo. Teams of F-86Fs were invited from Argentina, Peru (Talara) and the United States (Luke AFB). An F-80 team from Uruguay could not participate due to technical difficulties. The FAA's team of three pilots included two Cruz del Sur members – Vicecomodoro Jorge Mones Ruiz and Capt Carlos Blasis. In addition, two Cruz del Sur F-86Fs, C-113 and C-116, in the full team colour scheme were used by the gunnery team. On completion of the competition, the FAA had won the overall team contest, the individual trophy for most points in gunnery (Mones Ruiz) and most points for dive-bombing. In celebration of their success, the two Sabres had the word Campeones (champions) added in white on the left side of the nose above the official badge of the meeting.

The FAA Sabres were used in action only once – during the April 1963 'Revolución de Azules y Colorados', in which mainly Naval personnel took up arms against the President José Marío Guido. In the early morning of 2 April they took control of the Punta Indio Navy base, and at 6pm the same day four FAA Sabres were deployed to Morón, near Buenos Aires. From 8 o'clock the next morning the Sabres, along with FAA Meteors, Lincoln bombers and Morane

During 1970 remaining Argentinian F-86Fs were repainted in a camouflage colour scheme at Cordoba. 1st Lt Puga is seen here climbing aboard aircraft C-123 which was later presented to the USAF Academy at Colorado Springs. Note the IV BA badge and simple 'Fuerza Aerea' inscription. J.F.N. Padin

Paris trainers, carried out bombing raids against Punta Indio. By midday, the rebels had surrendered, at a cost of forty lives, and twenty-four naval aircraft had also been destroyed on the ground. No FAA aircraft were lost in this brief but bloody revolt, the Sabres being credited with at least one C-54 transport destroyed on the ground.

During 1964 FAA Sabres were deployed to Peru to take part in Operativo Ayacucho, an exercise designed to bring together the forces of Argentina, Colombia, Paraguay, Peru, Venezuela and the United States in a simulated joint operation to combat a left-wing insurgent movement in Peru. In the exercise FAA Sabres operated as Escuadrón de Caza 110, and carried out simulated bombing of rebel positions. Operativa Ayacucho was followed upon the Sabres' return by

further tactical exercises in the Argentine provinces of Formosa and Cordoba. In particular, the rising tensions between Argentina and Chile led to the deployment of seven FAA F-86Fs to Comodoro Rivadavia during August 1967. This deployment was named Operativo Comprobación.

Until 1970 FAA Sabres had worn a nondescript, natural metal colour scheme, but in line with FAA policy, aircraft going through overhaul at Area Material Rio Cuarto in Cordoba were gradually painted in a camouflage of dark green, tan and grey upper surfaces with semi-gloss white undersides. On these aircraft the Argentine flag was painted on the tail, as was the serial number, in white, but curiously, no national roundels were ever carried on these Sabres.

The F-86s soldiered on with IV BA

Green and white checked Sabre 32 of Royal Australian Air Force's 77 Squadron. The unit was based at Butterworth in Malaya for ten years from February 1959. A94-988 later passed to the Indonesian AF.
Jon Lake

until 1976, when it was decided to withdraw the fifteen surviving Sabres from service, of which a dozen were to be passed to the air force of Uruguay. However, this deal fell through as a result of pressure from the United States, and, though FAA Sabres took part in an Air Force exercise over the Las Lajas gunnery range on 11 May 1978, this was probably the last time they did so. The remaining Sabres took on an operational training role, one which became more important with the start of the Falklands/Malvinas conflict in 1982. The deployment of A-4 Skyhawks in that conflict left a gap in the domestic defence requirement and the ten FAA F-86Fs available were kept airworthy, despite a further two aircraft being lost in flying accidents the previous year. The Sabres were operated until 19 June 1986, when C-120/52-4963 broke up over Rivadavia during a routine three-ship sweep, killing the pilot. Wing failure was the cause of this crash and the accident led to the permanent grounding of the remaining FAA Sabres on 3 July, marking the end of a colourful era in Argentina's history.

Seventeen Sabres were lost in FAA service, the first being C-103 which was destroyed in a crash on 13 June 1961 at Isla Grande. In addition, C-121 was lost in a ground fire on 5 October 1972; it donated parts to become a composite display aircraft 'C-113' at Mendoza. Many of the FAA's surviving Sabres

subsequently returned to the United States, and have now been restored to airworthy condition in private hands.

Australia

The Royal Australian Air Force (RAAF) received its first CA-27 at Laverton in August 1954 and began Sabre operations during November when CA-27 Mk 30s were delivered to the Sabre Trials Flight of No. 2 Operational Training Unit (OTU) at Williamtown. 2 OTU, commanded by Wg Cdr R.C. Cresswell, began training RAAF Sabre pilots on 1 January 1955, and these aircraft flew alongside Wirraway and Vampire trainers at Williamtown. 2 OTU was renamed 2 Operational Conversion Unit (OCU) on 1 September 1958.

Once they had been passed out from the OTU, the first RAAF Sabre pilots were posted to 75 Squadron at Williamtown, the first operational unit to receive the type, equipping during April 1955. Next to receive Sabres was 3 Squadron in March 1956 and then 77 Squadron in November, also at Williamtown. Two further units, 76 and 79 Squadron, received Sabres in 1960 and 1962, respectively, the latter at Ubon Air Base in Thailand. The Thai deployment was part of the Australian air-defence commitment to the South-East Asia Treaty Organization (SEATO) during the Vietnam War. Sabres from 79 Squadron

regularly took part in simulated combat missions with USAF 7th TFS F-4 Phantoms, and these sorties successfully helped the F-4 crews to develop tactics to combat MiG-17 and 19 aircraft over Vietnam. The Squadron left Thailand in July 1968; aircraft and personnel were absorbed by 77 Squadron.

The Sabres of 3 and 77 Squadron also deployed overseas, to RAAF Butterworth in Malaya during November 1958 in support of Malayan emergency operations. To carry out the movement of the aircraft, Operation Sabre Ferry was initiated. With 3 Squadron's twenty-one Sabres departing at the beginning of November, the operation was supported by seven Canberra weather and navigation ships, four search-and-rescue Neptunes and seven Dakota transports to move the equipment. Routing via Townsville, Garbutt and Darwin, the aircraft were ferried in flights of three or four on odd-numbered days of the month beginning on 1 November. Crossing the Australian coast, the flights would then fly to Biak in Dutch New Guinea, Guiuan in the Philippines, and from Labuan in Borneo to Butterworth. 77 Squadron followed in early February 1959, and the two units became part of the British Commonwealth Strategic Reserve, alongside other RAAF types, notably the Canberras of 2 Squadron. The Sabres took part in only a few strikes against Communist insurgents during the emergency, beginning in February 1959 and continuing until July 1960. At the end of the emergency the Sabre squadrons took over garrison duties, participating in a number of SEATO air exercises and also being ready in case of a flare-up during the confrontation with Indonesia in 1963-64.

The discovery of metal fatigue in the wings of RAAF Sabres during 1964 necessitated a high priority being given to a modification programme – the Sabre at the time being the RAAF's only fighter. Modification kits were drawn up in the United States and, as the Sabres were scheduled for inspection and maintenance, the wing modifications were carried out. It appears that this may well have coincided with the fitting of Sidewinder missile launch rails.

The Australian-built Mirage IIIO began to replace the Sabre as the RAAF's main fighter during August 1965 when 75 Squadron at Williamtown officially converted. 76 Squadron followed suit in

A94-928 of 2 Operational Conversion Unit at RAAF Williamtown. The small retractable cooling vent, unique to the CAC Sabre, can be seen atop the fuselage. This aircraft also has the external oil pipe fitted to aerobatic team aircraft. Author

The last Sabres in RAAF service were those assigned to 5 Operational Training Unit. Most acquired a blue and white tail and intake trim, as seen on the machine in the background, as well as the new, slanted fin flash. J.M.G. Gradidge

September 1966, and in July 1967 3 squadron returned to Australia to re-equip with the type. At the same time, it was being proposed that RAAF Sabres could be converted for the ground-attack role; this never happened, and the Sabre was withdrawn from squadron service due to its remaining low fatigue life. As the last front-line RAAF Sabre unit, 77 Squadron under Wg Cdr K. Martin returned to Australia in April 1969 and converted to Mirages during July.

But the Sabre's days with the RAAF were far from over; 2 OCU continued to operate the type, having gained the best surviving aircraft from the squadrons. The unit used the Sabre as an advanced trainer alongside the first Mirage IIIOs from March 1964, and these were complemented by the arrival of AerMacchi MB326H aircraft in 1969. Mirage training became the sole responsibility of 2 OCU in 1970, and a new unit, 5 OUT, was reformed at Williamtown on 1 April 1970 to take over Sabre conversion and operational training for Mirage crews. In addition, 5 OTU Sabres often carried out banner-towing duties for the Mirages of 2 OCU. Having served its purpose, the unit was disbanded on 31 July 1971 and many of the Sabres withdrawn on that date were briefly stored at Williamtown before refurbishment and delivery to Indonesia.

In service, RAAF Sabres flew more than 210,600hr and, despite a generally good safety record, a total of thirty were lost as a result of flying accidents in RAAF service. The first loss was A94-911, which crashed on landing at Williamtown in May 1955. The final RAAF Sabre write-off occurred on 15 March 1971, when Plt Off Elsbury from 5 OTU ejected from A94-966 in a spin. Elsbury escaped unharmed and resumed flying duties two weeks later.

Bangladesh

The Bangladesh Defence Force (Bangladesh Biman Bahini/BDF) gained its five Canadair Sabre 6s from Pakistan in 1971. In fact, these were all that remained in airworthy condition at Tezgaon when Bangladesh (formerly East Pakistan) gained independence. These ex-14 Squadron, Pakistan Air Force aircraft were operated in natural metal finish, with a red intake ring, wing-tips and drop-tank noses. BDF roundels were applied in the usual six positions, with a Bangladesh flag on the tail fin and the Canadair construction number on the rear fuselage. All had Martin-Baker ejection seats fitted.

With a number of ex-Pakistan AF Sabre personnel in Bangladesh, the Sabres were kept airworthy despite a lack of spares support. In early 1973 twelve MiG-21MF fighters were delivered to the BDF at Chittagong and these Soviet-supplied aircraft operated alongside the Sabre 6s for a period before the latter were finally withdrawn in late 1973.

Belgium

It appears that a small number of F-86Fs were loaned to Belgium in 1955 for trials in line with finding a new fighter for its Air Force (Force Aerienne Belge). These aircraft were tested between 25 June and 5 December 1955, but little can be found on the results of the test. At this point Belgian air crews were also undergoing

Bolivia

Nine ex-Venezuelan AF F-86F-30s were delivered in October 1973 for use with Bolivia's 1 Grupo Aéreo de Caza at Santa Cruz/El Trompillo (the unit was later renamed Grupo Aéreo de Caza 32). Fuerza Aérea Boliviana (FAB) Sabres were supplied from Venezuela in an overall silver paint scheme and were given serials ranging from 650 to 658, inclusive. These machines were regularly overhauled and modified in Argentina, though the Bolivian aircraft did not benefit from the VOR radio fit of the FAA machines. This proved a costly omission when, in 1978, a pair of FAB Sabres became lost over the Amazon jungle; their pilots were forced to eject into the rainforest below.

In the mid-1980s four of the remaining six Sabres were routed through Taller Regional Rio IV at Cordoba in Argentina for overhaul. At the same time they were painted in a camouflage scheme similar to that worn by Argentinian F-86Fs. The FAB cam-

On 11 July 1984 disaster struck the small Sabre unit when a civilian Cessna crashed into the FAB hangar at Santa Cruz; it is thought that one of the F-86Fs was written off as a result. Shortage of spare parts for the Bolivian Sabres began to be felt at this time, Peru being approached in addition to Argentina in an effort to keep the aircraft in an airworthy condition. This lack of materiel support resulted in the withdrawal of three Sabres from use in August 1983 when canopy-jettison cartridges became unavailable. Despite this setback, FAB continued to support the aircraft and, by 1987, four Sabres were in service with Grupo Aereo de Caza 32.

Bolivia had hoped to receive the last of Argentina's Sabres in the mid to late 1980s, but the FAA's continued use of the Sabre as a result of the Falklands conflict made this impossible. In any case, Argentina's Sabres were withdrawn from use in 1987 with fatigue problems. The FAB's Sabres lasted only a few years longer, for when F-86F serial no. 652 exploded in flight in 1992, the remaining three aircraft were withdrawn. At this time four pilots were qualified on the aircraft. During the 1980s Lockheed T-33ANs supplemented the Sabres of GAC 32, and it is thought that these aircraft survive the F-86F as Bolivia's only jet offensive force.

Soon after their withdrawal all three surviving Bolivian Sabres were purchased by David Clark of Texas Air Command in Arlington. Clark was instrumental in the restoration of these aircraft, one of which was flying again by November 1995. The aircraft were put up for sale with fresh engine hot sections, paint, IRAN and radio at $325,000 each, plus a spare engine. These Sabres had actually been obtained from the Bolivians with full military equipment – including the gunsights.

It is rare to see photographs of any Bolivian Sabres in the air, much less four. These aircraft are all in the natural metal delivery colour scheme of around 1973. The leading machine, 656, was one of the three surviving FAB F-86Fs withdrawn in 1993 – the last front-line Sabres in use. *via Mike Fox*

Sabre conversion at Williams AFB, and so clearly the aircraft was a serious contender.

However, in the end, the Belgians decided to procure the British-designed Hunter and took up a licence to produce it in-house. The F-86Fs were returned to the United States, where they had nominally been on the charge of Warner Robins Air Materiel Area.

ouflage consisted of dark bronze-green, tan and light grey upper surfaces with semi-gloss white undersides. The Bolivian roundels were retained, but otherwise the aircraft were generally devoid of squadron or personalized markings, though the silver aircraft did at this time display a red-painted, intake lip.

Brazil

During 1966 the Brazilian Força Aérea Brasileira were reported as 'interested' in the supply of ex-Luftwaffe Sabre 6s, no doubt to replace the Meteor F-8s of 1 Grupo Aviaçao de Caça (GAvCa) and the F-80C Shooting Stars of 4 GAvCa. However, these Sabres were sold to Iran instead and no agreement was ever reached. The Meteors soldiered on until

1974, when they were replaced by Northrop F-5Es; the F-80Cs had earlier been withdrawn from service in 1970.

Canada

The first 'foreign' air force to receive Sabres, the Royal Canadian Air Force (RCAF) received entirely indigenously-built F-86s, beginning in 1951. Following ad hoc training with USAF Sabre units, RCAF pilots began to be more formally assigned to F-86 training with the Mobile Training Unit at Chatham. This unit also started the induction of Sabre ground crews and received the second production Sabre 2 for this purpose, before moving on to Chatham, New Brunswick in early 1952. At Chatham, No.1 (Fighter) Operational Training Unit (OTU) began to receive Sabre 2s in February 1952 for

the commencement of RCAF flying training on the type. Prospective pilots then graduated from the Harvard to T-33 and then on to the Sabre itself. No.1 (F) OTU also began the training of Greek and Turkish airmen before their countries each received the Canadair Sabre. As Sabre 5s became available a few years later, the unit then converted on to the type and took over the training requirements for Orenda-engined Sabre 5 and 6 units of the RCAF.

The first RCAF squadron to receive the Sabre was 410 Squadron at Dorval, which gained one Sabre 2 briefly in April 1951 before conversion from the British Vampire began in earnest during May. With the Squadron up to full strength, 410 was then earmarked for deployment to the United Kingdom later in the year, and thirty-five Sabre 2s were flown to Norfolk, Virginia for cocooning by the US

Navy before disembarking aboard HMCS Magnificent during November. Arriving in England, 410 Squadron moved into RAF North Luffenham, followed by 439 and 441 Squadrons in June and February 1952, respectively. Unlike its fellow units within 1 Wing at North Luffenham, 439 Squadron flew in its Sabres as part of 'Leapfrog 1', a series of RCAF operations tasked with deploying aircraft across the Atlantic.

To support the Canadian Sabres in Europe, the Bristol Aeroplane Company in England was engaged to undertake servicing tasks for the RCAF. Repairs which could be handled at North Luffenham were carried out there by Bristol's technicians, while extensive overhauls and other servicing were completed at its Filton airfield near Bristol. Company engineers travelled to the Canadair plant during September 1951 for training, and the first RCAF Sabre was accepted for routine servicing at North Luffenham on 10 March 1952. Bristol also undertook J47 engine overhaul for RCAF Sabres, while Airwork

The first Royal Canadian Air Force squadron to receive the Sabre was 410 Squadron at Dorval. The unit moved to RAF North Luffenham in England during late 1951. These 410 Squadron Sabre 2s are taxiing at 'North Luff' soon after arrival. DND via Jon Lake

One of the last RCAF Sabres in service, 23422 was aptly assigned to 422 Squadron at Söllingen until April 1963. Dave McLaren

Ltd at Speke Airport in Liverpool was also contracted, this time for rapid servicing and modification of RCAF Sabres. Both companies gathered important experience of Sabre servicing, and this ultimately paid dividends when both Airwork and Bristol were later tasked with RAF Sabre support and maintenance.

Further RCAF units at home moved up to the Sabre, including 413, 414 and 431 Squadrons at Bagotville, 416, 422 and 434 at Uplands, 421, 427 and 444 Squadrons at St. Hubert, and 430 at North Bay, all with Sabre 2s. Of these, 431 quadron disbanded in October 1954 after little more than ten months of Sabre flying. Another unit, 413 Squadron, was initially formed at Bagotville in 1951 as an all-weather unit, but problems with its intended CF-100 equipment led to a redesignation and its receipt of Sabre 2s in December 1951.

Considerable upheaval among the Sabre units followed, with the deployment of several squadrons overseas, starting with 416, 421 and 430

The 'AS' code of 416 Squadron, Royal Canadian Air Force was seen only briefly on its Sabre 6s. One of a number of European-based RCAF squadrons to convert to the CF-100, 416 lost its Sabres in 1957. This aircraft was transferred to 421 Squadron. MAP

Squadrons, which all flew across the Atlantic to Grostenquin in France with Leapfrog 2 beginning in late September 1952. The Leapfrog route left Goose Bay, then took the aircraft via fuel stops at Bluie West 1 (Greenland), Keflavik (Iceland), Prestwick (Scotland) and then into France. Leapfrog 3 then took 413, 427 and 434 Squadrons over to Zweibrucken in Germany during March 1953, and, in August, Leapfrog 4 deployed 414, 422 and 444 Squadrons to Söllingen, also in Germany. The consolidation of the RCAF Sabre squadrons in continental Europe was completed in December 1954 when the last of the squadrons from North

the United Kingdom and the North Luffenham-based Sabres effectively formed the front-line defence against this onslaught. Exercise *Ardent* confirmed that the RAF was in dire need of more modern interceptors, such as the Swift, Hunter and Javelin.

In May 1954 the first Sabre 5s arrived in Europe, and slowly the Sabre 2s were returned to Canadair for overhaul and upgrading before being passed on to the air forces of Greece and Turkey. The arrival of Orenda-engined Sabres in Europe signalled the start of intense rivalry between the NATO-assigned fighter squadrons. Only when F-86Hs arrived with the USAF squadrons would

The Sabre 6s started to be ferried into Europe during April 1955 on *Random* missions flown by the Overseas Ferry Unit. The first unit to receive the aircraft was 2 Wing at Grostenquin, and the old Sabre 5s were routed through Scottish Aviation at Prestwick, most returning to Canada for use by the Auxiliary Squadrons. The replacement process was completed in July 1956, 439 Squadron at Marville in France being the last unit to get Sabre 6s. However, almost immediately four squadrons were disbanded, one from each wing, and replaced by CF-100 Canuck units. The Sabre squadrons involved (410, 413, 414 and 416) were transferred 'on paper' back to Canada and later reformed as Norad CF-100 units. The NATO-assigned RCAF Sabre squadrons began to be run down in July 1962 with the disbanding of 421 Squadron for conversion to the CF-104. The other units swiftly followed suit, leaving 439 and 441 Squadrons at Marville as the final RCAF Sabre units in Europe. Eventually only 439 remained, and its personnel comprised disestablished pilots from all of the other RCAF Sabre units. In November 1963 this unit was also reluctantly disbanded, passing its Sabre 6s through Prestwick, where many were scrapped.

Back in Canada, the arrival of surplus Sabre 5s from Europe had allowed a number of Auxiliary Squadrons to convert in October 1956 using these aircraft. Moving over from antiquated Vampires, 400 and 411 Squadron at Downsview, 401 and 438 Squadron at St. Hubert plus 442 and 443 Squadron at Sea Island in Vancouver all began Sabre operations at about the same time. Similar in principle to US Air National Guard units, the Auxiliaries' use of the Sabre was short-lived. In 1958 a change in policy took away the fighter capability from these units, and in October all six squadrons reluctantly handed in their Sabres and began flying Beech Expeditors.

At Chatham, with the operational RCAF Sabre commitments reducing, No.1 (F) OTU disbanded in late 1961. However, immediately a new formation, the Sabre Transition Unit (STU), took over aircraft and personnel and began flying the Sabre 5 as an advanced trainer for prospective RCAF CF-104 Starfighter pilots. Tasked with the training of low-level navigation and bomb delivery, STU

These Sabre 5s in flight above Toronto were assigned to 400 and 411 Auxilliary Squadrons in October 1956. They were in service for just two years; in 1958 all six Canadian auxilliary Sabre units converted to the Beech Expeditor. MAP

Luffenham arrived in Germany. During their time in Europe, the Sabres took part in many NATO exercises, beginning with *Ardent*, designed to test the air defences of Great Britain. This began on 5 October 1952, with attacking forces comprising British-based F-84s from RAF Manston, escorting three B-50D squadrons of the 2nd Bomb Wing, which were on TDY at Upper Heyford. The British-based bomber effort was backed up by the permanently stationed B-45As and RB-45Cs from 47th Bomb Wing at Sculthorpe as well as RAF bombers in the shape of Lincolns, Washingtons (RAF B-29s) and Canberras. NATO-assigned units provided aircraft to attack

the balance be redressed and international dogfights over the continent would prove who was the best. It was usually the RCAF's Sabres that came out on top. In the spring of 1955 all NATO-assigned RCAF Sabres were routed back to England for the application of camouflage. The scheme was basically the same camouflage applied earlier to RAF Sabre 4s, and consisted of gloss dark green and dark sea-grey upper surfaces, with cerulean (PRU) blue undersides. This colour scheme was generally not applied to Canadian-based RCAF Sabres, but later Sabre 6s for assignment with the European squadrons had the scheme applied by Canadair before delivery.

One of the first Sabres to operate on the US Civil Register, N186X was one of two ex-Golden Hawks Sabres owned by Flight Test Research of Long Beach, California. This aircraft was lost in a crash at Cantil, CA on 19 June 1968; the piloted ejected safely. MAP

Now preserved at Bogota, this Columbian Sabre 6 was one of half a dozen delivered straight from Canadair in 1956. The wrap-around camouflage is not typical of the service FAC Sabre colour scheme. Peter R. Foster, November 1996

Sabres had their machine-guns removed as they were no longer needed for this mission. In late 1968, with the formation of other units to undertake CF-104 transition, the STU was stood down. To mark the end of RCAF Sabre operations, Gp Capt A.J Bauer led a pair of STU Sabre 5s on 'Sabre Swan', beginning on 9 December. The mission took the aircraft to Cold Lake, returning to Chatham on 17 December. The unit took in its last training duty on 13 December and in early 1969 twenty-one remaining Sabre 5s were ferried out to Mountain View for storage.

Chile

The Fuerza Aerea de Chile (FACh) received the first twenty-one of over thirty Hawker Hunter Mk F.71 and T-72s in 1964 to replace the squadron of F-80Cs with Grupo No. 7 at Los Cerillos. The FACh had expected that twenty-five F-86Fs would be supplied under MDAP to replace another squadron of F-80s (possibly Grupo 6 at Punta Arenas). The Sabres were due to arrive during the latter half of 1966, but, for unknown reasons, this did not happen and the Chilean AF turned to further supplies of Hunters to fill this shortfall.

Colombia

During World War II Colombia had been one of the first South American nations to offer use of its military bases to the United States. As a result, reciprocal Lend-Lease aircraft deliveries began in 1942, aided by a US military mission to reorganise the air force – the Fuerza Aérea Colombiana (FAC), which became an independent service in 1943.

Fighter deliveries of F-47Ds began in 1947, and the first jets arrived during 1954, in the shape of six T-33As. However, unusually for a Latin American country, it was Canada that beat the United States in supplying jet fighters to Colombia; the US government had been reluctant to nurture an arms race in the area.

Canadair agreed to sell six new Sabre 6s to the FAC at a total and reasonable cost of $3 million, and, in preparation for delivery, the Colombians sent seven pilots and a number of ground crew to Canadair's Cartierville plant for conversion training. Aircraft were supplied in the standard RCAF camouflage colour scheme. On 31 May 1956 the Sabres were accepted from Canadair by Col Carlos Uribe, and on 4 June the aircraft departed for Colombia. Arriving four days later, the aircraft had staged through Greenville in South Carolina, to Opalocha in Florida and on to the American base at Guantanamo Bay in Cuba.

The six aircraft went to equip 1° Grupo de Combate at Germán Olano Air Base at Palanquero, replacing and initially operating alongside survivors of the thirty-five F-47Ds supplied from the US and a number of F-80s. Apart from these fighters, the unit also operated a lone C-45 for communications duties. In FAC service the Sabres were serialled 2021 to 2026, curiously following on from the T-33As in the 'fighter' sequence of allocations.

During 1963 up to three F-86Fs were delivered to the FAC, having been withdrawn from use by the Spanish Air Force in April 1962 and subsequently passed to US charge. Their use must have been a mixed blessing, the J47 engines being no match for the performance of Orenda-engined Sabre 6s. In addition, the spares commonality between the two types was at best limited. Nonetheless, by June 1965 the FAC declared three Sabre 6s and two F-86Fs as combat-ready. The

FAC F-86Fs were serialled 2027 and 2028, the third aircraft apparently serving as a spare parts source. Along with T-33s operated by an advanced training squadron at Germán Olano, the Sabres often flew with rockets, light bombs and napalm, as necessary. However, only two Colombian airfields were considered capable of handling jet operations, the other being at Eldorado.

Inevitably, accidents reduced the effectiveness of the Sabre force, one aircraft being involved in a landing accident on the day of its delivery in June 1956. This machine was repaired on site at Palanquero. The first actual loss of an FAC Sabre was on 18 September 1956 (aircraft 2026), with further crash write-offs on 22 June 1960 (2022) and 6 September 1961 (2021 at Germán Olano). In total, six Colombian Sabres were lost in service.

All FAC Sabres were retired in 1966, though their fighter role was not filled again until the arrival of Mirage 5COAs in 1972.

Denmark

In 1949 Denmark became a founder member of NATO, and on 27 May 1950 the Danish parliament agreed to form an Air Force, independent of Army or Naval input. The Kongelige Danske Flyvevaben (Royal Danish Air Force, RDAF) officially came into being on 1 October and inherited a variety of mainly British-supplied types, with the most modern fighters being a number of Gloster Meteor F.4s.

As a NATO signatory, Denmark became the recipient for MDAP aid although equipment arrived slowly to begin with. Six F-84Es were delivered in August 1951 as a precursor for more than 200 further Thunderjets over the next few years. For training use, a few T-33s followed, but the RDAF still persevered with British-supplied Meteor fighters and interceptors.

All that changed in 1958 when Denmark became one of the first overseas nations to receive the F-86D. Initially, thirty-eight ex-USAFE F-86D-30 and -35 aircraft were overhauled and supplied, beginning on 26 June, in order to begin the conversion of Eskadrille (Esk) 723 at Aalborg. Esk 723 converted from Meteor NF.11s. Esk 726 was the next unit to

receive Sabres, having moved from Karup to Aalborg on 10 June in order to consolidate RDAF Sabres at one base. The Squadron had previously flown F-84Gs and received its first F-86D on 23 August 1958.

In line with most RDAF aircraft, the Sabres at first carried few marking variations, other than the Danish roundel in the usual six positions and a stylized Danish flag on the vertical fin. In order to distinguish different units, code letters were used, painted in large figures on the forward fuselage. Esk 723 Sabres carried consecutive codes from AB-A to AB-T, while Esk 726 was allotted the codes AL-A to AL-T.

In May 1960 a further batch of twenty-one F-86Ds arrived, enabling Esk 728, flying F-84Gs at Skrydstrup, to re-equip, starting in August. As space was tight at Aalborg, Esk 728 remained at Skrydstrup. The Squadron aircraft briefly carried code letters in the SI-A to Z range, but late in 1960 the whole RDAF serial number

The Sabres also began to be converted to carry the improved British Martin-Baker Mk 5 ejector seat, along with TACAN navigation equipment and launch rails for Sidewinder missiles.

One third of RDAF Sabres were written off in service, beginning on 1 December 1958 when 51-6090 (AB-M) of Esk 723 crashed at Hvorup, the last being F-128 (51-6128), which was lost at Ramstein AB in Germany on 14 April 1965. To provide spares backup for the RDAF Sabre fleet three F-86D-40 and 45 models were supplied from the Chateauroux depot in France in March 1962.

Withdrawal from front-line use began in June 1965 when both Esk 723 and 726 converted to F-104G Starfighters. With insufficient Starfighters to equip further squadrons fully, Esk 728 reluctantly disbanded on 31 March 1966, ending Denmark's association with the Sabre. The Sabres generally remained on the Danish bases, acting for many years as decoy aircraft.

These Royal Danish AF F-86Ds carry the Sidewinder rails fitted to many MAP Sabres, as well as the Martin-Baker Mk 5 ejector seat. F-977 was previously USAF 51-5977 and is today used for battle-damage repair at Kjevik in Norway. Phil Adams

system was changed. In future, all F-86Ds would be serialled 'F-', followed by the 'last three' of the USAF serial number.

A further change in RDAF colours occurred soon after, when most of the Air Force's tactical aircraft were repainted in an overall dark green camouflage scheme.

Dominican Republic

In early 1955 the Dominican Government expressed a desire to procure twenty-five MAP F-86Fs to equip the air force, the Fuerza Aérea Dominicana

(FAD). These may well have been to replace a similar number of F-47 Thunderbolts supplied under MAP in 1948. However, nothing further came of the Sabre order.

Ethiopia

Early in World War II, when Ethiopia had been ruled by the Italians, the country reluctantly gained new masters – first the British and then the United Nations (Sweden), governed the peace. Sitting on the Horn of Africa, Ethiopia was later found to be oil-rich, and American interests were strengthened in the country. During 1952 Eritrea was brought into federation with Ethiopia by the UN and forcibly became one state ten years later. Ports on the coast of Eritrea were often used by the US Navy as a base in the Indian Ocean. The union of Ethiopia and Eritrea was unpopular and led to a succession of coups, which ended in the ousting and execution of Emperor Haile Selassie in 1974.

During 1958 a US Military Aviation Advisory Group (MAAG) of around fifteen personnel arrived in Ethiopia and paved the way for the receipt of MAP-funded aircraft deliveries. Previously, mainly Swedish types, such as the SAAB B-17A bomber and the Safir trainer, had been supplied to Ethiopia, along with some British aircraft, such as the Fairey Firefly. The US MAP-supplied aircraft, which began to be delivered in 1960, consisted of sixteen T-28A and five T-33 trainers, a number of C-47 and C-54 transports plus an initial total of twelve F-86F Sabres. Some of the MAAG personnel flew the Sabres and, along with maintenance crews, trained Ye Ityopya Ayer Hayl (Imperial Ethiopian Air Force, IEAF) personnel on their new machines. At this time the IEAF had a strength of about 4,000, plus some Swedish advisers. No Swedish pilots were ever converted on to the F-86 and the last of the Swedish Air Force contingent left at the end of 1961. This left a few Swedish civilian technicians who were contracted direct to the Ethiopians.

The IEAF received its first three Sabres on 29 July 1960, when 51-13173, 52-5331 and 52-5448 were delivered, having been assigned to 1172nd Field Maintenance Squadron in Addis Ababa on 25 July, presumably for IEAF Sabre induction training. By 30 July six aircraft had been delivered (though it is not known whether these included the two 'training' airframes). A further six F-86Fs followed during September, with both batches being sent through USAF overhaul with 3140th Maintenance Group at Getafe in Spain. It seems likely that all this batch were F-30s, being fitted with slatted 6-3 dual store wings. These dozen aircraft (minus one, which crashed in the summer of 1960 soon after delivery) were used to form a fighter squadron which was based at Debre Zeit outside Addis Ababa. A further IEAF F-86F was written off before October 1962.

In their early service IEAF Sabres were unpainted except for the national insignia in the usual six positions and an IEAF serial number on the forward fuselage, below the gun ports. The serial number was also painted below the horizontal stabilizer, aft of the air brake. In line with other IEAF jets, the Sabres were serialled in the 200 range, the first dozen being allotted serials from 251 to 262.

It was not long before the F-86s were put into action and, on 15 and 16 December 1960, they attacked rebel positions in Addis Ababa, during a failed coup by the Swedish (UN)-trained Imperial Guard. The anti-rebel attacks were backed up by ancient SAAB B 17A bombers. It seems that these attacks had a quite profound effect on the rebels and they surrendered within a few days. It is not known whether Ethiopian pilots were trained on the Sabres by this time; US instructors were originally tasked with setting up the Sabre squadron and then bringing IEAF pilots up to operational readiness on the aircraft.

Congo: a Bitter Experience

Less than a year later, the Air Force became involved in the UN peace-keeping operation in the Congo. Ethiopia agreed to send four Sabres to the region to provide fighter support and, in late September 1961, the aircraft arrived at Elizabethville (now known as Kinshasa). The IEAF regarded the airfield as the only suitable base in the Congo capable of operating Sabres and refused to relocate their aircraft at Luluaborg, where Swedish SAAB J 29s and Indian Canberras were based. However, on 16 December the IEAF contingent, who along with the other jets in country were by now titled the 'All Fighter Group Unit', moved to another base at Kamina, where they stayed for the remainder of their operations in the Congo. The Sabres came under the control of Swedish Col Sven Lampell, whose title was Chief Fighter Operations Officer, UN Air Division. Lampell's aircraft were briefed to carry out four main areas of operations:
1. Air combat (F-86 and J 29)
2. Ground strafing (all aircraft)
3. Co-operation with UN ground forces (all aircraft)
4. Reconnaissance (Indian Canberras, later supplemented by two J 29s).

The Ethiopian Sabres suffered from spares shortages which affected their operational effectiveness. During the last three months of 1961 the F-86Fs had flown fewer hours than either the Swedish or the Indian aircraft, which broke down as follows:

October 1961:   J 29 (146hr, 100 per cent serviceability)
  Canberra (125hr/98 per cent)
  Sabre (51hr/72.3 per cent)
November 1961: J 29 (57hr/97.5 per cent)
  Canberra (97hr/78 per cent)
  Sabre (39hr/75 per cent)
December 1961: J 29 (132hr/82.6 per cent)
  Canberra (194hr/82.7 per cent)
  Sabre (45hr/88.8 per cent).

During the spring of 1962, Ralph Bunche, the UN Assistant General Secretary, reported of the Ethiopian unit that,

logistic back-up is complex because of obtaining spares through various channels. Aircraft performance requires longer runways than other types. Personnel experience is lower than other units by virtue of relatively short time aircraft have been in service with Ethiopian Air Force. Keenness and willingness of personnel does not make up for lack of experience.

It therefore seems ironic that, in the summer of 1962, a request was made to Ethiopia to supply further Sabres to the UN effort in the Congo. As a result, two more IEAF F-86Fs were to be flown out to Kamina in October.

On 12 May 1962 Sir P. Dean at the British Mission to the UN wrote to the Foreign Office expressing his concern for the UN air operation in the Congo. In particular, he revealed comments made by

This Imperial Ethiopian Air Force F-86F-30 pictured on UN duties in the Congo is equipped with a full load of ferry tanks. It is highly likely that this scene depicts the IEAF's departure from the Congo in ignominious circumstances during October 1962. *Per Björkner via Leif Hellström*

Brig I.J. Rikhye, the Military Adviser to the UN Secretary-General. Rikhye had asked if more Indian Canberras with 1,000 lb bombs could be provided to destroy Katangese aircraft on the ground, as he 'could not rely on the Ethiopians [to destroy them in the air]'.

In the autumn of 1962 the IEAF lost an F-86F in a non-operational accident, neither aircraft or pilot being recovered. The Ethiopians had long nurtured the belief that they were considered a second-rate unit by the other UN units in the Congo (a belief which seems to be borne out by the above comments), and, now that one of their pilots had been lost, those same IEAF personnel felt that not enough effort was made by the UN in searching for him. Thus, in late October, ferry tanks were fitted to the remaining F-86Fs, on the pretext of carrying out a long-range navigation exercise. The Ethiopians flew straight home, never to return. Officially, the Sabres were returned because they were needed back

in Ethiopia, Gen Assefa not approving of the drain on his Air Force's strength. But the brief and eventful stint in the Congo had left a bitter taste.

Despite their earlier comments, the UN saw this as a grave development, especially now that the Katangese Air Force had managed to obtain two Vampire jets and at least one Fouga Magister. But the damage had been done, and it was with some luck that the Swedish offered to supply SAAB J-29s and, additionally, in December 1962 the Italian government offered a number of Sabres to replace the Ethiopian aircraft, but minus pilots. Ironically, it was planned to crew these Italian Sabres with IEAF pilots, but nothing seems to have come of this. F-86F fighter cover was taken over by Iranian aircraft.

Back Home

The IEAF's small Sabre fleet saw action again in the 1964 Horn of Africa war

between Ethiopia and Somalia. It seemed that the United States had expected such action and, in August 1962, the American Embassy in Ethiopia had urged Washington to supply two or three further F-86Fs each year to make up for IEAF attrition losses. However, the British got wind of the suggestion and made firm representations to stop any further deliveries, as it could have raised the stakes with Somalia. This in turn would have led to further Soviet involvement with the Somalis. As it happened, the Americans had earlier brought pressure on the British over the proposed supply of Canberra bombers for the same reasons. It seems that the Ethiopians in turn had asked the United States for fifteen additional Sabres, but this was turned down. To placate the Ethiopians, in 1964 deliveries of F-5 fighters were promised under MAP for the 1966-67 period. However, on 10 October the IEAF's Gen Merid stated that he no longer had any confidence in the US offer, and, in any case, that the F-5s were two years away from delivery, by which time it would be too late.

Clearly, the Ethiopians were becoming dissatisfied with deliveries under MAP. In addition, many UN members felt that, as a result of the unauthorized withdrawal of its Sabres from the Congo, Ethiopia had behaved unacceptably. As a result, the MAP stream of arms began to dry up and, by the late 1960s, more Sabres were required to augment the dwindling number still in IEAF service, and it appears that further F-86Fs (possibly up to twenty-two) were supplied from the Imperial Iranian Air Force during November 1970. Some of these were ferried through Dharan Air Base in Saudi Arabia, wearing a sand/green and brown camouflage, with light grey undersides. This batch of aircraft went to equip a second fighter squadron, based at Asmara, and received serial numbers subsequent to the original batch of twelve Sabres. Thus IEAF serials up to and including 284 have been noted.

By 1976 it was reported that the Ethiopian AF had eleven F-86Fs left operational. It seems that these remaining aircraft were withdrawn in 1977, when the US Military Advisory Group was finally expelled. The Sabres were retired at the bases of Asmara (now in independent Eritrea) and Debre Zeit. IEAF Sabres were rumoured to have been used in the 1977-78 war with Somalia, which resulted in the supply of Russian MiG-21s to the Ethiopians. If true, this would have seen the somewhat strange prospect of F-86Fs and MiG-21s teamed together against Somali MiG-15s, 17s and 21s. Whatever the situation, the Somalis soon capitulated and the Sabre era in the Horn of Africa came to an end.

France

Following the Second World War, French industry took some time to recover, and this was especially true in the aircraft manufacturing industries. Thus, to begin rebuilding the French Air Force – the Armée de l'Air, many foreign types were purchased, and in 1951 F-84Gs and T-33 trainers started to arrive from the United States and, later on, F-84Fs and F-100Ds began to equip French squadrons. These machines were supplied under MAP since France was a NATO member at this point. (France withdrew from NATO in 1966, much to the chagrin of other members, not least the United States.)

In the interceptor role, France had planned to deploy the Dassault Mirage,

the prototype of which flew in 1955. However, delays in getting the production Mirage IIIC and Vautour IIN into service saw the Armée de l'Air looking to buy an interim aircraft off the shelf. The F-86K was chosen for this requirement.

A new unit was formed to receive these Sabres, 13e Escadre de Chasse Tout Temps (ECTT – All-Weather Fighter Wing). The unit was activated on 1 March 1955 at Lahr AB in West Germany under the leadership of Commandant Risso. However, delivery of the first F-86Ks did not begin until some time later, and originally eight T-33s were assigned so that crews could begin blind flying instrument training. To familiarize themselves with the F-86K, five 13e ECTT pilots were also detached to Istrana AB in Italy, while ground personnel were trained by four USAF instructors who set up a Field Training Detachment at Lahr. Finally, in June 1956 two Erco MB-18 flight simulators arrived at Lahr so that flight training could be carried out.

This situation continued until 4 September 1956 when the first of sixty FIAT-built F-86Ks – 55-4814 – arrived at Lahr, being officially accepted by the French the following day. The delivery of F-86Ks triggered the formation of two Escadrons (squadrons) within 13e ECTT on 1 October: Escadron 1 'Artois' with commanding officer Capt Fonvielle and Escadron 2 'Alpes' under Capt Brisset. In French service, these units were known as EC.1/13 and EC.2/13, respectively, denoting their assignment to 13e ECTT.

By the end of 1956 the unit had flown 189hr in the F-86K, comprising 196 missions. On 1 April 1957 13e ECTT moved into a new purpose-built base at Colmar-Mayenheim in France, at this time possessing fifty-three of the planned sixty machines. Delivery was completed in June with the arrival of 55-4816 and 4818 at Colmar.

To differentiate between the two Escadrons, the aircraft were assigned individual codes: EC.1/13 using 13-GA to GZ and EC.2/13 having 13-HA to HZ. In practice, however, these code allocations were reversed and, rather than completely repaint all codes, it was decided in late 1958 that a stroke of the brush would change EC.2/13's '13-G' to '13-Q' and EC.1/13 '13-H' to '13-P', thus restoring the alphabetic order of the squadron codes. This gave only fifty-two code permutations, and aircraft that were

'spare' took on codes in the '13-SA' range.

Armée de l'Air F-86Ks were immediately involved in NATO exercises, participating in *Counter Punch* in late 1957, followed by *Rebecca* in which 13e ECTT took up a 24hr alert posture. By the end of 1957 more than 2,000hr had been flown on the F-86K fleet. This was tempered by the first loss of a French F-86K when, on 13 April, 1957 55-4842 landed short at Colmar, causing the left undercarriage leg to break, Plt Lt Cavat was uninjured but it would not have been economical to repair the Sabre. A further landing accident on 11 June involved 55-4855, the aircraft running off the runway at Colmar. This time no damage was incurred.

The start of 1958 also marked the first and only fatal F-86K accident in French service. On 7 January a radio mechanic was sucked into the intake of a running Sabre and killed. At the end of May 1958 Exercise *Full Play* began, to simulate a large-scale attack by nuclear bombers. F-86Ks were the main adversary and, at the end of the exercise on 5 June, had flown 174 sorties by day and 50 at night. The concentrated flying schedule was continued when 13e ECTT deployed to Cazaux on 16 June for gunnery practice. The F-86Ks fired at targets trailed by Ouragan and B-26 aircraft.

On the night of 3 November 1958 EC.2/13 was just reaching the end of a mass night sortie. No doubt eager to get back safely on the ground, Lt Hervouet landed wheels-up at Colmar. The crash started a small fire and also blocked the runway, Hervouet managing to jump clear while the fire was put out. However, with the runway blocked, the airborne remainder of the squadron was forced to divert to Lahr, where the night's misfortune was compounded when the nosewheel of Capt Mayot's F-86K broke on landing. Mayot was uninjured and, fortunately, both Sabres, 55-4867 and 4843, respectively, were repaired.

During 1959 all F-86Ks began to be routed through FIAT in Turin for IRAN (Inspect and Repair As Necessary) overhaul and modification of mainplanes to 'F-40' specification, with extended leading edges and increased span. At about the same time, many French F-86Ks had a long red/white/red band applied to each fuselage side in an effort to increase their visibility in the air. This had a valid purpose: despite the application of these markings, on 28 October 1961 55-4855 and 55-4867 collided in flight, though both machines and pilots recovered safely to base. Another problem encountered by French F-86Ks was that of engine failure, sometimes caused by fuel system faults. This resulted in five crashes, four pilots ejecting successfully and another surviving the subsequent forced landing.

Further modification began at FIAT in June 1960 with the fitting of Sidewinder missile launch rails; at least twenty-nine aircraft were eventually converted, starting with 55-4820. This modification extended the useful life of the aircraft, but, in June 1961 at a fighter meet at Colmar, two new Mirage IIICs were unveiled in 13e ECTT markings. The writing was on the wall for the French F-86Ks, but it was not until January 1962 that EC.1/13 relinquished its Sabres, passing them to EC.2/13 to begin Mirage

conversion. EC.2nd13 then also gave up its F-86Ks in April, but at this time it was decided to form a third Escadron, EC.3/13, to operate the Sabres while the Mirage conversion was completed. EC.3/13 took over the 13-SA to SZ code range.

The transfer of a number of French F-86Ks to Italy began in early 1962 with the departure of thirteen aircraft to 51° Aerobrigata on 27 January; a further nine went on 13 July.

The F-86K remained in service until 4 October 1962, when, their usefulness at an end, they were transferred to USAF control under the terms of MAP. At the beginning of June 1963 fifteen airworthy F-86Ks were transferred to Chateauroux for storage, joining sixteen more F-86Ks already at the base. In March 1964 all these aircraft were destroyed by explosives. Only one aircraft survived in France: 55-4841, which was given to the French and placed on display at the

entrance to Colmar AB. It is now displayed in the Musée de l'Air in Paris.

Germany

At the end of World War II Germany's armed forces lay battered and defeated. Front-line aircraft of the Luftwaffe were either destroyed or shipped overseas for investigation by the former Allied powers. When the German surrender was signed on 7 May 1945 all military activity was curtailed literally overnight and many talented designers were either seconded to research projects abroad or moved voluntarily to other countries to continue their work.

At a NATO meeting in Paris on 23 October 1954 member states agreed to allow the formation of a new German army, navy and air force. When it came to rebuilding Germany's armed forces, the aircraft procured for the new Luftwaffe were all purchased from overseas as a result of the post-war provisions. None the less, progress was rapid. Luftwaffe planning was originally for twenty wings to be formed, including four of day fighters and three of all-weather fighter by

A small number of Sabre 5s for the Luftwaffe were incorrectly painted at Renfrew in Scotland before delivery. These aircraft featured a small cross on the fuselage, small German fin flash and oversized serial number. All were repainted before handover. 'F86 798' was the fourth Sabre delivered to Waffenschule 10 at Oldenburg on 6 March 1958. MAP

Above: **Luftwaffe Sabre 6s of JG 71 carried this stylish 'tulip' design on the intake and tail fin. 1 Staffel aircraft also received red nose and tail trim. JA-108 was c/n 1622 and, in line with other Luftwaffe Sabres, did not receive camouflage until late 1960.** Author

1960. A number of aircraft types were investigated to fill these roles, including the F-86F and the F-100D in the former and the F-94 Starfire in the latter. Eventually, the choice came down to Canadair Sabres in the day fighter mission and F-86Ks as all-weather interceptors.

Personnel for the new Luftwaffe were mainly drawn from wartime pilots and ground crews, though they had all invariably had little aircraft experience in the intervening ten years. To make a start, six pilots, including Johannes Steinhof, were trained in the United States, culminating in F-86F flight training at Nellis AFB. However, during 1955 the 7330th Flying Training Wing at Furstenfeldbruck AB began the training of Luftwaffe pilots, using USAFE F-86Fs.

The Luftwaffe was able to begin its own dedicated Sabre flying training in 1957 when the first German aircraft arrived from the Royal Canadian Air Force.

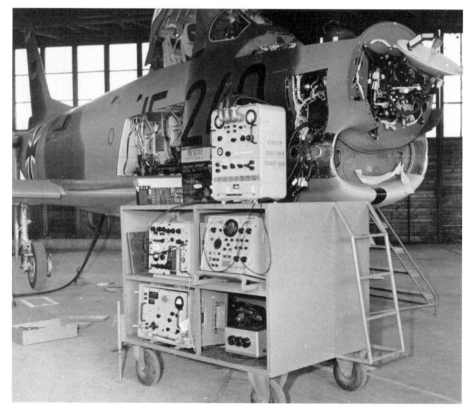

Right: **The complex fire-control system (FCS) and radar of the F-86K necessitated the need for complex diagnostic and test apparatus. This Jagdgeschwader 75 aircraft is plugged into an FCS analyser. Coded JE-240, this F-86K was ex-56-4142. It later saw service in Venezuela.** Peter Sickinger

Late in their Luftwaffe service, a number of Sabre 6s were modified to incorporate the Martin-Baker ejector seat. However, the extra bulk of the seat meant that the canopy retraction rails had to be modified to clear the headrest. This aircraft from JaboG 43 was visiting RAF Leuchars in Scotland during July 1966.

Breeze via Dave McLaren

These machines, seventy-five Sabre 5s, were put through an overhaul at Renfrew in Scotland and then assigned to the Luftwaffe, the first three being delivered on 18 February. All these aircraft equipped just one unit, the Waffenschule 10 (WS10), a training school formed at Oldenburg to convert potential Luftwaffe Sabre pilots for the tactical fighters – Canadair Sabre 6s and FIAT-built F-86Ks. With about sixty-five aircraft on hand, WS10 used the Sabre 5s until 1959 when new Sabre 6s began to arrive from Canadair. The first Sabre 6 had, in fact, arrived at Oldenburg on 2 September 1958, and the type served initially with a third squadron – 3 Staffel, though eventually it replaced Sabre 5s throughout WS10. The unit then flew these aircraft until March 1962 when Luftwaffe day fighter Sabre training ceased.

The 225 Luftwaffe Sabre 6s were crated at Canadair for shipment to Germany, where they were then transported to the Dornier plant at Oberpfaffenhofen for reassembly and test flying. To receive these aircraft, three F-86 wings were formed in 1959, beginning with Jagdgeschwader (JG) 71 at Aalhorn on 6 June 1959. JG72 and JG73 formed soon afterwards, at Leck and Oldenburg, respectively. Roughly equating to a squadron, the Luftwaffe Staffeln within the wings began applying squadron colours to their aircraft, and, although the Sabre 6s were delivered in natural metal colours, the standard NATO camouflage was also soon applied to the aircraft. Unit codes were also applied, followed by three numbers, the first of which indicated the assigned Staffel. JG-71 aircraft were coded 'JA', with JG-72 and 73 machines gaining 'JB' and 'JC' codes. The WS10 Sabres were applied with 'BB' identifying letters.

While the day fighter units were coming to operational effectiveness, the delivery of 88 F-86Ks from FIAT began in 1957. Arriving at Oberpfaffenhofen from Italy in pairs, the first two were flown in on 22 July, with delivery completed just less than a year later on 23 June 1958. All these aircraft carried USAF markings for the ferry flight, and, in the event, only fifty-seven actually entered Luftwaffe service. The remaining F-86Ks were crated, still in USAF colours, until they were disposed of with the operational aircraft. WS10 began F-86K training in July 1959, enabling pilots then to proceed to JG74 and JG75, the two units formed to operate the type. WS10 ceased all Sabre training in July 1962. JG75 was formed at Oldenburg in October 1960,

but moved to Leipheim that same month. The unit's aircraft carried 'JE' codes, but they were short-lived, and on 5 May 1961 JG75 disbanded and passed its Sabres to JG74, the only other wing to operate the F-86K. Activated at Neuberg in April 1961, JG74 was assigned to NATO in October of the following year. All unit aircraft were camouflaged, the scheme having been introduced during late 1960. Thus only a few of JG75's aircraft were thus painted before the wing disbanded. Luftwaffe use of the F-86K was fairly brief. Slated for conversion to the F-104G Starfighter, JG74 performed its last F-86K flight on 5 January 1966. Surviving aircraft and the crated spares – still in USAF colours – were passed to the Venezuelan Air Force.

The Sabre 6 continued in service for a while longer though, and in the early 1960s many aircraft were modified to carry the AIM-9 Sidewinder missile, though JG71 machines did not receive this capability. Other modification involved the incorporation of the Martin-Baker Mk 5 ejector seat, a bulky piece of equipment that necessitated a redesign of the canopy rails to clear the headrest. The Mk 5 seat was only modified into JG72 aircraft. With the impending arrival of the F-104, JG71 formed a third Staffel to consolidate F-86 operations before complete disbanding in August 1964. The remaining Sabre wings became fighter-bomber units and, as a result, were renamed in October 1964, JG72 becoming Jagdbombergeschwader (JaBoG) 43 and JG73 being transformed into JaBoG 42, having moved to Pferdsfeld two years previously. The original unit codes were retained despite the change in assignment. JaBoG 42 then relinquished its Sabres in favour of the FIAT G 91 beginning in April 1966, followed by JaBoG 43, with the last Sabre leaving the unit on 22 December 1966.

Small-scale use of the Sabre in Germany continued, however. At Westerland on Sylt island, a civilian contractor, Condor Flugdienst, had set up an operation to provide target-towing facilities for the Luftwaffe. Seven Sabre 6s were modified by Dornier starting in 1966, to carry on the wing pylon the Delmar RadOp plastic/foam target, a Dayglo-painted, bomb-shaped item. Trailed up to 7,300yd (8,000m) behind the Sabre tow aircraft, the target could amplify radar signals to represent a large, four-engined bomber and operations began on 1 October 1966. Condor operated these aircraft until April 1974 when Sabre flying in Germany finally ceased.

Great Britain

The Royal Air Force (RAF) began to feel the need for a swept-wing fighter soon after the beginning of the Korean War. The straight-wing, British-built Gloster Meteors, in particular, were outclassed by the MiG-15s in the early days of that conflict; their role quickly became that of fighter-bombers. However, as no British aircraft designs were immediately available, it fell to a foreign aircraft to meet the stop-gap needs of the RAF. That aircraft was the F-86 Sabre, and an initial assessment of the F-86A was made during October 1950 (the test pilot Roland Beamont had been the first Briton to fly a Sabre when he took the second XP-86 aloft at Muroc on 21 May 1948). Two aircraft were used by, among others, the Aircraft & Armament Experimental Establishment at Boscombe Down, the Royal Aircraft Establishment at Farnborough and the Central Fighter Establishment at West Raynham. The first of these, 49-1296, was written off on 14 August 1952 and replaced by 49-1279.

It soon became apparent that North American were working full-out to provide Sabres for the USAF and there was no spare capacity to fulfil an order for the RAF. Fortunately, on 26 October 1950, at a meeting of the Western European Air Advisory Committee, the Canadian representative disclosed that licence production of the Sabre by Canadair at Montreal was due to begin and that Sabres could be made available from this production line. These aircraft would be supplied under the Mutual Defense Assistance Program (MDAP) and, as such, could be used only in a tactical role: when the first of the initial order for 370 F-86E-equivalent Sabres arrived for the RAF they would be allocated to 2nd Allied Tactical Air Force (ATAF) squadrons in Germany.

The Sabres which the RAF received were generally Canadair CL-13 Mk 4s, roughly equivalent to the F-86E-10, and referred to in RAF parlance as the Sabre F. Mk 4. However, three CL-13 Mk. 2s were the first Sabres ferried to Britain for the RAF, during October 1952, and these were

This Sabre 6, D-9539, was operated by Condor Flugdienst as a target tug from the late 1960s. It carries a Del Mar SK-460 target under its left wing, complete with FK-460D acoustic body. Peter Sickinger

designated Sabre F. Mk 2. These were based at North Luffenham and were used to train the first cadre of RAF pilots who would be ferrying Sabres from Canada. During November 1952 a further sixty Sabres were offered to the RAF through MDAP. These Canadair machines were originally intended for the USAF, but were considered surplus to requirements. More importantly, it was agreed that this batch of aircraft could be used for the defence of the United Kingdom; two squadrons would therefore be equipped. By mid-1953 the RAF had laid plans for their Sabre fleet: the two squadrons of Fighter Command Sabres (nominally set at forty-four aircraft) would come into service during September 1953 and be phased out in March 1955. The 2 ATAF Sabres would equip a maximum of ten squadrons (220 aircraft), dropping to eight, which would be supported to March 1958 with 176 aircraft. This plan provided for a 'worst-case' scenario, assuming development difficulties with the Hunter fighter – the Sabre was to be in service only as long as the indigenous fighter force required bolstering.

As an interesting footnote, the RAF were offered a further fifty-four Sabres – this time ex-RCAF Mk 2s – which would have been available as Mutual Aid from March 1954. These Sabres were stated as being from British- and Europe-based RCAF squadrons. The British Government did not warm to this proposition as

it was felt that storage would cause problems, in addition to spares incompatibility with the RAF Sabre 4s. None the less, Air Cdr Costello suggested that, if cannibalized, the aircraft could provide valuable sources for much-needed radio sets and gunsights. In reality, the Canadians appeared to be giving the British first refusal on their Sabres before offering them to NATO. The offer was not taken up and they were transferred to Turkey and Greece instead.

With the impending arrival of nearly 430 Sabres for the RAF, the trio of Sabres at North Luffenham were reassigned to RAF Abingdon to form No.1 Overseas Ferry Unit on 4 December. No.1 OFU then became No. 1 (Long Range) Ferry Unit on 1 January 1953. Further ferry pilots were then trained, and the first delivery flight began on 9 December 1952, starting at St. Hubert in Quebec, and routing via Goose Bay, Bluie West 1, Keflavik and Prestwick. These ferry missions were named 'Becher's Brook', after the famous jump at the Aintree racecourse. No.1 (LR) FU was retitled No. 147 Squadron on 1 February 1953 and moved to RAF Benson on 4 May.

Arriving in natural metal finish, Sabres for RAF squadron use were camouflaged at several Maintenance Units before allocation. Aircraft for RAF Germany had camouflage consisting of gloss dark green and dark sea-grey uppers, with cerulean (PRU) blue undersides. The upper/lower camouflage demarcation was located so that the underside blue came up to the bottom of the machine-gun blast panel. On Sabres which were to be based in Britain the same upper-side colours were used, but this time the undersides were painted silver. In addition, the demarcation line was much lower, running forward from the wing root/fuselage junction. Finally, a few Sabres assigned to the Sabre Conversion Flight at Wildenrath and to test duties retained their natural metal finish.

RAF Sabres were allocated serial numbers in the ranges XB530 to XB532 (Sabre F. Mk 2s), XB533 to XB551, XB575 to XB650, XB664 to XB713, XB726 to XB775, XB790 to XB839, XB851 to XB900, XB912 to XB961, XB973 to XB999 (RAF Germany F. Mk 4s) and XD706 to XD736, XD753 to XD781 (British-based F. Mk 4s). Included among the XB batch were a number of aircraft which were initially delivered as XD102-138, apparently for allocation to British-based Sabre squadrons. However, this did not happen and these machines were reallocated out-of-sequence XB-serials instead. There is also evidence to suggest that serials XB962 to XB972 were painted on Sabres allotted to Becher's Brook 9 and 10, but this may have been a mistake made by Canadair.

On all RAF Sabres these serials were applied to the rear of the fuselage speed brake in black figures and spanwise beneath the port (left wing) to be read from the front, and beneath the starboard (right) wing to be read from the rear. RAF roundels were painted at the six normal locations, those beneath the wing being located outboard of the serial number.

To train RAF pilots in the numbers required to equip the squadrons, the Sabre Conversion Flight (SCF) was set up at RAF Wildenrath, Germany in March 1953. SCF then trained 353 pilots until June 1954, when it handed over the role to 229 Operational Conversion Unit (OCU) at RAF Chivenor in the south-west of England.

The former RAF Sabre pilot Air Cdr Desmond Browne recalls that the aircraft heralded a new era for the service:

The Sabre was a vital transition to powered controls, ejection seats, radar gunsights and transonic flight for the Hunter, Javelin and Lightning era. The Sabre had, however, many limitations: lack of firepower; limited high-speed low-level manoeuvrability (wing warp), poor radius of action without the use of underwing drop tanks, also no independent engine start-up facility. Still, it was a lovely aircraft to fly.

All the servicing requirements were based on US methods, resupply and management systems; these were controlled by and dependent on voluminous servicing manuals. The retraining of all ground personnel to the US systems meant a complete locking-in to these systems at a time of National Service. The RAF system was largely lost, unless servicemen were retained – hence a loss of flexibility in posting airmen throughout the service. In fact, it was a bit of a 'sprat to catch a mackerel' scheme. In most of NATO Europe it succeeded, but France and the UK opted out to retain their national aircraft industries and their overseas sales programmes.

The 2nd ATAF squadrons began to re-equip with Sabres as they arrived off the Becher's Brook ferry missions. No. 4 Squadron at Wildenrath received the first Sabre for squadron use, completing their first sorties on 6 March 1953. No. 3

A trio of 234 Squadron Sabre 4s in the unit's early Sabre markings – black and red checks on the nose. In 1955 the unit repainted the checkered motif in a band on either side of the fuselage roundel and the nose scallop was then painted entirely red. MAP

1953), 234 Squadron, Oldenburg (November 1953), 112 Squadron, Bruggen (December 1953), 130 Squadron, Bruggen (January 1954), and finally 93 Squadron at Jever, which received its first Sabre in March 1954. With the arrival of the second MDAP batch of Sabres the British-based squadrons formed in December 1953 (No. 66 Squadron, converting from Meteor F.8s at RAF Linton-on-Ouse) and February 1954 (No. 92 Squadron, also at Linton).

Numerous moves now followed in an effort to rationalize the squadrons, and also to ease congestion at Wildenrath. No. 3 squadron was the first to move – to Geilenkirchen in July 1953. 234 Squadron then also moved in to Geilenkirchen on 13 January 1954. No. 93 Squadron moved to Jever alongside 4 Squadron between 13 and 16 November 1954. In June 1955 Nos 67 and 71 Squadrons went on Armament Practice

Coded 'EWW' on the tail, this Sabre 4 was the personal mount of Wg Cdr Eric W. Wright at RAF Linton-on Ouse. Note that the Sabres based in England had a lower camouflage demarcation line (and silver undersides) in comparison with those RAF Sabres based in Germany. MAP

XB540 was one of a small number of aircraft assigned to the Central Gunnery School at RAF Leconfield. Withdrawn from RAF use, it was sent to Aviation Traders at Stansted Airport for conversion to F-86E(M) on 16 August 1955, where this photograph was taken. It appears to have been scrapped following conversion. A.J. Jackson

Squadron at Wildenrath then received its first Sabre on 11 May (XB614), replacing Venom aircraft. No. 67 Squadron was the next to receive a Sabre (XB674 on 18 May) at Wildenrath, and then began converting from the Vampire 5. During

the summer of 1953 the Wildenrath squadrons worked up on the Sabre, but other squadrons soon followed: No. 71 Squadron at Wildenrath (October 1953), 20 Squadron, Oldenburg (October 1953), 26 Squadron, Oldenburg (November

Camp (APC) to RAF Akrotiri, Cyprus. When they returned to Germany on 5 July they flew straight into Bruggen, their new base.

Among the feats performed during their brief time with the Sabre, it was probably the flypast for the Queen's Coronation Review at RAF Odiham which stands out. Soon after the arrival of their Sabres, aircraft from 3 and 67 Squadrons were deployed to RAF Duxford on 20 June 1953 to begin practising. These practice flights had begun on 4 June as elements (the RAF Sabre formation comprising twenty-four aircraft), followed by mass flypasts daily from 23 to 26 June and on 29 and 30 June, followed by further rehearsals on 1 to 3 and 6 to 9 July. Full-dress rehearsals were then flown across Odiham on 10, 12 and 13 July. In total, there were 643 aircraft in the flypast, ranging from a Sycamore helicopter to examples of the RAF's latest V-bombers, the Vulcan, the Valiant and the Victor; clearly, the organization of such an event was massive. The full flypast went off without a hitch on 15 July. In addition to the airborne display, both Sabre squadrons provided two aircraft each for the ground display. The Sabres returned to Germany on 16 July.

The so-called '6-3' hard-edge wing began to be fitted to RAF Sabres during late 1954 at station level, the first examples arriving with the squadrons soon after. The characteristics of this wing gave increased manoeuvrability at altitude, but also a higher stalling speed. In addition, the stall was more violent and more than one crash was attributed to this phenomenon. However, the 6-3 wing was better from a formation-flying point of view, and it was generally the arrival of this modified wing which signalled the formation of aerobatic teams. From the technical aspect, the RAF Sabres were generally reliable, but numerous special technical instructions (STIs) were necessary to keep on top of this. In the summer of 1955, for instance, there was a crippling series of fuselage fuel-tank cracks on many of the Sabres. An STI was quickly issued to rectify this problem, but during one eleven-day period during August, 71 Squadron had only one serviceable aircraft. Other modifications, such as the thickening of the upper wing skins to prevent under-carriage shimmy, were carried out at around the same time. If the aircraft could be flown away, this work was carried out at No. 5 Maintenance Unit (MU) at Kemble or No. 33 MU at Lyneham.

Inevitably, the arrival in service of indigenous fighters such as the Hawker Hunter spelled the end for the RAF's Sabre force. The first squadron to re-equip was No. 26 in August 1955, followed by 4 Squadron (September 1955), 67 Squadron (March 1956), 93 Squadron (March 1956), 20 Squadron (May 1956), 66 Squadron (May 1956), 92 Squadron

In 1958 many ex-RAF Sabres, having been converted to F-86E(M) configuration, were declared surplus to requirement and scrapped. These forlorn hulks at Lasham in Hampshire even wear their USAF delivery colours. None survived the cutting torch. MAP

The sole Sabre to be powered by the Bristol Siddeley Orpheus engine, XB982 was withdrawn from use at Bristol's Filton aerodrome in 1962 and eventually scrapped. Peter R. March

(May 1956), 130 Squadron (May 1956), 71 Squadron (June 1956), 112 Squadron (June 1956), 234 Squadron (June 1956), and finally, 3 Squadron, which lost its last Sabre in late June 1956. The 2nd ATAF Sabres were ferried back to the UK in some cases by squadron pilots, but usually by personnel from 147 Squadron at Benson. The last Sabre to leave Germany – XB670 – was flown from Geilenkirchen to Benson on 21 June 1956 by Flt Lt Burton of 147 Squadron. It is pertinent to note that many RAF Sabre pilots considered the early Hunters to be a retrograde step from the Sabre, the former exhibiting alarming tendencies to flame-out when the internal cannon armament was fired. However, the Hunter matured into a fine fighter and served the RAF until the mid-1990s.

With so little use on the Sabres, they were immediately gathered at Maintenance Units for storage. Under the rules of MDAP, the Sabres had to either be scrapped or passed back to the USAF, but US deals were soon closed with both the Italian and the Yugoslav Air Force for the majority of the aitrcraft, the remainder passing to Lasham for scrapping. MDAP Sabres for Italy and Yugoslavia were flown from the MUs or direct through Benson by 147 Squadron pilots and overhauled by Westlands at Yeovilton (and test flown from Merryfield), Aviation Traders at Stansted and Airwork at Ringway, Dunsfold and Speke. Aircraft which had not received the 6-3 wing modification in RAF service were brought up to standard and, after a thorough overhaul – of up to twelve months – emerged with white washable USAF markings for their delivery flights. All export aircraft were redesignated F-86E(M) – the M signifying 'modified'. USAF test pilots were assigned to the several rework facilities, and it was these men who carried out the delivery flights.

One former RAF Sabre did remain flying in Britain, however. In the mid-1950s Bristol-Siddeley Engines was busy developing its Orpheus 12 engine for use in NATO's new lightweight fighter aircraft, which was eventually won by the FIAT G.91. In order to provide flight-test data for this engine, Bristol-Siddeley loaned ex-RAF Sabre 4 XB982, which had been overhauled by Westland and released to the MDAP on 6 March 1957. Ferried to Bristol's Filton airfield, the Sabre was converted to Orpheus power, and emerged in the summer of 1958. The first 25min Orpheus-powered flight was carried out on 3 July by company test pilot Tom Frost; further flights were piloted by Mike Webber. With a more advanced design than the J47 engine, the Orpheus featured variable compressor inlet guide vanes and a two-stage turbine. Lighter in weight than the J47, the Orpheus none the less produced 6,810lb (3,095kg) of thrust at sea level in the Sabre test bed. In a test programme

F-86E(M) s/n 19242 was the personal mount of Maj Protopappas, commanding officer of 343 Squadron at Elefsina, Greece. The three fuselage bands are red, as is the tail fin. Themis Vranas

accounting for 25 flying hours, the Sabre test bed proved the Orpheus to be a safe and powerful engine, one that went on to power the Indian Hindustan HF.24 fighter. The Orpheus was also the powerplant of the Folland Gnat/Ajeet, an aircraft that gave Pakistan AF Sabres a hard time a few years later. XB982 ceased flying in 1960 and was put into storage at Filton. In 1962 the aircraft, along with the fuselage from a spares aircraft XB900/19788, was scrapped.

Greece

The Greek Air Force (Elliniki Polemiki Aeroporia) operated both the Canadair Sabre 2 [F-86E(M)] and the F-86D, unlike its NATO neighbour Turkey, which flew only the Canadair variant. It appears that, for whatever reason, Turkey was offered F-100s and the Greeks F-86Ds; this is one exception to the 'whatever Greece gets, so does Turkey' argument.

The first of 104 overhauled Canadair Sabre 2s was delivered to Elefsina Air Base on 2 July 1954. Forming 112 Pterighe (Wing), these aircraft initially went to equip 341 Day Fighter Squadron (Mire) and replaced F-84 Thunderjets. Soon after their arrival, a three-week

training course began, using Canadian instructors to train the first ten Greek AF pilots. Greek technicians, having earlier completed training at Canadair, instructed on maintenance subjects. The first 20hr of Sabre flying was, in effect, a basic flying course, followed by another 60hr of conversion flying. These first Greek Sabre pilots then became instructors themselves.

In 1955 further Sabres equipped 342 and 343 Squadrons at Elefsina, and the following year all F-86E units moved to Tanagra. There the F-86E units were often detailed with air-to-air and air-to-ground gunnery missions at Marathonas and over Andros Island. With intense training activity, it was inevitable that accidents should occur. Indeed, on 20 September 1954, not long after the first aircraft arrived, a Greek pilot ejected from his Sabre after experiencing severe porpoising. There were also a number of crashes involving pairs of aircraft, including one on 20 January 1962. Just before midnight two young airmen, 2nd Lts K. Nanopoulos and J. Demangos crashed into a hill shortly after taking off from Tanagra. They were both killed. The two remaining F-86E(M) squadrons converted to F-5s, 341 Mire in 1965, followed by 342 in January 1966.

This Greek Air Force F-86D, 51-8305 was transferred through MAP in May 1960 and used by 343 Squadron at Elefsina. The aircraft is to typical export standard with Sidewinder rails and Tacan fitted. The lower fuselage has also had an aluminized lacquer finish applied. Themis Vranas

The first of thirty-five F-86Ds arrived on 17 May 1960, and first unit to equip was 337 Squadron at Elefsina. On 12 May 1961 343 Squadron converted from the F-86E(M), and operated the F-86D until November 1965. 337 Squadron, as the last Greek 'Dog' unit, retired their machines in May 1967. In 1964 a number of Greek F-86Ds and E(M) aircraft were painted in a 'NATO' camouflage colour scheme. Still in these colours, many of the F-86Ds were then used as decoy aircraft at a number of air bases until the early 1990s.

Honduras

With a relatively small armed force, the Fuerza Aérea Hondureña (FAH) had for many years been supplied with only sporadic deliveries of American MAP aircraft. Following the infamous 1969 'Soccer War' with El Salvador, Honduras endeavoured to build up its air force, and the purchase of eighteen ex-Israeli Dassault MD.450 Ouragan fighter-bombers by El Salvador in 1973 marked the start of a small arms race. The FAH also managed to negotiate a contract for a number of ex-Israeli aircraft, this time for Dassault Super Mystère B2s. But delivery was not immediate and, desperate to obtain fighter aircraft, Honduras decided not to wait for the slow negotiations with the Israelis. Instead, eight ex-Yugoslav Air Force

This F-86E(M) was the first machine delivered to the Honduran AF. Subsequent aircraft were not so smartly painted. The photograph was taken at NAS Key West in July 1976. Patrick Martin via Mike Fox

Canadair CL-13 Mk 4s [F-86E(M) standard] were bought in 1976, just ahead of an Israeli agreement for the supply of the Super Mystères. Despite this, the sale of the Sabres went ahead, the aircraft having been shipped in crates to Fort Lauderdale in Florida, where they were readied for flight. At least two

F-86Fs were also supplied (possibly from Venezuela) at this time.

Bob Murray, a former CIA pilot, was employed to ferry overhauled F-86E(M)s from Florida to Honduras:

The total number delivered was ten. Assembly of the '86s was done in a warehouse on the north side of Fort Lauderdale International Airport. The aircraft were then towed down a vehicular road to the ramp area. The aircraft were fully equipped (0.50-cal), had 120gall drop tanks installed, and were painted a medium blue, but not glossy. [They] were delivered individually one every two to three weeks, spring and summer of 1976. The Hondurans cracked one up almost immediately, and I heard they had about five or six left [in 1989]. In 1974, while on leave from Air America, I delivered their first jet, a T-33 No. 222. At that time they were flying F4U Corsairs. Got some cockpit time in one at San Pedro Sula. That is where all the Sabres were delivered.

The Sabres were ferried via two routes. Initially, because it was thought that Cuba would not permit overflight, the aircraft were flown to Boca Chica NAS in Key West, refuelled and flown around the western tip of Cuba non-stop to San Pedro Sula. On my suggestion, as I had been flying twice a week in a DC-3 to Nicaragua over Cuba, permission

was requested to fly the 86s over. This was granted for three aircraft deliveries and then cut off for reasons unknown. The route was direct Marathon, direct Varadero, Giron Corridor to Giron, direct to Grand Cayman for refuelling. The next leg was direct Swan Island, direct San Pedro Sula.

The Sabres' arrival coincided with that of the Israeli aircraft. Former Israel Defense Force/Air Force Lt Col Shlomo Shapira was assigned to the FAH, under Israel Aircraft Industries charge, to train the Honduran pilots. It appears that the earlier [A] involvement with Iranian F-86Fs came to good use, for Lt Col Shapira also trained the Hondurans in the use of the Canadair CL-13 Sabres. But with the Super Mystères forming the main air-defence component of the air force, the Sabres were rendered largely superfluous and were assigned to Escuadrilla de Caza-Bombardeo (simply, 'fighter-bomber squadron') at Base Aérea

Coronel Héctor Caracciolo Moncada, La Ceiba. During the same period four F-86K all-weather fighters were presented to the FAH by the Venezuelan government, and these were also, curiously, assigned to Escuadrilla de Caza-Bombardeo. The F-86Ks carried natural metal finish throughout their short service life, but the F-86Es and Fs soon gained a camouflage paint scheme.

In 1980 four air force F-86Es were detailed to carry out a flypast over the capital Tegucigalpa to mark the FAH's twenty-fifth anniversary. Unfortunately, the exuberant formation leader managed to take his formation in too low and the number four aircraft hit a number of trees and cables in the city. The pilot managed to regain control of his Sabre, only to suffer a total hydraulics failure on his return to base. Compounding his woes, the ejection seat failed and he had to bail out manually, breaking his left leg in the process. This sorry episode led to the incorporation of Martin-Baker ejection seats in all remaining FAH Sabres.

It is not known when the Honduran F-86Ks were retired; it can only be

Ex-Yugoslav F-86E(M) FAH 3005 was photographed at Fort Lauderdale in 1976. Finished in an overall light gray colour scheme, it was on delivery to the Honduran Air Force. MAP

Seen on delivery to the Indonesian Air Force in 1973, Sabre 32 A94-963 became F-8608 in TNI-AU service.
J.M.G. Gradidge

Air Forces Day Ceremony to be held on 5 October 1978. The team aircraft acquired a special colour scheme, consisting of a red fuselage stripe and were fitted with equipment to enable hydraulic oil to be sprayed into the exhaust efflux, creating white smoke. The 14 Squadron Sabres experienced few accidents in service, though two aircraft were scrapped as a result of starter-motor explosions. A further machine, F-8610/A94-969, crashed on approach to Iswahyudi in November 1974. Although the pilot ejected safely, his seat killed a farm worker below. Another Sabre, F-8613/A94-975, was lost in an accident during March 1979. The Sabres served until late 1980 when the Squadron began flying the F-5E and F. Many Sabres were then assigned to a ground training role, gaining a TS prefix, referring to the aircraft's new mission.

assumed that their complexity and limited numbers precluded all but the briefest of operational use. However, the F-86Es did remain in service into the 1980s, thanks to maintenance support from Venezuela. They were finally retired in 1986.

Indonesia

On 21 April 1972 the Australian government announced that it would be presenting the Indonesian Air Force [Angkatan Udara Republik Indonesia (AURI) – renamed Tentara Nasional Indonesia-Angkatan Udara (TNI-AU) in mid-1974] with eighteen CAC Sabres. The aircraft – all Mk 32s – were refurbished at RAAF Williamtown where a number of AURI personnel received flying and maintenance training during 1972. At the same time, a number of Australian officers and airmen were detached to Indonesia in order to install the navigational and air-traffic equipment required at the Iswahyudi Air Base. In December 1972 a non-flying training aircraft, A94-370, was delivered to Indonesia aboard the MV *Gunung Kerintij* so that AURI personnel could begin familiarization.

The delivery of the mission aircraft in 1973 was undertaken in two groups, routing via RAAF Amberley, Mount Isa, Darwin and Bali, before arriving in Indonesia on 19 and 21 February 1973. The mission was accompanied by two RAAF Orions, while a pair of Canberras

flew ahead of the formations to provide weather information. Aircraft A94-352 was damaged on take-off at Bali during the ferry flight; a replacement (A94-970, Indonesian serial F-8618) arrived on 23 February and it appears that one other aircraft was also added to the AURI batch at this time. The aircraft were handed over officially by Mr Lance Barnard on 9 April 1973 in a ceremony at Iswahyudi AB to mark Indonesia's National Aviation Day. In AURI service they were given F-86- serials, followed by sequential numbers from 01 to 18. These were allotted in ascending RAAF serial number order, except for the last pair of aircraft which arrived out of sequence.

The Sabres all served with 14 Squadron (previously a MiG-21 unit) at Iswahyudi AB, near Madiun in East Java. After the 1974 AURI/TNI-AU reshuffle, the Squadron was renamed Sat-Sergap F-86 Squadron, and in 1976 five further Sabres were transferred to the Squadron from the Royal Malaysian Air Force. The colour scheme for the Sabres was fairly plain: overall silver with the TNI-AU pentagonal marking in six places, and an Indonesian flag on the tail. One exception to this was aircraft F-8614/A94-980, which was the personal aircraft of the 14 Squadron commanding officer. This aircraft carried a lurid red lightning flash on the fuselage and a striking yellow and red starburst design on the tail.

An aerobatic team was formed in July 1978 on the orders of the TNI-AU Chief of Staff, in preparation for the Indonesian

Iran

Previously little has been published of the Iranian involvement with the Sabre; many are keen to ignore the Air Force's use of large numbers of F-86Fs, which spanned a number of years, and quite separately from the equally large number of ex-Luftwaffe Canadair Sabre 6s which passed to the Pakistan AF. Their stories are intertwined, but it is important to explain some of the reasons for what appears to have been a well-generated smoke screen over Iranian Sabre operations.

Fifty-two MAP-supplied F-86F-25 and 30s were assigned to the Imperial Iranian Air Force (IIAF) during 1960, passing through overhaul with FIAT at Turin. These same machines had been transferred to FIAT from storage at Chateauroux AB in France, where many had been since their withdrawal from USAF service in 1956. One such aircraft (52-4724) was flown from the 50th FBW in Germany by H.O. Malone:

I did ferry one of our F86Fs to Chateauroux in May 1956 after we had converted to the H model. It was our understanding that the F models were going to Spain [partially true; others in this batch did indeed go to the Spanish AF]. The trip from Hahn took two hours, but I suspect we did some type of training en route because the flight should not have taken that long simply from point to point. We spent the night in France, then returned to Hahn aboard a C47 which was sent down the next day to fetch us. Some other pilots in the 81st squadron – the last one to get rid of its F models – flew Sabres direct to Madrid, sometimes with Spanish AF pilots as members of the flight, but I was not involved in that.

Assigned to MAP beginning in mid-March 1960, the Sabres were ferried into Iran through Brindisi, and in IIAF service new serials were allocated in the range 3-100 to 3-151. Before the arrival of the Sabres, the IIAF had operated around sixty-four F-84Gs in the ground attack role, with 1st and 3rd Fighter Bomber Squadrons at Mehrabad, plus F-47 Thunderbolts. 2nd FBS at Qalegh Murgeh operated twenty-seven T-6 trainers. In preparation for the arrival of Sabres, twenty-five pilots underwent training in the USA, completing the course in 1961; a further sixty-two officers and a hundred airmen completed ground-based training in this period. In addition, large numbers of US military personnel backed up the MAP effort in Iran, and they were the first to fly the aircraft before going on to qualify IIAF pilots. During the early 1960s an RAF detachment of about seven officers and thirteen airmen also provided fighter-control and radar-defence training.

The Sabres quickly replaced Thunderjets in 1st Tactical Fighter Squadron at Mehrabad, as well as 3rd Tactical Fighter Squadron, which moved to Vahdati Air Base with the arrival of the F-86Fs. Two further squadrons also re-equipped; 2nd TFS, previously flying T-6 trainers at Qalegh Murgeh moved to Mehrabad with F-86Fs, and 4th Tactical Fighter Squadron, an F-47 Thunderbolt unit, converted to Sabres at Vahdati. This complete re-equipping with Sabres was finished by August 1961, the F-84s and the Thunderbolts being scrapped at the same time. It appears that further F-86 deliveries were slated for the IIAF but were not followed up, ostensibly due to the imminent arrival of F-5A Freedom Fighters. At Mehrabad the 1st and the 2nd TFS, along with an RT-33 reconnaissance squadron, formed the 1st Tactical Fighter Wing, commanded by Col A. Rafat. The two Sabre squadrons at Vahdati came under 2nd TFW, with Brig Gen M. Naimi-Rod at its head. Brief mention should be made of the official IIAF Sabre aerobatic team, the Golden

In 1963, the Imperial Iranian Air Force sent four F-86Fs to the Congo for UN duties there. Operating as 103rd Tactical Fighter Squadron, these four aircraft are seen here in the Congo at that time. These immaculate aircraft are unusual in having semi-gloss mid-green anti-dazzle panels. Gilbert Casselsjö via Leif Hellström

Crown. The team originally flew F-84Gs but converted to Sabres in 1960. The six-aircraft team was commanded by Maj Nader Djahanbani and flew the Sabres until they were replaced by Northrop F-5s from 1966.

From 1961 the IIAF concentrated on getting operational with the F-86F squadrons. Formation flying, gunnery, rocket firing and napalm drops were all practised, not only for border defence but also as a show of force to those bent on subversion within Iran. To reinforce the message, regular firepower demonstrations were carried out and, on 20 September 1961, a large number of F-86Fs, led by Gen M.A. Khatami, the IIAF commander, put on one such show at Vahdati to mark Iranian Air Force Week. The demonstration showed Sabres completing rocketry, dive bombing and low-level bombing from altitudes ranging from 500 to 1,000ft (150-300m). Spectators watched in awe from just 400yd (370m) away as further Sabres carried out napalm drops. By this time, a number of IIAF Sabres had already been fitted with Sidewinder missile launch rails.

But the early effectiveness of the IIAF's

Sabre units was questioned by the British Air Attaché at the time. He cited the lack of fighter-interception exercises and the inability of IIAF pilots to co-ordinate their missions with the ground radar site at Doshan Tappeh as the prime causes for this. In joint exercises, RAF Canberra bombers often had to operate at 35,000ft (10,700m), somewhat lower than usual, because the IIAF's Sabre crews complained that the radar sites could not cover them above that altitude. Exasperated, the USAF colonel in charge of the MAP mission took a flight of IIAF Sabres safely up to 48,000ft (14,600m); when the Iranian Sabre pilots flew a subsequent mission unescorted they complained that they could only reach 42,000ft (12,800m). Such problems were not helped by Gen Khatami's order that Sabre wing commanders could not fly in case they killed themselves.

During 1963 the IIAF sent four F-86Fs (3-133, 140, 146 and 150) to the Congo to support UN operations there. The unit was apparently numbered 103rd Tactical Fighter Squadron for the duration of the attachment and, with the return of the F-86Fs to Iran, some personnel remained in the Congo, assigned to the UN-owned F-86E(M)s.

Re-equipment with more modern types had been on the Iranians' mind for some time – even since the arrival of the Sabres. The situation was only muddied when, on a visit to Iran in 1961, Senator Symington had stated that upon his return to the United States he would be pressing for IIAF re-equipment with F-105 Thunderchiefs. This caused some embarrassment, and the head of the US Military Advisory Group in Iran, Maj Gen Hayden, strongly opposed any further aid until the Iranians showed a degree of self-sufficiency. With this in mind, the Iranians began to look for suitable overhaul facilities for the Sabre fleet.

In 1966 Israel Aircraft Industries (IAI) landed the contract for overhauling IIAF F-86Fs at Lod airport in Israel. The first two Sabres had been seen at Lod on 26 October 1965 by a British Embassy official, Wg Cdr Goring-Morris, though no markings were visible. According to Goring-Morris's informant in Tehran, it had been planned to overhaul the aircraft in Pakistan, but the war with India had made this impossible. IAI had also been tasked to train thirty IIAF engineers so that overhauls could be done in Iran. On 26 April 1966 another unmarked F-86F was seen at Lod, and a US Embassy colleague confirmed to Goring-Morris that it was an IIAF Sabre awaiting air test after overhaul and that between forty and fifty aircraft were involved. Goring-Morris also reported that there had been numerous sightings of Israeli AF Boeing Stratocruisers at Mehrabad during 1966.

It seems that IAI were involved in another further overhaul contract for IIAF F-86Fs, and this contract, for thirty-five Sabres, was signed in November 1966. Zeev Tavor was one of two Israel Aircraft Industries (IAI) pilots tasked with test-flying the Sabres at Lod:

As I recall, this operation was not published. The aircraft carried no markings, they only had IAI [assigned] numbers. No photos were taken. The aircraft were flown by Iranian pilots to and from Israel, landing on their way in a third state [probably Turkey]. They couldn't fly direct because of Arab states on the way with no diplomatic relations with Israel.

Except myself, there was another pilot who checked out on the F-86F. This pilot passed away a few years ago. This guy checked out in

Iran and I checked out in Israel on the F-86F. I first flew the F-86F on 29 November 1966. My last flight was on 13 August 1968. Aircraft number was BK25. I logged a total of 15.45 flight hours on the F-86F. These were the only F-86Fs I flew.

I don't remember how many F-86s were involved in this operation, but I pulled out of my log book the aircraft numbers I flew on. The numbers were: BK-3, 4, 5, 6, 7, 11, 12, 13, 14, 16, 17, 18, 19, 25 (BK stands for Bedek-IAI code).

I flew a total of twenty flights on fourteen aircraft. The aircraft arrived in Israel in pairs and flew back in pairs. The other pilot's name was Yahalom Nachum. The only F-86s that went through IAI were the Iranians. The only anecdote I recall is that the F-86 had no parking brakes and we had to wait for the ground crews to chock the aircraft at the end of every flight. Beside this fact it was a friendly and easy aircraft to fly.

It would make sense that the Iranians would want to keep their connection with the Jewish state a secret from their Middle Eastern colleagues. This goes some way to explaining the secrecy surrounding IIAF Sabres. One thing is certain: the US were fully aware of all these developments.

During 1965 the IIAF began to receive its first contemporary MAP fighters, with the arrival of Northrop F-5s. The first aircraft arrived early in the year and, by 12 January 1965, all thirteen aircraft for the first squadron had arrived, with another four for the second F-5 squadron arriving on 31 December. In total, 117 aircraft were thought to have been assigned, of which twenty-six were purchased by the Iranians (as opposed to supplied under MAP/MDAP). It must have seemed strange, therefore, that in February 1966 the Iranians confirmed, through the Swiss government, that ninety ex-Luftwaffe Sabres had been bought, for use only in Iran, and that they would be permanently stationed there. This proved to be merely a diversionary tactic – the Sabres were not for Iran; they passed to the Pakistan Air Force. Their story is detailed in that section.

By the end of 1965 the IIAF still managed to declare between forty-two and forty-four F-86Fs in airworthy condition. The new F-5s equipped squadrons at Mehrabad, but also moved into a new purpose-built airfield at Sharokhi. The arrival of the F-5s appears to have marked a reorganization of the

Sabre squadrons, those at Mehrabad moving to Vahdati, where four new Sabre squadrons were formed: 201st, 202nd, 203rd and 204th TFS, all under 2nd TFW control. A detachment of four F-86Fs remained at Mehrabad to provide defence for the base during the conversion process, and also continued to give intercept practice for the radar controllers. The detachment returned to Vahdati in December 1965.

Little is known of the later service of IIAF Sabres; it is thought that they were finally withdrawn from service in 1971. Today only one Iranian Sabre is thought to survive, an unmarked example displayed in Tehran.

Iraq

The IAF received five F-86Fs in July 1958, just before the overthrow of King Faisal. These aircraft were either unserviceable upon delivery or very soon after and saw no operational use. They were reportedly bulldozed off the ramp and broken up. At this time the Iraqi AF (Al Quwwat Al Jawwiya Al Iraqiya) were operating thirteen Hunter F.6s, fourteen Venom FB. 1s and eight Vampire F. 52s in the day fighter role.

As a result of the coup, the United States refused to supply further F-86Fs and, turning to Russia, the IAF were supplied with thirteen Il-28 bombers and forty MiG-15/17 Fresco/Fagots in early 1959. The serial numbers are thought to have been 52-5209, 52-5222, 52-5231, 52-5235 plus one other, all delivered on 14 June 1958 under MAP project 8F653. All except the last aircraft were delivered from Chateauroux AB in France.

Israel

The Israeli Government began negotiations with Canadair in 1955 for the supply of 24 Sabre 6s. These aircraft were to equip a squodron of the Israeli Air Force, and a numbe of aircraft were allotted for delivery: C/Ns 1520, 1523 to 1526, 1531 to 1532 and 1534.Israeli serial numbers assigned to these machines were 6030-6037. At least six Sabres were painted in Israeli colours at Cartierville, the scheme consisting of the standard NATO camouflage, but with pale grey undersides. The Star of David roundel was applied in the six usual positions, and the serial number was applied in large figures aft of the fuselage roundel. Israeli personnel were soon being rotated through Canadair for pre-delivery training.

Unfortunately, this deal came to nothing. With the outbreak of the Suez Crisis in 1956, the Canadian Prime Minister intervened and cancelled the deal during October. The Sabres were stored until early 1957 and then delivered to RCAF units. But it seems that the Israelis still made good use of their Sabre training, and this may have led to their involvement with Sabre support for Iran and, to a lesser extent, Honduras.

Italy

The Italian Air Force (Aeronautica Militare Italiana – AMI) gained Sabre capability in 1955 with the arrival of the first ex-RAF Sabre 4s. These aircraft had been upgraded to F-86E(M) standard before delivery, although one Sabre 2 was also assigned to AMI, and this sole example remained in the 'slatted' configuration.

A number of AMI Vampire units then quickly began Sabre conversion as part of two separate Aerobrigata (Wings); 2° Aerobrigata Intercettori Diurni (fighter day wing) at Montichiari and 4°

Aerobrigata Intercettori Diurni at Pratica di Mare. 4° Aerobrigata had transferred from Napoli-Capodichino on 16 June 1956 as the airfield was unsuitable for Sabre operations. Constituent squadrons (gruppi – gruppo being singular) within 2° Aerobrigata painted their camouflaged Sabre intake lips identifying colours, comprising 8° (red), 13° (green) and 14° gruppi (white). It seems that the 4° Aerobrigata squadrons

– 9°, 10° and 12° Gruppi did not adopt this practice.

With FIAT building F-86Ks, it was only natural that the AMI would be first to receive the type in NATO, and 1° Stormo Caccia Ogni Tempo (1st All-Weather Fighter Group) formed at Istrana in late 1955 for this purpose. The first squadron to receive the F-86K was 6° Gruppo, which formed in October 1955 and received its first aircraft on 2 November.

This F-86K, MM6214/53-8302 was assigned to 6° Gruppo of 1° Stormo Caccia Ogni Tempo at Istrana on 24 February 1956 and is seen here at that time. On 31 January 1958 this aircraft suffered an engine fire on landing at Pisa and was burnt out. The pilot Magg. Francesco Terzani escaped unharmed. J.M.G. Gradidge

This natural metal F-86E(M) was assigned to 2° Aerobrigata at Cameri. Lionel N. Paul via Mike Fox

17° and 23° Gruppi then received the aircraft in 1956, the latter initially operated as a Sezione (Flight) of 1° Stormo Caccia Ogni Tempo at Pisa from 1 December 1956, and was finally redesignated as a Gruppo on 30 March 1957.

Some considerable upheaval then affected the Sabre units, not least the conversion of 1° Stormo to guided missile operations in May 1959. This precipitated the move of the F-86Ks to a pair of units previously flying F-84Fs: 21° Gruppo (gaining ex-17° Gruppo Sabres) and 22° Gruppo (taking over 6° Gruppo aircraft). 23° Gruppo remained an F-86K unit, and all three numerically-consecutive units were reassigned to 51° Aerobrigata control at Istrana. 21° Gruppo converted to the F-104G in September 1963, passing its F-86Ks to 12° Gruppo.

Meanwhile, the F-86E units were also realigned, 4° Aerobrigata deploying to Grosseto starting in March 1959, with 10° Gruppo being detached to Grazzanise in December 1961. 9° and 10° Gruppi then converted to F-104s, beginning in March 1963. This left 12° Gruppo, which converted to F-86Ks at Gioia del Colle in September 1963. The 2° Aerobrigata F-86Es were lost in October 1962 with the disbanding of the wing, having moved gruppi to Cameri and Rimini in 1957. However, 13° Gruppo continued as an autonomous squadron, the last in the AMI to operate F-86Es. The unit flew the last AMI F-86E mission at Cameri on 15 August 1965, then moved to Treviso for conversion to the FIAT G.91R.

The last AMI F-86K had been delivered from the factory on 31 October 1957, but further examples were obtained from France, which passed twenty-two F-86Ks to 51° Aerobrigata, starting in January 1962. By 1967 the Italian AF had three F-86K squadron-sized units remaining, 23° Gruppo having moved to Rimini-Miramare in July 1964 and 12° Gruppo reassigning to the newly-formed 36° Stormo on 1 August 1966. With F-104S deliveries beginning, 22° Gruppo moved to Cameri on 9 June 1969 for conversion to the type, passing its remaining Sabres to 12° and 23° Gruppi. In December 1971 12° Gruppo also converted to the Starfighter, and any viable F-86Ks were ceded to the only AMI Sabre unit remaining: 23° Gruppo at Rimini-Miramare. With inevitable conversion to the F-104 in sight, 23° Gruppo was

assigned to 5° Stormo on 25 March 1973, receiving its first F-104S on 19 March. The last AMI F-86K flight was flown on 27 July 1973 by Capt Mario Pinna. In service, the F-86Ks had flown 162,396hr.

Japan

For Japan, the Korean conflict proved that every cloud has a silver lining. The massive US build-up in the country allowed Japanese industry to recover from wartime destruction in support of the military, notably in aircraft manufacturing. The reconstruction of an armed Japanese fighting force, to be used in a purely defensive role, was also easier to implement when the time came. With the end of the Korean War, tensions still remained in the Far East, and a Japanese Self-Defense Law was passed on 2 June 1954, followed by the formation of an air arm, the Japanese Air Self-Defense Force (JASDF) on 1 July. The growth of the fledgling JASDF centred around the rebuilt airfield at Hamamatsu. By the end of 1954 a training unit with T-34 Mentor aircraft was already in operation there.

To equip the planned seven fighter-interceptor and two all-weather interceptor wings (each with three squadrons, and as interceptors, with a pure defence role), the JASDF expected to procure 526 F-86Fs and 150 F-86Ds. In addition, to

fulfil the tactical reconnaissance mission the Japanese planned for three squadrons of RF-86Fs, totalling fifty-four machines. These types were procured for the JASDF, but the actual numbers delivered were significantly reduced.

In August 1955 the first five Japanese Sabre pilots – all wartime veterans – began F-86F flight training at Nellis AFB in Nevada, having completed basic refresher training in Japan. These crews then returned to Japan following training in February 1956. Concurrent training was accomplished at Hamamatsu using USAF F-86Fs of 6024th Flying Training Group, beginning in July 1955.

Meanwhile, beginning on 10 December 1955, thirty ex-FEAF F-86F-25 and -30 aircraft were delivered to JASDF for assignment to training duties with 1st Hikotai (Squadron), which had formed at Tsuiki on 1 December. Placed under the control of 1st Kokudan (Wing) under Maj Gen Minoru Genda, 1st Hikotai served as the JASDF Sabre conversion unit, and managed to graduate sixty Japanese pilots by June 1956. The unit then moved into Hamamatsu at the end of the year after the base's runway had been extended from 4,000 to 7,000ft (1,120 to 2,133m). To complete the order for 180 US-supplied Sabres, 150 FY55 F-86F-40s arrived, starting in April 1956. With a lack of trained JASDF personnel, forty-five of these were then returned to the United

Visiting RAF Luqa in Malta during 1970, this 12° Gruppo F-86K carries the code of 36° Stormo at Gioia del Colle. This is one of the aircraft originally delivered to the French Air Force and ceded back to Italy in July 1962. MAP

This 1956 photograph shows one of the first F-86Fs supplied to Japan. The natural metal scheme shows traces of the former USAF identity, 55-3829. Black and yellow are the colours of 1st Hikotai. Mike Fox

This shot of QF-86F 55-5091 shows the damage done by a non-warhead Sidewinder missile on 7 November 1990. The aircraft was repaired and flew again. USN

States in February 1959. Thus, in effect, 135 F-86Fs were supplied from American stocks, plus a further 300 under licence from Mitsubishi.

On 25 August 1956 the first tactical F-86F unit, 2nd Hikotai, was formed under 1st Kokudan, and based at Hamamatsu AB. The activation and equipping of squadrons then began to speed up, with 2nd Kokudan forming at Chitose on 1 October 1956, at the same time activating its first squadron, the 3rd Hikotai with F-86Fs and then in February 1957 also adding the 4th Hikotai.

The first of 122 all-weather F-86D interceptors arrived during January 1958 to equip four all-weather interceptor squadrons at Tsuiki and Chitose. The first unit to equip was 101st Hikotai, which activated on 1 August 1958 under 3rd Kokudan. By the end of 1962 the four interceptor hikotai were in place and fully equipped. Completing the JASDF Sabre inventory, the first of eighteen RF-86F Sabre conversions was assigned to 501st Hikotai in 1962. Formed on 1 December 1961 at Matsushima AB, 501st Hikotai moved to Iruma AB in 1962, also gaining a small number of standard F-86Fs to perform training missions. Special mention should be made here of the Blue Impulse F-86F aerobatic team. The world's longest-serving Sabre aerobatic team, Blue Impulse was formed in March 1960 at Hamamatsu AB. Among the feats performed by it was the drawing of the multicoloured rings in smoke above the opening ceremony of the Tokyo Olympic Games. The team flew their last F-86F display on 8 February 1981 before converting to the Mitsubishi T2 for the 1982 season.

In June 1959 the National Defense Agency decided to improve the performance of JASDF Sabres in order to offset the delay in the ordering of supersonic fighters. It was proposed that, by the installation of booster rockets, the top speed of the F-86F could be increased to 1.2 Mach and the service ceiling to 60,000ft (18,300m). This may well have been the impetus behind the testing of an F-86F in the USA with a Rocketdyne AR2-3 motor. In 1964 the Defense Agency advanced another Sabre modification: the Air Staff Office proposed that a hundred F-86Fs could be modified for use in the ground-attack role. This project went no further: the Ground Staff Office – which favoured the Mitsubishi Mu-2 – won the day.

In 1964 the JASDF began to apply popular names to its aircraft. Under this system, the F-86F became known as 'Kyokko' (Morning Sunshine) and the F-86D 'Gekko' (Moonlight). With the completion of Hyakuri AB in December 1965, the F-104s based there took over the defence of Tokyo from F-86Fs based at Iruma. Briefly, with the formation of the last F-86F hikotai in November 1961, the JASDF possessed ten squadrons with the type. The arrival of more modern aircraft, such as the F-104, relieved the burden on the Sabres and it was inevitable that units would begin to relinquish their aircraft. Thus, on 20 November 1965 2nd Hikotai disbanded, with 9th Hikotai following suit one month later.

The next units to draw down were those operating the F-86D. The JASDF had planned to withdraw the F-86Ds from service during 1967 and to suspend all repair and overhaul during the 1965 Fiscal Year. However, the phase out was staggered, with 102nd and 105th Hikotai disbanding on 1 December 1967 and the remaining units on 1 October the following year. These units slowly handed in their Sabres, 5th Hikotai disbanding in July 1971 and 4th Hikotai in June 1975. But, even by the beginning of 1977, the JASDF still possessed six front-line F-86F units and an RF-86F recce squadron. The RF-86Fs were finally withdrawn in April 1977, and the final F-86F squadron, 6th Hikotai, moved to Misawa AB in 1979 for conversion to the Mitsubishi F.1. However, a small number of F-86Fs were retained by specialized units such as the Koku Sotai Shireibu Hikotai (Headquarters Squadron) at Iruma AB. The HQ Squadron had the honour of performing the JASDF's last Sabre flight with F-86F 62-7497 on 15 March 1982. Under the terms of MAP, most of the surviving F-86Fs were then shipped back to the United States where the Navy had them slated for use in the QF-86F drone programme at China Lake in California. After conversion to target drones, many were blown out of the sky in order to test the latest offensive weaponry. With regular maintenance and responsible operation the aircraft had lasted well and the point was not lost on the Navy. They chose the best airframes for conversion and, despite having a choice of many ex-MAP Sabres from other nations besides Japan, it is worth noting that the majority of QF-86F conversions were performed on ex-JASDF airframes. It thus seems ironic that the careful and professional maintenance carried out by the Japanese on their F-86Fs should ultimately be responsible for their destruction.

Korea

Following the end of the Korean War in 1953, many USAF units remained in the country to counter any further aggression from the North. Among these were the Sabre-equipped 4th FIW, 8th FBW, 18th FBW, 51st FIW and 58th FBW. However, many of these Wings moved out during 1954, leaving just the 58th FBW at Osan-Ni.

In order to fill the gap left by these departing USAF units, the Republic of Korea Air Force (ROKAF) would therefore re-equip with the F-86F and, to prepare them to receive the Sabres, five F-86Fs were initially assigned to the USAF's 6146th Air Depot Group at Sach'On on 20 June 1955. The Group moved to Seoul on 3 August, simultaneously being redesignated as 6146th Field Training Group, charged with further USAF indoctrination and the flying training of ROKAF personnel on US-supplied types. Finally, on 1 September 1955, the Group

52-4858 was one of a small number of RF-86Fs supplied to the Republic of Korea from Taiwan; most other RoKAF recce Sabres came direct from US supply. The colours are those of 32nd Squadron.
Davis via Mike Fox

moved into Suwon and was assigned a further batch of Sabres on 19 September. These aircraft were USAF-owned, and were used by ROKAF personnel until the delivery of their own aircraft. In early 1956 the Field Training Group's Sabres were reassigned back to their USAF units or to maintenance; only a few were then returned to the ROKAF.

The first of the F-86Fs for the Koreans

arrived at Suwon under MAP Project 5F558 on 28 December 1955 from Kisarazu in Japan. The ROKAF received further deliveries of Sabres until mid-1956, when eighty-five aircraft had been delivered. These Sabres went to equip the three-squadron 10th Fighter Wing at Kimpo. During 1958 a further twenty-seven F-86Fs were delivered, and between 11 April and 2 May 1958, ten RF-86Fs were also delivered ex-USAF, plus at least one further aircraft from Taiwan. The RF-86Fs were assigned under MAP project 7F740, and served with a separate unit – 32nd Squadron – at Suwon. The latter delivery of F-86Fs enabled another wing to be formed so that, by 1958, there were two Fighter Wings – 10th and 11th – operating out of Kimpo. At this stage the ROKAF had no infrastructure to support the RF-86Fs, and there were no photo-developing or interpretation capabilities in the country. Major F-86 maintenance was accomplished in Japan.

During 1960 forty F-86Ds were delivered from Shin Meiwa at Komaki, Japan, to equip two interceptor squadrons under 10th Fighter Wing. A further delivery of five or more aircraft was made in November 1960.

By the beginning of 1962 the ROKAF had 133 F-86Fs, operating with 102nd and 103rd Fighter Squadrons, under 10th Fighter Wing at Suwon, and 101st, 111th and 112th Fighter Squadrons, under 11th Fighter Wing at Kimpo. An F-86F training unit – 17th Advanced Flying Training Squadron – was based at Taegu. In addition, the thirty-two surviving F-86Ds flew with 108th and 109th Fighter Squadrons (All-Weather) under 10th FW at Suwon. The 10th FW's commanding officer was Col Yoon Eung Yul; 11th FW was commanded by Col Choo Young Bock.

On 30 April 1965 the ROKAF received its first Northrop F-5A at Suwon; it was planned that these aircraft would supplant and eventually replace the F-86Fs. By 1976 it was reported that 130 Sabres of all types were still in service with the ROKAF, but that in 1978-79, the remaining fifty F-86Fs and eighteen F-86Ds were finally retired. However, as late as 1987, F-86Fs and RF-86Fs were still in service at Taegu AB, and it may well be that a number remained in service with the photoreconnaissance squadron, plus some F-86F continuation trainers. Many ROKAF Sabres were subsequently passed to the US Navy for the QF-86F programme; their poor condition meant that most were cannibalized for spares.

Malaysia

In April 1969 the Australian Prime Minister John Gorton announced that the government would be presenting the Royal Malaysian Air Force (Tentara Udara Diraja Malaysia – TUDM) with ten Sabre 32s. This deal was worth Aus$10 million, and included spare parts, a Sabre flight simulator and ninety RAAF personnel, who would be attached to the Malaysian base at Butterworth to begin training. A Sabre Advisory Flight was formed at Butterworth in April 1969 to begin the training of TUDM personnel.

To receive the Sabres, a new unit, 11 (Cobra) Squadron, was formed at Butterworth, and in August 1969 the first combat aircraft arrived. They originally carried an overall silver colour scheme, but this soon gave way to a camouflage scheme of overall olive-green upper surfaces with pale blue-grey undersides. In TUDM service the Sabres were allotted

These Royal Malaysian AF Sabre 32s were lined up at Butterworth in December 1969, soon after delivery from Australia. Assigned to 11 'Cobra' Squadron, they gained a green and light gray camouflage scheme in later service. Roger Brooks

Malaysian serial numbers, apparently being FM1 followed by the 'last three' of the RAAF serial, but later the whole batch were renumbered in the FM1900 series.

In November 1971 a further Sabre, A94-357, was presented as a non-flying training aid, and in the same month a further six Sabres were given to the TUDM from Australian stocks. The Australian Sabre Advisory Flight was disbanded in February 1972. Finally, in February 1974 the last TUDM Sabre was assigned, A94-356, a second training airframe.

On 31 May 1975, 12 (Kilau, Lightning) Squadron was formed, and apparently took over surviving aircraft from 11 Squadron. 12 squadron converted to the F-5 in April 1976, ending the TUDM Sabre's active service. Many Malaysian Sabres remained in the country as training airframes and five TUDM Sabres were passed to Indonesia in July 1976.

The Netherlands

In 1951 the Dutch parliament approved a plan whereby an independent air force would be created as part of the country's new NATO commitment. The plan suggested that nine day fighter squadrons plus six night fighter, six fighter-bomber and four observation/communications squadrons would be required. However, later in 1951 NATO air force arrangements were revised, and the Paris Plan, approved in February 1952, put forward an increase in the aircraft assigned to each squadron, at the same time reducing the number of actual squadrons. Thus the Royal Air Force (Koninklijke Luchtmacht, KLu), created on 27 March 1953, would feature six day fighter squadrons and three all-weather squadrons.

The original equipment of the KLu comprised Gloster Meteor F.8 fighters and F-84G fighter bombers, the latter marking the arrival of the first MDAP-funded aircraft. Finally, in 1954 the all-weather requirement was filled with the decision to equip the KLu with F-86K Sabres. This proved to be a controversial move; many high-ranking politicians and air force officers had expected a two-seat machine to be chosen.

In order to prepare the Air Force for Sabre operations, 700 Squadron was formed at Soesterburg on 1 August 1955 to begin training, the unit at first calling upon three Meteor trainers to keep aircrews up to date. At the same time, 328 Squadron at Woensdrecht was disbanded and personnel transferred into Soesterburg to form 702 Squadron. Even at this late date navigators were being trained in anticipation of the arrival of two-seat interceptors. 702 Squadron transferred to Twenthe in December in order to accept the first KLu F-86Ks, and on 1 June 1956 701 Squadron formed at Twenthe, completing the trio of Dutch Sabre units.

The first fifteen NAA-built F-86Ks arrived in Holland on 1 October 1955 aboard the USS Tripoli, and a further eight had been received by the end of the year. Following assembly and test flight, the first pair of KLu Sabres, 54-1277 and -1278, were accepted by 702 Squadron on 8 December. In total, fifty-six NAA-built F-86Ks were assigned to the Dutch AF, completing delivery in April 1957. A further six FIAT-built examples were accepted in April and May, falling somewhat short of being able to fulfil the ideal twenty-five-aircraft squadron strength. Squadron assignment was roughly nineteen F-86Ks for 700 and 701 Squadron, with 702 Squadron, officially established as the F-86K operational conversion unit on 1 January 1957, having an average strength of sixteen machines. During 1959 KLu Sabre operations were consolidated at Twenthe with the arrival of 700 Squadron from Soesterburg.

Delivered in natural metal finish, KLu Sabres carried markings to denote squadron assignment in the form of letter/number codes. 700 Squadron aircraft carried 6A- codes, 701 Squadron aircraft bore Y7- and 702 Squadron ZX-codes, each aircraft being then assigned an individual suffix number. In the early 1960s the code system was changed so that all F-86Ks, irrespective of their squadron, carried a Q, followed by the 'last three' of the USAF serial number. From 1961 Sidewinder launch rails were also incorporated on most aircraft, known affectionately as the 'Kaasjager' ('K'-fighter).

The service life of the KLu F-86Ks was relatively short, and a total of thirteen F-86Ks were lost in flying accidents. With the advent of the F-104 Starfighter, the Sabre fleet began to wind down, and 702 Squadron, their training commitment complete, disbanded on 1 April 1962. The surviving aircraft were mostly passed to the remaining squadrons, but from 21 June 1962 a number of high-time Sabres were permanently withdrawn from use and sent to FIAT for reconditioning. At the time it was thought that they would be passed on to the Turkish Air Force, but all these aircraft (up to ten) were instead assigned to the Italian AF. The next Dutch unit to disband was 701 Squadron which was inactivated during 1963, and 700 Squadron then disbanded on 30 June 1964. The F-86K was officially withdrawn from KLu service on 31 October 1964. Many of the Sabre personnel converted

F-86K 54-1252 in 701 Squadron's early 'Y7' coded colours. The pilot in bowler hat is Lt R. Fry, a USAF exchange officer. J.M.G. Gradidge

en masse to the Starfighter, but the old F-86K squadron numbers were never reactivated.

Norway

The Royal Norwegian Air Force (RNoAF) began to replace its F-84G Thunderjets with the arrival of the first F-86Fs on 30 March 1957. These were the first of some ninety Sabres delivered under MAP project 7F037, thirty being delivered before the end of the year. Delivery of the whole batch was completed in May 1958. The first unit to receive the F-86F was 332 Skvadron at Rygge, which converted from F-84Gs in April 1957. Further Sabre squadrons then quickly converted from Thunderjets; 331 and 334 Skv at Bodø, 336 Skv at Lista and 338 Skv at Ørland.

Attrition deliveries of F-86Fs then followed, six in May and June of 1960 and nineteen more by sea from the United States in January 1961. During later years persistent wing centre-section cracks restricted F-86F operations; indeed, other Sabre fleets were grounded by this same problem. Norwegian F-86Fs had severe flying restrictions placed on their airframes to see out their remaining service.

Interceptors Arrive

Starting in September 1955, sixty American-built F-86Ks were supplied, though one of these aircraft was lost during acceptance trials in the USA. It was not replaced until early 1960. The RNoAF's F-86K capability suffered another blow on 10 March 1956 when four aircraft were destroyed in a hangar fire at Gardermoen AB near Oslo. These machines were replaced by four FIAT-built F-86Ks during June. The F-86Ks began to equip the squadrons in September 1955, with the formation of 337 Skv at Gardermoen. A second unit, 339 Skv, then formed with F-86Ks at Gardermoen in July 1956. These units were then disbanded in September 1963 and merged their aircraft and personnel into 332 and 334 Skv, respectively. Two F-86F units had earlier converted to the F-86K: 332 Skv, which moved into Bodø in the autumn of 1962 for conversion and then took over 337 Skv F-86Ks, and 334 Skv which converted to F-86Ks in August

F-86F 53-1096 of 336 Skv, Royal Norwegian Air Force has many features associated with MAP-supplied Sabres. The extended-span 'F-40' dual-store wing, is typical, as are the just visible Tacan aerial on the nose and the Martin-Baker ejector seat. Author

1960 and then also gained 339 Skv machines in 1963.

Replacement of the F-86Fs began in April 1963 when 331 Skv received its first F-104G Starfighters, and F-5s also began arriving in early 1966. As they were replaced, F-86Fs were largely put through overhaul and sent on to further MAP assignment. Many RNoAF F-86Fs served with the Royal Saudi AF and in a spares capacity with the Portuguese AF.

The F-86Ks were withdrawn beginning in the autumn of 1964 when 332 Skv was disbanded. 334 Skv was then the last RNoAF unit to operate Sabres, and retired its last F-86Ks on 15 July 1967. With little further use, the majority were then scrapped.

Pakistan

In 1947 the newly-independent nation of Pakistan sought to nurture close relations with the United States in order to gain military support, having originally been equipped with military equipment ceded by India and later by fairly ancient British-supplied machines. With the United States as the driving force, Pakistan and Turkey concluded a security treaty in 1954, known as the Turko-Pakistan Pact. This immediately enabled the US to offer military assistance to

Pakistan under the Mutual Defense Assistance Agreement signed the same year. Pakistan also became a member of the South-East Asia Treaty Organisation (SEATO) in 1954 and joined the Baghdad Pact, later renamed the Central Treaty Organization (CENTO) in 1959. Pakistan had little interest in SEATO and joined mainly to appease Washington; however, the SEATO/CENTO links with other countries (especially Iran) later proved fruitful.

Between 1954 and 1965 the United States provided Pakistan with $630 million in direct-grant assistance and over $670 million in concessional sales and defence-support assistance. The bottom line was that, in addition to military and naval equipment, the Pakistan Air Force (PAF) also received equipment to establish six squadrons of modern jet aircraft. These would be F-86F Sabres, and a purpose-built base was constructed at Sargodha to house the fighters.

The PAF received a total of 120 F-86Fs from the USA, though the initial batch was for just one hundred. The first fourteen of these were accepted at Drigh Road (Faisal), Karachi in August 1956, having arrived at Karachi as part of a larger batch of thirty-eight Sabres aboard a US carrier. The first PAF Sabres went to 11 Squadron at Masroor, replacing the survivors of thirty-six British-supplied Supermarine Attackers in September.

Further units converted at this time, including 5 Squadron at Peshawar which had been flying the Hawker Fury and a number of squadrons were activated to operated Sabres, including 15 Squadron, which was created on 15 June at Masroor. To provide conversion training, No. 2 Fighter Conversion Unit/Jet Conversion School at Masroor and Drigh Road was redesignated No. 2 Fighter Conversion Squadron on 1 June 1957 and received F-86Fs to operate alongside the T-33s already with the unit.

On 23 March 1957 the PAF celebrated Republic Day in style; having received sixty-four Sabres by this time, the Air Force succeeded in getting every aircraft into the air for a formation flypast. This was all the more impressive because of two factors: first, the most junior pilots in the formation had less than 2hr on Sabres and, secondly, a lack of drop tanks meant that all the Sabres flew without them, giving them only 30min to take off, assemble and accomplish the flypast before recovering successfully.

Delivery of this batch of F-86Fs concluded in 1958, many under MAP contract 7F039 and comprising a good number of ex-USAFE machines. In addition, many newly-built F-86F-40s were sent to the PAF straight from NAA. These aircraft allowed further squadrons to form on the type, including 18 and 19 Squadrons at Masroor, the latter having formed on 1 February 1958 with just twelve F-86Fs.

The PAF was quickly transformed into a fairly modern, well-equipped fighting unit and was substantially reorganized along American lines, with hundreds of Pakistani officers being trained by US officers, either in Pakistan or at schools in the United States. Although many British traditions remained, much of the tone of the Army, especially the officer corps, was Americanised.

1965: War with India

Having long fought border skirmishes with India, it was somewhat inevitable that full-scale conflict should break out. The Sabres formed a useful deterrent to air incursion into Pakistan, but, even so, on 10 April 1958 Indian Air Force (IAF) Canberra IP988 was shot down over Rewat by Flt Lt M. Yunus of 15 Squadron. Yunus's kill was taken while flying F-86F 55-5005. But it was not until 1965 that

full-scale war loomed. The first air engagements took place on 1 September, when four Vampires were claimed by PAF Sabres and the Indian ground offensive marked the start of 'The Seventeen Day War' on 6 September. On that day twenty-seven Sabre combat air patrol missions were flown and seven IAF Hunters were claimed shot down. Other Sabres launched ground-attack missions against Indian airfields, seven MiG-21s and five Mystères being destroyed on the ground at Pathankot.

On 7 September one of the most controversial missions in Sabre lore was launched. As the official Pakistan version put it:

At 0605 hours six Hunters were reported heading for Sargodha; CAP aircraft were alerted, and the first visual contact by four F-86s and one F-104 was established when the enemy was in the process of diving at a target at the Sargodha airfield. Two pairs of F-86s and one F-104 finally queued up behind the enemy Hunters, which were in a formation of four with one straggling Hunter. Sqn Ldr M.M. Alam, who was in the leading formation, first engaged the straggler with [Sidewinder] missiles. The first missile went into the ground; the Hunter saw the F-86s behind him and pulled up to break. Another missile was fired and this connected; the enemy aircraft exploded. The leader then followed the enemy formation of four aircraft. The Indians saw our F-86s and threw a hard turn, but Sqn Ldr Alam closed in on the Hunter formation and picked off one Hunter after another until he destroyed all four in high-g shots. The first Hunter was shot down just short of the Chenab river, while the other four were knocked down about 30 miles further east.

Mahmood Alam, commander of 11 Squadron, thus claimed five Hunters and ace status in one mission – but had he indeed performed this feat? Knowing the ineffectiveness of the Sabre's machine-gun armament in Korea, it seems highly improbable. Alam's first victim was claimed to be Sqn. Ldr Kacker, commanding officer of the IAF's 27 Squadron. Though he was indeed downed on that day, following his repatriation, Kacker claimed that he had been 93 miles (150km) east of Sargodha when his engine failed due to booster pump failure, many miles from Alam's 'kill' site. The wreckage of two 7 Squadron Hunters was subsequently discovered near the Sangla

Hill railway station, but none other was found. The IAF convincingly announced that the remaining pair of Hunters returned safely, which seems likely considering the lack of otherwise substantiating wreckage. Therefore it would seem that Alam actually downed two IAF Hunters on this mission – a good score none the less.

The Seventeen Day War ended with a ceasefire on 23 September. Pakistan claimed at least twenty-six IAF aircraft lost to Sabre combat alone while admitting to at least nine F-86Fs lost to both air and ground fire.

Post-war Rearmament

With the end of the war, Pakistan feverishly looked for more equipment to bolster its armed forces. Obviously, Sabres were high on the shopping list, but with the conflict just ended, the UN forbad member states to sell arms to the opposing sides. Pakistan therefore turned to its CENTO partner Iran to subvert the embargo. Iran in turn approached the German government with a view to buying ninety surplus Luftwaffe Sabre 6s. Though initially claimed by the Iranian government to have been purchased for their Air Force, it soon became apparent that the Sabres were just being routed through Iran for the Pakistan Air Force. This was a ruse designed to fool the NATO countries into unwittingly supplying a warring nation with arms. On 2 June 1966 the British Embassy revealed that the Germans knew the ex-Luftwaffe Sabres were being sent to Pakistan 'for a fortnight or so' as a display of CENTO solidarity. It was also revealed that the Sabres had been flown in Iran by Pakistan AF pilots. This seems reasonable, and no doubt this represented the period in which the first PAF pilots converted to the Orenda-engined Sabre 6. By June twenty aircraft were believed to have been flown to Karachi for 'modification' (according to the IIAF), and on 6 July the US Assistant Air Attaché noted two Sabres dogfighting over Peshawar. One aircraft was camouflaged, the other silver (natural metal). The camouflaged aircraft had the better of the exchange; it seemed to have more thrust. The Asst Air Attaché reported that 'all Pakistan Air Force Sabres are silver', indicating that the camouflaged aircraft was one of the newly-delivered ex-Luftwaffe, ex-IIAF

This Pakistan Air Force F-86F-40 wears an unusual colour scheme: mid-gray upper surfaces and pale blue undersides. Something of an anomaly, 55-3855 was supposedly delivered to the Japanese Air Self-Defense Force on 17 May 1956 and lost in an accident on 21 November 1957. MAP

Sabre 6s. Clearly, dogfighting would not be included in a post-'modification' air test.

In July 1966 the IIAF assured the German government that the missing IIAF (ex-Luftwaffe) Sabres had gone to Israel 'for repairs'. As we now know that the IIAF F-86Fs were undergoing overhaul in Israel during this period, this statement represents a ruse to deflect attention away from what was a really happening. The Canadian Embassy also reported at this time that engines may have been sent from Pakistan to Israel for overhaul. Deliveries of the ex-Luftwaffe Sabres to the IIAF were said to have begun in March 1966. Later in July, while on a visit to Germany, the IIAF's Lt Gen Toufanian openly admitted to the Chief of ARMISH-MAAG, Gen Jablonsky, that the IIAF had received eighty (rather than ninety) F-86s from Germany and passed sixty to Pakistan. Despite this, on 7 September the IIAF told the Germans that all but sixteen of the sixty Sabres sent to Pakistan 'for overhaul' had been returned to Iran. On the same day, Gen Toufanian told Col Ludwig Hauswedel of the Luftwaffe that only twelve remained in Pakistan! He stated that the remainder would be flying in the IIAF Air Day on 17 October. Needless to say, all the Sabre 6s were assigned to the PAF, supplementing and eventually replacing the F-86Fs.

By the end of 1966 only forty or so of the original batch of F-86Fs remained in service. The arrival of Dassault Mirages and Shenyang F.6s in the late 1960s began the conversion of a number of units, including 5 and 11 Squadron at Sargodha. Additionally, in March 1965 a Fighter Leader School had been formed at Peshawar, the unit being redesignated 26 Squadron on 30 August 1967. 16 Squadron then took over as the Fighter Leader School at Sargodha in April 1970 operating Sabre 6s; this was inactivated in October 1972. At this point, 19 Squadron took over FLS duties before converting to Shenyang F.6s in May 1977. 17 Squadron also converted to the Shenyang F.6 following the 1971 war, followed by 15 Squadron in 1975.

1971: War Again

With East Pakistan destabilized in late 1971, India picked this time to launch an all-out attack on Pakistan, with air engagements beginning on 22 November. PAF Sabres came up against a formidable force of Indian fighters, including MiG-21s, Hunters and Sukhoi Su-7s. However, it was the diminutive Folland Gnat (or licence-built Hindustan Ajeet) that seemed to pose the biggest threat. Highly agile, the Gnat could outmanoeuvre the Sabre, which was by far the PAF's best dogfighter. Indeed, the aircraft was so small, with a wingspan of only 24ft (7.3m), that the F-86 pilots had trouble

even seeing it. In East Pakistan, with only 14 Squadron's Canadair Sabres defending, the PAF held out against overwhelming odds: ten Indian squadrons faced them. Though the runway at their Tezgaon base was cratered so badly that Sabre operations there ceased on 8 December, eleven 14 Squadron F-86s survived. Airworthy examples were then taken over by the Bangladesh Air Force when East Pakistan gained independence. With a stalemate becoming clear, the Indian government agreed to a ceasefire on 17 December. Again, it is difficult to assess accurate claims, the Pakistan AF declaring ninety-five kills in the first four days of fighting and 141 in total for fewer than twenty Sabres lost.

Final Days

Despite being warned by the United States that the Sabre 6s were reaching the end of their fatigue life in 1974, the PAF continued to use the aircraft, though by the late 1970s only two units – 18 and 26 Squadron – were still flying them. Some efforts at wing strengthening were made, but, despite this, two aircraft were destroyed in 1980 following catastrophic wing failures, leading to the enforced withdrawal of the Sabre from service. Wing cracks proved a problem area for high-time Sabres throughout the world and are known to have troubled not only the Pakistani aircraft but those with air forces as far afield as Norway and Peru. Following their withdrawal, the surviving PAF Sabres were stored at the bases of Peshawar and Masroor in the unlikely event that they could be returned to flying condition in an emergency. They were never again needed.

Peru

The Peruvian Air Force (Fuerza Aérea del Peru – FAP) received its first F-86Fs on 15 September 1955. These aircraft were delivered under MDAP contract 5F214 from McLellan AFB and, by the end of the year, a dozen of the type had been delivered. They went to equip 11 Escadrone de Caza (11 Fighter Squadron) of Grupo de Caza 12 at Talara Limatambo, serving alongside up to forty-seven F-47D Thunderbolts with 12 Esc de Caza. FAP Sabre pilots had been trained in the

United States, first at Lackland AFB and then at Nellis AFB. Two F-86Fs were written off in 1956, one by the father of Roque Garcia, Jr:

My father's name is Roque A. Garcia. He is a retired colonel of the Peruvian Air Force. He graduated from the USAF Class 55-N as a 2nd lieutenant in 1955, thanks to the MDAP Program for foreign cadets. Back in Peru in 1955, he was stationed with the 11th Fighter Squadron in Talara, a coastal desert surrounded city 350 miles [560km] north of the Peruvian capital, Lima.

On 10 April 1956, during a routine escort mission his squadron was scheduled to take off around 5:20 in the afternoon. He was flying a North American Sabre F-86F-25. He was the left wing man in a three-way formation. During take-off, he encountered a serious mechanical problem that prevented the plane from taking off. On the first attempt, after gaining the required speed, he felt a sluggish sensation, kind of a heavy nose during take-off. After pulling the stick back, the aircraft could not stay airborne and dropped to the ground. He checked the trim set and power and found them normal. After the first failed attempt, he radioed the control tower informing them of the situation and gave his other two companions the go ahead to continue while he tried a couple of more times. While in the struggle, he realized that he had used about

two-thirds of the 3,800ft [1,150m] runway, which incidentally had no crash barrier. The runway was being enlarged to accommodate the modern Sabres at that time.

Suddenly, he noticed a worker crossing the runway with a one-wheel handcart full of rocks. When the worker saw the plane coming, he dropped the handcart and fled. By that time, my father decided to abort the mission. He pulled back the throttle and turned the switches off, and ground looped the aircraft to the left to avoid killing the worker. Smoke and fire were coming out of the tail while the plane was jumping up and down the desert. On the first jump he tried to control the plane but the nose landing-gear broke. On the second jump he lost the left landing gear causing the plane to start rolling over toward the left wing. Fearing for his life and thinking about the full load of ammo and fuel he was carrying and in a split-second decision he made up his mind to eject himself out of that situation. He raised his left arm rest and at the same time placed his foot on the foot rest securely and the canopy jettisoned. He raised his right arm rest and squeezed the ejection trigger, feeling the tremendous blow on his butt and body. Which, incidentally, caused the plane to go back into horizontal position. Seconds passed and he was going up very fast and when he reached the top of the jump, he heard the automatic harness release engaging and he kicked the non 'zero-zero'-type ejection seat and started a free fall.

Tumbling with arms and legs extended, he embraced himself in the foetal position, becoming a human ball ready for impact and waited till the last moment to try to hit the ground with his feet down.

When he touched down, he bounced once and then tried to stand up and run away from the aircraft already in flames 50ft away and fell. Each machine-gun was loaded with 180 rounds of ammo and the bullets started to explode like firecrackers. He realized that he was not going to be able to get away by himself, so he looked around for help and found at a short distance to his left the young man who crossed his path on the runway. He yelled at him, asking him to pull him out of the close fire. With the help of the worker, he tried to take the first steps but then realized he had a broken leg and his body gave away and fell to the ground. The fractured bones from his right femur perforated the skin and came out in the upper part of his right leg. By that time, a fire engine reached the accident as well as an ambulance. The fire lasted 3hr and it consumed the plane. The ambulance took him to a city hospital where a 14in long wound was cleaned and the bones aligned with a stainless-steel plate and then put in a cast from the waist down.

After the accident, it was determined that the probable cause of the accident was a misalignment of the variable position empennage [all-flying tail]. All that remained from the plane were charred pieces of metal. In November 1956 he was sent to the Walter Reed Army Hospital in Washington, DC for specialized medical treatment.

Though preserved, this Peruvian AF F-86F displays the 11th Fighter Squadron 'Tiger' badge on its tail. Peter R. Foster, Las Palmas

The arrival of British Hunter fighters in 1956 signalled an increase in Sabre fatigue; the F-86F pilots were trying to outmanoeuvre the Hunters in practice dogfights. By the end of the year the FAP possessed thirty-two F-47Ds, ten F-86Fs, sixteen Hunter F.4s and nine T-33s. The FAP strength at this time was about 6,000 of which 380 were aircrew. Officer cadets were trained at the Officers School in Las Palmas, then received basic flying instruction on the PT-17. Following this, they received further flying instruction over a three-year period and passed to T-37Cs for advanced flying training. After graduation, FAP pilots passed on to the T-33, the F-86 or the B-26. Only experienced crews were allowed to fly the Hunter and, later, Canberra aircraft. To replace a number of F-86Fs lost in accidents, a further 'attrition' delivery of Sabres was made during September 1960, these aircraft going direct to MAP from storage at Davis Monthan AFB.

In the early 1960s FAP bases were named in honour of leading military figures and the units were also realigned. The Sabres then came under 11 Air Group control at Talara/Capitán Montes Air Base, led by Col Guillermo L. Berckemeyer. The group consisted of No. 111 Escadrone de Caza-Bombardero with thirteen F-80Cs and No. 112 Escadrone de Caza-Bombardero with fifteen F-86Fs.

The F-80s had arrived during 1958, and all F-47Ds were then reallocated with No. 721 Escadrone de Caza-Bombardero at Piura/Capitán Concha. The Hunters were assigned to No. 611 Escadrone de Caza at Chiclayo/Tte Col. Ruiz. In the period from July 1963 to May 1965, the FAP lost a further four Sabres, including one on 7 July 1964, the pilot being killed and another on 16 September 1964, the pilot then managing to eject.

In late 1966 Peru was reportedly offered a number of English Electric Lightning interceptors by the British, though this was strongly denied by government officials in Lima. An American counter-offer was then made of a further twenty-five F-86Fs, apparently in an attempt to calm a perceived 'arms race' in South America. Neither offer was pursued, but the Peruvians did buy a number of aircraft from France instead.

The introduction of the 'Conte-Long' amendment to the US FY68 foreign aid legislation had a profound effect on the Peruvian military. The amendment called for obligatory cuts in US military assistance to any country buying 'sophisticated' arms from a 'foreign' nation. As the Peruvian AF had just bought a number of French Mirage 5Ps, the FAP was thus precluded from a MAP-supplied batch of Northrop F-5s. In 1976 the FAP was equipped with Soviet Sukhoi Su-22 Fitters; these replaced any remaining Sabres left in service.

Philippines

Formed in 1947, the Philippine Air Force (PAF), or Hukbong Himpapawid ng Pilipinas, has always been heavily reliant on US aid. Beginning with F-51D fighters, the first jets, Lockheed T-33s, were delivered in August 1955. But it was not until 1957 that jet fighters began to arrive. The Philippine AF, like many other MAP-supported air forces, was promised a number of F-86Fs to replace the ageing Mustangs and, on 31 January, the first four Sabres were handed over to the PAF. Part of an initial batch of thirty F-86F-30s, further small groups were delivered up to the end of July. These machines came through a variety of routes: the first four from overhaul by Shin Meiwa in Japan, and subsequent aircraft from Kisarazu. At least fifteen more F-86F-30s were delivered during June 1958, eighteen or more in June 1959 and a small number

ex-Spanish AF Sabres were received following their withdrawal in Spain on 10 April 1962.

PAF personnel underwent USAF ground and flight training with F-86Fs at Clark AB, while the runway at Basa AB was extended for Sabre operations. The delivery of large numbers of F-86Fs allowed 6th Tactical Fighter Squadron 'Cobras' to convert from F-51Ds under 5th Fighter Wing. Based at Clark AB, the Sabres of 6th TFS were joined soon after by further deliveries into 7th TFS 'Bulldogs', which also converted from F-51Ds under 5th Fighter Wing. These units later moved into Basa AB when building there was completed. While still at Clark, the PAF lost its first Sabre and pilot when Capt Antonio Roig hit the ground following an engine flame-out.

The Air Force gained an all-weather capability on 12 August 1960 with the delivery of twenty F-86D-35s. Formed at Basa as the sole interceptor unit within PAF, 8th Fighter Interceptor Squadron later acquired a few more aircraft, including a number of F-86D-50s. Assigned to 5th Fighter Wing, the F-86Ds were phased out of PAF service in July 1968. One further Sabre unit, the 9th Tactical Fighter Squadron 'Limbas', was activated under 5th Fighter Wing at Basa AB with F-86Fs in 1963. Pilots from this Squadron flew UN Sabres in the Congo beginning in February 1963. In total, seventy-seven PAF personnel, commanded by Lt Col Jose Rancudo served in

Two of the first quartet of F-86Fs delivered to the Philippine Air Force, 52-4828 and -4796, are seen here being prepared in January 1957 at Clark AB. Both were ex-8th FBW and had gone through overhaul by Shin Meiwa at Itami in Japan. via Mike Fox

Seen at Basa AB during the 1960 'Flying Brothers' gunnery meet, these PAF F-86F-30s belonged to 5th Fighter Wing. All were part of a batch supplied from the USA in June 1959. Alberto Anido via Adrian Balch

the Congo, returning to the Philippines in June. Their aircraft were actually ex-Italian Sabre Mk 4s, unique in being owned by the UN. When the PAF personnel returned home, Iranian Sabre crews from 103rd TFS took them over.

Civil unrest in the Philippines during 1972 led to the imposition of martial law, and this coincided with a further twenty F-86Fs' being transferred from Taiwan as part of the Military Assistance Program. With the unrest turning into armed conflict between Muslim and Christian factions, PAF Sabres were put into action in the following months to suppress any uprisings. The job was not without danger. On 4 January 1974 Col Antonio Bautista, Commander of 9th TFS, was hit by ground fire while on a bombing run over Jolo. Though he ejected safely, Bautista was killed on the ground by Muslim rebels.

In PAF service a number of F-86Fs acquired an overall two-tone green and sand camouflage scheme, as well as the usual Sidewinder capability. With the arrival of the Northrop F-5As in August 1965, 6th TFS became the first PAF squadron to convert to the type, though 7th and 9th TFS remained with Sabres until at least 1974. It is thought that the remaining F-86Fs were formed into a reserve squadron at Nichols AB, serving until as late as 1978, when around twenty machines still remained.

Portugal

Under the renewal negotiations for the Azores (Açores) air base with the United States in 1955, the Força Aérea Portuguesa (FAP) asked for a number of F-84 Thunderjets, in addition to the fifty already delivered. The American response overwhelmed the Portuguese: they would supply not only enough aircraft to make up four F-84 squadrons, but also two

squadrons-worth of F-86Es. The main condition was that one of the F-86 squadrons would be based on the Azores (though this never happened). The agreement was signed in November 1957, but the FAP received the F-86F rather than the E version in the original proposal.

The first of sixty-five North American F-86F Sabres for the FAP were delivered, ex-USAFE, from August 1958 to Ota Air Base, under the Mutual Defence Assistance Program. Ota Air Base was designated as BA 2 (Basa Aérea 2 – Air Base 2). Until this time, the only offensive jet equipment of the FAP was the F-84G Thunderjet, also based at Ota.

In order to receive the new F-86Fs, a new esquadra (squadron) was formed on 4 February 1958: Esquadra 50, though the unit initially possessed no Sabres and flying training was carried out on the F-84G aircraft. Air and ground crews also undertook training on the F-86F, the latter going through courses in four groups of fifteen between March and June 1958. USAF Capt Billy D. Brown plus six non-commissioned officers led this training. Two American pilots, Maj T.H. Akkola and Capt David L. Brown, supported the conversion of Portuguese pilots to the F-86F. Maj Moura Pinto became Esq 50's first commanding officer; the first F-86F arrived at Ota on 24 August and was assigned to the unit in September. Pinto became the first Portuguese to break the

As delivered, Portuguese F-86Fs were finished in natural metal with the coloured nose band on the exterior of the intake only. In addition, the 'Cruz del Cristo' roundel was slightly redesigned in later service. This Esquadra 51 aircraft, ex-52-5207, was destroyed in an accident on 23 October 1962. Author

Following withdrawal from service, many Portuguese AF F-86Fs were stored, pending exchange by the PAF Museum. 5338/52-5204 is seen at BA2 Ota. MAP

sound barrier in an FAP F-86F on 24 September.

With the formation of the Grupo Operacional system during September 1958 (where the Grupo number would contain the figure zero) Esq 50 was renumbered as Esq 51 – in future, no FAP squadron numbers would end in a zero to prevent any confusion. Furthermore, during October 1959 a second unit, Esquadra 52, was formed at Ota to receive further Sabres, but due a shortage of aircraft it started flight operations only on 12 December. Both units came under the command of Grupo Operacional 501. To differentiate between the two Esquadra, Esq 51 Sabres were painted with blue tail fins (but not the rudder), wing and tail plane tips and intake rings, with Esq 52 aircraft being painted red in these areas. Aircraft in this early scheme did not have the inside of the intake lip painted. In line with FAP tradition, the two Esquadras were given names; Esq 51 was given the title 'Falcões' (Falcons) and the motto 'Guerra ou paz tanto nos faz' (It makes no difference to us whether it's war or peace), Esq 52 receiving the name 'Galos' (Cockerels). The Esq 52 motto was 'Acometer para vencer' (loosely: Attack to win). In February 1959 the Chief of Air Staff established F-86F pilot flying rate at 15hr per pilot per month. The FAP quickly got to grips with the F-86F, and, as

a result of outstanding weapon delivery scores, in August 1959 the Esq 52 commander Maj Brochado de Miranda and 2nd Sgt Cartaxo were deployed to Cazaux in France as referees in the NATO Guynemer Trophy air-to-air gunnery competition.

FAP Sabres (all F-86F-35s) were transferred from the USAF in two main batches: thirty-three delivered to MAP in July-September 1958, and thirty between July 1959 and March 1960. A final pair of F-86F-30s, 52-5083 and 5084, were delivered from the United States in July 1961. All other F-86F were supplied direct through FIAT in Italy from USAFE squadrons. All FAP Sabres were brought up to F-40 standard before delivery. In addition to these aircraft, at least six more F-86F-35s were transferred to Portugal for spares use: three from Norway and three from Saudi Arabia. In FAP service F-86Fs were given serials in the 5301 to 5365 range; Esq 51 aircraft, being the first twenty-five delivered, were generally in the range 5301 to 5325, with Esq 52 receiving 5326 to 5350. The serials 5351 to 5365 were given to the later deliveries; it is thought that none of these aircraft served with Esq 52.

FAP serials were painted in figures 15cm (5.9in) high on the tail fin in white (rounded font) over the Esquadra colour. Additionally, the last three numbers of

the serial was applied in black 0.5m (20in) figures on the forward fuselage below the cockpit, this time in the 'squared-off' style of lettering. The full serial number was also painted in black below the left wing and above the right (0.75m – 30in – figures) this time in the rounded style. Portuguese 'Cruz de Cristo' roundels were applied on either side of the fuselage, and on the opposite wing to that of the serial numbers. Finally, the Portuguese fin flash was positioned on the tail 10cm (3.9in) below the serial number. FAP Sabres originally operated in a natural metal finish, with the majority of the airframe stencils remaining in English. Those stencils which were applied in Portuguese were generally located around the cockpit area or related to regular servicing items such as fuel fillers and power receptacles. In this 'original' scheme, no anti-dazzle panel was applied. During the mid-1960s, the Cruz de Cristo was slightly redesigned with a narrower white portion to the cross and more pointed ends to the red portions. During 1968-69 the FAP F-86Fs were painted overall satin pale grey (FS 26473), with the same markings, except that the Esquadra band on the intake lip extended on to the inner surface and a small, black, anti-dazzle panel was applied. In FAP service, Sabres normally carried the 200gall finless drop tank and have been rarely seen with the 120gall tank with 'Stuka' fins.

On 4 October 1959 BA 5 at Monte Real was opened for operations, and all FAP Sabres moved straight in under the control of Grupo Operacional 501 (the first figure of the Grupo Operacional number signifying the Base number, in this case, the 5 in 501 representing Monte Real). Largely as a result of the FAP's commitments in Africa and the escalation of operations there, Esq 52 was disbanded on 12 June 1961. Its twenty-six pilots were posted to other tasks, and all remaining aircraft were absorbed into Esq 51. The unit also maintained a quick reaction alert (QRA) force with two aircraft and one spare to perform daylight intercepts. For these duties the FAP received AIM-9B Sidewinder infra-red homing AAMs in 1962. These complemented the Sabre's six internal 0.50 calibre machine-guns. Flying training was intensive and cross-country navigation exercises were flown to Denmark, Germany, Italy and Spain. A number of

F-86F s/n 5347 was one of the last Portuguese Sabres in service. Ex-USAF 53-1083, it was withdrawn from use in September 1981 and stored for the FAP Museum. FAP

T-33s were also used by Esq 51 for similar training tasks, and further examples, assigned to the reformed Esq 52, towed gunnery targets for the Sabres. During the mid-1960s a number of FAP Sabres were withdrawn from use and stored at the Ota depot, presumably for spare part reclamation to support the remaining FAP fleet.

Action in Africa

The presence of Portuguese military aviation in Africa can be traced back to 1917, when a unit was formed briefly in Mozambique. The following year another unit formed in Angola, but by 1923 these had disbanded and for nearly 40 years no Portuguese military aircraft would be based in the colonies. However, on 15 March 1961 masses of terrorists from the Congo crossed into Angola and began the slaughter of blacks and whites alike. Within two months, forty-eight villages in northern Angola had been abandoned and several thousand people had been killed. A stop-gap volunteer unit was hastily formed to counter the terrorist operations, but , armed only with Piper Cubs and Austers, they were generally ineffectual.

Clearly, Portugal would have to act to prevent further carnage in the colony. Thus from June 1961 FAP Thunderjets were deployed from BA 2 to Luanda (activated as FAP base BA 9 on 1 June) to become the newly-formed Esq 93. These aircraft remained in Angola until 1973. Even before the arrival of the F-84s, a solitary Lockheed PV-2 Harpoon was operated by the FAP from Luanda International Airport following its arrival there on 19 May 1960. In order to prevent similar terrorist problems in Portuguese Guinea, it was then decided to deploy a number of F-86Fs to the colony as a show of force. On 9 August 1961 eight F-86Fs from BA 5 began their ferry flight from Monte Real to Gando, and then on via Cape Verde island to Bissalanca aerodrome near Bissau in Portuguese Guinea. The total flight time was 6hr 10min, with 3,800km (2,400 miles) covered – a record for FAP aircraft at that time. The aircraft involved were nos 5307, 5314, 5322, 5326, 5354, 5356, 5361 and 5362. The Sabres on this mission – code-named *Atlas* – arrived on 15 August and became confusingly known as Detachment 52. The detachment was commanded by Maj Ramiro de Almeida Santos. As a civil aerodrome, Bissalanca was named in FAP parlance as AB 2 (AB – Aerodrome Base), and it was planned that the Sabres would stay at AB 2 for eight days before returning to Portugal.

However, the events in Angola dictated that the Sabres stayed in Guinea for a time and, as a result, they were ideally positioned to act when Communist guerrillas from the PAIGC organization began activities in the country. But it was not until the summer of 1963, when the south of the colony was evacuated due to terrorist activity, that the Sabres went into action. Flying mainly in the ground-attack/close air support role, FAP Sabres flew 577 missions between August 1963 and October 1964. Four hundred and thirty of these were in the ground-attack role. Seven of the eight Sabres were hit by ground fire during this period, but all bar one were recovered to base. Two Sabres were lost in Guinea-Bissau; 5314 on 17 August 1962, which was destroyed by fire after performing an emergency landing with bombs still attached, and 5322 on 31 May 1963 as a result of enemy action. Both pilots were rescued, the second one ejecting from his aircraft.

The last operational mission was flown by Maj Barbeitos de Sousa on 20 October 1964. Political pressure from the United States resulted in the need to return the Sabres to Portugal, they having been supplied under the MAP solely for NATO use. Thus, at the end of October 1964, the Sabres flew back to Monte Real and Detachment 52 was disbanded. From October ground-attack missions in Guinea were flown by armed FAP FIAT G-91s and T-6s.

One more aspect concerning the conflicts in Africa deserves a mention. In late 1961 guerrilla activity in Mozambique flared up. Between May and December 1962 the FAP dispatched four PV-2 Harpoons to supplement a single PV-2 already in Mozambique, and six Nord Noratlas transports were dispatched at the end of 1962. All these aircraft operated from BA 10 at Beira, Mozambique to cover the hostilities. It was soon realized, however, that fighter-bomber aircraft would be required in the colony and an approach was made to the West German government to acquire surplus Canadair Sabre 6s. This deal was agreed by the Portuguese and the German air staff, and it was envisaged that one Esquadra of Canadair Sabres would operated under Grupo Operacional 1001 at Beira. However, the intervention of the US Government forced the West Germans to cancel the deal and forty ex-Luftwaffe FIAT G-91R/4s were offered instead and received in 1966. At around this time, an offer of unknown origin was made to Gen Machado de Barros for a hundred Sabres, but was not taken seriously by FAP Chiefs of Staff. It is interesting to note that, in a comparison made in January 1965 between the F-86F and the G-91R/4 in a battlefield scenario, Col Gomes do Amaral came down firmly on the side of the G-91.

Withdrawal

The revolution of 25 April 1974 brought the Communist Party firmly into the forefront of Portuguese politics. Several cases of sabotage among FAP aircraft were recorded, but it appears that the Sabres escaped unharmed; by this time they were considered obsolete in any case. However, a fall in morale in the FAP, allied to critical spares shortages and further acts of sabotage, brought the force to its knees. The military actions in Africa were abandoned and large numbers of aircraft were left there. Another attempted Communist coup of November 1975 had little effect on the FAP, and within two days the uprising was quelled without a mission being flown from BA 5. The FAP took a long time to recover from these crises and by the late 1970s only six F-86Fs remained in service. However, the cessation of hostilities in Africa meant an end to the arms embargo on Portugal and American aid was resumed, starting with six Northrop T-38 Talons in 1977. In 1979, under yet another reorganization, Esq 51 was renumbered as Esq 201 and flew a mixture of F-86Fs and T-38 Talon trainers, in anticipation of an F-5 delivery. All remaining FAP Sabres were retired on 31 July 1980, the last flight being undertaken by Tenente Col Victor Silva in 5347/53-1083 and Capt Roda in 5360/53-1190. Their 1hr 25min flight took them over many FAP installations. Many of the surviving Sabres were then passed to scrapyards at Alverca and Palhais, with the best aircraft being retained by the FAP's Museu do Ar as 'currency' for future exchanges for other aircraft for the museum. The 'Galos' badge worn by Esq 201 Sabres was taken over by the A-7P Corsairs of Esq 302.

Rhodesia

During 1975 the Rhodesian Government began negotiations with Venezuela for the purchase of twenty-eight surplus F-86Ks. The deal never came to fruition, presumably again as a result of US Government intervention.

Saudi Arabia

Before the late 1940s Saudi Arabia had possessed little in the way of an air force; the few aircraft that were available came under the control of foreign advisers, mainly Britain. But by the start of the 1950s this situation had changed – thanks to the revenue being generated from Saudi Arabia's newly -developed oil fields.

Naturally, it was the British who attempted to bid for the lucrative contract to build up a new Royal Saudi Air Force (RSAF) or Al Quwwat Al-Jawwiya Assa'udiaya; but in the end, this first battle was won by the USA. From 5 August 1945 the USAF had been given permission to use Dharan AB as a staging post, when it signed a five-year agreement with the Saudis. The USAF at the time had no other bases in the region, so the Dharan post had great significance in moving troops from the European to the Pacific theatre. The base was activated and assigned to Air Transport Command (ATC) on 20 February 1946, later passing to USAFE control, back to ATC (by then renamed MATS), and finally to USAFE again in 1953.

A British mission had arrived in Saudi Arabia during 1950 with a view to setting up the foundations of an air force, followed by a US mission on 1 January 1951. However, when, on 18 June, the Dharan agreement came up for renegotiation the Saudis realized that they were in a strong bargaining position with the United States, and asked for a number of aircraft and resources in return for the continued use of Dharan. Thus, in 1952, ten Temco T-35A Buckaroos arrived, along with US personnel to set up a training syllabus for the RSAF, together with a Military Assistance Advisory Group (MAAG). Before this, in 1949, the Saudis had sent nine pupils to England for pilot training; these pilots would then be the first RSAF aircrews. Soon after the arrival of the decidedly non-standard Buckaroos, a number of T-6 Texan aircraft were acquired by the RSAF so that relevant training could begin, though the establishment of a combat training unit was not accomplished until 1957.

The Saudis, keen to obtain front-line aircraft as soon as possible, cited disputes between themselves and Egypt and Yemeni Royalists as grounds for strengthening their Air Force. Despite there being no provision for offensive aircraft in the US–Saudi Dharan Agreement, constant pressure from the Saudis saw the delivery of six B-26 Invaders begin in February 1954, though they saw little use.

Further aircraft arrived during the late 1950s to bring the RSAF strength up to a reasonable level, with four Vampire jets arriving from Egypt during July 1957 and more later. But it was the resigning of the Dharan Airfield and Base rights agreement with the United States on 2 April 1957 which provided the impetus to speed up the arming of Saudi Arabia. First, a number of US-supplied T-28 advanced trainers, ten T-33 jet trainers and some T-34 Mentor trainers were acquired, along with C-47, C-54 and six C-123B transports. Finally, during August and September 1957 the RSAF received the first of sixteen Sabres. The Saudis finally had a fighter force. These aircraft were loaned to the USAF's 7244th Air Base Group at Dharan for the induction and training of Sabre pilots and ground crews and were not transferred to the Saudis (under MAP) until 11 March 1961. During this early period at least two Sabres were lost, one on 1 January 1959 and a second on 8 December. The Sabres in this batch were ex-USAFE, and had been modified to F-40 standard, with the extended span 6-3 wing, equipped with unfinned 200gall drop tanks.

It appears that, at this stage, the RSAF had reached the point of numbering their squadrons in a sequence related to the serial numbers of the aircraft which they flew:

T-35 Buckaroo 1 Squadron (serialled from 100 up)
T-6 Texan, T-34 2 Squadron (serialled from 200 up)
A-26 Invader 3 Squadron (serialled from 300 up, but withdrawn from use)
C-47, C-123 and C-54 4 Squadron (serialled from 400, 430 and 450 up, respectively)
Vampire and F-86F 5 Squadron (serialled from 500 and 550 up, respectively)
Chipmunk 6 Squadron (serialled from 600 and up)
T-33 7 Squadron? (serialled from 700 and up)

It is not known which serials/units were assigned to the T-28 aircraft. When the F-86Fs were officially transferred to the Saudis in 1961, they continued to operate out of Dharan AB. It has been reported that RSAF Sabres were frequently grounded due to lack of spares and that, in any case, these aircraft were delivered with no armament, but no evidence has been found to support the latter claim. What is certain is that the Saudis lacked the overhaul facilities to properly maintain the F-86s, and in 1963 a number were sent to West Germany for thorough IRAN (inspect and repair as necessary) overhauls; this process was completed in 1964. In 1967 the Saudi Sabres were again overhauled in Germany. It is worth mentioning at this point that the Dharan agreement with the United States was allowed to lapse in 1962, and the USAF pulled out soon after the 1 April deadline.

5 Squadron's Sabres regularly flew missions to stave off Egyptian border incursions during this period, but they were ranged against more potent MiG-19 and later MiG-21 interceptors, and were largely a token force. In January 1966 the Saudi government decided that a major upgrade of the previously ineffectual air-defence system was required. This would be based around British-supplied BAC Lightning interceptor/ground-attack and BAC 167 (Strikemaster) light ground-attack aircraft. American Raytheon Hawk surface-to-air missiles were also planned for the defence system, with the ground radar and infrastructure coming from Associated Electrical Industries in Britain. However, continued border attacks by Egypt resulted in a requirement for fast deliveries, and, by the end of 1966, several stop-gap items of equipment had arrived in Saudi Arabia. Among these were small numbers of refurbished Hawker Hunter and ex-RAF Lightning aircraft plus thirty-seven Thunderbird surface-to-air missiles. The Hunters were requested to fill a gap in transition between the Jet Provost trainer and the Lightning. When, in February 1966, the Saudis had asked for a number of Hunters, the British Foreign Office in turn questioned why the Sabre could not fulfil this task. The Saudi reply was simple: in their view the Sabres were by that time of little value. Nonetheless, in the latter part of 1966 the British company Airwork, among the other requirements of its new engineering contract with the Saudis,

began to provide maintenance support for the Saudi Sabres. In a letter dated 7 December 1965 Airwork had estimated that the contract to support Saudi C-123s, T-33s and F-86Fs would be based on 8,700 man-months. Previously, a limited spares supply contract for the Sabres had been set up with California-based Kindred Aviation. This contract lapsed on 2 August 1966.

Despite this relative disruption in the RSAF, the Sabres remained in service. Indeed, during 1966-67 further F-86Fs were delivered as part of the Military Aid Program, a number from the Royal Norwegian Air Force and further examples ex-USAF. The last named had come through NAA Palmdale, having previously been in use with 4520th Combat Crew Training Wing at Nellis AFB. These Sabres equipped 7 Squadron, alongside the remaining T-33s and survivors from the original batch of F-86Fs. 7 Squadron effectively became a jet operational conversion unit for the RSAF. During October 1968 three RSAF F-86Fs were passed to the Portuguese Air Force, where they were reclaimed for spare parts. In total, it is thought that the RSAF received more than thirty Sabres.

In December 1969 RSAF Sabres saw action on the borders with Yemen after the British pull-out from Aden. Together with Saudi Lightnings, the RSAF aircraft were based at Khamis Mushayt and attacked fortified positions along the southern border of Saudi Arabia. It has been reported that the RSAF Sabres were supported by Pakistani personnel at this time. With the cessation of hostilities in January 1970, the Sabres of 7 Squadron returned to Dharan, and it seems that 5 Squadron disbanded around this time, its surviving Sabres being passed to 7 Squadron and renumbered in the 700 series. It was at this point that the serviceability of the RSAF Sabres took a downturn, four F-86Fs being lost in 1969–70 alone. However, the aircraft soldiered on with 7 Squadron until a suitable replacement could be arranged.

Finally, during 1971 numbers of F-5B and F-5E aircraft began to arrive in Saudi Arabia, the former eventually going to 7 Squadron, the RSAF's fighter weapons-conversion unit. The acquisition of numbers of F-5F fighter trainers in 1977 signalled the end of the RSAF's experience with the Sabre. Most of the remaining aircraft were unceremoniously

dumped at the edge of Dharan AB and may still be seen there.

As originally delivered, it appears that the RSAF F-86Fs were applied with an overall silver colour scheme. The Royal Saudi Air Force title was emblazoned along the fuselage, below its equivalent in Arabic. On the vertical fin the Saudi flag was positioned against a broad white band, which was itself bordered by bands of green, outlined in white. Saudi roundels were positioned in the normal fuselage locations, with a larger version above the right wing and below the left one. The opposite upper and lower wings carried a large RSAF. All lettering except the serial numbers was in green. At first USAF serials and buzz numbers were carried, the serial number positioned below the Saudi flag, but these were soon replaced by the 550 and 700 serials on the fin, each with the Arabic equivalent number above it. Buzz numbers were then removed. It seems that all RSAF Sabres had green-painted drop-tank noses. At least one aircraft (presumably from 5 Squadron) had its nose applied with white/green/white/green/white bands, extending back to the front of the machine-gun muzzle panel, and this treatment was repeated on the wing-tips.

In later service (possibly after the 1963 IRAN), RSAF Sabres received an overall pale grey paint scheme (similar to that applied to Portuguese Sabres), with just the machine-gun panel left unpainted. In addition, a small, black, anti-dazzle panel was painted forward of the cockpit, extending to the rear of the intake ring. At this time the green bands on the nose, wings and tail were removed, as were the green drop-tank noses.

South Africa

The South African Air Force (SAAF) sent its No. 2 Squadron to Korea during 1950, flying F-51D Mustangs as part of the USAF 18th Fighter Bomber Wing. The Mustangs were retired on 31 December 1952, and No. 2 Squadron then moved from K-10 Chinhae to K-55 Osan, to receive the first of eighteen F-86Fs on loan from the USAF. The first five F-86Fs, renumbered 601-605, were delivered in late January 1953, and the Squadron resumed operations on 16 March 1953, when the first mission was undertaken by Commandant Gerneke. As part of 18th

FBW, the SAAF Sabres had their fin flashes extended to the top of the vertical fin, but with the South African flag's orange replacing the 18th's red. Code letters were applied to the mid fuselage, running from A to I for odd-numbered machines and J to R for even numbers. When four further aircraft were obtained to make good attrition, the letter codes of the lost aircraft were then applied to the subsequent 619-622 serialled machines.

Fighter sweeps and bombing missions took place in MiG Alley near the Yalu and the Chong Chong river, two Sabres being lost to ground fire. The Squadron flew 2,032 sorties during the period to 27 July 1953, when the armistice was signed. All the SAAF F-86Fs were then returned to the USAF, and 2 Squadron went home

Seen in the company of a Fleet Air Arm Sea Fury over Korea, this 2 Squadron South African AF F-86F was previously 52-4315. 2 Squadron operated the F-86F from January 1953 until the cease-fire in July. *Jon Lake*

Nearly half of the South African Air Force's Sabre 6 fleet was airborne for this fourteen-ship formation. Aircraft are from 2 Squadron at Waterkloof and wear the 'castle' national markings introduced in 1956 and the red fuselage band applied from 1959. *Jon Lake*

to South Africa in October 1953 for conversion to Vampires. The Korean episode earned the Squadron a Presidential Unit Citation.

Beginning in 1954 SAAF looked at several fighter types with a view to replacing the Vampires. It was no surprise that they eventually decided on the Sabre, signing a contract with Canadair for thirty-four Sabre 6s for delivery in 1956. As a result, in February Capt Larry Eager, Capt Ronnie Nienaber, Lt Edwin Pienaar and one other began Course 50 at the Chatham OTU in Canada. The first

of the Sabre 6s for the SAAF (the thirty-four aircraft were serialled 350 to 383) was shipped to South Africa in August 1956 for assembly at No. 1 Air Depot, and aircraft 350 flew for the first time in South Africa on 4 September, piloted by Eager. Before the end of the year, he had taken 350 through the sound barrier – the first time in South Africa.

Two units operated the Sabres, No.1 and No. 2 Squadron, both based at Waterkloof AB, and they began to receive their Sabres in 1956. No. 2 Squadron thus renewed their acquaintance with the

F-86, having flown Vampire FB.52s in the intervening period. No. 2 Squadron remained at Waterkloof and converted to Mirage IIICZs in late 1963, passing its Sabres to No. 1 Squadron, which moved into Pietersburg AB in 1967. No.1 Squadron converted on to the Mirage F.1AZ in October 1975, and moved back to Waterkloof. It transferred its remaining Sabres to 85 Advanced Flying School (AFS).

This Flying School had the distinction of flying the Sabre for the remainder of its SAAF service; its pilots loved the machine and appreciated the opportunity. Based at Pietersburg AB, 85 AFS had formed a Sabre flight in 1975, flying alongside Impalas and Mirage IIIDZ, D2Z and EZ aircraft. The Sabres were finally grounded on 10 October 1979, but not officially retired until April 1980.

SAAF Sabre 6s initially flew in natural metal, with the national insignia in six places. In addition, the SAAF serial number appeared on the rear fuselage under the horizontal stabilizer, and the Canadair construction number was painted on the forward fuselage below the cockpit. Squadron code letters were painted on both sides mid-fuselage, forward of the national insignia and also on top and bottom of the fuselage. These letters were painted in the squadron colours: blue for 1 Squadron and red for 2 Squadron. The tail fin of all aircraft displayed the large fin flash seen on SAAF Sabres in Korea. In 1959 squadron-coloured bands began appearing on all aircraft: blue outlined in orange for 1

Camouflaged South African Air Force Sabre 6 serial number 350 was the first aircraft delivered, and also the first aircraft to break the sound barrier in South Africa. The aircraft is finished in the unusual olive drab and deep buff over light gray SAAF camouflage scheme. The tail marking is of the No. 85 Advanced Flying School at Pietersburg. Author

Squadron and red outlined in black for 2 Squadron. A diagonal band was applied to the fuselage, while further bands appeared at the wing and tailplane tips and on drop tanks. As a result, the code letter on the fuselage top was deleted. From 1971 SAAF Sabres began to be painted in the standard SAAF camouflage colour scheme: olive drab (BSC 298) and deep buff (BSC 360) upper surfaces with light admiralty grey (BSC 697) undersides. This scheme lasted until the withdrawal of the Sabre from service.

Following their retirement, on 12 January 1981, a deal was struck whereby ten of the retired Sabres were sold to Flight Systems, Inc. of Mojave in California for for £110,000 sterling, but only one of these was returned to flying status with FSI, the rest sitting in storage at Mojave, still wearing their SAAF camouflage. By the early 1990s the majority of these Sabres had been sold on to civilians.

Spain

During the early post-war years, Spain had operated significant numbers of German-built or -designed aircraft, the majority being obsolete even at this early stage. It was not until 26 September 1953 that the Spanish signed a defence agreement with the United States, and this allowed more modern types to enter the inventory. The North American F-86F was chosen as Spain's first jet fighter.

On 30 June 1955 the first two Sabres arrived at Getafe airfield near Madrid for the Ejército del Aire (Air Force – EdA). These machines, F-86F-25s 51-13194 and -13239, had been received from the USAF's 86th FBW in Germany, and were assigned EdA serials C.5-1 and C.5-2, respectively. The 'C.5' stood for Caza (Fighter) type 5, the Spanish designation for the F-86F. On 14 September a further five Sabres arrived at Getafe and, by the end of the year, twenty-three had been assigned, all of this batch and up to 125 others being supplied through Chateauroux AB in France under MAP project 5F546. In total, 270 F-86Fs were

forwarded to EdA, the latter group under MAP project 6F643. Beginning in October 1955 CASA at Getafe began the conversion of these aircraft to F-40 specification, and then undertook the periodic repair and overhaul of the aircraft once in service. The final Spanish Sabres arrived with CASA from Chateauroux in June 1957, the two hundred and seventieth F-86F then being assigned to the EdA from Getafe on 31 May 1959. A mixed bunch of aircraft, the Spanish AF batch comprised 18 F-86F-20s, 155 F-86F-25s, 32 F-86F-30s and 65 new FY55 F-86F-40s.

The first EdA unit to receive the F-86F was Ala de Caza (Fighter Wing) 1 at Manises Air Base, which formed on 6 September 1955. Two Escadrón (Squadrons) were formed under Ala 1: 11 and 12 Escadrón, on 1 October 1955 and 1 April 1956, respectively. To differentiate between these units, 11 Esc Aircraft carried a red nose band, with blue for 12 Esc. The first Ala 1 Sabres arrived at Manises on 5 October 1955. Further wings were then quickly activated with the F-86F under the Mando de la Defensa Aérea (Air Defence Command): Ala de Caza 2 at Zaragosa on 19 September 1956 (with 21 Esc, black nose band), and Ala de Caza 4 at Son San Juan also on 19 September (41 Esc, with green nose band). To provide operational conversion on to the F-86F, Escuela de Reactores (Jet School), which had flown T-33s for a number of years at Talavera la Réal, also received

Seen here taxiing at Son San Juan, this white-nosed 61 Escadrón aircraft was normally based at Torrejón. C.5-104 was ex-55-3990, delivered in October 1956. Author

Sabres, beginning with the first two on 11 January 1959. Two further Sabre wings then formed, completing the equipping of the EdA: Ala de Caza 5 at Morón on 8 May 1959 (51 Esc, orange nose band) and Ala de Caza 6 at Torrejón on 6 June (61 Esc, white nose band).

During the early 1960s a Sidewinder missile capability began to be incorporated on to a number of EdA Sabres, but not all units operated aircraft in this configuration; among those that did, 41 Esc at Son San Juan was the first to equip, in 1960, and Ala de Caza 1 received their first aircraft in 1963. Many EdA Sabres were then returned to USAF control during 1962 for reallocation under the MAP system, at least thirty-two F-86Fs being lost in this manner. Furthermore, at the same time more than seventeen mainly early model aircraft were broken up for spares. 41 Esc was disbanded during 1963.

One further unit operated the F-86F: 98 Esc based at Torrejón. Formed in 1957 after a budget increase, the Squadron operated independently and operated a mixed bag of thirteen aircraft and helicopters at first. The first Sabre was assigned to the unit on 26 June 1959, and in April 1965 the Squadron became 981 Esc. F-86Fs remained with 981 Esc until November 1967, but their function is not known.

On 1 April 1965 General Order 31 was put into action, which redesignated a number of EdA units. At Manises the two Sabre Escadróns now came under Ala de Caza 11, with 101 Esc and 112 Esc taking over the new designations. These Escadrón designations did not last long, however. On 20 October 101 Esc became 111 Esc, while, somewhat confusingly, 112 Esc took over the name of 101 Esc. Though still assigned to Ala 11, the two units took up different missions: the new 101 Esc under the Mando de la Defensa Aérea and 112 Esc subordinate to Mando del la Aviación Táctica (Tactical Aviation Command). Further reorganizations involved Ala 2, which became Ala 12 (with 121 Esc subordinate) and Ala 5, which became Ala 15 (151 Esc). Ala 6, Escadrón 61 then became 161 Esc, an F-104 Starfighter unit, and 102 Esc was created to fly the Sabres under the Mando del la Aviación Táctica. With the creation of the Escadrón de Aplicacion y Tiro (Application and Gunnery Squadron) at Talavera in April

Still bearing the colours of Zaragosa-based 102 Escadrón, C.5-223 was previously assigned to the USAF's 36th Fighter Day Wing as 51-13450. Author

Though bearing Chinese markings, this F-86F was actually loaned to the Thunder Tiger aerobatic team by the USAF for a series of displays in the United States during 1958. Most of these Nellis-based aircraft were returned to 4530th CCTW. J.M.G. Gradidge

Serialled F-86081 in Republic of China AF service, this F-86F-1 has not received the 'F-40' wing modification of most MAP-supplied machines. It was supplied to the RoCAF in February 1956. Lionel Paul via Mike Fox

1965, Escuela de Reactores F-86Fs gained 732 codes, while the T-33s wore 731 on their tails. In its time, the school trained 372 EdA Sabre pilots, and ceased F-86F flying in June 1969.

These units were further rearranged with the gradual rundown in EdA Sabre activity. In February 1967 111 Esc was inactivated, while on 3 November 101 Esc became a unit independent of Ala 11, though still under the Mando de la Defensa Aérea. Also in November, Ala 12 was inactivated, the Sabres at Zaragosa being reassigned to the newly created 102 Esc, while Ala 15 was also stood down at Morón, 103 Esc being created in its place. Finally, 102 Esc at Torrejón transferred its designation to Zaragosa, simultaneously becoming 201 Esc in its place, still with F-86F equipment as a tactical unit.

During 1970 many of the remaining Sabre squadrons were disbanded – 101 Esc at Manises in February and 103 Esc at Morón in the previous month, converting to F-5Bs as 202 Esc. Then on 26 February 1971, 201 Escadrón at Torrejón gave up its final Sabre, C.5-76/55-3957, leaving just one EdA unit operating the F-86F: 102 Esc at Zaragosa. Yet further unit redesignations then took place, Ala 13 being activated at Zaragosa on 13 April 1972, at which point 102 Esc became 131 Esc. The unit then underwent one further change with the creation of Ala 41 on 31 October as an operational conversion unit with T-33s and the last remaining Sabres. Ala 41 F-86F C.5-70 flew the last EdA Sabre flight on 7 December 1972 with its official withdrawal from service following on 31 December.

Switzerland

During 1956, Canadair bailed three European-based RCAF Sabre 6s for use in Switzerland's fighter evaluation. Three contenders were involved: the Sabre, the Hawker Wunter and the Dassault Mystère.

The Sabres made extensive flight trails, including weapons delivery; they were flown by both Candair and Swiss Air Force pilots. In that period 18 February to 1 March 1957, forty-one flights were carried out.

However, in the final reckoning, the Hunter's superior internal armament won out and the Swiss bought British fighter instead. Only in recent years have these aircraft been withdrawn.

Taiwan

Outside of the United States and Canada, the Republic of China Air Force (RoCAF) was undoubtedly the largest Sabre operator, initially gaining 320 F-86Fs and seven RF-86Fs between 1954 and the end of 1958. However, many more F-86Fs arrived after that, as well as a small number of F-86Ds. Thus the RoCAF may well have operated in excess of 500 Sabres.

Under MAP project 4F343, a number of early F-86Fs were assigned to RoCAF on 27 November 1954, and the first four were delivered two days later. The Sabres were given RoCAF serials, beginning with the first machine delivered, 51-2893 an F-86F-1. By June 1956 171 F-86Fs had arrived, including thirty-eight F-86F-1s, nine F-86F-5s and twenty-three F-86F-10s.

In RoCAF service the aircraft was given the serial F-86001, all subsequent aircraft numbering upwards from this. The arrival of these aircraft allowed the 5th Fighter Wing's 27th Fighter Squadron at Taoyuan AB to convert from F-47Ds in late 1954. During 1955 the remaining pair of 5th FW Thunderbolt squadrons also converted to the F-86F. Wing aircraft were identified by a yellow, vertical, fuselage band, bordered in red, plus bands in the same colour on the wings and nose.

The 2nd Fighter Wing at Hsinchu AB then converted its three Thunderbolt squadrons in late 1955, followed by the 3rd Fighter Wing at Pingtung AB in 1956. 2nd FW Sabres were distinguished by having an angled, yellow, fuselage band, bordered in red, similar to the Korean War identification bands. In addition, the aircraft sported a red nose, bordered by a yellow lightning flash. 3rd Fighter Wing F-86Fs carried a sharkmouth nose scheme and a red and white checked tail. Fuselage bands were also applied, though this time with a black centre band.

The RF-86Fs were at first operated by 12th Squadron of 5th Fighter Wing, based at Taoyuan AB, receiving the first aircraft in 1955 to replace RF-51D Mustangs. On 31 January 1956 a RoCAF RF-86F piloted by Li Sheng-Lin was detailed with a recce mission over China. Entering Chinese airspace at Yunsiao in Fukien Province, the Sabre was intercepted by fighters, but Li managed evade them and diverted into Kai Tak airport in Hong Kong. A statement from Taiwan said that the aircraft had diverted following engine trouble. The pilot and the aircraft were immediately impounded by the British authorities and the Chinese government pressed for the retention of the pilot in custody. However, on 12 March Li was returned to Taiwan. The same could not be said of the Sabre. The whole affair apparently presented the British in Hong Kong with a dilemma – how to dispose of the aircraft without raising protests from China and Taiwan? It was at first suggested that the aircraft could be returned to Britain for the RAF, but, as the service had by that time replaced its Sabres, this was not done. It was also suggested to return the aircraft to the USA.

Although the Hong Kong government agreed to release the aircraft to Taiwan on 19 October, no moves were made to comply with this. The authorities at Kai Tak were by this time complaining that the aircraft took up hangar space. The Taiwan government then paid $HK 26,000 for the aircraft, but by January 1957 it had still not been returned, and the several parties entered into negotiations for its return. Finally, on 9 February 1957 the British Secretary of State for the Colonies agreed to the release of the Sabre. Low-key arrangements were then made to have the RF-86 shipped in four crates declared as 'four cases of machinery' at Kaohsiung docks aboard the steamer Chiao Hang. However, upon loading, it was found that this ship was unable to carry the heaviest case and all were then embarked upon the Teh Hu on 22 March, bound for Tamsui in Taiwan. The Taiwanese Government were charged a further $HK 16,805.80 for the shipping. Despite the time that had elapsed since the start of the affair, the return of the aircraft led to further protests from China. By this time, of course, it was too late to do anything about it.

In 1957 all RF-86Fs were transferred to 4th Squadron of 5th Fighter Wing also at Taoyuan AB. Although the unit subsequently received RF-100As in 1959, the RF-100 was not fully operational in RoCAF service and RF-101s were used instead.

Airliner Interception

On 4 October 1957 a Hong Kong Airways Viscount was intercepted by two RoCAF

This 13 Squadron Royal Thai AF Sabre was based at Don Muang AB near Bangkok. Fuselage code '1334' represents 13 Squadron, the tail number being the 'last four' of its USAF serial, 52-4942. Jon Lake

These F-86Ls of 12 Squadron Royal Thai Air Force were all ex-US Air National Guard aircraft supplied in 1964. The F-86L SAGE equipment was removed before delivery. Tail markings are pale blue and white with a black border. Jon Lake

F-84Gs near the KW beacon; less than a fortnight later another Hong Kong Airways Viscount was subjected to quarter attacks by a pair of Thunderjets off the coast of Formosa. Finally, on 8 November another of the airline's aircraft was again intercepted, this time by a RoCAF F-86F (F-86093). The captain of the Viscount, E.T.J Pridmore, reported that he had been flying along Airway Red 3 at the time of the attack, near the FK beacon. The whole episode lasted 3 to 4min. Following this latest attack, the British Civil Aviation Authority were contacted and firm protests made. However, despite assurances from the Foreign Office and the Taiwan Government, this was not the last of the matter.

On 30 January 1959 two RoCAF F-86Fs buzzed a BOAC Comet with fifty passengers and crew aboard, off the coast of Taiwan. The Comet had been travelling from Hong Kong to Tokyo, and one of the Sabres reportedly came within 6ft (2m) of the Comet's starboard wingtip. This incident would have received little attention except that one of the passengers had taken photographs and leaked them to the press. However, despite complaints to the Taiwan government they continued to deny that anything had taken place. On 16 February Rear-Adm Liu Hohtu stated, 'Nothing like that ever happened. Our chaps have a lot of other things to do. Why should they interfere with an airliner?' This typified the Taiwanese attitude, but the photographic evidence was irrefutable. One of the Sabres involved was 52-

4517/F-86172 with the sharkmouth markings and chequered tail of the 3rd Fighter Wing.

Quemoy and Matsu Again

Sparked off by Chiang Kai-shek's movement of troops into the islands of Quemoy and Matsu during 1954, this crisis was ended in May 1955 with a truce between Red and Nationalist China. But tensions remained and sporadic confrontations continued. On 21 July 1956 a flight of four RoCAF F-86Fs engaged three MiG-15s over the Formosa Straits. Two of the Communist fighters were claimed as 'probables' for no Sabre losses. With renewed open conflict in 1958, the RoCAF's Sabres were in the front line of defence, also providing fighter cover for bomber raids on the mainland. Now equipped with early Sidewinder missiles, RoCAF Sabres did not always have the upper hand; on 29 July 1958 two F-86Fs were shot down, apparently by MiG-19s over the Straits. But in the period from 14 August 1958 to 10 October 1959 in nine major battles thirty-one MiG-17s were downed, most of these by F-86Fs. RoCAF Sabre losses for the period are not known. During an engagement on 24 September 1958 a RoCAF F-86F fired an AIM-9B Sidewinder at a Chinese MiG-17. The missile failed to explode and was presented to the Russian Ivan Toropov's design team at OKB-134, Tushino. The Sidewinder taught the Soviets many lessons.

Again, irregular skirmishes continued after the cessation of hostilities. On 16 February 1960 four F-86Fs on a mission over Fukien Province were intercepted by ten Chinese MiG-17s. During the ensuing battle 20 miles (32km) east of Tungshan Island, one MiG was shot down and a Sabre was damaged. Credit for the MiG kill was shared by Capt Yeh Chuan-Hsi and Col Lo Hua-Ping. The latter had tried to fire a Sidewinder but had declared his equipment inoperative. However, upon return to base, the Sabre was inspected by an American expert and declared fully serviceable. Col Lo had confused his cockpit switches in the heat of battle. Lo, the leader of the Sabre wing, also commanded the Thunder Tiger aerobatic team. In this engagement, two Sidewinders were fired but both were reported as having missed their targets.

F-86Ds Arrive, Re-equipment Begins

In 1959 an undisclosed number of F-86Ds (possibly twenty) arrived to equip 44th TFS at Hsinchu AB, the unit converting from F-86Fs. The Dogs were retired in 1966, when 44th Squadron became a training unit. The RoCAF received its first F-5As at Tainan on 9 December 1965. They were handed over to Gen Gsu Huan Sheng, Commander-in-Chief of the RoCAF; these aircraft initially went to 1st Squadron of 1st Fighter Wing at Tainan. The F-86Fs were gradually replaced by Northrop F-5s, though F-104 Starfighters had also begun to replace the Sabres of

3rd Fighter Wing in 1960. It has been reported that the 'Taiwan Air Reserve' equipped two Sabre squadrons – no evidence can be found to support this. The last RoCAF Sabre unit – the 2nd Fighter Wing at Hsinchu – retired its F-86Fs during 1971 in favour of F-100As. The official retirement of the Sabre F-86F was completed on 3 April 1971. A number of RoCAF F-86Fs were acquired by the US Navy for the QF-86F drone programme at China Lake. Like the Korean machines, they were generally in poor condition and used only for parts reclamation.

Thailand

In line with many Far Eastern nations, the United States viewed Thailand as an essential link in the control of Communist expansion in the area. However, unlike some of the 'front-line' nations, the supply of MAP equipment to Thailand was not considered so urgent. Beginning in 1950, a Joint US Military Advisory Group was established in order to set up training and support for the arrival of new equipment for the armed forces, especially the Royal Thai Air Force (RTAF). In 1951 the first MAP-supplied fighters arrived on the USS *Cape Esperance*, comprising fifty Grumman Bearcat propeller-driven machines. But it was not until 1957 that the Thais obtained their first jet aircraft: thirty F-84G Thunderjets and a number of T-33 trainers.

The RTAF gained its first Sabres in 1960, and these aircraft were supplied direct from US stocks. Starting on 25 May 1960, twenty F-86F-30s were ferried into NAA's Inglewood plant for conversion to F-86F-40 standard from Davis Monthan and McLellan AFBs. Then, after conversion, these aircraft were assigned to MAP, fifteen on 20 October, one on the 27th, a further example on the 29th and three on 30 October. These first twenty F-86Fs for the RTAF were delivered in November and replaced the F-84s in 12 Squadron as well as beginning the equipping of 13 Squadron at Don Muang AB near Bangkok. The latter unit relinquished its F-8F-1 Bearcats at this time, both Squadrons coming under 1st Wing control.

A further twenty F-86Fs were delivered on 7 March 1962, bringing the total

RTAF F-86Fs delivered at that point to forty. This batch were entirely drawn from storage at Davis Monthan AFB and overhauled and upgraded to F-86F-40 specification by North American, but this time at Palmdale beginning in February 1961. They were assigned to MAP on 21 August 1961, though it is not known why there was a six-months gap until their official acceptance by the Thai AF. Further 'attrition' deliveries were made, often singly, from such diverse locations as Norway, Taiwan and Saudi Arabia; the final total of RTAF F-86Fs appears to have been around forty-seven. The F-86F was referred to as the B.Kh.17 (Boh Khoh – aircraft, fighter) in Thai service.

In order to establish an all-weather fighter capability, the RTAF received twenty F-86Ls in 1964, and these aircraft were all assigned to 12 Squadron at Don Muang. These machines were all ex-US Air National Guard, comprising mainly ex-124th FIS Iowa ANG aircraft. Having all arrived at Davis Monthan in March and April 1962, they had only recently been retired when the Thai requirement was approved. Many were overhauled at Inglewood before their assignment to MAP in September 1963. They were referred to as B.Kh.17K in RTAF service, Thailand being the only nation outside the United States to operate this type. However, the country was not supplied with the SAGE equipment to support their intended role. The delivery of the F-86Ls then allowed 12 Squadron's F-86Fs to be assigned to a new unit, 43 Squadron,

which was activated at Takhli AB under 4th Wing for this purpose, moving to Don Muang later. 13 Squadron began to receive Northrop F-5As in April 1966, losing its F-86Fs soon afterwards. 43 Squadron continued to use F-86Fs until 1972 when they were replaced by Cessna A-37Bs at Nakhon Phanom. The Sabres were left at Don Muang AFB as decoys. The F-86Ls were replaced by F-5Es in 1976.

Tunisia

Twelve FY55 F-86F-40s were delivered to Tunisia during 1969. These aircraft were all among a number of Sabres returned to the United States from the Japanese Air Self-Defense Force on 22 May 1964 and stored at Davis Monthan AFB. Following their overhaul at McLellan AFB, the aircraft were delivered in two batches of six, the first being accepted on 13 August 1969 and the following batch on 17 November.

A US military advisory team accompanied the Sabres, among them George Getchell, who was seconded from Williams AFB, having flown F-86Fs as part of the MAP training programme at Nellis AFB until 1965:

In 1969 I was tagged, because of my relatively recent F-86 time, to be part of a twenty-man team (three pilots and seventeen maintenance) to go to Bizerte, Tunisia and check out a Tunisian Air Force squadron in F-86Fs. After

The last Sabres supplied under MAP were these F-86F-40s delivered to the Tunisian Air Force in November 1969. These aircraft were all ex-Japanese and were painted in smart south-east Asia-type camouflage. MAP

we finished our training program, the Tunisians were starting to form and train an acro team. I know one of the pilots crashed and was killed while practising a low-level inverted pass over the airport. Too bad, he was one of their best pilots.

The Sabres were delivered in a camouflage scheme and were apparently assigned to 11 Squadron at Sidi Ahmed AB, near Bizerte. They were eventually replaced by Italian-built MB-326Ks, which were operated by 11 Squadron in the fighter/ground-attack role alongside F-5E/Fs of 15 Squadron. With a small air force, Tunisia possessed only two other large bases, at La Karouba (helicopters) and Sfax (13 and 14 Squadron with SF-260).

Shark-mouthed Sabre 19215 was part of a Turkish aerobatic team that visited Bierset Air Base in Belgium for the 1958 Meeting des Nations. The aircraft and its pilot were lost on 1 April 1959 when it dived into the ground 30 miles east of Eskisehir AB. Robert Verheggen

Turkey

The Turkish Air Force (Turk Hava Kuvvetleri – THK) received the first of its 107 Canadair Sabres in June 1954, all being enhanced to F-86E(M) standard with '6-3' wing modifications. Delivery comprised thirty-four Sabres in 1954, sixty-three in 1955 and ten in 1956, although two were lost on delivery. They equipped squadrons at 4th Air Base (Hava Ussu), Eskisehir. The first to receive Sabres was 141 Interceptor Squadron (Filo), commanded by Maj I. Ildir. Reformed on 7 September 1954, 141 Filo was declared fully equipped on 1 November. 142 Filo then reformed on 1 February 1955 with F-86Es, followed by 143 Filo during that summer.

All Sabre units moved to Merzifon in 1956 as part of 44th Fighter Bomber Group (Ucus Grubo). By this time, each squadron nominally had twenty-five combat-ready Sabres available; the actual figures were twenty-four, twenty-two and fifteen. In addition, the three squadrons at that time had thirty-four, twenty-six and twenty-three qualified pilots, though fewer than twenty in each squadron were declared as combat-ready. The three squadrons each carried a lightning flash on the aircraft's nose, painted a particular colour to signify ownership: red for 141 Filo, yellow for 142 Filo and blue for 143 Filo.

During September 1964 it was reported that all the Dutch AF's 700 Squadron F-86Ks were being sold to Turkey. Despite continuing reports that this happened, no F-86Ks (or F-86Ds, for that matter) ever served with the Turkish AF.

By 1960 the THK Sabre inventory stood at eighty, a large number having been lost in accidents in the five or so intervening years. As newer equipment began to arrive from the United States, the squadrons slowly relinquished their Sabres, starting with 141 Filo, which converted to F-104Gs in August 1964. 142 Filo then received F-5As in 1967 and 143 Filo retired its twenty remaining F-86Es during 1968, also converting to the F-5A.

Uruguay

In late 1976 the Air Force of Uruguay (Fuerza Aérea Uruguaya – FAU) was on the verge of accepting a dozen ex-Argentinian F-86Fs. These aircraft would have been the first FAU fighters since the withdrawal of Grupo de Aviación's F-80Cs in 1971. However, as MAP-supplied aircraft, US State Department permission had to be granted before transfer and this was not forthcoming. Instead the Sabres saw further limited use in Argentina.

Venezuela

In early 1955 the Venezuelan Air Force (Fuerza Aerea Venezolanas – FAV) requested twenty-two MAP-funded F-86Fs to replace a number of obsolete Vampire fighters. Responding quickly, the United States delivered seven F-86Fs to the FAV on 6 August, followed by a further six on 3 October. Eight more followed on 19 February 1957, with one single aircraft being assigned on 20 February. All these aircraft were delivered under MDAP project 5F753 from McLellan AFB. Some reports state that other F-86Fs were delivered to FAV in December 1960, though this is thought unlikely.

All F-86Fs were assigned to Escadron de Caza 36 'Jaguares' of Grupo Aerea de Caza 12 at Mariscal Sucre. At this time the VAF possessed a strength of 163 pilots, 96 other officers, 238 officer cadets, 610 non-commissioned officers and 365 NCOs and airmen undergoing training. The Sabres were serialled to reflect the aircraft number (first digit), the Esquadrilha within the Esc de Caza 36 (A, B or C) and the 36 representing the Esc de Caza.

On 1 January 1958 four F-86Fs joined in an attempted revolt, making a number of low-level flights over Caracas. They strafed the Presidential Palace at Miraflores, the Ministry of Defence and the National Security Headquarters, at least one aircraft being hit by anti-aircraft fire. This revolt had serious repercussions for the armed forces, the majority of the Air Force's command posts changing as a result.

By mid-1959 the disruptions of the January 1958 coup and further unsuccessful revolts had weakened the

FAV to a shadow of its former self. Though the Air Force had nineteen F-86Fs on strength (according to the British Air Attaché's report of 13 July), at best six F-86Fs were in an airworthy condition. They were all in dire need of IRAN overhaul, which was beyond the scope of the FAV's limited maintenance capacity. Clearly, the best solution would be to return the Sabres to the USA for overhaul. By this time, Esc de Caza 36 had moved from Mariscal Sucre to Palo Negro's El Liberatador Air Base.

The 1959 total of FAV Sabres would indicate that, by that point, three had been lost in accidents, a relatively low figure due in part to the small number of flying hours being put on the Sabre fleet. About six F-86Fs were written off during FAV service, of which one flew into the ground on 24 April 1956 and another was lost at Virginia in Carabo State on 10 February 1965.

During 1965 the FAV began negotiations with the West German Government for the purchase of all 'seventy-three' surviving Luftwaffe F-86Ks, including the unflown examples. Export licences were approved for fifty-one aircraft (presumably the airworthy ones) and the sale was worth £50,000 ($140,000) per aircraft, including spares. It was also reported at the time that the deal included the fitting of recce equipment in some aircraft, but no evidence can be found to substantiate this. A total of seventy-eight F-86Ks were eventually supplied, including many unused, non-flyable aircraft as spares sources. At least four aircraft were impounded at the docks in Curaçao on delivery and never entered service – they were eventually scrapped, still in their USAF delivery markings. F-86Ks flew with Escuadróns de Caza 34 and 35, and later apparently replaced the F-86Fs of Esc de Caza 36. Four aircraft are reported to have passed to the Honduran AF in 1969 following overhaul, but it seems more likely that this event occurred some time after 1975. The FAV F-86Ks encountered many maintenance problems, a large number being grounded in July 1969 for hydraulic hose problems. Around twenty-seven were reported to have been written off, with the remainder being withdrawn at Palo Negro around 1974. Most are still there, slowly rotting away. Nine F-86Fs later passed to the Bolivian AF during 1973, though any F-86Fs surviving in FAV service were replaced by Dassault Mirage IIIEVs in 1971.

Yugoslavia

Before 1948 the Ratnog Vazduhoplovstva i ProtivVazdusne Odbrane Jugoslavije (RV i PVO – Yugoslav Air Force and Anti-Aircraft Defence) had relied heavily upon Soviet-built aircraft for its inventory. However, following the ending of Soviet trade with Yugoslavia in 1948, it soon became obvious that major modernization was necessary if the RV i PVO was to fulfil its task of national defence.

Thus, in 1951, the Yugoslav Government obtained Republic F-47D Thunderbolts from the United States, and De Havilland Mosquitos from Britain. But these aircraft were already considered obsolete, and jet-powered aircraft were required to meet the threat of the potent MiG-15 fighters being supplied to the Warsaw Pact countries. The first jet aircraft for Yugoslavia, four T-33s, arrived at Batajnica Air Base near Belgrade on 10 March 1953, supplied by the US Mutual Defense Assistance Program (MDAP). In June the first offensive jets – Republic F-84G Thunderjets – arrived for the Yugoslav Air Force.

The F-84G fighter bomber was unsuited to the fighter task for which it had been purchased, being grossly inferior to the MiG-15, and again the US MDAP came to the assistance of the Yugoslavs. To bolster the region against Communist aggression, the RV i PVO would begin to equip with the Sabre fighter. The introduction of the Sabre signified the beginning of a new era with the formation

Pictured here on delivery (probably at McLellan AFB), this Venezuelan F-86F, coded 4B36, went to serve with Escadron de Caza 36 at Mariscal Sucre in 1955. Note that the aircraft carries the maximum external fuel tankage of two 120 and two 200gall drop tanks for the ferry flight south. *Jon Lake*

The Fuerza Aerea Venezolanas (FAV) acquired as many as seventy-eight F-86Ks from Germany in 1965. Only fifty or so actually entered FAV service, the rest serving as spare parts sources. The F-86Ks initially served with Esc de Caza 34 and 35 in an overall light gray colour scheme. *Jon Lake*

of the first modern fighter-interceptor unit of the RV i PVO, and, in March 1956, technical classes were organized to convert pilots and the technical personnel of 117 vuzduhoplovni puk (aircraft wing). These technical classes lasted seventeen days for pilots and twenty-one for technicians. The RV i PVO would receive ex-Royal Air Force Canadair Sabre 4s, brought up to later specification by, among other things, the fitting of the 'hard edge' 6-3 wing with wing fence. The modification of these aircraft was carried out under contract in Britain by Aviation Traders at Stansted, Airwork at Dunsfold, Gatwick and Speke and by Westlands at the Merryfield factory. Following modification, these aircraft became known as F-86E(M) – the M signifying 'modified'. The aircraft were delivered in standard RAF colours, with washable white USAF markings and serial numbers. They were then handed over to the USAF as part of the MDAP programme and sent to Yugoslavia through Naples.

The first two Sabres were delivered on 21 May 1956, with a further four the following month. However, as the majority of the MDAP F-86E(M)s were being delivered to the Italian Air Force at that time, it was not until May 1957 that further deliveries to the RV i PVO resumed, when another four aircraft were accepted. Upon their arrival, the Sabres were painted in Yugoslav colours, which consisted of the standard RAF camouflage

of dark green (640) and dark sea-grey (638) upper surfaces and PRU blue undersides, with colour demarcation high up on fuselage sides. Black, rounded-style, serial numbers were used, all aircraft carrying a large, black, anti-dazzle panel. The 75cm (29in) diameter Yugoslav roundels were placed on either side of the fuselage, above the left wing and below the right. The red/white/blue national flash appeared on the tail fin with a red star superimposed. F-86E(M) aircraft delivered to the RV i PVO were allotted new serial numbers in the 11XXX range, the last three figures beginning with 001 and numbering consecutively thereafter in order of delivery. The RV i PVO serial number appeared above the fin flash in 18cm (7in) high black numbers. Finally, the last three numbers of the serial number (often referred to by the Yugoslavs as an eskadrille number) appeared in 50cm (19in) high black figures on the forward fuselage. This number was repeated below the left wing and above the right, aligned with the leading edge of the wing.

The small number of Sabres initially available led to their high utilization, and the first accident occurred on 8 August 1956, when 19459 (believed to be 11003) was written off in a landing accident at Batajnica. One other notable event occurred soon after the arrival of the first batch of Sabres: the breaking of the sound barrier for the first time by a Yugoslav. This honour fell to Pukovnik (Wing

Commander/Colonel) Nikola Lekic, the commander of 44 Vazduhoplovne Divizije (Air Division) on 31 July 1956. Two days before the event, an American instructor pilot had demonstrated the breaking of the sound barrier over Batajnica aerodrome. Inspired to repeat the feat, and to demonstrate the capability of his pilots, Lekic declared to the American pilot that, after only two or three solo flights in the F-86E, he would also break the barrier. This was indeed an ambitious boast, considering that a pilot needed around 60hr of F-86E sortie time as well as ground school to be considered fully proficient.

Lekic immediately began his theoretical training on the F-86E during the afternoon of 29 July, and the next day carried out his first Sabre flight. In the early morning of 31 July, he carried out a second flight after which, to the astonishment of the American instructors, Lekic declared that he was ready to break the barrier. And so, later the same morning, Lekic, flying Sabre serial number 11005, took off accompanied by an American pilot in a second Sabre. Soon after take off, this 'chase' aircraft had to return to base because of an unserviceable canopy seal. Lekic then climbed to 49,000ft (15,000m) to start his dive. Watching his air-speed indicator and Machmeter in the cockpit, he soon passed through an indicated Mach number of 1.0. However, the control tower at Batajnica reported that it had not heard the resultant sonic boom, at which point Lekic repeated his climb and dive and managed to produce the required boom for the observers on the ground. In breaking the barrier Lekic earned much praise, and on 8 September he received a gold medal and letter of thanks from the Canadair company, as well as a Mach Busters Club certificate.

With the continuation of F-86E(M) deliveries in May 1957, the RV i PVO began to equip its first wing with the aircraft – 117 vp from 44 Air Division at Batajnica. By the end of the year, a total of thirty-seven Sabres had been delivered to the Wing, which started training on to the new jet during July, when up to fifteen Sabres were on strength. The F-84G fighter bombers which had previously equipped 117 vp were passed to other Air Force units. Initially, only three pilots from 117 vp carried out training on to the Sabre. These three pilots then in turn

One that got away. When Yugoslavia turned to the United States with a view to purchasing Sabres in 1959 (rather than being MAP-supplied, as were the Yugoslav's first forty-three Sabres), the continued availability of ex-RAF aircraft meant that they were delivered quickly. 19587, seen in storage at Avio Diepen in Ypenburg, Holland became 11060 with the Yugoslavs. J.M.G. Gradidge, June 1957

Delivered in 1957, this ex-RAF F-86E(M) served with 117 vp at Batajnica. The delivery colour scheme is the same as that used for both British and Canadian-operated Sabres. Mitja Marusko

trained the remaining thirty-one pilots of the Wing, as well as seven more from 44 Air Division's other Wing, 204 vp, which was due to receive the F-86E(M) in the near future.

The warming of relations with the Soviet Union during the mid-1950s inevitably led to a worsening of links with the West, and in particular the United States. Deliveries of MDAP-supplied aircraft soon slowed down, and on 15 July 1957 the Yugoslav Government issued a statement to the effect that, from December of that year, all military aid from the USA would cease. By this time only forty-three F-86E(M) Sabres had been delivered. Despite this lack, in March 1958 204 vp carried out its conversion to the F-86E at Batajnica, having received twenty Sabres from 117 vp, where it had previously carried out the training of its personnel. In turn, the F-84Gs which had previously been flown

by 204 vp were passed to other RV i PVO units. In 1958 Sabres from 44 Air Division took part in flypasts to mark May Day and a visit of the Indonesian premier.

The requirement to perform all maintenance and repair of Sabres in Yugoslavia led in late 1958 to the first IRAN (Inspect and Repair as Necessary) survey of F-86Es by Vazduhoplovno-Tehnickog Remontnog Zavoda (Air Force Technical Repair Institute/VTRZ) 'Jastreb' (Hawk) at Zemun. The high level of technical competence gained by these VTRZ units greatly assisted the largely isolated Yugoslavs in keeping their jets airworthy. But it soon became apparent that further deliveries of fighters were required by the RV i PVO.

The government then came to an agreement with the United States for the purchase of seventy-eight ex-RAF F-86E(M), in addition to those donated under MDAP. The new batch were to be

supplied from 1959, at a price ranging from $5,000 to $15,000 per aircraft. In addition, 130 ex-USAFE F-86Ds were acquired to fulfil the need for all-weather interceptors. These latter aircraft were purchased at the equivalent and reasonable price of £3,570 sterling each. In preparation for their entry into service, four RV i PVO pilots undertook flying training at the Perrin AFB All-Weather Flying School in Texas. In addition, one officer and four airmen undertook maintenance training at Perrin.

Some of the seventy-eight F-86E(M) aircraft in this commercially-acquired batch passed through Avio Diepen at Ypenburg in Holland, where they had been in storage from as early as June 1957. Some were then allotted straight to operational units, while the remainder went into pre-issue maintenance with VTRZ 'Jastreb'. This later group of Sabres wore a different colour scheme from their MDAP counterparts. This consisted of a natural metal finish with a smaller, black, anti-dazzle panel (in comparison with the RAF scheme). Roundels were carried in

This camouflaged F-86D-41, serial 14029, is having its oxygen system replenished via the access door just aft of the boarding step. Note also the open brake chute door at the base of the vertical tail. The aircraft was ex-USAF 52-3717. Ostric

the normal positions, but the red/white/blue fin flash was positioned higher up on the tail fin. Serial numbers (commencing 11044) were of a black 'squared-off' type, as was the eskadrille number on the forward fuselage. The eskadrille number was again repeated on the wings, but this time it was positioned at 90 degrees to the aircraft's centreline. At the end of 1959 these Sabres then began to re-equip 83 vp at Zemun and 94 vp at Skopje, both previously being equipped with F-84G Thunderjets. The two wings took from four to six months to reach operational status, assisted by 117 and 204 vp, and their conversion was completed at the beginning of June 1960. As both the early MDAP-supplied camouflage F-86E(M)s and the later batch of natural metal aircraft passed through maintenance, the colour scheme

was standardized with a natural metal finish, 'rounded' numbers, the small, black, anti-dazzle panel and the lower positioned fin flash. In addition, RV i PVO F-86Es received matt black-painted canopy rails. From the early 1960s many aircraft received a gloss camouflage colour scheme, consisting of light olive (FS 34102) and medium sea-grey (FS 36187) upper surfaces, with PRU blue (FS 35164) undersides. The colour demarcation was much lower on the fuselage than in the RAF scheme. The small anti-dazzle panel was retained, along with the black canopy rail, but all numbers were repainted white in their original positions.

The newly-acquired F-86D aircraft were delivered straight from the 3130th Air Base Group at Chateauroux AB in France starting in late July 1961 and initially passed to VTRZ 'Jastreb' for

repair and maintenance. Immediately thirty aircraft from this batch were used for spares reclamation. The Yugoslavs found to their dismay that none of the aircraft had the E-4 fire-control system fitted, which was essential for the aircraft's operation. Also, there were no supplies of Mighty Mouse rockets which were the F-86D's only armament. Following protests from Yugoslavia, the US Government arranged for the delivery of this missing equipment.

The first unit of the RV i PVO to receive the F-86D was 117 vp at Batajnica, which converted from the F-86E. Wing personnel completed their F-86D ground training at VTRZ 'Jastreb' during August 1962, with flying training beginning on 5 September. By the end of 1962 this training had in turn been successfully completed, by which time the eskadrilles of 117 vp had ten D-models in service. Further F-86Ds were delivered to the Wing in 1963, when 117 vp displayed the aircraft to the public for the first time at the May Day parade in Belgrade. By the end of 1963 117 vp had thirty-one F-86Ds at its disposal. Because of the complexity of the F-86D's electrical systems and its relatively advanced engine systems, the RV i PVO aircraft technicians were not entirely enamoured with the aircraft. Frequent unserviceabilities required an inordinate amount of time to maintain the F-86D and cannibalization was common. Even though the Yugoslavs had purchased 130 F-86Ds, the number in operational service rarely exceeded forty. RV i PVO F-86Ds were generally left unpainted, with serial and eskadrille numbers in the 'rounded' style and national insignia placed as on the F-86E. Anti-dazzle panels were either olive drab or black. A camouflage scheme was also adopted, again with the same colouring as the later F-86E scheme, but camouflaged F-86Ds were often seen without the anti-dazzle panel.

In 1963 204 vp at Batajnica began to receive the first Russian MiG-21F-13 fighters and to phase their Sabres out. The purchase of these aircraft then led to a total ban on military sales to Yugoslavia by the USA. Clearly, the days of the Sabre in Yugoslavia were numbered, and by the end of 1963 only sixty-seven F-86E(M) aircraft from a total of 121 remained in service. However, the poor radar performance of the early MiG-21s meant that the F-86Ds were retained until later versions, such as the MiG-21 PFM, became available.

Around this time, the first reconnaissance conversions of the F-86D were being modified. These photo-equipped aircraft were designated IF-86D (I for izvidacki – reconnaissance) in Yugoslav service. The conversion entailed the removal of the Mighty Mouse rocket pack, and three K-24 cameras were installed in its place. In addition, two pylons were installed under the forward fuselage for carrying FOTAB (Foto Avio Bombe/photo-aerial bomb) and SAB (Svetlece Avio Bombe/light-illuminating aerial bomb) flares. The modification of thirty-two such aircraft was carried out by VTRZ 'Zmaj' (Dragon) at Pleso, near Zagreb, the first IF-86D being delivered before the end of 1963. It was originally thought that these conversions were carried out on a new batch of RV i PVO Sabres, but it now seems that some if not all the aircraft were from existing Yugoslav F-86Ds stocks. In the first half of 1964 184 ivp (Reconnaissance Wing) at

Though preserved, this photograph clearly shows the photo flare racks fitted beneath the forward fuselage of the IF-86D reconnaissance Sabre. The Yugoslavs converted thirty-two aircraft to IF-86D configuration, featuring three K-24 cameras mounted in place of the Mighty Mouse rocket pack. Author

Pleso received the first of its twenty IF-86D aircraft. The Wing also used modified RF-84Gs and IT-33As at this time. During 1965 184 ivp was disbanded, although the IF-86D element, 352 reconnaissance eskadrille, was retained independently. This unit converted to MiG-21R reconnaissance fighters in 1971. IF-86Ds retained their natural metal colour scheme until they were retired from service.

The 1960s saw a rationalization of RV i PVO units and resources. During 1964 several units were disbanded, and from these wings two strengthened eskadrilles equipped with F-86Es were retained. Additionally, the remaining F-86Es were assigned to fighter-bomber duties. During 1967 a reconnaissance eskadrille was formed at Pleso, equipped with IF-86Ds, and came under the command of the F-86D Wing (thought to be 83 vp) based there. The Wing then began to train for the reception of new MiG-21F fighters. The F-86Ds were then passed to 94 vp at Skopski Petrovac, whose F-86Es were retired. With the large number of F-86Ds at Skopski Petrovac, a new fighter wing was formed and this new unit completed training on the F-86D to operational status within three months.

Brief mention should be made here of the use of Puk and Eskadrille badges during the RV i PVO service of the

F-86E(M) and F-86D. These appeared from 1966, along the same lines as the squadron badges applied to the aircraft of Western air forces. Though no details are known of which eskadrilles or wings these badges belonged to, a few examples are: otter (IF-86D), penguin, shark, eagle's head and seal (all F-86E), griffin vulture diving (F-86D based at Pleso) and griffin vulture with open wings (F-86D based at Pleso). These symbols usually appeared on the forward fuselage, contained in a large circle, and often replaced or were superimposed on the eskadrille number. To further confuse matters, these markings were often retained on an aircraft even after it passed to another unit.

With the growth of the domestic aircraft manufacturing industry, which produced the Soko Galeb trainer and the Jastreb fighter-bomber variant, the F-86Es were withdrawn from service in 1971. The F-86Ds lingered on slightly longer with 83 vp, and shortly before their final withdrawal from operational service in late 1974, took part in the Autumn 1973 exercises between the RV i PVO and Yugoslav Army units. Six former RV i PVO F-86Es were subsequently sold to the Fuerza Aerea Hondureña in 1976. These aircraft were shipped in crates to Fort Lauderdale in Florida, where they were readied for flight and ferried to Honduras.

APPENDIX

The Three Prototypes

The first prototype XF-86 was painted in this gloss pearl grey scheme during NAA tests in 1948 to further improve top speed; the no.3 XF-86 was painted in a 'Super Fine' finish at the same time. As no appreciable benefit was observed, and hydraulic fluid was found to degrade the paint, both aircraft were returned to natural metal finish.

Soon after delivery to the USAF in December 1948, the no.1 XF-86 was repainted with block-style serials and buzz numbers. By this time, the tail mounted fuel drain had been re-positioned slightly rearwards to the location favoured on production aircraft. 45-59597 was tested to destruction with 4901st Support Wing at Kirtland AFB on 31 August 1952.

Still bearing the 'PU' buzz number of an XP-86, this view of the no.2 machine shows the tail-mounted bumper attached for landing and take-off trials during early 1948. Also of note is the opened engine compressor discharge duct, just forward of the tail fin. On production models, the duct was a simple fixed outlet.

Though it was used by NAA as an armament test aircraft, by the time of its handover to the USAF in December 1948, the machine guns had been removed from this, the third XF-86. Mainly used in the test support role at Edwards AFB, after a short period of modification at Norton AFB, the aircraft was tested to destruction at Kirtland AFB during August 1952.

The third XP-86, 45-59599, bore more of a 'production' appearance than other prototypes, though it still carried the fin-mounted navigation lights and airspeed probe. It did, however, feature the electrically-operated gun blast doors and incorporated provision for external stores to be carried. Here it carries twenty High Velocity Air Rockets (HVAR), mounted in pairs. Production F-86As could only carry sixteen HVARs.

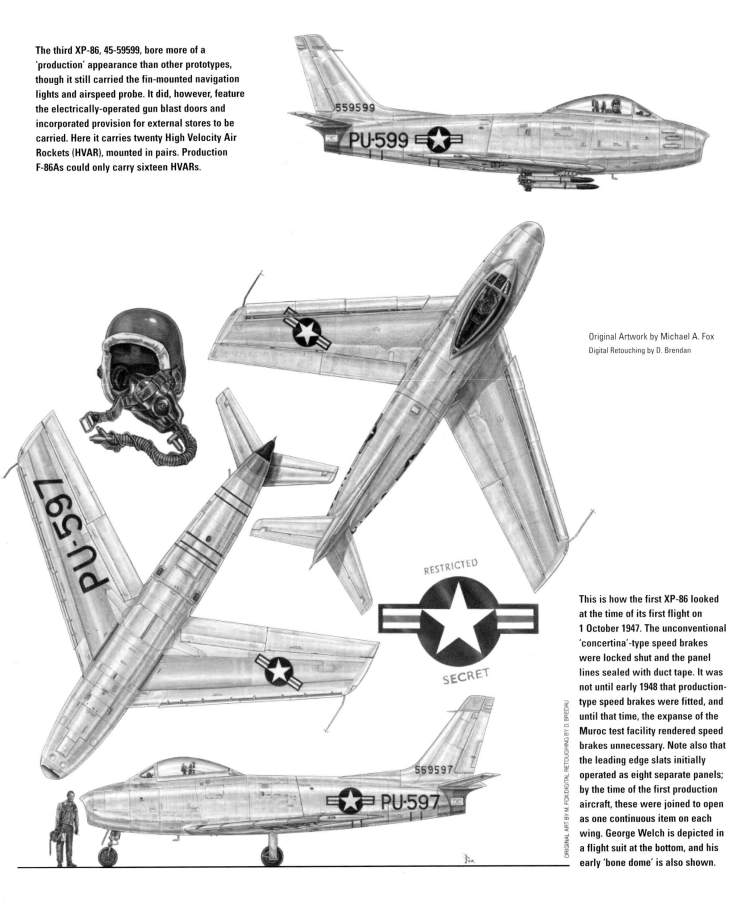

Original Artwork by Michael A. Fox
Digital Retouching by D. Brendan

ORIGINAL ART BY M. FOX/DIGITAL RETOUCHING BY D. BREDAU

This is how the first XP-86 looked at the time of its first flight on 1 October 1947. The unconventional 'concertina'-type speed brakes were locked shut and the panel lines sealed with duct tape. It was not until early 1948 that production-type speed brakes were fitted, and until that time, the expanse of the Muroc test facility rendered speed brakes unnecessary. Note also that the leading edge slats initially operated as eight separate panels; by the time of the first production aircraft, these were joined to open as one continuous item on each wing. George Welch is depicted in a flight suit at the bottom, and his early 'bone dome' is also shown.

Index